You Read to Me, I'll Read to You

Very Short Fairy Tales to Read Together

(in which wolves are tamed, trolls are transformed, and peas are triumphant)

by

MARY ANN HOBERMAN

Illustrated by

MICHAEL EMBERLEY

Megan Tingley Books

LITTLE, BROWN AND COMPANY

New York ❧ An AOL Time Warner Company

To the unknown authors of these tales, with love and gratitude
—M. A. H.

*To all the hardworking, unheralded comic artists — a constant source
of inspiration and humility*
—M. E.

Also to read together:

You Read to Me, I'll Read to You: Very Short Stories to Read Together

First Edition

Library of Congress Cataloging-in-Publication Data

Hoberman, Mary Ann.
    You read to me, I'll read to you : very short fairy tales to read together / by Mary Ann
Hoberman ; illustrated by Michael Emberley — 1st ed.
      p. cm.
    "Megan Tingley books."
    ISBN 0-316-14611-0
    1. Readers (Primary) 2. Fairy tales. [1. Fairy tales.] I. Emberley, Michael, ill. II. Title.

PE1119.H63 2004
428.6 — dc21   2003047445

10 9 8 7 6 5 4 3 2

TWP

Printed in Singapore

The illustrations for this book were done in gel pen, watercolor, and dry pastel on
90-lb. hot-press watercolor paper.
The text was set in Horley Old Style, and the display type is Shannon.

Table Of Contents

Author's Note:

Here is a sequel to the first *You Read to Me, I'll Read to You.* As in the preceding book, the short rhymed stories are like little plays for two voices that sometimes speak separately, sometimes in unison. However, the subject matter of these stories differs from the first book: Here, each one is a variation on a familiar fairy tale. But once again each story ends with a version of the same refrain:

> *You read to me!*
> *I'll read to you!*

As I said in the first book, I see the book's users as either a pair of beginning readers (two children, or a child and a parent who is in a literacy program) or one beginning and one more-advanced reader (either an older child or an adult). When you think about it, that includes just about every reader there is!

The stories in this book ring changes on eight traditional fairy tales. Therefore I recommend that parents and teachers make sure that their new readers are familiar with the original versions before going on to the stories in this book.

Once again I would like to acknowledge Literacy Volunteers of America. My work with them has provided me with the inspiration for these books, whose ongoing purpose is to encourage literacy by reading to, and listening to, each other.

Introduction

Here's another book,
Book two—

You read to me!

        I'll read to you!

We'll read each page
To one another—

You'll read one side,

        I the other.

But who will read—
Now guess this riddle—
When the words
Are in the middle?

The answer's easy!

        Plain as pie!

We'll read together,
You and I.

The Three Bears

I'm Goldilocks.

       I'm Baby Bear.

What pretty fur!

       What pretty hair!

Why are you here?

       You're in my bed.

I'm in your bed?

       That's what I said.
       Why are *you* here?

I lost my way.
I found your house
And thought I'd stay.

       And then you ate
       My porridge up
       And drank my milk
       Right from my cup.

Why, yes, I did.
You weren't there
And I was hungry,
Baby Bear.

       Well, now I'm very
       Hungry, too.

Oh, goodness me!
What shall we do?

       Where do you live?

Not very far.
A mile or two
From where we are.

I know the forest
Very well.
I'll take you home.
I'll trace your smell.

Why, Baby Bear,
You're very smart!

Get out of bed
And then we'll start.

When I get home,
Here's what I'll do:
I'll make some porridge
Just for you.

Will you add honey
For a treat?
(That's my favorite
Thing to eat.)

I'll add some honey
If you wish.
(You can even
Lick the dish.)

Yummy yum!
I love to lick!
What comes next?

I'll let you pick.

I pick a picture book
To share.

Why, that is perfect,
Baby Bear!

The Three Bears is
The one we'll do!
You'll read to me!
I'll read to you!

The Princess and the Pea

I'm the princess!

        I'm the pea!

Look at me!

        No, look at me!

Pea, you made me
Black and blue.

        I am flat
        Because of you.

I stayed up
The whole night long,
Wondering
Just what was wrong.

        I stayed up
        The whole night through,
        Squished and squashed
        Because of you.

I'm a princess,
Toe to chin.
Princesses
Have tender skin.

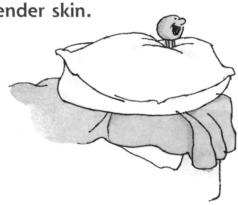

I'm the one
That proved you're real.
Think about
The way I feel.

You are just
A silly pea!
I'm a princess!
Look at me!

I'm not silly!
Not at all!
I can't help it
If I'm small.
Peas have feelings
Just like you.

Do they, Pea?

They do. It's true.

If it's true,
What can I do?

Put me in
Your wedding ring.
That would be
A special thing.

In my ring?
Oh, goodness me!
Not a diamond?

No, a pea.

Such a ring
I've never seen.
Still, you are
A pretty green.

Green and gold
Is really grand.
I'll look handsome
On your hand.

And every time
I look at you,
I'll think about
Our story, too.

Our story? Tell me
What you mean?

A story all about
A queen
Who made a princess
Just like me
Go to sleep
Upon a pea.

> And was the pea
> A pea like me?

Why, yes it was.
The very same.
The Princess and
The Pea's its name.

> I'd like to read it.

I would, too.

> You read to me.
> I'll read to you.

11

Jack and the Beanstalk

My name is Jack,
The beanstalk lad.

And I'm the ogre
Jack made mad.

I lost our milk cow
In a trade.

You got five beans.
That's all you made.

My mother threw them out
That night
And in the morning
What a sight!
A beanstalk grew
That was so tall
We couldn't see
The top at all.

You climbed it
To the top and then
You stole my magic
Laying hen.

Your hen that lays
Gold eggs. Why, yes.
I stole your hen,
I do confess.

My bags of gold,
You stole them, too,
And then my golden harp.

That's true.

That was a naughty
Thing to do!

Now Mister Ogre,
Don't be mad.
I do admit
That I was bad,
But we were poor
And hungry, too.

You give them back
Or I'll eat *you!*

I'll give them back
If you agree
To sometimes lend
Your hen to me.

You're asking me
To lend my hen?

Not all the time.
Just now and then.
And also for
A special treat,
Please lend your harp.
It sounds so sweet.

Why, yes, it has
A lovely tone.
But don't forget,
It's just a loan!

A bag of gold
Perhaps you'd share?

A half-bag's all
That I can spare.

Now that's all settled
And we're friends
And that's the way
Our story ends.

Let's write it down.

        Let's write it now.

We'll tell about
The beans and cow

        And how the beanstalk
        Grew and grew

And when our story
Is all through,
You'll read to me!
I'll read to you!

Little Red Riding Hood

Little Red Riding Hood's my name.
My grandma made my hood.
I'm visiting her house today.
She lives inside this wood.

> My name is Big Bad Wolf, it is,
> And I'm in Grandma's bed,
> Pretending to be Grandma.
> Her nightcap's on my head.

Why, Grandma dear, you're looking strange.
Your eyes are big and wide!

> Oh, never mind, Red Riding Hood.
> Just sit down by my side.

But Grandma dear, you look so odd.
Your teeth are very long!

> Why, no, they're not, Red Riding Hood.
> Believe me, nothing's wrong.

You're not my grandma! Not at all!
Just look me in the eye.

> I am! I am! I really am!
> I wouldn't tell a lie!

Oh, yes, you would! You mean old wolf,
I should have known it's you!

> But see the nightcap on my head.
> I'm Grandma through and through!

16

Now, Big Bad Wolf, tell me the truth.
What did you have to sup?

> Well, if you really have to know,
> I ate your grandma up.

You ate her up? You naughty wolf!

> I ate her in one bite.

Well, hurry, cough her up again!
I hope she's still all right.

> *Ahem! Ahaw! Kerchoo! Kerchaw!*

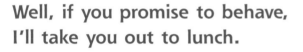

Oh, Grandma, you're not dead!
Now, Wolf, give Grandma back her cap
And give her back her bed.

> But I'm still starved, Red Riding Hood.
> What can I have to munch?

Well, if you promise to behave,
I'll take you out to lunch.

> We'll go out to a restaurant
> And while our dinners cook,
> We'll read a special story
> Out of a special book.

It's called *Little Red Riding Hood.*

> Just like your name, I see.

> Now let's begin. I'll read to you
> And then you'll read to me.

Cinderella

Cinderella
Is my name.

She's our sister.
What a shame!

All day long
I do my chores,
Washing clothes
And scrubbing floors.

All day long
We gobble sweets—
Candies, cakes,
And other treats.

I can't please them,
Though I try.

We are jealous.
That is why.

When the palace
Had a ball
And the King did
Ask us all,

We both played
A clever trick.
We pretended
She was sick.

When they left me,
Guess who came?
Fairy Godmother's
Her name!
My rags became
A gorgeous gown.
A carriage took me
Into town.

A beauty came
Into the ball.
The prince preferred her
To us all.

They didn't know
That it was I.
As midnight struck
I said good-by.
But as I hurried
Down the stair,
I lost one slipper
Of my pair.

Next day the prince
Sent out a crew
To find the owner
Of the shoe.

All day long
They looked for her
Until they came
To where we were.

We thought to get
Our feet to fit
We'd just chop off
A little bit.

Oh, don't do that!
Stepsisters, stop!
You'll hurt yourselves!
You mustn't chop!
It's not your fault
You wear size nine.
The only foot it fits
Is mine.

It's just not fair!
It's just not right!
You should have stayed
At home last night.

Now don't be selfish.
Don't be mean.
You're talking to
The future queen.

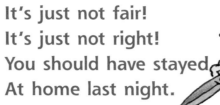

20

You'll be the queen?
Why, that is true!
All right, we'll both
Be nice to you.

Well, if you're nice
As nice can be,
I'll let you both
Come live with me.

In the palace?
Oh, what fun!
All our naughty
Days are done!

But we can read
The old tale, too—
Cinderella—
Read it through.
You read to me.
I'll read to you.

The Three Little Pigs

I'm Big Bad Wolf.

       I'm Little Pig.

You're very small.

       You're very big.
       But now I've got you
       In my pot.

The water's getting
Very hot.

       I'll cook you up
       And make a stew.

Why, that's an awful
Thing to do.

       Now that's a silly
       Thing to say.
       You ate my brother
       Yesterday.

Why, so I did!
I had forgot.
(This water's getting
Really hot.)

And on the day before
It's you
Who ate my other
Brother, too.

Did I do that?
That wasn't nice.
(Could you put in
A little ice?)

They built their houses
In the town.
You huffed and puffed
And blew them down.

Well, they were made
Of straw and sticks
While yours is made
Of good strong bricks.

First I built
My house of bricks,
And then I fooled you
With my tricks.

And now you've got me
In your pot.
This water's really
Really hot!

23

Say you're sorry
Loud and clear.

I'm sorry. Let me
Out of here!

Louder! Clearer!
Give a shout!

I'M SORRY, PIG!
NOW LET ME OUT!

Now do you promise
To be nice?

I promise, Pig.

Then here's some ice.
Sit down and cool
Yourself a bit.
I'll read you something
While you sit.

24

What will you read?

A tale that's true.
A tale about
Both me and you.

Can I read, too?

If you know how.

Of course I do.

Then let's start now.

We'll read *Three Little Pigs*
Right through.
You'll read to me.
I'll read to you.

The Little Red Hen and the Grain of Wheat

I'm Little Red Hen.
I planted the wheat.
I dug up the soil
In the dust and the heat.

And I am the Duck
And I have to admit
That I did not help her,
Not one little bit.

I'm Little Red Hen.
With my rake and my hoe
I weeded my garden
And helped it to grow.

And I am the Cat
And all through the spring
I did nothing either,
Not one little thing.

I'm Little Red Hen.
I watered my grain
All summer long
And I did not complain.

And I am the Dog.
I stayed in my bed
And pulled all my covers
Right over my head.

I worked in my garden
Until it was fall
And the small grain of wheat
Had grown ripe and quite tall.

We watched as she worked
While the harvest time passed
And she threshed it and ground it
And baked it at last.

And then when the bread
Was baked golden and nice,
I went and I asked you
If you'd like a slice.

And all of us answered,
As you may well guess,
With a shout and a cheer
And a great big loud YES!

But you didn't help me.
I worked all alone
And cared for my garden
Until it was grown.

And all of us answered,
We're sorry indeed!
We'll help you the next time
When you plant a seed.

Is that a true promise?
Do all of you swear
To help me the next time
And do your fair share?

And all of us answered,
Why, Little Red Hen,
We'll never be lazy
And selfish again!

Well, if you are sure
That you'll do as you say,
Then here are your slices.

Oh, hip, hip, hooray!
This bread is delicious,
So golden and brown,
And now that we've eaten,
We think we'll sit down.

I think I'll sit with you
And take a short rest.
I'll read you a story,
The one I like best.

What story is that, Hen?

A story I know.
We'll read it together.
We'll go nice and slow.

And what is it called, Hen?

Why, something quite sweet.
The Little Red Hen and
The Small Grain of Wheat.

Why, that sounds like you, Hen.

You're all in it, too.

You'll read it to me and
I'll read it to you.

29

The Three Billy Goats Gruff

I am the biggest billy goat.

> I am a great big troll.
> I'm standing guard upon my bridge.

I'm going for a stroll.

> But I won't let you cross my bridge.
> Unless you pay a toll.

Why, I'm the biggest billy goat!
You can't do that to me!

> But I'm an old ferocious troll
> As you can plainly see.

Do you charge lots of money, Troll?

> I only charge a cent.

What do you use your money for?

> I have to pay my rent.

I pay bills for my brothers, Troll.
They both depend on me.

> And I support my two young trolls.
> I, too, must work for three.

You poor old troll, if I had known
Your worries and your woes,
I never would have bothered you
Or scared you, goodness knows!

And Billy Goat, if *I* had known
Your troubles and your cares
I never would have frightened *you*
Or given *you* such scares.

Why, thank you, Troll.
That's very nice.

         I'd like to thank you, too.

And now that we've become good friends,
What would you like to do?

         Why, I would like to dip my toes
         Into the mountain brook.

And I would like to poke my nose
Into a storybook
About three billy goats named Gruff
Who took a mountain stroll
And went across a mountain bridge
And fooled a great big troll.

         You fool me in that story?

Why, yes, I fear we do.

         Well, never mind, you read to me
         And I will read to you.

GET YOUR GOAT

The End

And so our fairy tales
Are through.

We've read them all.
What shall we do?

We could reread them.

Yes, we could.

That might be fun.

That might be good.

But then, again,
We could read some
Of those old tales
That these are from.

And I know something else
As well.
There are more fairy tales
To tell.

Other ones
We haven't read?
Other ones
To read instead?

Many more
That we can add.
Funny, scary,
Happy, sad,
Short ones, long ones,
Old and new.

Well, why not start
To read a few?
You read to me.
I'll read to you.

DATE DUE

JUN 1 4 2001	

BRODART, CO.

Cat. No. 23-221-003

The Social and Economic Views

of

Mr. Justice Brandeis

LOUIS D. BRANDEIS
JUSTICE OF THE SUPREME COURT OF THE UNITED STATES

THE SOCIAL
AND ECONOMIC VIEWS
OF
MR. JUSTICE BRANDEIS

Collected, with Introductory Notes, by
ALFRED LIEF

With a Foreword by
CHARLES A. BEARD

NEW YORK: THE VANGUARD PRESS

Manufactured in the United States of America by the H. Wolff Estate

CONTENTS

[v]

CONTENTS

INTRODUCTION: A BACKGROUND.

ONE evening in 1916, at a dinner party given by a certain rich man in New York City, a former cabinet officer, then a successful practising attorney, made a long discourse on what he called the "outrage" committed by President Wilson in nominating Louis D. Brandeis to a place on the Supreme Bench. With the outward calm of a gentleman determined to control his feeling, he expounded the reasons for his vigorous opposition to this stroke of state. He was a Republican and Mr. Brandeis was a Democrat, but of course he was sure that this fact had "nothing to do with the matter." The truth was that Mr. Brandeis had been active in politics; he had served as counsellor and advisor for labor unions, reform leagues, and other "radical" organizations pressing for judicial rulings this way or legislation that way; he had expressed decided opinions on most of the great issues likely to come before the Supreme Court for adjudication, especially rate regulation; in arriving at decisions as a judge he would not follow the law and the precedents but would be swayed by his already matured convictions; and finally Mr. Brandeis had been guilty of violating the ethics of the bar. Fortunately, concluded the orator, "all the best people in business and the legal profession" were standing solidly together against the nomination, and the machinations of the wicked might be defeated. With an air of triumph he looked around at his dining colleagues and quite naturally received a salvo of approval.

For strange reasons, not necessary to recount here, there

happened to be among the company a professor grown weary of teaching freshmen, listening to baccalaureate sermons, and observing commencement ceremonials. Possessed by a disputative temper, derived probably from much study of Socrates, the professor applied the elenchus to the statesman's oracular propositions. "You would admit," he ventured, "that quite a number of Supreme Court judges were active in politics previous to their elevation. John Marshall was an ardent Federalist; he was appointed an envoy to France by a Federalist President; he ran for Congress on the Federalist ticket and after a campaign of extreme virulence was elected; later he served as Secretary of State; and then was made Chief Justice by a Federalist President. He had certainly expressed forceful opinions on many of the great issues likely to come before him as judge and it was well known that he entertained positive views as to the nature of the Union and the rights of property, which would control his judicial decisions. In fact, it was principally for this reason that he was selected for the Court at the very moment when the Federalists were being driven out of the elective branches. And as for following the law and precedents, Marshall's greatness lay in his superb ability to make both, for the law was vague and there were but few precedents to serve as guides. Taney likewise was active in politics before Jackson nominated him— Democratic politics; he entertained decided views—in the main contrary to Marshall's; it was for this reason that he was selected. Other examples are not necessary. And then, by the way, what are the ethics of the bar?" At that point the host, who had inherited his fortune and looked with genial amusement on both lawyers and professors, saw that the temperature was rising and suggested that the company adjourn to the library for coffee.

It is difficult at this distance to imagine the bitterness of the battle that raged over the nomination of Mr. Brandeis to the Supreme Court. A vast array of respectable citizens attacked it from every angle. Seven former presidents of the American Bar Association, including William H. Taft, Joseph H. Choate, and Elihu Root, vigorously opposed it. A delegation representing Boston eminence appeared before the Senate committee to assail his public and private life and demand his exclusion from the bench. With a keen eye for tactics, his critics concentrated on his alleged infractions of professional ethics, accused him of making "false and misleading statements," representing "interests opposed to public welfare," and resorting to "duplicity in the performance of his professional duties." From January until Spring the battle raged. Even the Democrats were disconcerted by the heavy and continuous fusillade. For a time it looked as if O'Gorman of New York, Reed of Missouri, Shields of Tennessee, and Smith of Georgia would vote against reporting the nomination favorably to the Senate.

So high did the waves of passion toss that President Wilson was moved to write a special letter to the chairman of the judiciary committee urging immediate and favorable action. The investigation, he insisted, had demonstrated that the charges against Mr. Brandeis were "unfounded," that they "threw a great deal more light on the character and motives of those with whom they originated than upon the qualifications of Mr. Brandeis." They had come largely from men who hated him because he refused to promote "their own selfish interests" and from people prejudiced and misled by propaganda. Such, the President said, were the conclusions to which he had come after making personal inquiries into the allegations that had been so freely bruited abroad. "The propaganda in this matter," he continued, "has been very extraordinary and very distressing to those who love fairness and value the dignity of the great professions."

Having disposed of the business of professional ethics, President Wilson proceeded to give his grounds for selecting Mr. Brandeis in the beginning. "I nominated Mr. Brandeis for the

Supreme Court," he said, "because it was and is my deliberate judgment that, of all the men now at the bar whom it has been my privilege to observe, test, and know, he is exceptionally qualified. I cannot speak too highly of his impartial, impersonal, orderly, and constructive mind, his rare analytical powers, his deep human sympathy, his profound acquaintance with the historical roots of our institutions and insight into their spirit, or of the many evidences he has given of being imbued, to the very heart, with our American ideals of justice and equality of opportunity; of his knowledge of modern economic conditions and the way they bear upon the masses of the people, or of his genius in getting persons to unite in common and harmonious action and look with frank and kindly eyes into each other's minds, who had before been heated antagonists. This friend of justice and of men will ornament the high Court of which we are all so justly proud. I am glad to have had the opportunity to pay him this just tribute of admiration and of confidence; and I beg that your committee will accept this nomination as coming from me, quick with a sense of public obligation and responsibility." In the end the nomination was confirmed by a vote that was almost strictly partisan in character and the outcome may be principally attributed to the resolute stand of President Wilson.

Who was this man that he should arouse such intense hostility in an immense sector of American respectability? Louis Dembitz Brandeis was born in Louisville, Kentucky, in 1856. His father and mother, with a small band of Jews from Bohemia, like so many other Europeans of the liberal faith, had fled to America after the Revolution of 1848 collapsed and sought liberty in "the Valley of Democracy." On both sides of his house there were heritages of culture, learning, and humanity and in the New World the old traditions were revitalized and expanded. His father and mother espoused the cause which Lincoln led, and his maternal uncle, Louis Dembitz, whose name the Justice bears, was an Abolitionist, a member of the Republican convention at Chicago in 1860, and one of the stalwart band of Lincoln supporters. Thus, although his father was a successful merchant, Louis D. Brandeis was brought up in no rarified counting-house atmosphere but in an environment of elevating aspirations, enriched by the high hopes of two hemispheres.

At the age of sixteen, young Brandeis was taken by his parents to Europe and while they travelled he spent three winters in a *Realschule* in Dresden where the rigid German discipline only served to emphasize his American individualism and make him more eager than ever to cast his lot in with the land of his birth, choosing the law as his profession. Undeterred by the wreck of his father's business in the panic of 1873, which forced him to earn his way, he entered the Harvard Law School in 1875, tutoring youngsters to pay his bills. Though plagued by bad eyesight and compelled to devote weary hours to the business of earning a living, he won for himself a reputation for extraordinary brilliance in legal studies and graduated with exceptional honors.

After a brief experiment in law practice at St. Louis, Brandeis returned to Boston and within less than ten years gathered a large clientele and won a high position in the community. Personally gifted, interested in the arts and music, acquainted with the masterpieces of the Old World, he easily found a wide circle of delightful acquaintances in Boston and, had he chosen, might have lived luxurious days full of ease, plenty, and contentment. But to a man of his spirit this gradual sinking into the downy couch of futility was so repugnant as to be impossible. When he married Alice Goldmark in 1891 he explained to her that by continuing his frugal habits he would be able henceforward to devote himself to many aspects of public life in which he was already interested; and with her full cooperation he set out on a course that led through colorful, if tempestuous, experiences to the Supreme Court of the United States.

A mere enumeration of the various enterprises in which Mr. Brandeis participated would fill more pages than are allotted to this Introduction, but a few incidents that help to give a clue to his thinking and temper may be brought out in perspective. Late in the eighties, when the American Federation of Labor was just getting under way, he became deeply impressed with the importance of trade unions in raising the standards of life for industrial workers, and held many long conferences with John F. O'Sullivan and his wife, who is perhaps better known as Mary Kenney. Very soon he was drawn in a professional way into a labor dispute as the representative of an employer and on making an inquiry into the facts of the case was struck by the ignorance of his client respecting wages and conditions in his own industry. In the end Mr. Brandeis acted as an arbiter and effected a satisfactory settlement.

This was the beginning of his long services as a mediator in industrial disputes. In all these cases, including the great dress and shirt makers' strike in New York, Mr. Brandeis operated on certain definite principles: organization on both sides as a necessary condition to the establishment and enforcement of standards, high wage-levels, preference for union workers, permanent machinery for the adjustment of disputes, and the impartial arbitration of controversies. Certainly there was nothing revolutionary in this creed, except to employers who believed that they were entitled to run their business in their own way without regard to the welfare of the workers under their jurisdiction. But moderate as the program may seem to genial liberals, it was decidedly distasteful to most industrial leaders at the time it was proposed and is by no means universally accepted today as the golden rule of political economy.

Fully aware that the trade union had definite limitations as an instrument for raising standards of industrial life all along the line, Mr. Brandeis gave equal attention to the political aspects of his interest. He early accepted woman suffrage on its merits as a human right and as a phase of women's effort to secure a firmer footing in our world of harsh conflict. From this it was but a step to supporting certain types of social legislation, respecting the hours of labor for women, the conditions of their industry, and minimum wages. Again and again he acted as counsel in cases involving the constitutionality of such legislation; and in connection with the preparation of his arguments he supplemented his study of legal precedents by a microscopic analysis of the material, economic, physiological, and psychological factors in each situation. In brief after brief he piled up facts, facts, facts, bearing on health, fatigue, and productivity, all designed to show the grim human necessity for the laws which he was defending. If a single illustration of the new approach be chosen, it may well be the brief in the Oregon case, prepared by Josephine Goldmark under the direction of Mr. Brandeis, reprinted in part below (pp. 337-348)—a plea which by common consent is an outstanding achievement in the development of American constitutional law. To make a long story too short, he was in 1916 the outstanding authority in the realities and jurisprudence of social legislation—legislation which appears mild enough now but made many great industrialists and college presidents fairly froth at the mouth in the spacious years of the early twentieth century.

Widening his range of concern, Mr. Brandeis gave attention to various phases of insurance so vital to masses of wage earners without economic reserves and dependent upon the hazards of industry and life. Those whose memories are long, or who have read a little history, know about the life insurance scandals which Charles E. Hughes investigated with such skill and acumen in New York that the people made him governor of the state. During this inquiry, Mr. Brandeis became deeply interested in a constructive way in the whole subject, and turning to his own commonwealth of Massachusetts he worked out and ardently championed, against embattled insurance companies, the Savings Bank Insurance Act under which safe insurance is sold at low rates to wage earners, and competing concerns are compelled to be more circumspect in their operations. And this he regarded as a step toward a wider system of insurance founded on mutual assistance, not profit-making. "The economic menace of past ages," he said in defending his program, "was the *dead* hand which gradually acquired a large part of all available lands. The greatest menace of today is the very *live* hand of these great insurance companies which control so large a part of our quick capital"—words by no means palatable to powerful persons in the financial streets of the country.

Reaching still further into the body politic, Mr. Brandeis attacked the question of public utility regulation. Did not street-car fares, gas bills, and electric-light charges go deeply into the pockets of the masses for whom he spoke? But here too his program was never utopian. He believed that fair terms could be worked out by reasonable men, on precise rules susceptible of mathematical expression. Taking his work in connection with the Boston Consolidated Gas Company case and the Elevated Railway contest as illustrative, in both of which he worked valiantly, we may generalize his principles somewhat in the following form: short-term franchises, careful safeguards for municipal rights over streets, prudent investment, standard dividends, reasonable charges adjusted on a sliding scale to dividends, and a mutuality of interest between stockholders and consumers. These ideas definitely realized would, he thought, eliminate the roots of political corruption in this connection and turn managerial energy into efficient management.

In a similar spirit Mr. Brandeis entered into the struggle over the regulation of railway rates and services which ran so high at the opening of the twentieth century. With characteristic zeal and penetration he made himself thoroughly informed on the subject of railroad management; in fact, one of the first masters in the field. And when the New York, New Haven, and Hartford Railway directors, under the leadership of Mr. Morgan and Mr. Mellon, opened their spectacular career of buying and consolidating, Mr. Brandeis, speaking as "the people's attorney" for the Public Franchise League, began a searching inquiry into their operations. By a study of their methods he became convinced that they were paying prices too high for the enterprises they were absorbing and that only by a death-grip monopoly of transportation in New England could they possibly earn dividends on the inflated bonds and stocks which they were issuing. Moreover, he concluded from his investigations that mere bigness made for inefficiency and that American railways were being wastefully conducted, so wastefully indeed that they were throwing to the winds at least a million dollars a day. Though he was defeated in his attempts to prevent certain mergers, he had the unhappy satisfaction of seeing his predictions realized in the crash of the New Haven line, so ruinous to the public and its stockholders. Moreover, everything he had said about the willful, blundering, and shortsighted management of the Company was more than confirmed by the investigations and reports of the Interstate Commerce Commission.

Less spectacular but more effective in immediate results were the labors of Mr. Brandeis as counsel for shippers and then as counsel for the Government in contests before the Interstate Commerce Commission over advances in freight rates. In 1910 a number of railway companies announced proposed increases in their charges and the Commission in reply made a thorough investigation into the reasonableness of their demands. In elaborate arguments buttressed by serried arrays of statistics and revealing a piercing insight into the finances and operations of the companies in question, Mr. Brandeis convinced the Commission that the public could not be expected to pay for imprudent capitalization and inefficient management. When the companies, dissatisfied with the rulings in the first set of cases, applied to the Commission again in 1913 for advances in rates, a similar process was followed and in the end its order granting a few increases was accompanied by a detailed bill of particulars showing how the railways might add to their net earnings by introducing better operating methods. For these constructive proposals, which time proved to be sound in many respects, Mr. Brandeis was in a large measure personally responsible. Here he made manifest once more his passion for facts and his power of penetrating into the realities of situations which give special distinction to his thinking and his manner of approaching problems.

Although constantly preoccupied with practical affairs, Mr. Brandeis found time to write voluminously on labor, trusts, railroads, insurance, and finance, always crowding his pages with facts and figures. In 1913-14, for example, he published a noteworthy series of articles in *Harper's Weekly* on "Our Financial Oligarchy," later reprinted under the title of *Other People's Money and How Bankers Use It*. In this systematic study he explained with great wealth of citations and statistics how bankers effected great combinations in business, established interlocking directorates, pumped water into values, skimmed commissions off of business coming and going, and then proved inefficient in management for the simple reason that the capacity to make financial deals did not carry with it ability in industrial administration. His remedy for this state of affairs was the dissolution of illegal industrial corporations which served as feeders for "the Money Trust." To accomplish this end he proposed that "the Sherman law should be supplemented both by providing more efficient judicial machinery and by creating a commission with administrative functions to aid in enforcing the law." Thus he foreshadowed the Clayton Anti-trust law and the Federal Trade Commission Act.

As if his hands were not already full, Mr. Brandeis undertook to serve as counsel in what amounted to the prosecution of the Secretary of the Interior, Richard A. Ballinger, led by Gifford Pinchot and Norman Hapgood, then of *Harper's Weekly*, before a joint congressional committee investigating charges of fraud in the disposition of public lands in the West and Alaska. It would not be possible here to attempt an analysis of the issues in this tangled controversy or to describe the angry political passions that accompanied it. Whatever the merits of the dispute, it is certain that Mr. Brandeis emerged as the champion of conservation, another one of the political problems of the time, and displayed an amazing knowledge of the workings of the Department of the Interior, which was exceedingly disconcerting to the defense.

Nor is it possible here to go deeper into the other activities of this remarkable man; to speak of his innumerable arguments on behalf of public interest before the courts of law, committees of Congress, state legislative committees, and the Interstate Commerce Commission, of his varied labors with private associations formed to realize social purposes, of his scattered writings and speeches on the questions of his time, or of his rôle in the Zionist movement in which he has been such a prominent figure. Some day the review will be made but this is not the time for it. It would also be out of place here to attempt a summary of Mr. Brandeis' judicial opinions—those printed in this volume and others which have been omitted from this limited collection. That is a task for a skilled lawyer with ample space at his disposal.

What may properly be undertaken is a summary picture of the idealized social order mirrored in the mind of the man who became a Justice of the Supreme Court in June, 1916. Admittedly it must be fragmentary at best and fail to satisfy those who feel it necessary to range themselves as friends or foes in this world of turmoil which, philosophically speaking, permits of no dichotomy. And it will also fall far short of the truth;

such is the fallibility of the best intentions. But this picture, faulty as it may be in perspective and detail, is the best contribution which a student can make to an understanding of Mr. Brandeis as a jurist and the rôle of the Supreme Court in the development of American economy, public and private. If to many lawyers the proceeding seems to be "immaterial and irrelevant," the great body of laymen who have given some thought to the evolution of American constitutional law will certainly find it germane to the issues of the present volume.

To be sure, the tradition of bar associations runs to the effect that the law is definite and explicit and that it is the business of judges to state the law, not to make it. And apparently this dubious proposition is widely taught in law schools as a canon binding on the faithful. But natural reason and inference from facts fail to support it. If the law is explicit and clear as the multiplication table, then why all this bother to keep Mr. Brandeis or Mr. Hughes or Mr. Parker off the Supreme Bench? Why all this exploration of the earlier opinions and affiliations of men proposed for the Supreme Court? If the law is precise, then any trained mind in a sound body ought to be able to find it and expound it; one disciplined lawyer ought to be as good as another and a stiff legal examination would be a more certain way of discovering competence than presidential searching and senatorial scrutiny. If the law is clear and has nothing to do with private convictions of the judges, why call their expositions "opinions"? Above all, if this assumption is well founded, why are the nine judges, all able, all trained, all informed, all under an oath to uphold the Constitution so often divided five to four over the meaning of the document they expound? "General propositions do not decide concrete cases," remarked Mr. Justice Holmes in Lochner *vs.* New York. "The decision will depend on a judgment or intuition more subtle than any articulate major premise." And from what does that judgment or intuition spring except from the mind of the judge made up, as Locke told us long ago, out of his experience—his whole cultural heritage with its wide-ramifying social affiliations?

Mr. Justice Brandeis, like every other judge, entered upon his responsibilities with a fairly coherent picture in his mind of what he wished American society to represent and become. It is true that he wrote no systematic treatise on sociology before taking on the ermine. Nor was he given to that logical perfection which usually eventuates in Utopia. Yet from his writings and activities so briefly surveyed above can be constructed in bold outlines a mosaic of the convictions and facts that largely determined his approach to controversial questions before the Court.

American society, as Mr. Brandeis then conceived it, should not be dominated by huge monopolies and trusts, but should be the home of "the new freedom," in which small, individual enterprises can flourish under the defensive arm of the government. The relations of the great utilities and the public should be adjusted on principles of prudent investment, efficient capitalization, scientific management, and fair earnings equitably shared with the public under sliding-scale rules. Trade unions are necessary to the upholding of decent living standards among the mass of workers, and in the weighting of judicial opinion they should be given the benefit of the doubt unless the mandate of the law is too clear to be mistaken or the end sought is undesirable as ascertained by an inquiry into facts. The weakness of wage-earners in our industrial society must be offset by state and federal legislation of a social character, and since the Constitution is blessed by "a convenient vagueness," such legislation should be sustained if the facts indicate that it is fairly calculated to accomplish a reasonable purpose. Perhaps in the future, to conclude the summary, our capitalistic order may be materially supplemented by the development of cooperation along the lines so successfully followed in Great Britain. And from this picture can be drawn the antithesis which explains why Mr. Justice Brandeis, along with his colleague, Mr. Justice Holmes, is so often found on the dissenting side.

If from the substance of Mr. Brandeis' mind, we turn to his intellectual methods—by no means as separable as logicians sometimes imagine—we find certain characteristics just as well marked. All his reasoning is orderly, representing a clear-cut course of thought. His speeches, arguments, and judicial opinions march. They have a point of departure, a route, and a terminus; never do they wander through oceans of words along uncertain ways to irrelevant ends. He has a sense for the precision of language and uses it as a fine-edged tool. He has a passion for concrete things, rather than abstractions, pertinent data revealing the intimate relation of laws and judicial decisions to practical affairs. Above all he seeks to draw his jurisprudence out of the realities of life—its work, its economy, and its social arrangements. For the copious citation of more or less dubious precedents, which are seldom exactly apposite, he has little affection, preferring, it seems, to substitute for the show of authority a display of stubborn and irreducible facts knit closely together in a pattern of thinking. A minimum of legal legerdemain and a maximum of data and logic—there is his method as revealed in his written words, which are at bottom confessions of the man.

And what of his place in American constitutional development? That, as of every other statesman, will depend not upon the purity of his spirit, the logic of his mind, nor his arrangement of materials, but upon the degree to which he has divined the future—the upshot of the things in which he has been immersed. Is the America of tomorrow to be the society of "the new freedom" so effectively portrayed by Mr. Brandeis and the President who appointed him? Or will the march of integration in finance and industry override the small enterprises which they sought to preserve against extinction? Here we all see

through a glass darkly. Those who have thought most about
it may be inclined to say with Henry Adams that, given our
ignorance, silence is best. And yet, even though the year 2000
may be far from the picture which Mr. Brandeis has idealized
in his mind, we may be sure that the realistic, fact-burdened
method which he has employed in all his thinking about legal
and economic affairs will have an increasing influence on coming
generations of students, lawyers, and judges. Humanity and
ideas, as well as things, are facts, and a jurisprudence which
takes them into account cannot perish from the earth.

CHARLES A. BEARD.

The series of dots that recur in the Opinions indicate the citations of Court decisions. As these are only of technical interest, the editor has thought best to omit them for the sake of smooth reading. Where asterisks occur, they indicate omissions that occur in the original, except in the excerpts, where they denote editorial selection.

Although the numerous footnotes which in the original accompany these Opinions are also omitted, attention must be called to their exhaustive marshalling of proof in demonstration of the views expressed in the text.

I. Labor Problems

"The Chronic Problem of Unemployment"

(Dissenting Opinion, *Adams* v. *Tanner*, 1917)

IMMEDIATELY AFTER THE VOTERS OF THE STATE OF WASHINGTON adopted a measure prohibiting employment agencies from taking fees from workers, a private agency sued in a Federal District Court to prevent enforcement of the law on the ground that it violated the due process clause of the Fourteenth Amendment. An injunction was denied and the bill dismissed, but on appeal the Supreme Court upheld the contention of the agency by a vote of five to four.

The State contended that the business is "economically . . . non-useful, if not vicious, because it compels the needy and unfortunate to pay for that which they are entitled to without fee or price, that is, the right to work." To this Mr. Justice McReynolds, writing for the majority of the Court, replied that the abuses in the business justified its regulation, but that the statute brought about its destruction. Since, when properly conducted, the private agency is useful, to destroy it, he said, is "arbitrary and oppressive."

Justice McKenna, dissenting, simply stated his view that, under prior decisions, the law was a valid exercise of the police power of the State. Justices Holmes and Clarke concurred in the following opinion of Justice Brandeis:

"To DECLARE the statute of a State, enacted in the exercise of the police power, invalid under the Fourteenth Amendment, is a matter of such seriousness that I state the reasons for my dissent from the opinion of the Court.

"The statute of the State of Washington, commonly known as the 'Abolishing Employment Offices Measure,' was proposed

[3]

by Initiative Petition No. 8, filed July 3, 1914, and was adopted November 3, 1914, at the general election; 162,054 votes being cast for the measure and 144,544 against it. In terms, the Act merely prohibits the taking of fees from those seeking employment.

"Plaintiffs, who are proprietors of private employment agencies in the city of Spokane, assert that this statute, if enforced, would compel them to discontinue business and would thus, in violation of the Fourteenth Amendment, deprive them of their liberty and property without due process of law. The Act leaves the plaintiffs free to collect fees from employers; and it appears that private employment agencies thus restricted are still carrying on business. But even if it should prove, as plaintiffs allege, that their business could not live without collecting fees from employees, that fact would not necessarily render the Act invalid. Private employment agencies are a business properly subject to police regulation and control. . . . And this Court has made it clear that a statute enacted to promote health, safety, morals, or the public welfare may be valid, *although* it will compel discontinuance of existing businesses in whole or in part. Statutes prohibiting the manufacture and sale of liquor present the most familiar example of such a prohibition. But where, as here, no question of interstate commerce is involved, this Court has sustained also statutes or municipal ordinances which compelled discontinuance of such business as (*a*) of manufacturing and selling oleomargarine . . . , (*b*) of selling cigarettes . . . , (*c*) of selling futures in grain or other commodities . . . , (*d*) of selling stocks on margin . . . , (*e*) of keeping billiard halls . . . , (*f*) of selling trading stamps.

"These cases show that the scope of the police power is not limited to regulation as distinguished from prohibition. They show also that the power of the State exists equally, whether the end sought to be attained is the promotion of health, safety, or morals, or is the prevention of fraud or the prevention of general demoralization. 'If the State thinks that an admitted evil cannot be prevented except by prohibiting a calling or transaction not in itself necessarily objectionable, the courts cannot interfere, unless in looking at the substance of the matter, they can see that it "is a clear, unmistakable infringement of rights secured by the fundamental law." ' *Otis* v. *Parker*, 187 U. S. 606, 609. Or, as it is so frequently expressed, the action of the Legislature is final, unless the measure adopted appears clearly to be arbitrary or unreasonable, or to have no real or substantial relation to the object sought to be attained. Whether a measure relating to the public welfare is arbitrary or unreasonable, whether it has no substantial relation to the end proposed, is obviously not to be determined by assumptions or by *a priori* reasoning. The judgment should be based upon a consideration of relevant facts, actual or possible—*Ex facto jus oritur*. That ancient rule must prevail in order that we may have a system of living law.

"It is necessary to inquire, therefore: What was the evil which the people of Washington sought to correct? Why was the particular remedy embodied in the statute adopted? And, incidentally, what has been the experience, if any, of other States or countries in this connection? But these inquiries are entered upon, not for the purpose of determining whether the remedy adopted is wise, or even for the purpose of determining what the facts actually were. The decision of such questions lies with the legislative branch of the Government. . . . The sole purpose of the inquiries is to enable this Court to decide whether, in view of the facts, actual or possible, the action of the State of Washington was so clearly arbitrary or so unreasonable that it could not be taken 'by a free government without a violation of fundamental rights.' See *McCray* v. *United States*, 195 U. S. 27, 64.

"*1. The Evils.*

"The evils with which the people of Washington were confronted arose partly from the abuses incident to the system of

[5]

private employment agencies and partly from its inadequacy.

"(*a*) The abuses.

"These are summarized in a report published by the United States Bureau of Labor in October, 1912. [Brandeis' opinion quotes from the bureau's Bulletin No. 109, p. 36, listing fraudulent methods used by agencies, including collusion with employers who discharge workers after a few days and collusion with keepers of immoral houses.]

"In the report to Congress of the United States Commission on Industrial Relations, created by Act of August 23, 1912 (chap. 351, 37 Stat. 415) which gave public hearings on the subject of employment offices in May, 1914, the abuses are found to be as follows. [The opinion then quotes from the report, which emphasizes extortionate fees, discrimination, fee-splitting with foremen who discharge men constantly in order to hire more, and misrepresentation of terms and conditions of employment.]

"(*b*) The inadequacy.

"But the evils were not limited to what are commonly called abuses—like the fraud and extortion described above. Even the exemplary private offices charging fees to workers might prove harmful, for the reason thus stated in the report to Congress of the United States Commission on Industrial Relations, cited *supra*. [The next quotation declares that the agencies congest the labor market, increase irregularity of employment, fill vacancies with people already employed elsewhere so as to earn more fees; keep men idle by imposing fees which erect barriers to jobs, and make the weakest and poorest classes of wage-earners pay "the largest share for a service rendered to employers, to workers, and to the public as well."]

"*2. The Remedies.*

"During the fifteen years preceding 1914 there had been extensive experimentation in the regulation of private employment

[6]

agencies. Twenty-four States had attempted *direct* regulation under statutes, often supplemented by municipal ordinances. Nineteen States had attempted *indirect* regulation through the competition of municipal offices. Other experiments in indirect regulation through competition were made by voluntary organizations, philanthropic, social, and industrial. The results of those experiments were unsatisfactory. The abuses continued in large measure; and the private offices survived to a great extent the competition of the free agencies, public and private. There gradually developed a conviction that the evils of private agencies were inherent and ineradicable, so long as they were permitted to charge fees to the workers seeking employment. And many believed that such charges were the root of the evil.

"On September 25, 1914, the American Association of Public Employment Offices adopted at its annual meeting the following resolutions [favoring the elimination of all private employment agencies operating for a profit within the United States.]

"The United States Commission on Industrial Relations declared in its report to Congress [that State attempts to remove the abuses had proved futile and that officers in charge of State regulation favored total abolition of private labor agencies.]

"But the remedies proposed were not limited to the suppression of private offices charging fees to workers, and the extension of the system of State and municipal offices. The conviction became widespread that, for the solution of the larger problem of unemployment, the aid of the Federal Government and the utilization and development of its extensive machinery was indispensable. During the seven years preceding 1914 a beginning had been made in this respect. The Immigration Act of February 20, 1907 (chap. 1134, 34 Stat. 898, 909), created within the Bureau of Immigration and Naturalization a Division of Information, charged with the duty of promoting 'a beneficial distribution of aliens.' The services rendered by this

[7]

division included, among others, some commonly performed by employment agencies. While it undertook to place in positions of employment only aliens, its operations were national in scope. The Act of March 4, 1913, creating the Department of Labor, resulted in a transfer of the Bureau of Immigration, including the Division of Information, to that department. . . . By this transfer the scope of the division's work was enlarged to correspond with the broad powers of the Labor Department. These were declared by Congress to be:

'to foster, promote, and develop the welfare of the wage-earners of the United States, to improve their working conditions, and to advance their opportunities for profitable employment.'

"Then its efforts 'to distribute' (that is, both to supply and to find places for) labor were extended to include citizens as well as aliens; and much was done to develop the machinery necessary for such distribution. In the summer of 1914, and in part before the filing in the State of Washington of the proposal for legislation here in question, action had been taken by the Department of Labor which attracted public attention. It undertook to supply harvest hands needed in the Middle West and also to find work for the factory hands thrown out of employment by the great fire at Salem, Massachusetts, June 25, 1914. The division was strengthened by cooperation with other departments of the Federal Government (Agriculture, Interior, Commerce, and the Post Office, with its 60,000 local offices) and with State and municipal employment offices. As early as June 13, 1914, the United States Department of Labor had also sought the cooperation in this work of all the leading newspapers in America, including those printed in foreign languages.

"*3. Conditions in the State of Washington.*

"The peculiar needs of Washington emphasized the defects of the system of private employment offices.

"(*a*) The evils.

"The conditions generally prevailing are described in a report recently published by the United States Department of Labor, thus: [The opinion quotes Bureau of Labor Bulletin No. 211, pp. 17, 18, which mentions the casual, short-time jobs and the frequent shifting of workers in the Pacific States.]

"The reports of the Washington State Bureau of Labor give this description: [Report 1913, 1914, pp. 27, 28; Report 1915, 1916, p. 120. The condition of imposing high fees, sending men long distances and setting them adrift after a few days' work is described as obnoxious.]

"The abuses and the inadequacy of the then existing system are also described by State officials in affidavits included in the record.

"(*b*) The remedies.

"Washington had not tried direct regulation of private employment offices, but that method was being considered as late as 1912. Its people had had, on the other hand, exceptional opportunities of testing public employment offices. The municipal employment office established at Seattle in 1894 under an amendment of the city charter is among the oldest public offices in the United States. Tacoma established a municipal office in 1904, Spokane in 1905, and Everett in 1908. The continuance and increase of these municipal offices indicate that their experience in public employment agencies was at least encouraging. And the low cost of operating them was extraordinary. In Spokane the fees charged by private agencies ranged from $1 upward, and were usually about $2. In the Seattle free municipal agency the cost of operations, per position filled, was reduced to a trifle over four cents. The preliminary steps for establishing 'Distribution Stations' under the Federal system, including one at Seattle, had been taken before the passage of the Washington law. Later branch offices were established in thirteen other cities.

"4. The Fundamental Problem.

"The problem which confronted the people of Washington was far more comprehensive and fundamental than that of protecting workers applying to the private agencies. It was the chronic problem of unemployment,—perhaps the gravest and most difficult problem of modern industry,—the problem which, owing to business depression, was the most acute in America during the years 1913 to 1915. In the State of Washington the suffering from unemployment was accentuated by the lack of staple industries operating continuously throughout the year and by unusual fluctuations in the demand for labor, with consequent reduction of wages and increase of social unrest. Students of the larger problem of unemployment appear to agree that establishment.of an adequate system of employment offices or labor exchanges is an indispensable first step toward its solution. There is reason to believe that the people of Washington not only considered the collection by the private employment offices of fees from employees a social injustice, but that they considered the elimination of the practice a necessary preliminary to the establishment of a constructive policy for dealing with the subject of unemployment.

"It is facts and considerations like these which may have led the people of Washington to prohibit the collection by employment agencies of fees from applicants for work. And weight should be given to the fact that the statute has been held constitutional by the Supreme Court of Washington and by the Federal District Court (three judges sitting),—courts presumably familiar with the local conditions and needs.

"In so far as protection of the applicant is a specific purpose of the statute, a precedent was furnished by the Act of Congress, December 21, 1898, 30 Stat. 755, 763 (considered in *Patterson* v. *The Eudora*, 190 U. S. 169), which provides, among other things:

" 'If any person shall demand or receive, either directly or indirectly, from any seaman or other person seeking employment as seaman, or from any person on his behalf, any remuneration whatever for providing him with employment, he shall for every such offense be liable to a penalty of not more than $100.'

"In so far as the statute may be regarded as a step in the effort to overcome industrial maladjustment and unemployment by shifting to the employer the payment of fees, if any, the action taken may be likened to that embodied in the Washington Workmen's Compensation Law (sustained in *Mountain Timber Co.* v. *Washington,* 243 U. S. 219), whereby the financial burden of industrial accidents is required to be borne by the employers.

"As was said in *Holden* v. *Hardy,* 169 U. S. 366, 387:

" '. . . in view of the fact that from the day Magna Charta was signed to the present moment, amendments to the structure of the law have been made with increasing frequency, it is impossible to suppose that they will not continue, and the law be forced to adapt itself to new conditions of society, and particularly to the new relations between employers and employees as they arise.'

"In my opinion, the judgment of the District Court should be affirmed."

Adams, et al. v. *Tanner, Attorney General*
of the State of Washington, et al.
244 U. S. 590, 597

Curbing Efforts to Unionize

(The "Yellow Dog" Contract)

(Dissenting Opinion, *Hitchman Coal Co.* v. *Mitchell*, 1917)

A WEST VIRGINIA COAL MINING COMPANY OBTAINED AN INJUNCTION in a District Court restraining agents of the United Mine Workers of America from interfering with its labor relations to compel the company to unionize its mine. All its employees had been given work on condition that they would join no union while in the company's employ.

The District Court based its decree on two grounds: the union was a common-law conspiracy in unreasonable restraint of trade, and its organizers were unlawfully attempting to induce breach of contract. The decree was reversed in the Circuit Court of Appeals, which held that the evidence failed to show the use of unlawful methods, but the Supreme Court reversed once more, and reinstated the decree of the District Court.

Mr. Justice Pitney, for the majority of the Court, said that the company had a legal right to run a non-union mine, and that the union organizers were motivated, not by a bona fide interest in increasing the membership of the union, but by the illegal desire to compel the company to change its method of operation. The absence of violence did not make their methods legal. "In our opinion, any violation of plaintiff's legal rights contrived by defendants for the purpose of inflicting damage, or having that as its necessary effect, is as plainly inhibited by the law as if it involved a breach of the peace. A combination to procure concerted breaches of contract by plaintiff's employees constitutes such a violation."

Mr. Justice Brandeis dissented (Holmes and Clarke, JJ., concurring). He rehearsed the facts and gave these conclusions:

[12]

"FIRST: The alleged illegality of the United Mine Workers of America under the law of West Virginia.

"The United Mine Workers of America does not appear to differ essentially in character and purpose from other international unions which, like it, are affiliated with the American Federation of Labor. Its membership is said to be larger than that of any other; and it may be more powerful. But the common law does not limit the size of unions or the degree to which the individual workmen may by union increase their bargaining power. As stated in *Gompers* v. *Buck Stove & Range Co.,* 221 U. S. 418, 439: 'The law, therefore, recognizes the right of workingmen to unite and to invite others to join their ranks, thereby making available the strength, influence and power that comes from such association'.

"We do not find either in the decisions or the statutes of West Virginia anything inconsistent with the law as declared by this Court. The union is not an unlawful organization, and is not in itself an unlawful conspiracy. We have no occasion to consider the legality of the specific provisions contained in its constitution or by-laws.

"*Second*: The alleged illegality of the United Mine Workers of America under the Federal Anti-Trust Act.

"The District Judge undertook to pass upon the legality of the United Mine Workers of America under the Federal Anti-Trust Act; but the question was not in issue in the case. It had not been raised in the bill or by answer. Evidence bearing upon the issue was properly objected to by defendants and should have been excluded.

"*Third*: The alleged conspiracy against the West Virginia mines.

"It was doubtless the desire of the United Mine Workers of America to unionize every mine on the American continent and especially those in West Virginia which compete directly with the mines of Western Pennsylvania, Ohio, Indiana, and other States already unionized. That desire and the purpose to effect it were not unlawful. They were part of a reasonable effort to improve the condition of workingmen engaged in the industry by strengthening their bargaining power through unions, and extending the field of union power. No conspiracy to shut down or otherwise injure West Virginia was proved, nor was there any averment in the bill of such conspiracy, or any issue otherwise raised by the pleadings which justified the consideration of that question by the District Court. [In a footnote the dissenting opinion adds: "This alleged conspiracy not being in issue, the District Court improperly allowed the introduction of, and considered, a mass of documents referring to various mine workers' conventions, and joint conventions of miners and operators held years previous to the filing of the bill. Judge Dayton laid great stress on reported declarations of the delegates to these conventions, although the declarations of alleged co-conspirators were obviously inadmissible, there being no foundation for the conspiracy charge".]

"*Fourth*: 'Unionizing plaintiff's mine without plaintiff's consent'.

"The fundamental prohibition of the injunction is against acts done 'for the purpose of unionizing plaintiff's mine without plaintiff's consent.' Unionizing a shop does not mean inducing the employees to become members of the union. It means inducing the employer to enter into a collective agreement with the union governing the relations of the employer to the employees. Unionizing implies, therefore, at least *formal* consent of the employer. Both plaintiff and defendants insisted upon exercising the right to secure contracts for a closed shop. The plaintiff sought to secure the *closed non-union shop* through individual agreements with employees. The defendants sought to secure the *closed union shop* through a collective agreement with the union. Since collective bargaining is legal,

[14]

the fact that the workingmen's agreement is made not by individuals directly with the employer, but by the employees with the union and by it, on their behalf, with the employer, is of no significance in this connection. The end being *lawful*, defendants' efforts to unionize the mine can be illegal only if the methods or means pursued were unlawful; unless indeed there is some special significance in the expression 'unionizing without plaintiff's consent.'

"It is urged that a union agreement curtails the liberty of the operator. Every agreement curtails the liberty of those who enter into it. The test of legality is not whether an agreement curtails liberty, but whether the parties have agreed upon something which the law prohibits or declares otherwise to be inconsistent with the public welfare. The operator by the union agreement binds himself: (1) To employ only members of the union; (2) to negotiate with union officers instead of with employees individually the scale of wages and the hours of work; (3) to treat with the duly constituted representatives of the union to settle disputes concerning the discharge of men and other controversies arising out of the employment. These are the chief features of a 'unionizing' by which the employer's liberty is curtailed. Each of them is legal. To obtain any of them or all of them men may lawfully strive and even strike. And, if the union may legally strike to obtain each of the things for which the agreement provides, why may it not strike or use equivalent economic pressure to secure an agreement to provide them?

"It is also urged that defendants are seeking to 'coerce' plaintiff to 'unionize' its mine. But coercion, in a legal sense, is not exerted when a union merely endeavors to induce employees to join a union with the intention thereafter to order a strike unless the employer consents to unionize his shop. Such pressure is not coercion in the legal sense. The employer is free either to accept the agreement or the disadvantage.

[15]

Indeed, the plaintiff's whole case is rested upon agreements secured under similar pressure of economic necessity or disadvantage. If it is coercion to threaten to strike unless plaintiff consents to a closed union shop, it is coercion also to threaten not to give one employment unless the applicant will consent to a closed non-union shop. The employer may sign the union agreement for fear that *labor* may not be otherwise obtainable; the workman may sign the individual agreement for fear that *employment* may not be otherwise obtainable. But such fear does not imply coercion in a legal sense.

"In other words an employer, in order to effectuate the closing of his shop to *union* labor, may exact an agreement to that effect from his employees. The agreement itself being a lawful one, the employer may withhold from the men an economic need—employment—until they assent to make it. Likewise an agreement closing a shop to *non-union* labor being lawful, the union may withhold from an employer an economic need—labor—until he assents to make it. In a legal sense an agreement entered into, under such circumstances, is voluntarily entered into; and as the agreement is in itself legal, no reason appears why the general rule that a legal end may be pursued by legal means should not be applied. Or, putting it in other words, there is nothing in the character of the agreement which should make *unlawful* means used to attain it which in other connections are recognized as *lawful*.

"*Fifth*: There was no attempt to induce employees to violate their contracts.

"The contract created an employment at will; and the employee was free to leave at any time. The contract did not bind the employee not to join the union; and he was free to join it at any time. The contract merely bound him to withdraw from plaintiff's employ if he joined the union. There is evidence of an attempt to induce plaintiff's employees to *agree* to join the union; but none whatever of any attempt to induce them to violate their contract. Until an employee actually joined the union he was not, under the contract, called upon to leave plaintiff's employ. There consequently would be no breach of contract until the employee both joined the union *and* failed to withdraw from plaintiff's employ. There was no evidence that any employee was persuaded to do that or that such a course was contemplated. What perhaps was intended was to secure agreements or assurances from individual employees that they would join the union when a large number of them should have consented to do so; with the purpose, when such time arrived, to have them join the union together and strike—unless plaintiff consented to unionize the mine. Such a course would have been clearly permissible under the contract.

"*Sixth*: Merely persuading employees to leave plaintiff's employ or others not to enter it, was not unlawful.

"To induce third persons to leave an employment is actionable if done maliciously and without justifiable cause although such persons are free to leave at their own will. . . . It is equally actionable so to induce others not to enter the service. The individual contracts of plaintiff with its employees added nothing to its right in this connection, since the employment was terminable at will.

"As persuasion, considered merely as a means, is clearly legal, defendants were within their rights if, and only if, their interference with the relation of plaintiff to its employees was for justifiable cause. The purpose of interfering was confessedly in order to strengthen the union, in the belief that thereby the condition of workmen engaged in mining would be improved; the bargaining power of the individual workingman was to be strengthened by collective bargaining; and collective bargaining was to be insured by obtaining the union agreement. It should not, at this day, be doubted that to induce workingmen to leave or not to enter an employment in order to advance such a purpose, is justifiable when the workmen are not bound by contract to remain in such employment.

"*Seventh*: There was no 'threat, violence, or intimidation.'

"The decree enjoined 'threats, violence or intimidation.' Such action would, of course, be unlawful though employed in a justifiable cause. But there is no evidence that any of the defendants have resorted to such means. The propaganda among plaintiff's employees was conducted almost entirely by one man, the defendant Hughes, a district No. 6 organizer. His actions were orderly and peaceable, consisting of informal talks with the men, and a few quietly conducted public meetings in which he argued the benefits of organization and pointed out to the men that, although the company was then paying them according to the union scale, there would be nothing to prevent a later reduction of wages unless the men united. He also urged upon the men that if they lost their present jobs, membership in the union was requisite to obtaining employment in the union mines of the neighboring States. But there is no suggestion that he exceeded the moderate bounds of peaceful persuasion, and indeed, if plaintiff's witnesses are to be believed, men with whom Hughes had talked, his argument made no impression on them, and they expressed to him their satisfaction with existing conditions at the mine.

"When this suit was filed no right of the plaintiff had been infringed and there was no reasonable ground to believe that any of its rights would be interfered with; and, in my opinion, the Circuit Court of Appeals properly reversed the decree of the District Court, and directed that the bill be dismissed."

Hitchman Coal & Coke Co. v. *Mitchel, et al.*
245 U. S. 229, 263

[18]

Inducing Workers to Boycott

(Dissenting Opinion, *Duplex Printing Press Co. v. Deering*, 1921)

A COMPANY MANUFACTURING PRINTING PRESSES IN MICHIGAN sought to enjoin the business agents of the New York local of the International Association of Machinists from interfering with its interstate trade by conspiring in violation of the Sherman Anti-Trust Law. Plaintiff charged that the union was attempting to induce the company's customers not to purchase, and the customers' workers not to haul, handle, or instal its presses. Before the suit was brought to hearing the Clayton Act was passed.

Section 20 of the Clayton Act restricts the granting of injunctions in cases "between an employer and employees . . . involving, or growing out of, a dispute concerning terms or conditions of employment." The two lower courts held that this section barred the grant of an injunction. But a majority of the Supreme Court, speaking through Mr. Justice Pitney, held that the restriction is limited to a case between the actual parties to such a dispute; that the 60,000 members of the machinists' union could not make a controversy at the Michigan factory their own; that plaintiff's business was a property right entitled to protection against unlawful interference, and that the union, by instigating sympathetic strikes and boycotts against employers who were purchasers of plaintiff's product, was a conspiracy in restraint of trade.

"Congress had in mind particular controversies, not a general class war," Justice Pitney said.

Holmes and Clarke, JJ., concurred in the dissenting opinion of Justice Brandeis:

THE DUPLEX COMPANY, a manufacturer of newspaper printing presses, seeks to enjoin officials of the machinists' and

[19]

affiliated unions from interfering with its business by inducing their members not to work for plaintiff or its customers in connection with the setting up of presses made by it. Unlike *Hitchman Coal & Coke Co.* v. *Mitchell* [*supra*], there is here no charge that defendants are inducing employees to break their contracts. Nor is it now urged that defendants threaten acts of violence. But plaintiff insists that the acts complained of violate both the common law of New York and the Sherman Act, and that, accordingly, it is entitled to relief by injunction under the State law and under §16 of the Clayton Act, October 15, 1914, c. 323, 38 Stat. 730, 737.

"The defendants admit interference with plaintiff's business but justify on the following ground: There are in the United States only four manufacturers of such presses; and they are in active competition. Between 1909 and 1913 the machinists' union induced three of them to recognize and deal with the union, to grant the eight-hour day, to establish a minimum wage scale, and to comply with other union requirements. The fourth, the Duplex Company, refused to recognize the union; insisted upon conducting its factory on the open shop principle; refused to introduce the eight-hour day and operated, for the most part, ten hours a day; refused to establish a minimum wage scale; and disregarded other union standards. Thereupon two of the three manufacturers who had assented to union conditions notified the union that they should be obliged to terminate their agreements with it unless their competitor, the Duplex Company, also entered into the agreement with the union, which, in giving more favorable terms to labor, imposed correspondingly greater burdens upon the employer. Because the Duplex Company refused to enter into such an agreement, and in order to induce it to do so, the machinists' union declared a strike at its factory, and in aid of that strike instructed its members and the members of affiliated unions not to work on the installation of presses which plaintiff had delivered in New York. Defendants insisted that by the common law of New York, where the acts complained of were done, and where this suit was brought, and also by §20 of the Clayton Act, 38 Stat. 730, 738, the facts constitute a justification for this interference with plaintiff's business.

"*First.* As to the rights at common law: Defendants' justification is that of self-interest. They have supported the strike at the employer's factory by a strike elsewhere against its product. They have injured the plaintiff, not maliciously, but in self-defense. They contend that the Duplex Company's refusal to deal with the machinists' union and to observe its standards threatened the interest, not only of such union members as were its factory employees, but even more of all members of the several affiliated unions employed by plaintiff's competitors and by others whose more advanced standards the plaintiff was, in reality, attacking; and that none of the defendants and no person whom they are endeavoring to induce to refrain from working in connection with the setting up of presses made by plaintiff is an outsider, an interloper. In other words, that the contest between the company and the machinists' union involves vitally the interest of every person whose cooperation is sought. May not all with a common interest join in refusing to expend their labor upon articles whose very production constitutes an attack upon their standard of living and the institution which they are convinced supports it? Applying common-law principles the answer should, in my opinion, be: Yes, if as a matter of fact those who so cooperate have a common interest.

"The change in the law by which strikes once illegal and even criminal are now recognized as lawful was effected in America largely without the intervention of legislation. This reversal of a common-law rule was not due to the rejection by the courts of one principle and the adoption in its stead of another, but to a better realization of the facts of industrial life. It is conceded that, although the strike of the workmen in plaintiff's factory injured its business, the strike was not an actionable wrong; because the obvious self-interest of the strikers constituted a justification. . . . Formerly courts held that self-interests could not be so served. . . . But even after strikes to raise wages or reduce hours were held to be legal because of the self-interest, some courts held that there was not sufficient causal relationship between a strike to unionize a shop and the self-interest of the strikers to justify injuries inflicted. . . . But other courts, repeating the same legal formula, found that there was justification, because they viewed the facts differently. . . .

"When centralization in the control of business brought its corresponding centralization in the organization of workingmen, new facts had to be appraised. A single employer might, as in this case, threaten the standing of the whole organization and the standards of all its members; and when he did so the union, in order to protect itself, would naturally refuse to work on his materials wherever found. When such a situation was first presented to the courts, judges concluded that the intervention of the purchaser of the materials established an insulation through which the direct relationship of the employer and the workingmen did not penetrate; and the strike against the material was considered a strike against the purchaser by unaffected third parties. . . . But other courts, with better appreciation of the facts of industry, recognized the unity of interest throughout the union, and that, in refusing to work on materials which threatened it, the union was only refusing to aid in destroying itself. . . .

"So, in the case at bar, deciding a question of fact upon the evidence introduced and matters of common knowledge, I should say, as the two lower courts apparently have said, that the defendants and those from whom they sought cooperation have a common interest which the plaintiff threatened. This view is in harmony with the views of the Court of Appeals of New York. For in New York, although boycotts like that in *Loewe* v. *Lawlor*, 208 U. S. 274, are illegal because they are conducted, not against a product, but against those who deal in it, and are carried out by a combination of persons, not united by common interest, but only by sympathy . . . , it is lawful for all members of a union by whomever employed to refuse to handle materials whose production weakens the union. . . .

"In my opinion, therefore, plaintiff had no cause of action by the common law of New York.

"*Second*. As to the anti-trust laws of the United States: §20 of the Clayton Act declares:

'Nor shall any of the acts specified in this paragraph be considered or held to be violations of any law of the United States'.

"The acts which are thus referred to are, whether performed singly or in concert:

'Terminating any relation of employment, or*** ceasing to perform any work or labor, or*** recommending, advising or persuading others by peaceful means so to do; or*** attending at any place where such person or persons may lawfully be, for the purpose of obtaining or communicating information, or*** peacefully persuading any person to work or abstain from working; or*** ceasing to patronize or employ any party to such dispute, or*** recommending, advising, or persuading others by peaceful and lawful means so to do; or*** paying or giving to, or withholding from, any person engaged in such dispute, any strike benefits or other moneys or things of value; or

[23]

peacefully assembling in a lawful manner and for lawful purposes; or*** doing any act or thing which might lawfully be done in the absence of such dispute by any party thereto'.

"This statute was the fruit of unceasing agitation, which extended over more than twenty years and was designed to equalize before the law the position of workingmen and employer as industrial combatants. Aside from the use of the injunction, the chief source of dissatisfaction with the existing law lay in the doctrine of malicious combination, and, in many parts of the country, in the judicial declarations of the illegality at common law of picketing and persuading others to leave work. The grounds for objection to the latter are obvious. The objection to the doctrine of malicious combinations requires some explanation. By virtue of that doctrine, damage resulting from conduct such as striking or withholding patronage or persuading others to do either, which without more might be *damnum absque injuria* because the result of trade competition, became actionable when done for a purpose which a judge considered socially or economically harmful and therefore branded as malicious and unlawful. It was objected that, due largely to environment, the social and economic ideas of judges, which thus became translated into law, were prejudicial to a position of equality between workingmen and employer; that due to this dependence upon the individual opinion of judges great confusion existed as to what purposes were lawful and what unlawful; and that in any event Congress, not the judges, was the body which should declare what public policy in regard to the industrial struggle demands.

"By 1914 the ideas of the advocates of legislation had fairly crystallized upon the manner in which the inequality and uncertainty of the law should be removed. It was to be done by expressly legalizing certain acts regardless of the effects produced by them upon other persons. As to them Congress was to extract the element of *injuria* from the damages thereby inflicted, instead of leaving judges to determine according to their own economic and social views whether the damage inflicted on an employer in an industrial struggle was *damnum absque injuria,* because an incident of trade competition, or a legal injury, because in their opinion, economically and socially objectionable. This idea was presented to the committees which reported the Clayton Act. The resulting law set out certain acts which had previously been held unlawful, whenever courts had disapproved of the ends for which they were performed; it then declared that, when these acts were committed in the course of an industrial dispute, they should not be held to violate any law of the United States. In other words the Clayton Act substituted the opinion of Congress as to the propriety of the purpose for that of differing judges; and thereby it declared that the relations between employers of labor and workingmen were competitive relations, that organized competition was not harmful and that it justified injuries necessarily inflicted in its course. Both the majority and the minority reports of the House committee indicate that such was its purpose. If, therefore, the Act applies to the case at bar, the acts here complained of cannot 'be considered or held to be violations of any law of the United States', and hence do not violate the Sherman Act.

"The Duplex Company contends that §20 of the Clayton Act does not apply to the case at bar, because it is restricted to cases 'between an employer and employees, or between employers and employees, or between employees, or between persons employed and persons seeking employment, involving, or growing out of, a dispute concerning terms or conditions of employment'; whereas the case at bar arises between an employer in Michigan and workingmen in New York not in his employ, and does not involve their conditions of employment.

[25]

But Congress did not restrict the provision to employers and workingmen *in their employ.* By including 'employers and employees' and 'persons employed and persons seeking employment' it showed that it was not aiming merely at a legal relationship between a specific employer and his employees. Furthermore, the plaintiff's contention proves too much. If the words are to receive a strict technical construction, the statute will have no application to disputes between employers of labor and workingmen, since the very acts to which it applies sever the continuity of the legal relationship. . . . The further contention that this case is not one arising out of a dispute concerning the conditions of work of one of the parties is, in my opinion, founded upon a misconception of the facts.

"Because I have come to the conclusion that both the common law of a State and a statute of the United States declare the right of industrial combatants to push their struggle to the limits of the justification of self-interest, I do not wish to be understood as attaching any constitutional or moral sanction to that right. All rights are derived from the purposes of the society in which they exist; above all rights rises duty to the community. The conditions developed in industry may be such that those engaged in it cannot continue their struggle without danger to the community. But it is not for judges to determine whether such conditions exist, nor is it their function to set the limits of permissible contest and to declare the duties which the new situation demands. This is the function of the Legislature which, while limiting individual and group rights of aggression and defense, may substitute processes of justice for the more primitive method of trial by combat."

Duplex Printing Press Co. v. *Deering, et al.*
254 U. S. 443, 479

Picketing and Property Rights

(Dissenting Opinion, *Truax* v. *Corrigan*, 1921)

SOON AFTER ARIZONA BECAME A STATE, ITS LEGISLATURE PLACED
strict limitations on the use of injunctions in cases arising out of labor
disputes; in effect permitting them to issue only against acts of violence.
Three years later, in 1916, a strike was called in a restaurant in Bisbee;
the public was informed by handbills, pickets, and banners that the
restaurant was unfair to organized labor. Receipts diminished, and the
owner of the restaurant, claiming that the law was unconstitutional,
sought an injunction against the activities of the strikers. When it was
denied in the State courts, he appealed to the Supreme Court.

Chief Justice Taft, writing for a majority of five, pointed out that
under the Duplex decision (*supra*) the business was a property right;
the intention to inflict a loss was clear; plaintiff's business was reduced
from $55,000 a year to $12,000. He said, "The real question here is:
Were the means used illegal?" and answered that the libelous attacks,
abusive epithets, threats, continuous patrolling of the premises, and loud
appeals of the pickets at the entrance to the restaurant "leave no doubt
of that." Despite the absence of violence, this was not lawful persuasion; a statute that attempted to make it legal deprived the employer
of his liberty and property without due process of law. And if the act
were construed merely to deprive the employer of the remedy of the
injunction, it denied the equal protection of the laws by arbitrarily
excluding one class of wrongs from such relief.

Justices Holmes, Pitney, Brandeis and Clarke dissented, the first
three writing separate opinions. Brandeis (with whom Holmes agreed)
wrote:

"THE FIRST Legislature of the State of Arizona adopted in 1913 a Civil Code. By title vi, chapter 3, it sets forth conditions and circumstances under which the courts of the State may or may not grant injunctions. Paragraph 1464 contains, among other things, a prohibition against interfering by injunction between employers and employees, in any case growing out of a dispute concerning terms or conditions of employment, unless interposition by injunction is necessary to protect property from injury through violence. Its main purpose was doubtless to prohibit the courts from enjoining peaceful picketing and the boycott. With the wisdom of the statute we have no concern. Whether Arizona in enacting this statute transgressed limitations imposed upon the power of the States by the Fourteenth Amendment is the question presented for decision.

"The employer has, of course, a legal right to carry on his business for profit, and incidentally the subsidiary rights to secure and retain customers, to fix such prices for his product as he deems proper, and to buy merchandise and labor at such prices as he chooses to pay. This right to carry on business— be it called liberty or property—has value, and he who interferes with the right without cause renders himself liable. But for cause the right may be interfered with and even be destroyed. Such cause exists when, in the pursuit of an equal right to further their several interests, his competitors make inroads upon his trade, or when suppliers of merchandise or of labor make inroads upon his profits. What methods and means are permissible in this struggle of contending forces is determined in part by decisions of the courts, in part by acts of the Legislature. The rules governing the contest necessarily change from time to time. For conditions change, and, furthermore, the rules evolved, being merely experiments in government, must be discarded when they prove to be failures.

"Practically every change in the law governing the relation of employer and employee must abridge, in some respect, the liberty or property of one of the parties, if liberty and property be measured by the standard of the law theretofore prevailing. If such changes are made by acts of the Legislature, we call the modification an exercise of the police power. And, although the change may involve interference with existing liberty or property of individuals, the statute will not be declared a violation of the due process clause, unless the Court finds that the interference is arbitrary or unreasonable or that, considered as a means, the measure has no real or substantial relation of cause to a permissible end. Nor will such changes in the law governing contests between employer and employee be held to be violative of the equal protection clause merely because the liberty or property of individuals in other relations to each other (for instance, as competitors in trade or as vendor and purchaser) would not, under similar circumstances, be subject to like abridgment. Few laws are of universal application. It is of the nature of our law that it has dealt, not with man in general, but with him in relationships. That a peculiar relationship of individuals may furnish legal basis for the classification which satisfies the requirement of the Fourteenth Amendment is clear. That the relation of employer and employee affords a constitutional basis for legislation applicable only to persons standing in that relation has been repeatedly held by this Court. The questions submitted are whether this statutory prohibition of the remedy by injunction is in itself arbitrary and so unreasonable as to deprive the employer of liberty or property without due process of law, and whether limitation of this prohibition to controversies involving employment denies him equal protection of the laws.

"Whether a law enacted in the exercise of the police power is justly subject to the charge of being unreasonable or arbitrary can ordinarily be determined only by a consideration of the contemporary conditions, social, industrial, and political, of the community to be affected thereby. Resort to such facts is necessary, among other things, in order to appreciate the evils sought to be remedied and the possible effects of the remedy proposed. Nearly all legislation involves a weighing of public needs as against private desires, and likewise a weighing of relative social values. Since government is not an exact science, prevailing public opinion concerning the evils and the remedy is among the important facts deserving consideration, particularly when the public conviction is both deep-seated and widespread and has been reached after deliberation. What, at any particular time, is the paramount public need, is necessarily largely a matter of judgment. Hence, in passing upon the validity of a law charged as being unreasonable, aid may be derived from the experience of other countries and of the several States of our Union in which the common law and its conceptions of liberty and of property prevail. The history of the rules governing contests between employer and employee in the several English-speaking countries illustrates both the susceptibility of such rules to change and the variety of contemporary opinion as to what rules will best serve the public interest. The divergence of opinion in this difficult field of governmental action should admonish us not to declare a rule arbitrary and unreasonable merely because we are convinced that it is fraught with danger to the public weal and thus to close the door to experiment within the law.

"In England a workingman struggling to improve his condition, even when acting singly, was confronted until 1813 with laws limiting the amount of wages which he might demand. Until 1824 he was punishable as a criminal if he combined with his fellow workmen to raise wages or shorten hours or to affect the business in any way, even if there was no resort to a strike. Until 1871 members of a union who joined in persuading employees to leave work were liable criminally, although the employees were not under contract and the persuasion was both peaceful and unattended by picketing. Until 1871 threatening a strike, whatever the cause, was also a criminal act. Not until 1875 was the right of workers to combine in order to attain their ends conceded fully. In that year Parliament declared that workmen combining in furtherance of a trade dispute should not be indictable for criminal conspiracy, unless the act, if done by one person, would be indictable as a crime. After that statute a combination of workmen to effect the ordinary objects of a strike was no longer a criminal offense. But picketing, though peaceful, in aid of a strike, remained illegal, and likewise the boycott. Not until 1906 was the ban on peaceful picketing and the bringing of pressure upon an employer by means of a secondary strike or a boycott removed. In 1906, also, the act of inducing workers to break their contract of employment (previously held an actionable wrong) was expressly declared legal. In England improvement of the condition of workingmen and their emancipation appear to have been deemed recently the paramount public need.

"In the British dominions the rules governing the struggle between employer and employed were likewise subjected to many modifications; but the trend of social experiment took a direction very different from that followed in the mother country. Instead of enabling the worker to pursue such methods as he might deem effective in the contest, statutes were enacted in some of the dominions which forbade the boycott, peaceful picketing, and even the simple strike and the lockout; use of the injunction to enforce compliance with these prohibitions was expressly sanctioned; and violation of the statute was also made punishable by criminal proceedings. These prohibitions were the concomitants of prescribed industrial arbitration through administrative tribunals by which the right of both employer and employee to liberty and property were seriously abridged in the public interest. Australia and New Zealand made compulsory both arbitration and compliance with the award. Canada limited the compulsion to a postponement of the right to strike until the dispute should have been officially investigated and reported upon. In these dominions the uninterrupted pursuit of industry and the prevention of the arbitrary use of power appear to be deemed the paramount public needs.

"In the United States the rules of the common law governing the struggle between employer and employee have likewise been subjected to modifications. These have been made mainly through judicial decisions. The legal right of workingmen to combine and to strike in order to secure for themselves higher wages, shorter hours, and better working conditions received early general recognition. But there developed great diversity of opinion as to the means by which, and also as to the persons through whom, and upon whom, pressure might permissibly be exerted in order to induce the employer to yield to the demands of the workingmen. Courts were required, in the absence of legislation, to determine what the public welfare demanded, whether it would not be best subserved by leaving the contestants free to resort to any means not involving a breach of the peace or injury to tangible property, whether it was consistent with the public interest that the contestants should be permitted to invoke the aid of others not directly interested in the matter in controversy, and to what extent incidental injury to persons not parties to the controversy should be held justifiable.

"The earliest reported American decision on peaceful picketing appears to have been rendered in 1888; the earliest on boycotting in 1886. By no great majority the prevailing judicial opinion in America declares the boycott as commonly practised an illegal means (see *Duplex Printing Press Co.* v. *Deering*), while it inclines towards the legality of peaceful picketing. . . . But in some of the States, notably New York, both peaceful picketing and the boycott are declared permissible. Judges being thus called upon to exercise a *quasi* legislative function and weigh relative social values, naturally differed in their conclusion on such questions.

"In England, observance of the rules of the contest has been enforced by the courts almost wholly through the criminal law or through actions at law for compensation. An injunction was granted in a labor dispute as early as 1868. But in England resort to the injunction has not been frequent and it has played no appreciable part there in the conflict between capital and labor. In America the injunction did not secure recognition as a possible remedy until 1888. When a few years later its use became extensive and conspicuous, the controversy over the remedy overshadowed in bitterness the question of the relative substantive rights of the parties. In the storms of protest against this use many thoughtful lawyers joined. The equitable remedy, although applied in accordance with established practice, involved incidents which, it was asserted, endangered the personal liberty of wage earners. The acts enjoined were frequently, perhaps usually, acts which were already crimes at common law or had been made so by statutes. The issues in litigation arising out of trade disputes related largely to questions of fact. But in equity issues of fact as of law were tried by a single judge, sitting without a jury. Charges of violating an injunction were often heard on affidavits merely, without the opportunity of confronting or cross-examining witnesses. Men found guilty of contempt were committed in the judge's discretion, without either a statutory limit upon the length of the imprisonment, or the opportunity of effective review on appeal, or the right to release on bail pending possible revisory proceedings. The effect of the proceeding upon the individual was substantially the same as if he had been successfully prosecuted for a crime; but he was denied, in the course of the equity proceedings, those rights which by the Constitution are commonly secured to persons charged with a crime.

[33]

"It was asserted that in these proceedings an alleged danger to property, always incidental and at times insignificant, was often laid hold of to enable the penalties of the criminal law to be enforced expeditiously without that protection to the liberty of the individual which the Bill of Rights was designed to afford; that through such proceedings a single judge often usurped the functions not only of the jury but of the police department; that in prescribing the conditions under which strikes were permissible, and how they might be carried out, he usurped also the powers of the Legislature; and that incidentally he abridged the constitutional rights of individuals to free speech, to a free press, and to peaceful assembly.

"It was urged that the real motive in seeking the injunction was not ordinarily to prevent property from being injured nor to protect the owner in its use, but to endow property with active, militant power which would make it dominant over men; in other words, that under the guise of protecting property rights, the employer was seeking sovereign power. And many disinterested men, solicitous only for the public welfare, believed that the law of property was not appropriate for dealing with the forces beneath social unrest; that in this vast struggle it was unwise to throw the power of the State on one side or the other, according to principles deduced from that law; that the problem of the control and conduct of industry demanded a solution of its own; and that, pending the ascertainment of new principles to govern industry, it was wiser for the State not to interfere in industrial struggles by the issuance of an injunction.

"After the constitutionality and the propriety of the use of the injunction in labor disputes was established judicially, those who opposed the practice sought the aid of Congress and of State Legislatures. The bills introduced varied in character and in scope. Many dealt merely with rights; and, of these, some declared, in effect, that no act done in furtherance of a labor dispute by a combination of workingmen should be held illegal, unless it would have been so if done by a single individual, while others purported to legalize specific practices, like boycotting or picketing. Other bills dealt merely with the remedy; and, of these, some undertook practically to abolish the use of the injunction in labor disputes, while some merely limited its use either by prohibiting its issue under certain conditions or by denying power to restrain certain acts. Some bills undertook to modify both rights and remedies. These legislative proposals occupied the attention of Congress during every session but one in the twenty years between 1894 and 1914. Reports recommending such legislation were repeatedly made by the judiciary committee of the House or that of the Senate, and at some sessions by both. Prior to 1914, legislation of this character had at several sessions passed the House, and in that year Congress passed and the President approved the Clayton Act, section 20 of which is substantially the same as paragraph 1464 of the Arizona Civil Code. . . .

"Such was the diversity of view concerning peaceful picketing and the boycott expressed in judicial decisions and legislation in English-speaking countries when in 1913 the new State of Arizona, in establishing its judicial system, limited the use of the injunction, and when in 1918 its Supreme Court was called upon to declare for the first time the law of Arizona on these subjects. The case of *Truax* v. *Bisbee Local No. 380*, 19 Ariz. 379, presented facts identical with those of the case at bar. In that case the Supreme Court made its decision on four controverted points of law. In the first place, it held that the officials of the union were not outsiders with no justification for their acts. . . . In the second place, rejecting the view held by the Federal courts and the majority of the State courts on the illegality of the boycott, it specifically accepted the law of New York, Montana, and California, citing the decisions of those States. . . . In the third place, it rejected the law of New Jersey, Minnesota and Pennsylvania that it is illegal to circularize an employer's customers, and again adopted the rule declared in the decisions of the courts of New York, Montana, California, and Connecticut. . . . In deciding these three points the Supreme Court of Arizona made a choice between well-established precedents laid down on either side by some of the strongest courts in the country. Can this Court say that thereby it deprived the plaintiff of his property without due process of law?

"The fourth question requiring decision was whether peaceful picketing should be deemed legal. Here, too, each of the opposing views had the support of decisions of strong courts. If the Arizona court had decided that by the common law of the State the defendants might peacefully picket the plaintiff, its decision, like those of the courts of Ohio, Minnesota, Montana, New York, Oklahoma, and New Hampshire, would surely not have been open to objection under the Federal Constitution; for this Court has recently held that peaceful picketing is not unlawful. . . . The Supreme Court of Arizona found it unnecessary to determine what was the common law of the State on that subject, because it construed paragraph 1464 of the Civil Code as declaring peaceful picketing to be legal. In the case at bar, commenting on the earlier case, the court said:

'The statute adopts the view of a number of courts which have held picketing, if peaceably carried on for a lawful purpose, to be no violation of any legal right of the party whose place of business is picketed, and whether as a fact the picketing is carried on by peaceful means, as against the other view taken by the Federal courts and many of the State courts that picketing is *per se* unlawful.'

[36]

"Shortly before that decision the Criminal Court of Appeals of Oklahoma had placed a similar construction upon a statute of that State, declaring that—

'The doctrine [that picketing is not *per se* unlawful] represents the trend of legal thought of modern times, and is specifically reflected in the statute above construed'. . . .

"A State, which despite the Fourteenth Amendment possesses the power to impose on employers without fault unlimited liability for injuries suffered by employees, and to limit the freedom of contract of some employers and not of others, surely does not lack the power to select for its citizens that one of conflicting views on boycott by peaceful picketing which its Legislature and highest court consider will best meet its conditions and secure the public welfare.

"The Supreme Court of Arizona having held as a rule of substantive law that the boycott as here practiced was legal at common law, and that the picketing was peaceful, and hence legal under the statute (whether or not it was legal at common law), necessarily denied the injunction, since, in its opinion, the defendants had committed no legal wrong and were threatening none. But even if this Court should hold that an employer has a constitutional right to be free from interference by such a boycott, or that the picketing practiced was not in fact peaceful, it does not follow that Arizona would lack the power to refuse to protect that right by injunction. For it is clear that the refusal of an equitable remedy for a tort is not necessarily a denial of due process of law. And it seems to be equally clear that such refusal is not necessarily arbitrary and unreasonable when applied to incidents of the relation of employer and employee. The considerations which show that the refusal is not arbitrary or unreasonable show likewise that such refusal does not necessarily constitute a denial of equal protection of the laws merely because some, or even the same property rights which are excluded by this statute from protection by injunction, receive such protection under other circumstances, or between persons standing in different relations. The acknowledged legislative discretion exerted in classification, so frequently applied in defining rights, extends equally to the grant of remedies. It is for the Legislature to say—within the broad limits of the discretion which it possesses—whether or not the remedy for a wrong shall be both criminal and civil and whether or not it shall be both at law and in equity.

"A State is free since the adoption of the Fourteenth Amendment, as it was before, not only to determine what system of law shall prevail in it, but also by which processes legal rights may be asserted, and in what courts they may be enforced. . . . As a State may adopt or reject trial by jury . . .; or, adopting it, may retain or discard its customary incidents . . .; as a State may grant or withhold review of a decision by appeal . . .; so it may determine for itself, from time to time, whether the protection which it affords to property rights through its courts shall be given by means of the preventive remedy or exclusively by an action at law for compensation.

"Nor is a State obliged to protect all property rights by injunction merely because it protects some, even if the attending circumstances are in some respects similar. The restraining power of equity might conceivably be applied to every intended violation of a legal right. On grounds of expediency its application is commonly denied in cases where there is a remedy at law which is deemed legally adequate. But an injunction has been denied on grounds of expediency in many cases where the remedy at law is confessedly not adequate. This occurs whenever a dominant public interest is deemed to require that the preventive remedy, otherwise available for the protection of private rights, be refused and the injured party left to such remedy as courts of law may afford. Thus, courts ordinarily refuse, perhaps in the interest of free speech, to restrain actionable libels. . . . In the interest of personal liberty they ordinarily refuse to enforce specifically, by mandatory injunction or otherwise, obligations involving personal service. . . . In the desire to preserve the separation of governmental powers they have declined to protect by injunction mere political rights, and have refused to interfere with the operations of the police department. . . . Instances are numerous where protection to property by way of injunction has been refused solely on the ground that serious public inconvenience would result from restraining the act complained of. Such, for example, was the case where a neighboring landowner sought to restrain a smelter from polluting the air; but that relief, if granted, would have necessitated shutting down the plant, and this would have destroyed the business and impaired the means of livelihood of a large community. There are also numerous instances where the circumstances would, according to general equity practice, have justified the issue of an injunction, but it was refused solely because the right sought to be enforced was created by statute, and the courts, applying a familiar rule, held that the remedy provided by the statute was exclusive.

"Such limitations upon the use of the injunction for the protection of private rights have ordinarily been imposed in the interest of the public by the court acting in the exercise of its broad discretion. But in some instances, the denial of the preventive remedy because of a public interest deemed paramount, has been expressly commanded by statute. Thus the courts of the United States have been prohibited from staying proceedings in any court of a State, Judicial Code, §265, and also from enjoining the illegal assessment and collection of taxes, Revised Statutes, §3224. . . . What Congress can do in curtailing the equity power of Federal courts, State Legislatures may do in curtailing equity powers of the State courts, unless prevented by the Constitution of the State. In other words, States are free since the adoption of the Fourteenth Amendment, as they were before, either to expand or to contract their equity jurisdiction. The denial of the more adequate equitable remedy for private wrongs is in essence an exercise of the police power, by which, in the interest of the public and in order to preserve the liberty and the property of the great majority of the citizens of a State, rights of property and the liberty of the individual must be remolded, from time to time, to meet the changing needs of society.

"For these reasons, as well as for others stated by Mr. Justice Holmes * and Mr. Justice Pitney, in which I concur, the judgment of the Supreme Court of Arizona should, in my opinion, be affirmed: First, because in permitting damage to be inflicted by means of boycott and peaceful picketing Arizona did not deprive the plaintiff of property without due process of law or deny him equal protection of the laws; and, secondly, because, if Arizona was constitutionally prohibited from adopting this rule of substantive law, it was still free to restrict the extraordinary remedies of equity where it considered their exercise to be detrimental to the public welfare, since such restriction was not a denial to the employer either of due process of law or of equal protection of the laws."

Truax, et al. v. *Corrigan, et al.*
257 U. S. 312, 354

* For the opinion of Holmes in *Truax* v. *Corrigan,* see *The Dissenting Opinions of Mr. Justice Holmes,* published by The Vanguard Press.

"The Qualified Right to Strike"

(Opinion of the Court, *Dorchy* v. *State of Kansas*, 1926)

"Section 17 of the Court of Industrial Relations Act (Laws of Kansas, Special Session 1920, c. 29), while reserving to the individual employee the right to quit his employment at any time, makes it unlawful to conspire 'to induce others to quit their employment for the purpose and with the intent to hinder, delay, limit, or suspend the operation of' mining. Section 19 makes it a felony for an officer of a labor union willfully to use the power or influence incident to his office to induce another person to violate any provision of the Act. Dorchy was prosecuted criminally for violating §19. The jury found him guilty through inducing a violation of §17; the trial court sentenced him to fine and imprisonment, and its judgment was affirmed by the Supreme Court of the State. . . . Dorchy claimed in both State courts that §19, as applied, was void because it prohibits strikes, and that to do so is a denial of the liberty guaranteed by the Fourteenth Amendment. Because this claim was denied, the case is here under §237 of the Judicial Code as amended.

"This is the second writ of error. When the case was first presented, it appeared that after entry of the judgment below, certain provisions of the Act had been held invalid by this Court in *Charles Wolff Packing Co.* v. *Court of Industrial Relations*. The question suggested itself whether §19 had not necessarily fallen, as part of the system of so-called compulsory arbitration, so that there might be no occasion to consider the

[41]

constitutional objection made specifically to it. That question being one of statutory interpretation, which had not been passed upon by the State court, the case was reversed, without costs, and remanded for further proceedings not inconsistent with the opinion of this Court (*Dorchy* v. *Kansas,* 264 U. S. 186). Thereupon the Supreme Court of Kansas decided that §19 is so far severable from the general scheme of legislation held invalid that it may stand alone with the legal effect of an independent statute, and it reaffirmed the judgment of the trial court. . . . By the construction thus given to the statute we are bound. The only question open upon this second writ of error is whether the statute as so construed and applied is constitutional.

"The State court did not, in either of its opinions, mention the specific objection to the validity of §19 now urged. In the second, it discussed only the question of statutory construction. In the first, it stated merely that the case is controlled by *State* v. *Howat,* 109 Kan. 376, *Court of Industrial Relations* v. *Charles Wolff Packing Co.,* 109 Kan. 629, and *State* v. *Howat,* 109 Kan. 779. In these cases, which came to this Court for review in *Howat* v. *Kansas,* 258 U. S. 181, and *Charles Wolff Packing Co.* v. *Court of Industrial Relations,* 262 U. S. 522; *Id.,* 267 U. S. 552, there was no occasion to consider the precise claim now urged—the invalidity of §19 when treated as an independent statute. Nor was this question referred to in any way. But the claims raised by Dorchy below properly raised it, and, as the judgment entered involves a denial of the claim, we must pass upon it. The question requiring decision is not, however, the broad one whether the Legislature has power to prohibit strikes. It is whether the prohibition of §19 is unconstitutional as here applied. . . . The specific facts out of which the strike arose must therefore be considered.

"Some years prior to February 3, 1921, the George H.

Mackie Fuel Company had operated a coal mine in Kansas. Its employees were members of District No. 14, United Mine Workers of America. On that day, Howat, as president, and Dorchy, as vice-president, of the union, purporting to act under direction of its executive board, called a strike. So far as appears, there was no trade dispute. There had been no controversy between the company and the union over wages, hours, or conditions of labor; over discipline or the discharge of an employee; concerning the observance of rules; or over the employment of non-union labor. Nor was the strike ordered as a sympathetic one in aid of others engaged in any such controversy. The order was made and the strike was called to compel the company to pay a claim of one Mishmash for $180. The men were told this; and they were instructed not to return to work until they should be duly advised that the claim had been paid. The strike order asserted that the claim had 'been settled by the joint board of miners and operators but [that] the company refuses*** to pay Brother Mishmash any part of the money that is due him.' There was, however, no evidence that the claim had been submitted to arbitration, nor of any contract requiring that it should be. The claim was disputed. It had been pending nearly two years. So far as appears, Mishmash was not in the company's employ at the time of the strike order. The men went out in obedience to the strike order, and they did not return to work until after the claim was paid, pursuant to an order of the Court of Industrial Relations. While the men were out on strike, this criminal proceeding was begun.

"Besides these facts, which appear by the bill of exceptions, the State presents for our consideration further facts which appear by the record in *Kansas* v. *Howat*, one of the cases referred to by the Supreme Court of Kansas in its first opinion in the case at bar. These show that Dorchy called this strike in violation of an injunction issued by the State court, and that the particular controversy with Mishmash arose in this way. Under the contract between the company and the union, the rate of pay for employees under 19 was $3.65 a day and for those over 19 the rate was $5. Mishmash had been paid at the lower rate from August 31, 1917, to March 22, 1918, without protest. On that day he first demanded pay at the higher rate, and claimed back pay from August 31, 1917, at the higher rate. His contention was that he had been born August 31, 1898. The company paid him, currently, at the higher rate beginning April 1, 1918. It refused him the back pay on the ground that he was in fact less than nineteen years old. One entry in the Mishmash family Bible gave August 31, 1898, as the date of his birth; another August 31, 1899. Hence the dispute. These additional facts were not put in evidence in the case at bar. *Kansas* v. *Howat*, 109 Kan. 376, was a wholly independent proceeding. Mere reference to it by the Court as a controlling decision did not incorporate its record into that of the case at bar. . . . And it does not appear that the Court treated these facts as matters of which it took judicial notice. We must dispose of the case upon the facts set forth in the bill of exceptions.

"The right to carry on business—be it called liberty or property—has value. To interfere with this right without just cause is unlawful. The fact that the injury was inflicted by a strike is sometimes a justification. But a strike may be illegal because of its purpose, however orderly the manner in which it is conducted. To collect a stale claim due to a fellow member of the union who was formerly employed in the business is not a permissible purpose. In the absence of a valid agreement to the contrary, each party to a disputed claim may insist that it be determined only by a court. . . . To enforce payment by a strike is clearly coercion. The Legislature may make such action punishable criminally, as extortion or otherwise. . . . And it may subject to punishment him who uses the power or influence incident to his office in a union to order the strike. Neither the common law, nor the Fourteenth Amendment, confers the absolute right to strike. . . .

Affirmed."

Dorchy v. State of Kansas
272 U. S. 306

Handling a Non-Union Product

(Dissenting Opinion, *Bedford Cut Stone Co.* v. *Stone Cutters'*
Ass'n, 1927)

THE JOURNEYMEN STONE CUTTERS' ASSOCIATION WAS TRYING TO
unionize the Bedford Stone Company and twenty-three other producers
of Indiana limestone. The union's method was to call upon the members
of all its locals to abstain from handling stone on which work had been
started by non-union labor.

Failing to obtain an injunction in the District Court, the companies
were again defeated in the Circuit Court of Appeals, but the Supreme
Court held that the companies were entitled to an injunction under
§16 of the Clayton Act. Mr. Justice Sutherland said that the opinion
in the *Duplex Co. Case* (*ante*) "might serve as an opinion in this case."

The order to strike against petitioners' product was coercive, Justice
Sutherland wrote; purchase was prevented; the union, although a
lawful group with a lawful end in view, by combining in the course
of conduct "necessarily threatened to destroy or narrow petitioners'
interstate trade."

Justice Sanford, concurring, could not distinguish the *Duplex Co.
Case*. Justice Stone, concurring, said he would have thought the union's
action reasonable but for the authority of the Duplex decision.

Justice Brandeis dissented again (Justice Holmes agreeing as
before):

"THE CONSTITUTION of the Journeymen Stone Cutters' Association provides: 'No member of this association shall cut,
carve, or fit any material that has been cut by men working in
opposition to this association'.

"For many years the plaintiffs had contracts with the association under which its members were employed at their several quarries and works. In 1921, the plaintiffs refused to renew the contracts because certain rules or conditions proposed by the journeymen were unacceptable. Then came a strike. It was followed by a lockout, the organization by the plaintiffs of a so-called independent union, and the establishment of it at their plants. Repeated efforts to adjust the controversy proved futile. Finally, the association urged its members working on buildings in other States to observe the above provision of its constitution. Its position was:

'that, if employers will not employ our members in one place, we will decline to work for them in another, or to finish any work that has been started or partly completed by men these employers are using to combat our organization.'

"The trial court dismissed the bill. The United States Circuit Court of Appeals affirming the decree said:

'After long negotiations and failure to reach a new working agreement, the union officers ordered that none of its members should further cut stone which had already been partly cut by non-union labor, with the result that on certain jobs in different States stone cutters, who were members of the union, declined to do further cutting upon such stone. Where, as in some cases, there were few or no local stone cutters, except such as belonged to the union, the completion of the buildings was more or less hindered by the order, the manifest object of which was to induce appellants to make a contract with the union for employment of only union stone cutters in the Indiana limestone district. It does not appear that the quarrying of stone, or sawing it into blocks, or the transportation of it, or setting it in the buildings, or any other building operation, was sought to be interfered with, and no actual or threatened violence appears, no picketing, no boycott, and nothing of that character.'

"If, in the struggle for existence, individual workingmen may, under any circumstances, cooperate in this way for self-protection even though the interstate trade of another is thereby restrained, the lower courts were clearly right in denying the injunction sought by plaintiffs. I have no occasion to consider whether the restraint, which was applied wholly intrastate, became in its operation a direct restraint upon interstate commerce. For it has long been settled that only unreasonable restraints are prohibited by the Sherman Law. . . . And the restraint imposed was, in my opinion, a reasonable one. The Act does not establish the standard of reasonableness. What is reasonable must be determined by the application of principles of the common law, as administered in Federal courts, unaffected by State legislation or decisions. . . . Tested by these principles, the propriety of the unions' conduct can hardly be doubted by one who believes in the organization of labor.

"Neither the individual stone cutters nor the unions had any contract with any of the plaintiffs or with any of their customers. So far as concerned the plaintiffs and their customers, the individual stone cutters were free either to work or to abstain from working on stone which had been cut at quarries by members of the employers' union. So far as concerned the association, the individual stone cutter was not free. He had agreed, when he became a member, that he would not work on stone 'cut by men working in opposition to' the association. It was in duty bound to urge upon its members observance of the obligation assumed. These cut stone companies, who alone are seeking relief, were its declared enemies. They were seeking to destroy it. And the danger was great.

"The plaintiffs are not weak employers opposed by a mighty union. They have large financial resources. Together, they ship seventy percent of all the cut stone in the country. They are not isolated concerns. They had combined in a local employers' organization. And their organization is affiliated with the national employers' organization, called 'International Cut Stone & Quarrymen's Association.' Standing alone, each of the 150 journeymen's locals is weak. The average number of members in a local union is only thirty-three. The locals are widely scattered throughout the country. Strong employers could destroy a local 'by importing scabs' from other cities. And many of the builders by whom the stone cutters were employed in different cities are strong. It is only through combining the 5,000 organized stone cutters in a national union, and developing loyalty to it, that the individual stone cutter anywhere can protect his own job.

"The manner in which these individual stone cutters exercised their asserted right to perform their union duty by refusing to finish stone 'cut by men working in opposition to' the association was confessedly legal. They were innocent alike of trespass and of breach of contract. They did not picket. They refrained from violence, intimidation, fraud, and threats. They refrained from obstructing otherwise either the plaintiffs or their customers in attempts to secure other help. They did not plan a boycott against any of the plaintiffs or against builders who used the plaintiffs' product. On the contrary, they expressed entire willingness to cut and finish anywhere any stone quarried by any of the plaintiffs, except such stone as had been partially 'cut by men working in opposition to' the association. A large part of the plaintiffs' product consisting of blocks, slabs, and sawed work was not affected by the order of the union officials. The individual stone cutter was thus clearly innocent of wrongdoing, unless it was illegal for him to agree with his fellow craftsmen to refrain from working on the 'scab'-cut stone because it was an article of interstate commerce.

"The manner in which the journeymen's unions acted was also clearly legal. The combination complained of is the co-operation of persons wholly of the same craft, united in a national union, solely for self-protection. No outsider—be he quarrier, dealer, builder, or laborer—was a party to the combination. No purpose was to be subserved except to promote the trade interests of members of the Journeymen's Association. There was no attempt by the unions to boycott the plaintiffs. There was no attempt to seek the aid of members of any other craft, by a sympathetic strike or otherwise. The contest was not a class struggle. It was a struggle between particular employers and their employees. But the controversy out of which it arose related, not to specific grievances, but to fundamental matters of union policy of general application throughout the country. The national association had the duty to determine, so far as its members were concerned, what that policy should be. It deemed the maintenance of that policy a matter of vital interest to each member of the union. The duty rested upon it to enforce its policy by all legitimate means. The association, its locals and officers, were clearly innocent of wrongdoing, unless Congress has declared that, for union officials to urge members to refrain from working on stone 'cut by men working in opposition' to it, is necessarily illegal if thereby the interstate trade of another is restrained.

"The contention that earlier decisions of this Court compel the conclusion that it is illegal seems to be unfounded. The cases may support the claim that, by such local abstention from work, interstate trade is restrained. But examination of the facts in those cases makes clear that they have no tendency whatsoever to establish that the restraint imposed by the unions in the case at bar is unreasonable. The difference between the simple refraining from work practiced here and the conduct held unreasonable in *Duplex Printing Press Co.* v. *Deering* appears from a recital in that opinion of the defendants' acts. [The quotation given by Justice Brandeis enumerates threats of sympathetic strikes in other trades, threats of injury to customers, and a variety of other means of preventing the sale of Duplex presses.]

"The character of the acts held in *Duplex Printing Press Co.* v. *Deering* to constitute unreasonable restraint is further shown by the scope of the injunction there prescribed. [It enjoined interference of purchase, transportation, carting, installation, use, display or repairing of the presses "in furtherance of the secondary boycott."]

"The difference between the facts here involved and those in the *Duplex* case does not lie only in the character of the acts complained of. It lies also in the occasion and purpose of the action taken and in the scope of the combination. The combination there condemned was not, as here, cooperation for self-protection only of men in a single craft. It was an effort to win by invoking the aid of others, both organized and unorganized, not concerned in the trade dispute. The conduct there condemned was not, as here, a mere refusal to finish particular work begun 'by men working in opposition to' the union. It was the institution of a general boycott, not only of the business of the employer, but of the businesses of all who should participate in the marketing, installation, or exhibition of its product. The conduct there condemned was not, as here, action taken for self-protection against an opposing union installed by employers to destroy the regular union with which they long had had contracts. The action in the *Duplex* case was taken in an effort to unionize an open shop. Moreover, there the combination of defendants was aggressive action directed against an isolated employer. Here it is defensive action of workingmen directed against a combination of employers. The serious question on which the Court divided in the *Duplex* case was not whether the restraint imposed was reasonable. It was whether the Clayton Act had forbidden Federal courts to issue an injunction in that class of cases. . . .

"In *Loewe* v. *Lawlor*, 208 U. S. 274 [and other cases cited by the majority], the conduct held unreasonable was not, as here, a refusal to finish a product partly made by members of an opposing union. It was invoking the power of the consumer as a weapon of offensive warfare. There, a general boycott was declared of the manufacturer's product. And the boycott was extended to the businesses of both wholesalers and retailers who might aid in the marketing of the manufacturer's product. Moreover, the boycott was to be effected, not by the cooperation merely of the few members of the craft directly and vitally interested in the trade dispute, but by the aid of the vast forces of organized labor affiliated with them through the American Federation of Labor.

"In *United States* v. *Brims*, 272 U. S. 549, the combination complained of was not the cooperation merely of workingmen of the same craft. It was a combination of manufacturers of millwork in Chicago with building contractors who cause such work to be installed and the unions whose members are to be employed. Moreover the purpose of the combination was not primarily to further the interests of the union carpenters. The immediate purpose was to suppress competition with the Chicago manufacturers. [Justice Brandeis quotes from the opinion in that case, where the Court named the incentives to combination.]

"In *United Mine Workers* v. *Coronado Co.*, 259 U. S. 344 [and other cases cited by the majority], the questions put in issue were not the reasonableness of the restraint, but whether the restraint was of interstate commerce.

"Members of the Journeymen Stone Cutters' Association

could not work anywhere on stone which had been cut at the quarries by 'men working in opposition' to it, without aiding and abetting the enemy. Observance by each member of the provision of their constitution which forbids such action was essential to his own self-protection. It was demanded of each by loyalty to the organization and to his fellows. If, on the undisputed facts of this case, refusal to work can be enjoined, Congress created by the Sherman Law and the Clayton Act an instrument for imposing restraints upon labor which reminds one of involuntary servitude. The Sherman Law was held in *United States* v. *United States Steel Corporation,* 251 U. S. 417, to permit capitalists to combine in a single corporation fifty per cent of the steel industry of the United States dominating the trade through its vast resources. The Sherman Law was held in *United States* v. *United Shoe Machinery Co.,* 247 U. S. 32, to permit capitalists to combine in another corporation practically the whole shoe machinery industry of the country, necessarily giving it a position of dominance over shoe manufacturing in America. It would, indeed, be strange if Congress had by the same Act willed to deny to members of a small craft of workingmen the right to cooperate in simply refraining from work, when that course was the only means of self-protection against a combination of militant and powerful employers. I cannot believe that Congress did so."

Bedford Cut Stone Co., et al.
v. *Journeymen Stone Cutters' Association*
of North America, et al.
274 U. S. 37, 56

II. Regulation of Business

A Property Right in News

(Dissenting Opinion, *International News* v. *Associated Press*, 1918)

WHEN THE INTERNATIONAL NEWS SERVICE COPIED NEWS ITEMS posted on bulletins and published in early editions of newspapers which were members of the Associated Press, the International was restrained from conveying that news to subscribers "until its commercial value as news to the complainant and all its members has passed away."

This order was affirmed by the Supreme Court, where Mr. Justice Pitney reasoned that news, being stock in trade, "must be regarded as *quasi* property." It retained its value as long as it was fresh. Gathered at great cost and skill, it was entitled to protection from appropriation at the point where profit was reaped. To the defense that news becomes common property upon being posted or published, Justice Pitney answered that a newspaper reader's right to tell others of the paper's contents bore no relation to the competitive rights of complainant and defendant. Here was interference with business, differing from the ordinary case of unfair competition principally in that the International sold the A. P.'s goods as its own instead of misrepresenting its goods as another's. The pirated news reached readers of the International's papers throughout the country as early as it was transmitted to rival papers of the Associated Press, without crediting the source.

In a separate opinion Mr. Justice Holmes * (with whom Mr. Justice McKenna concurred) wrote that the defendant's conduct created a subtle falsehood, an injury deserving a remedy; but "a suitable acknowledgement of the source is all that the plaintiff can require"; if express credit was not given, use of the news should be deferred a fixed number of hours after publication by the plaintiff.

Mr. Justice Brandeis dissented:

* See page 307, *The Dissenting Opinions of Mr. Justice Holmes.*

"THERE ARE published in the United States about 2,500 daily newspapers. More than 800 of them are supplied with domestic and foreign news of general interest by the Associated Press—a corporation without capital stock, which does not sell news or earn or seek to earn profits, but serves merely as an instrumentality by means of which these papers supply themselves at joint expense with such news. Papers not members of the Associated Press depend for their news of general interest largely upon agencies organized for profit. Among these agencies is the International News Service which supplies news to about 400 subscribing papers. It has, like the Associated Press, bureaus and correspondents in this and foreign countries; and its annual expenditure in gathering and distributing news is about $2,000,000. Ever since its organization in 1909, it has included among the sources from which it gathers news, copies (purchased in the open market) of early editions of some papers published by members of the Associated Press and the bulletins publicly posted by them. These items, which constitute but a small part of the news transmitted to its subscribers, are generally verified by the International News Service before transmission; but frequently items are transmitted without verification; and occasionally even without being rewritten. In no case is the fact disclosed that such item was suggested by or taken from a paper or bulletin published by an Associated Press member.

"No question of statutory copyright is involved. The sole question for our consideration is this: Was the International News Service properly enjoined from using, or causing to be used gainfully, news of which it acquired knowledge by lawful means (namely, by reading publicly posted bulletins or papers purchased by it in the open market) merely because the news had been originally gathered by the Associated Press and continued to be of value to some of its members, or because it did not reveal the source from which it was acquired?

"The 'ticker' cases, the cases concerning literary and artistic compositions, and cases of unfair competition were relied upon in support of the injunction. But it is admitted that none of those cases affords a complete analogy with that before us. The question presented for decision is new, and it is important.

"News is a report of recent occurrences. The business of the news agency is to gather systematically knowledge of such occurrences of interest and to distribute reports thereof. The Associated Press contended that knowledge so acquired is property, because it costs money and labor to produce and because it has value for which those who have it not are ready to pay; that it remains property and is entitled to protection as long as it has commercial value as news; and that to protect it effectively, the defendant must be enjoined from making, or causing to be made, any gainful use of it while it retains such value. An essential element of individual property is the legal right to exclude others from enjoying it. If the property is private, the right of exclusion may be absolute; if the property is affected with a public interest, the right of exclusion is qualified. But the fact that a product of the mind has cost its producer money and labor, and has a value for which others are willing to pay, is not sufficient to ensure to it this legal attribute of property. The general rule of law is, that the noblest of human productions—knowledge, truths ascertained, conceptions, and ideas—become, after voluntary communication to others, free as the air to common use. Upon these incorporeal productions the attribute of property is continued after such communication only in certain classes of cases where public policy has seemed to demand it. These exceptions are confined productions which, in some degree, involve creation, invention, or discovery. But by no means all such are endowed with this

[59]

attribute of property. The creations which are recognized as property by the common law are literary, dramatic, musical, and other artistic creations; and these have also protection under the copyright statutes. The inventions and discoveries upon which this attribute is conferred only by statute, are the few comprised within the patent law. There are also many other cases in which courts interfere to prevent curtailment of plaintiff's enjoyment of incorporeal productions; and in which the right to relief is often called a property right, but is such only in a special sense. In those cases, the plaintiff has no absolute right to the protection of his production; he has merely the qualified right to be protected against the defendant's acts, because of the special relation in which the latter stands or the wrongful method or means employed in acquiring the knowledge or the manner in which it is used. Protection of this character is afforded where the suit is based upon breach of contract or of trust or upon unfair competition.

"The knowledge for which protection is sought in the case at bar is not of a kind upon which the law has heretofore conferred the attributes of property; nor is the manner of its acquisition or use nor the purpose to which it is applied, such as has heretofore been recognized as entitling a plaintiff to relief.

"*First*. Plaintiff's principal reliance was upon the 'ticker' cases; but they do not support its contention. The leading cases on this subject rest the grant of relief, not upon the existence of a general property right in news, but upon the breach of a contract or trust concerning the use of news communicated; and that element is lacking here. [Justice Brandeis then gives extracts from the opinion in *Board of Trade* v. *Christie Grain & Stock Co.*, 198 U. S. 236, 250, in which case confidential price quotations were communicated to outsiders; the Court said that strangers obtaining the knowledge by inducing a breach of trust will be restrained, and that use of the knowledge during the time it was supposed to be confidential was the value involved.]

"The only other case in this Court which relates to this subject is *Hunt* v. *N. Y. Cotton Exchange,* 205 U. S. 322. While the opinion there refers to a general property right in the quotations, the facts are substantially the same as those in the *Christie Case,* which is the chief authority on which the decision is based. Of the cases in the lower Federal courts and in the State courts it may be said, that most of them too can, on their facts, be reconciled with this principle, though much of the language of the courts cannot be. In spite of anything that may appear in these cases to the contrary it seems that the true principle is stated in the *Christie Case,* that the collection of quotations 'stands like a trade secret.' And in *Dr. Miles Medical Co.* v. *Park & Sons Co.,* 220 U. S. 373, 402, this Court says of a trade secret:

> 'Any one may use it who fairly, by analysis and experiment, discovers it. But the complainant is entitled to be protected against invasion of its right in the process by fraud or by breach of trust or contract.'

"The leading English case, *Exchange Telegraph Co.* v. *Gregory & Co.,* [1896] 1 Q. B. 147, is also rested clearly upon a breach of contract or trust, although there is some reference to a general property right. The later English cases seem to have rightly understood the basis of the decision, and they have not sought to extend it further than was intended. Indeed, we find the positive suggestion in some cases that the only ground for relief is the manner in which knowledge of the report of the news was acquired.

"If the news involved in the case at bar had been posted in violation of any agreement between the Associated Press and its members, questions similar to those in the 'ticker' cases might have arisen. But the plaintiff does not contend that the posting was wrongful or that any papers were wrongfully issued by its subscribers. On the contrary it is conceded that both the bulletins and the papers were issued in accordance with the regulations of the plaintiff. Under such circumstances, for a reader of the papers purchased in the open market, or a reader of the bulletins publicly posted, to procure and use gainfully, information therein contained, does not involve inducing anyone to commit a breach either of contract or of trust, or committing or in any way abetting a breach of confidence.

"*Second*. Plaintiff also asks relief upon the cases which hold that the common-law right of the producer to prohibit copying is not lost by the private circulation of a literary composition, the delivery of a lecture, the exhibition of a painting, or the performance of a dramatic or musical composition. These cases rest upon the ground that the common law recognizes such productions as property which, despite restricted communication, continues until there is a dedication to the public under the copyright statutes or otherwise. But they are inapplicable for two reasons: (1) At common law, as under the copyright acts, intellectual productions are entitled to such protection only if there is underneath something evincing the mind of a creator or originator, however modest the requirement. The mere record of isolated happenings, whether in words or by photographs not involving artistic skill, are denied such protection. (2) At common law, as under the copyright acts, the element in intellectual productions which secures such protection, is not the knowledge, truths, ideas, or emotions which the composition expresses, but the form or sequence in which they are expressed; that is, 'some new collocation of visible or audible points—of lines, colors, sounds or words.' . . . An author's theories, suggestions, and speculations, or the systems, plans, methods, and arrangements of an originator, derive no such protection from the statutory copyright of the book in

[62]

which they are set forth; and they are likewise denied such protection at common law.

"That news is not property in the strict sense is illustrated by the case of *Sports and General Press Agency, Ltd.*, v. *'Our Dogs' Publishing Co., Ltd.*, [1916] 2 K. B. 880, where the plaintiff, the assignee of the right to photograph the exhibits at a dog show, was refused an injunction against defendant who had also taken pictures of the show and was publishing them. The court said that, except in so far as the possession of the land occupied by the show enabled the proprietors to exclude people or permit them on condition that they agree not to take photographs (which condition was not imposed in that case), the proprietors had no exclusive right to photograph the show and could therefore grant no such right. And it was further stated that, at any rate, no matter what conditions might be imposed upon those entering the grounds, if the defendant had been on top of a house or in some position where he could photograph the show without interfering with the physical property of the plaintiff, the plaintiff would have no right to stop him. If, when the plaintiff creates the event recorded, he is not entitled to the exclusive first publication of the news (in that case a photograph) of the event, no reason can be shown why he should be accorded such protection as to events which he simply records and transmits to other parts of the world, though with great expenditure of time and money.

"*Third.* If news be treated as possessing the characteristics not of a trade secret, but of literary property, then the earliest issue of a paper of general circulation or the earliest public posting of a bulletin which embodies such news would, under the established rules governing literary property, operate as a publication, and all property in the news would then cease. Resisting this conclusion, plaintiff relied upon the cases which hold that uncopyrighted intellectual and artistic property survives private circulation or a restricted publication; and it contended

[63]

that in each issue of each paper, a restriction is to be implied, that the news shall not be used gainfully in competition with the Associated Press or any of its members. There is no basis for such an implication. But it is, also, well settled that where the publication is in fact a general one, even express words of restriction upon use are inoperative. In other words, a general publication is effective to dedicate literary property to the public, regardless of the actual intent of its owner. In the cases dealing with lectures, dramatic and musical performances, and art exhibitions, upon which plaintiff relied, there was no general publication in print comparable to the issue of daily newspapers or the unrestricted public posting of bulletins. The principles governing those cases differ more or less in application, if not in theory, from the principles governing the issue of printed copies; and in so far as they do differ, they have no application to the case at bar.

"*Fourth*. Plaintiff further contended that defendant's practice constitutes unfair competition, because there is 'appropriation without cost to itself of values created by' the plaintiff; and it is upon this ground that the decision of this Court appears to be based. To appropriate and use for profit, knowledge and ideas produced by other men, without making compensation or even acknowledgement, may be inconsistent with a finer sense of propriety; but, with the exceptions indicated above, the law has heretofore sanctioned the practice. Thus it was held that one may ordinarily make and sell anything in any form, may copy with exactness that which another has produced, or may otherwise use his ideas without his consent and without the payment of compensation, and yet not inflict a legal injury; and that ordinarily one is at perfect liberty to find out, if he can by lawful means, trade secrets of another, however valuable, and then use the knowledge so acquired gainfully, although it cost the original owner much in effort and in money to collect or produce.

[64]

"Such taking and gainful use of a product of another which, for reasons of public policy, the law has refused to endow with the attributes of property, does not become unlawful because the product happens to have been taken from a rival and is used in competition with him. The unfairness in competition which hitherto has been recognized by the law as a basis for relief, lay in the manner or means of conducting the business; and the manner or means held legally unfair, involves either fraud or force or the doing of acts otherwise prohibited by law. In the 'passing off' cases (the typical and most common case of unfair competition), the wrong consists in fraudulently representing by word or act that defendant's goods are those of plaintiff. . . . In other cases, the diversion of trade was effected through physical or moral coercion, or by inducing breaches of contract or of trust or by enticing away employees. In some others, called cases of simulated competition, relief was granted because defendant's purpose was unlawful; namely, not competition but deliberate and wanton destruction of plaintiff's business.

"That competition is not unfair in a legal sense, merely because the profits gained are unearned, even if made at the expense of a rival, is shown by many cases besides those referred to above. He who follows the pioneer into a new market, or who engages in the manufacture of an article newly introduced by another, seeks profits due largely to the labor and expense of the first adventurer; but the law sanctions, indeed encourages, the pursuit. He who makes a city known through his product, must submit to sharing the resultant trade with others who, perhaps for that reason, locate there later. . . . He who has made his name a guaranty of quality, protests in vain when another with the same name engages, perhaps for that reason, in the same line of business; provided precaution is taken to prevent the public from being deceived into the belief that what he is selling was made by his competitor. One bearing a

name made famous by another is permitted to enjoy the unearned benefit which necessarily flows from such use, even
though the use proves harmful to him who gave the name
value. . . .

"The means by which the International News Service ob-
tains news gathered by the Associated Press is also clearly
unobjectionable. It is taken from papers bought in the open
market or from bulletins publicly posted. No breach of contract
such as the Court considered to exist in *Hitchman Coal & Coke
Co.* v. *Mitchell* [See p. 12] or of trust such as was present
in *Morison* v. *Moar,* 9 Hare, 241, and neither fraud nor force
is involved. The manner of use is likewise unobjectionable. No
reference is made by word or by act to the Associated Press,
either in transmitting the news to subscribers or by them in
publishing it in their papers. Neither the International News
Service nor its subscribers is gaining or seeking to gain in its
business a benefit from the reputation of the Associated Press.
They are merely using its product without making compensation. . . . That they have a legal right to do, because the product
is not property, and they do not stand in any relation to the
Associated Press, either of contract or of trust, which otherwise
precludes such use. The argument is not advanced by charac-
terizing such taking and use a misappropriation.

"It is also suggested that the fact that defendant does not
refer to the Associated Press as the source of the news may
furnish a basis for the relief. But the defendant and its subscribers, unlike members of the Associated Press, were under
no contractual obligation to disclose the source of the news;
and there is no rule of law requiring acknowledgement to be
made where uncopyrighted matter is reproduced. The International News Service is said to mislead its subscribers into
believing that the news transmitted was originally gathered
by it and that they in turn mislead their readers. There is, in
fact, no representation by either of any kind. Sources of infor-

[66]

mation are sometimes given because required by contract; sometimes because naming the source gives authority to an otherwise incredible statement; and sometimes the source is named because the agency does not wish to take the responsibility itself of giving currency to the news. But no representation can properly be implied from omission to mention the source of information except that the International News Service is transmitting news which it believes to be credible.

"Nor is the use made by the International News Service of the information taken from papers or bulletins of Associated Press members legally objectionable by reason of the purpose for which it was employed. The acts here complained of were not done for the purpose of injuring the business of the Associated Press. Their purpose was not even to divert its trade, or to put it at a disadvantage by lessening defendant's necessary expenses. The purpose was merely to supply subscribers of the International News Service promptly with all available news. The suit is, as this Court declares, in substance one brought for the benefit of the members of the Associated Press, who would be proper, and except for their number perhaps necessary, parties; and the plaintiff conducts the suit as representing their interests. It thus appears that the protection given by the injunction is not actually to the business of the complainant news agency; for this agency does not sell news nor seek to earn profits, but is a mere instrumentality by which 800 or more newspapers collect and distribute news. It is these papers severally which are protected; and the protection afforded is not from competition of the defendant, but from possible competition of one or more of the 400 other papers which receive the defendant's service. Furthermore, the protection to these Associated Press members consists merely in denying to other papers the right to use, as news, information which, by authority of all concerned, had theretofore been given to the public by some of those who joined in gathering it; and to which the law denies the attributes of property. There is in defendant's purpose nothing on which to base a claim for relief.

"It is further said that, while that for which the Associated Press spends its money is too fugitive to be recognized as property in the common-law courts, the defendant cannot be heard to say so in a court of equity, where the question is one of unfair competition. The case presents no elements of equitable title or of breach of trust. The only possible reason for resort to a court of equity in a case like this is that the remedy which the law gives is inadequate. If the plaintiff has no legal cause of action, the suit necessarily fails. . . . There is nothing in the situation of the parties which can estop the defendant from saying so.

"*Fifth.* The great development of agencies now furnishing country-wide distribution of news, the vastness of our territory, and improvements in the means of transmitting intelligence, have made it possible for a news agency or newspapers to obtain, without paying compensation, the fruit of another's efforts and to use news so obtained gainfully in competition with the original collector. The injustice of such action is obvious. But to give relief against it would involve more than the application of existing rules of law to new facts. It would require the making of a new rule in analogy to existing ones. The unwritten law possesses capacity for growth; and has often satisfied new demands for justice by invoking analogies or by expanding a rule or principle. This process has been in the main wisely applied and should not be discontinued. Where the problem is relatively simple, as it is apt to be when private interests only are involved, it generally proves adequate. But with the increasing complexity of society, the public interest tends to become omnipresent; and the problems presented by new demands for justice cease to be simple. Then the creation or recognition by courts of a new private right may work serious injury to the general public, unless the boundaries of the right are definitely established and wisely guarded. In order to reconcile the new private right with the public interest, it may be necessary to prescribe limitations and rules for its enjoyment; and also to provide administrative machinery for enforcing the rules. It is largely for this reason that, in the effort to meet the many new demands for justice incident to a rapidly changing civilization, resort to legislation has latterly been had with increasing frequency.

"The rule for which the plaintiff contends would effect an important extension of property rights and a corresponding curtailment of the free use of knowledge and of ideas; and the facts of this case admonish us of the danger involved in recognizing such a property right in news, without imposing upon news-gatherers corresponding obligations. A large majority of the newspapers and perhaps half the newspaper readers of the United States are dependent for their news of general interest upon agencies other than the Associated Press. The channel through which about 400 of these papers received, as the plaintiff alleges, 'a large amount of news relating to the European war of the greatest importance and of intense interest to the newspaper-reading public' was suddenly closed. The closing to the International News Service of these channels for foreign news (if they were closed) was due not to unwillingness on its part to pay the cost of collecting the news, but to the prohibitions imposed by foreign governments upon its securing news from their respective countries and from using cable or telegraph lines running therefrom. For aught that appears, this prohibition may have been wholly undeserved; and at all events the 400 papers and their readers may be assumed to have been innocent. For aught that appears, the International News Service may have sought then to secure temporarily by arrangement with the Associated Press the latter's foreign news service. For

[69]

aught that appears, all of the 400 subscribers of the International News Service would gladly have then become members of the Associated Press, if they could have secured election thereto. It is possible, also, that a large part of the readers of these papers were so situated that they could not secure prompt access to papers served by the Associated Press. The prohibition of the foreign governments might as well have been extended to the channels through which news was supplied to more than a thousand other daily papers in the United States not served by the Associated Press; and a large part of their readers may also be so located that they cannot procure prompt access to the papers served by the Associated Press.

"A Legislature, urged to enact a law by which one news agency or newspaper may prevent appropriation of the fruits of its labors by another, would consider such facts and possibilities and others which appropriate inquiry might disclose. Legislators might conclude that it was impossible to put an end to the obvious injustice involved in such appropriation of news, without opening the door to other evils, greater than that sought to be remedied. Such appears to have been the opinion of our Senate which reported unfavorably a bill to give news a few hours' protection [Senate Bill No. 1728, 48th Congress, First Session]; and which ratified on February 15, 1911, the convention adopted at the Fourth International American Conference (38 Stat. 1785, 1789, Article xi); and such was evidently the view also of the signatories to the International Copyright Union of November 13, 1908, as both these conventions expressly exclude news from copyright protection.

"Or legislators dealing with the subject might conclude, that the right to news values should be protected to the extent of permitting recovery of damages for any unauthorized use, but that protection by injunction should be denied, just as courts of equity ordinarily refuse (perhaps in the interest of free speech) to restrain actionable libels, and for other reasons decline

[70]

to protect by injunction mere political rights; and as Congress has prohibited courts from enjoining the illegal assessment or collection of Federal taxes. If a Legislature concluded to recognize property in published news to the extent of permitting recovery at law, it might, with a view to making the remedy more certain and adequate, provide a fixed measure of damages, as in the case of copyright infringement.

"Or again, a Legislature might conclude that it was unwise to recognize even so limited a property right in published news as that above indicated; but that a news agency should, on some conditions, be given full protection of its business; and to that end a remedy by injunction as well as one for damages should be granted, where news collected by it is gainfully used without permission. If a Legislature concluded (as at least one court has held, *New York and Chicago Grain and Stock Exchange* v. *Board of Trade*, 127 Ill. 153) that under certain circumstances news-gathering is a business affected with a public interest, it might declare that, in such cases, news should be protected against appropriation only if the gatherer assumed the obligation of supplying it at reasonable rates and without discrimination to all papers which applied therefor. If legislators reached that conclusion, they would probably go further and prescribe the conditions under which and the extent to which the protection should be afforded; and they might also provide the administrative machinery necessary for insuring to the public, the press, and the news agencies, full enjoyment of the rights so conferred.

"Courts are ill-equipped to make the investigations which should precede a determination of the limitations which should be set upon any property right in news or of the circumstances under which news gathered by a private agency should be deemed affected with a public interest. Courts would be powerless to prescribe the detailed regulations essential to full enjoyment of the rights conferred or to introduce

[71]

the machinery required for enforcement of such regulations. Considerations such as these should lead us to decline to establish a new rule of law in the effort to redress a newly disclosed wrong, although the propriety of some remedy appears to be clear."

International News Service v. Associated Press
248 U. S. 215, 248

Unfair Methods of Competition

(Dissenting Opinion, *Federal Trade Commission* v. *Gratz*, 1920)

THE FEDERAL TRADE COMMISSION ORDERED A COMPANY TO CEASE and desist from the practice of requiring purchasers of steel ties for binding bales of cotton to buy an equal amount of jute bagging. The order was annulled by the Circuit Court of Appeals, which found no evidence that such practice was general and held that the Commission was without jurisdiction to determine the merits of specific individual grievances.

In affirming the Circuit Court's judgment Mr. Justice McReynolds said that the complaint failed to show any unfair method of competition. There was no allegation of monopoly, misrepresentation or oppression, and the prices were fair; there was nothing to justify the conclusion that the public suffered injury. "If real competition is to continue, the right of the individual to exercise reasonable discretion in respect of his own business methods must be preserved," said the majority opinion.

Mr. Justice Brandeis dissented (Mr. Justice Clarke concurring with him):

"FIRST. The Court disposes of the case on a question of pleading. This, under the circumstances, is contrary to established practice. The circumstances are these:

"The pleading held defective is not one in this suit. It is the pleading by which was originated the proceeding before the Federal Trade Commission, an administrative tribunal, whose order this suit was brought to set aside. No suggestion was made in the proceeding before the Commission that the com-

[73]

plaint was defective. No such objection was raised in this suit in the court below. It was not made here by counsel. The objection is taken now for the first time and by the Court.

"This suit, begun in the Circuit Court of Appeals for the Second Circuit, was brought to set aside an order of the Federal Trade Commission. Before the latter the matter involved was thoroughly tried on the merits. There was a complaint and answers. Thirty-five witnesses were examined and cross-examined. A report of proposed findings as to facts was submitted by the Examiner and exceptions were filed thereto. Then, the case was heard before the Commission, which made a finding of facts, stated its conclusions as to the law, and ultimately issued the order in question. The proceedings occupied more than sixteen months. The report of them fills 400 pages of the printed record. In my opinion it is our duty to determine whether the facts found by the Commission are sufficient in law to support the order, and also, if it is questioned, whether the evidence was sufficient to support the findings of fact.

"*Second.* If the sufficiency of the complaint is held to be open for consideration here, we should, in my opinion, hold it to be sufficient. The complaint was filed under §5 of the Federal Trade Commission Act which declares unlawful 'unfair methods of competition in commerce,' empowers the Commission to prevent their use, and directs it to issue and serve 'a complaint stating its charges in that respect' whenever it has reason to believe that a concern 'has been or is using' such methods. The function of the complaint is solely to advise the respondent of the charges made so that he may have due notice and full opportunity for a hearing thereon. It does not purport to set out the elements of a crime like an indictment or information, nor the elements of a cause of action like a declaration at law or a bill in equity. All that is requisite in a complaint before the Commission is that there be a plain statement of the thing claimed to be wrong so that the respondent may be put upon his defense. The practice of the Federal Trade Commission in this respect, as in many others, is modeled on that which has been pursued by the Interstate Commerce Commission for a generation and has been sanctioned by this as well as the lower Federal courts. . . .

"The complaint here under consideration stated clearly that an unfair method of competition had been used by respondents, and specified what it was, namely, refusing to sell cotton ties unless the customer would purchase with each six ties also six yards of bagging. The complaint did not set out the circumstances which rendered this tying of bagging to ties an unfair practice. But this was not necessary. The complaint was similar in form to those filed with the Interstate Commerce Commission on complaints to enforce the prohibition of 'unjust and unreasonable charges' or of 'undue or unreasonable preference or advantage' which the Act to Regulate Commerce imposes. It is unnecessary to set forth why the rate specified was unjust or why the preference specified is undue or unreasonable, because these are matters not of law but of fact to be established by the evidence. . . . So far as appears neither this nor any other court has ever held that an order entered by the Interstate Commerce Commission may be set aside as void, because the complaint by which the proceeding was initiated, failed to set forth the reasons why the rate or the practice complained of was unjust or unreasonable; and I cannot see why a different rule should be applied to orders of the Federal Trade Commission issued under §5.

"In considering whether the complaint is sufficient, it is necessary to bear in mind the nature of the proceeding under review. The proceeding is not punitive. The complaint is not made with a view of subjecting the respondents to any form of punishment. It is not remedial. The complaint is not filed with a view to affording compensation for any injury alleged to have resulted from the matter charged, nor with a view to protecting individuals from any such injury in the future. The proceeding is strictly a preventive measure taken in the interest of the general public. And what it is brought to prevent is not the commission of *acts* of unfair competition, but the pursuit of unfair *methods.* Furthermore, the order is not self-executory. Standing alone it is only informative and advisory. The Commission cannot enforce it. If not acquiesced in by the respondents, the Commission may apply to the Circuit Court of Appeals to enforce it. But the Commission need not take such action, and it did not do so in respect to the order here in question. Respondents may, if they see fit, become the actors and ask to have the order set aside. That is what was done in the case at bar.

"The proceeding is thus a novelty. It is a new device in administrative machinery, introduced by Congress in the year 1914, in the hope thereby of remedying conditions in business which a great majority of the American people regarded as menacing the general welfare, and which for more than a generation they had vainly attempted to remedy by the ordinary processes of law. It was believed that widespread and growing concentration in industry and commerce restrained trade, and that monopolies were acquiring increasing control of business. Legislation designed to arrest the movement and to secure disintegration of existing combinations had been enacted by some of the States as early as 1889. In 1890 Congress passed the Sherman Law. It was followed by much legislation in the States and many official investigations. Between 1906 and 1913 reports were made by the Federal Bureau of Corporations of its investigations into the petroleum industry, the tobacco industry, the steel industry, and the farm implement industry. A special committee of Congress investigated the affairs of the United States Steel Corporation. And in 1911 this Court rendered its decision in *Standard Oil Co.* v. *United States,* 221 U. S. 1, and in *American Tobacco Co.* v. *United States,* 221 U. S. 106. The conviction became general in America that the legislation of the past had been largely ineffective. There was general agreement that further legislation was desirable. But there was a clear division of opinion as to what its character should be. Many believed that concentration (called by its opponents monopoly) was inevitable and desirable; and these desired that concentration should be recognized by law and be regulated. Others believed that concentration was a source of evil; that existing combinations could be disintegrated, if only the judicial machinery were perfected; and that further concentration could be averted by providing additional remedies, and particularly through regulating competition. The latter view prevailed in the Sixty-Third Congress. The Clayton Act (Act Oct. 15, 1914, c. 323, 38 Stat. 730) was framed largely with a view to making more effective the remedies given by the Sherman Law. The Federal Trade Commission Act (Act Sept. 26, 1914, c. 311, 38 Stat. 717) created an administrative tribunal, largely with a view to regulating competition.

"Many of the duties imposed upon the Trade Commission had been theretofore performed by the Bureau of Corporations. That which was in essence new legislation was the power conferred by §5. The belief was widespread that the great trusts had acquired their power, in the main, through destroying or overreaching their weaker rivals by resort to unfair practices. As Standard Oil rebates led to the creation of the Interstate Commerce Commission, other unfair methods of competition, which the investigations of the trusts had laid bare, led to the creation of the Federal Trade Commission. It was hoped that, as the former had substantially eliminated rebates, the latter might put an end to all other unfair trade practices, and that it might prove possible thereby to preserve the competitive system. It was a new experiment on old lines; and the machinery employed was substantially similar.

"In undertaking to regulate competition through the Trade

[77]

Commission, Congress (besides resorting to administrative as distinguished from judicial machinery) departed in two im. portant respects from the methods and measures theretofore applied in dealing with trusts and restraints of trade:

"(1) Instead of attempting to inflict punishment for having done prohibited acts, instead of enjoining the continuance of prohibited combinations and compelling disintegration of those formed in violation of law, the Act undertook to preserve competition through supervisory action of the Commission. The potency of accomplished facts had already been demonstrated. The task of the Commission was to protect competitive business from *further* inroads by monopoly. It was to be ever vigilant. If it discovered that any business concern had used any practice which would be likely to result in public injury—because in its nature it would tend to aid or develop into a restraint of trade —the Commission was directed to intervene, before any act should be done or condition arise violative of the Anti-Trust Act. And it should do this by filing a complaint with a view to a thorough investigation; and, if need be, the issue of an order. Its action was to be prophylactic. Its purpose in respect to restraints of trade was prevention of diseased business conditions, not cure.

"(2) Instead of undertaking to define what practices should be deemed unfair, as had been done in earlier legislation, the Act left the determination to the Commission. Experience with existing laws had taught that definition, being necessarily rigid, would prove embarrassing and, if rigorously applied, might involve great hardship. Methods of competition which would be unfair in one industry, under certain circumstances, might, when adopted in another industry, or even in the same industry under different circumstances, be entirely unobjectionable. Furthermore, an enumeration, however comprehensive, of existing methods of unfair competition must necessarily soon prove incomplete, as with new conditions constantly arising novel unfair methods would be devised and developed. In leaving to the Commission the determination of the question whether the method of competition pursued in a particular case was unfair, Congress followed the precedent which it had set a quarter of a century earlier, when by the Act to Regulate Commerce it conferred upon the Interstate Commerce Commission power to determine whether a preference or advantage given to a shipper or locality fell within the prohibition of an undue or unreasonable preference or advantage. . . . Recognizing that the question whether a method of competitive practice was unfair would ordinarily depend upon special facts, Congress imposed upon the Commission the duty of finding the facts, and it declared that findings of fact so made (if duly supported by evidence) were to be taken as final. The question whether the method of competition pursued could, on those facts, reasonably be held by the Commission to constitute an unfair method of competition, being a question of law, was necessarily left open to review by the Court. . . .

"*Third.* Such a question of law is presented to us for decision; and it is this: Can the refusal by a manufacturer to sell his product to a jobber or retailer, except upon condition that the purchaser will buy from him also his trade requirements in another article or articles, reasonably be found by the Commission to be an unfair method of competition under the circumstances set forth in the findings of fact? If we were called upon to consider the sufficiency of the complaint, and that merely, the question for our decision would be, whether the particular practice could, under any circumstances, reasonably be deemed an unfair method of competition. But as this suit to set aside the order of the Commission brings before us its findings of fact, we must determine whether these are sufficient to support their conclusion of law that the practice constituted—

'under the circumstances therein set forth, unfair methods of competition in interstate commerce against other manufacturers, dealers, and distributors in the material known as sugar-bag cloth, and against manufacturers, dealers, and distributors of the bagging known as rewoven bagging and second-hand bagging in violation of' the statute.

"It is obvious that the imposition of such a condition is not necessarily and universally an unfair method; but that it may be such under some circumstances seems equally clear. Under the usual conditions of competitive trade the practice might be wholly unobjectionable. But the history of combinations has shown that what one may do with impunity, may have intolerable results when done by several in cooperation. Similarly what approximately equal individual traders may do in honorable rivalry may result in grave injustice and public injury, if done by a great corporation in a particular field of business which it is able to dominate. In other words, a method of competition fair among equals may be very unfair if applied where there is inequality of resources. Without providing for those cases where the method of competition here involved would be unobjectionable, Massachusetts legislated against the practice, as early as 1901, by a statute (chapter 478) of general application. Its highest court, in applying the law which it held to be constitutional, described the prohibited method as 'unfair competition.' . . . The (Federal) Bureau of Corporations held the practice, which it described as 'full-line forcing,' to be highly reprehensible. Congress, by §3 of the Clayton Act, specifically prohibited the practice in a limited field under certain circumstances. An injunction against the practice has been included in several decrees in favor of the Government entered in cases under the Sherman Law. In the decree by which the American Tobacco Company was disintegrated pursuant to the mandate of this

Court, each of the fourteen companies was enjoined from 're-fusing to sell to any jobber any brand of any tobacco product manufactured by it, except upon condition that such jobber shall purchase from the vendor some other brand or product also manufactured and sold by it***.' . . . The practice here in question is merely one form of the so-calling 'tying clauses' or 'conditional requirements' which have been declared in a discerning study of the whole subject to be 'perhaps the most interesting of any of the methods of unfair competition.' [*Unfair Methods of Competition and Their Prevention*, by W. H. S. Stevens.]

"The following facts found by the Commission, and which the Circuit Court of Appeals held were supported by sufficient evidence, show that the conditions in the cotton tie and bagging trade were in 1918 such that the Federal Trade Commission could reasonably find that the tying clause here in question was an unfair method of competition: Cotton, America's chief staple, is marketed in bales. To bale cotton, steel ties and jute bagging are essential. The Carnegie Steel Company, a subsidiary of the United States Steel Corporation, manufactures so large a proportion of all such steel ties that it dominates the cotton tie situation in the United States and is able to fix and control the price of such ties throughout the country. The American Manufacturing Company manufactures about forty-five percent of all bagging used for cotton baling; one other company about twenty percent; and the remaining thirty-five percent is made up of second-hand bagging and a material called sugar-bag cloth. Warren, Jones & Gratz, of St. Louis, are the Carnegie Company's sole agents for selling and distributing steel ties. They are also American Manufacturing Company's sole agents for selling and distributing jute bagging in the cotton-growing section west of the Mississippi. By virtue of their selling agency for the Carnegie Company, Warren, Jones & Gratz held a dominating and controlling position in the sale and

[81]

distribution of cotton ties in the entire cotton-growing section of the country, and thereby it was in a position to force would-be purchasers of ties to also buy from them bagging manufactured by the American Manufacturing Company. A great many merchants, jobbers, and dealers in bagging and ties throughout the cotton-growing States were many times unable to procure ties from any other firm than Warren, Jones & Gratz. In many instances Warren, Jones & Gratz refused to sell ties unless the purchaser would also buy from them a corresponding amount of bagging, and such purchasers were oftentimes compelled to buy from them bagging manufactured by the American Manufacturing Company in order to procure a sufficient supply of steel ties.

"These are conditions closely resembling those under which 'full-line forcing,' 'exclusive-dealing requirements' or 'shutting off materials, supplies, or machines from competitors'— well-known methods of competition, have been held to be unfair, when practiced by concerns holding a preponderant position in the trade.

"*Fourth.* The Circuit Court of Appeals set aside the order of the Commission solely on the ground that it was without authority to determine the merits of specific individual grievances, and that the evidence did not support its finding that Warren, Jones & Gratz had—

'adopted and practiced the policy of refusing to sell steel ties to those merchants and dealers who wished to buy from them unless such merchants and dealers would also buy from them a corresponding amount of jute bagging.'

"The reason assigned by the Circuit Court of Appeals for so holding was that the evidence failed to show that the practice complained of (although acted on in individual cases by respondents) had become their 'general practice.' But the power of the Trade Commission to prohibit an unfair method of competition found to have been used is not limited to cases where the practice had become general. What §5 declares unlawful is not unfair competition. That had been unlawful before. What that section made unlawful were 'unfair methods of competition'; that is, the method or means by which an unfair end might be accomplished. The Commission was directed to act, if it had reason to believe that an 'unfair method of competition in commerce has been or is being used.' The purpose of Congress was to prevent any unfair method which may have been used by any concern in competition from becoming its general practice. It was only by stopping its use before it became a general practice, that the apprehended effect of an unfair method in suppressing competition by destroying rivals could be averted. As the Circuit Court of Appeals found that the evidence was sufficient to support the facts set forth above, and since on those facts the Commission could reasonably hold that the method of competition here in question was unfair under the circumstances, it had power under the Act to issue the order complained of.

"In my opinion the judgment of the Circuit Court of Appeals should be reversed."

Federal Trade Commission v. *Gratz, et al.*
253 U. S. 421, 429

Misrepresenting to the Public

(Opinion of the Court, *Federal Trade Commission* v. *Winsted*, 1922)

"THE Winsted Hosiery Company has for many years manufactured underwear which it sells to retailers throughout the United States. It brands or labels the cartons in which the underwear is sold, as 'Natural Merino,' 'Gray Wool,' 'Natural Wool,' 'Natural Worsted,' or 'Australian Wool.' None of this underwear is all wool. Much of it contains only a small percentage of wool; some as little as ten percent. The Federal Trade Commission instituted a complaint under §5 of the Act of September 26, 1914, c. 311, 38 Stat. 717, 719, and called upon the company to show cause why use of these brands and labels alleged to be false and deceptive should not be discontinued. After appropriate proceedings an order was issued which, as later modified, directed the company to— [The "cease and desist" order is quoted, requiring an accurate designation of the materials used.]

"A petition for review of this order was filed by the company in the United States Circuit Court of Appeals for the Second Circuit. The prayer that the order be set aside was granted; and a decree to that effect was entered. That court said:

'Conscientious manufacturers may prefer not to use a label which is capable of misleading, and it may be that it will be desirable to prevent the use of the particular labels, but it is in our opinion not within the

[84]

province of the Federal Trade Commission to do so.'

"The case is here on writ of certiorari. . . .

"The order of the Commission rests upon findings of fact; and these upon evidence which fills 350 pages of the printed record. Section 5 of the Act makes the Commission's findings conclusive as to the facts, if supported by evidence.

"The findings here involved are clear, specific, and comprehensive: The word 'Merino,' as applied to wool, 'means primarily and popularly' a fine long-staple wool, which commands the highest price. The words 'Australian Wool' mean a distinct commodity, a fine grade of wool grown in Australia. The word 'wool' when used as an adjective means made of wool. The word 'worsted' means primarily and popularly a yarn or fabric made wholly of wool. A substantial part of the consuming public, and also some buyers for retailers and sales people, understand the words 'Merino,' 'Natural Merino,' 'Gray Merino,' 'Natural Wool,' 'Gray Wool,' 'Australian Wool' and 'Natural Worsted,' as applied to underwear, to mean that the underwear is all wool. By means of the labels and brands of the Winsted Company bearing such words, part of the public is misled into selling or into buying as all wool, underwear which in fact is in large part cotton. And these brands and labels tend to aid and encourage the representations of unscrupulous retailers and their salesmen who knowingly sell to their customers as all wool, underwear which is largely composed of cotton. Knit underwear made wholly of wool has for many years been widely manufactured and sold in this country and constitutes a substantial part of all knit underwear dealt in. It is sold under various labels or brands, including 'Wool,' 'All Wool,' 'Natural Wool' and 'Pure Wool,' and also under other labels which do not contain any words descriptive of the composition of the article. Knit underwear made of cotton and wool is also used in this country by some manufacturers who market it without any label or marking describing the material or fibres of which it is composed, and by some who market it under labels bearing the words 'Cotton and Wool,' or 'Part Wool.' The Winsted Company's product, labeled and branded as above stated, is being sold in competition with such all-wool underwear, and such cotton and wool underwear.

"That these findings of fact are supported by evidence cannot be doubted. But it is contended that the method of competition complained of is not unfair within the meaning of the Act, because labels such as the Winsted Company employs, and particularly those bearing the word 'Merino,' have long been established in the trade and are generally understood by it as indicating goods partly of cotton; that the trade is not deceived by them; that there was no unfair competition for which another manufacturer of underwear could maintain a suit against the Winsted Company; and that even if consumers are misled because they do not understand the trade signification of the label or because some retailers deliberately deceive them as to its meaning, the result is in no way legally connected with unfair competition.

"This argument appears to have prevailed with the Court of Appeals; but it is unsound. The labels in question are literally false, and, except those which bear the word 'Merino,' are palpably so. All are, as the Commission found, calculated to deceive and do in fact deceive a substantial portion of the purchasing public. That deception is due primarily to the words of the labels, and not to deliberate deception by the retailers from whom the consumer purchases. While it is true that a secondary meaning of the word 'Merino' is shown, it is not a meaning so thoroughly established that the description which the label carries has ceased to deceive the public; for even buyers for retailers, and salespeople, are found to have been misled. The facts show that it is to the interest of the public that a proceeding to stop the practice be brought. And they show also that the practice constitutes an unfair method of competition as against manufacturers of all-wool knit underwear and as against those manufacturers of mixed wool and cotton underwear who brand their product truthfully. For when misbranded goods attract customers by means of the fraud which they perpetrate, trade is diverted from the producer of truthfully marked goods. That these honest manufacturers might protect their trade also by resorting to deceptive labels is no defense to this proceeding brought against the Winsted Company in the public interest.

"The fact that misrepresentation and misdescription have become so common in the knit underwear trade that most dealers no longer accept labels at their face value does not prevent their use being an unfair method of competition. A method inherently unfair does not cease to be so because those competed against have become aware of the wrongful practice. Nor does it cease to be unfair because the falsity of the manufacturer's representation has become so well known to the trade that dealers, as distinguished from consumers, are no longer deceived. The honest manufacturer's business may suffer, not merely through a competitor's deceiving his direct customer, the retailer, but also through the competitor's putting into the hands of the retailer an unlawful instrument, which enables the retailer to increase his own sales of the dishonest goods, thereby lessening the market for the honest product. That a person is a wrongdoer who so furnishes another with the means of consummating a fraud has long been a part of the law of unfair competition. And trade-marks which deceive the public are denied protection although members of the trade are not misled thereby. As a substantial part of the public was still misled by the use of the labels which the Winsted Company employed, the public had an interest in stopping the practice as wrongful; and since the business of its trade rivals who marked their goods truthfully was necessarily affected by that practice, the Commission was justified in its conclusion that the practice constituted an unfair method of competition; and it was authorized to order that the practice be discontinued.

Reversed."

(Mr. Justice McReynolds dissented without opinion.)

Federal Trade Commission v. Winsted Hosiery Co.
258 U. S. 483

Manufacturers in Cooperation

(Dissenting Opinion, *American Column Co.* v. *United States*, 1921)

THE "OPEN COMPETITION PLAN" OF THE AMERICAN HARDWOOD Manufacturers' Association, by means of which members pooled information on sales, prices, supply on hand, and production, was held by the Court to be a combination in restraint of trade in violation of the Sherman Law.

Mr. Justice Clarke called this "abnormal conduct on the part of 365 natural competitors*** simply an expansion of the gentleman's agreement of former days, skilfully devised to evade the law." Daily reports, weekly reviews and forecasts, and frequent trade meetings were evidence of a purpose to suppress competition by restricting production and harmonizing prices. Despite the absence of a specific agreement to fix prices, the evidence showed concerted action to restrict production and large price increases. Justice Clarke cited previous decisions of the Court upholding the view that undue restraint of competition was restraint of trade within the meaning of the anti-trust law.

Holmes and McKenna, JJ., concurred in Justice Brandeis' dissent. Holmes also wrote a separate dissenting opinion.* Brandeis said:

"THERE are more than 9,000 hardwood lumber mills in that part of the United States which lies east of a line extending from Minnesota to Texas. Three hundred and sixty-five concerns—each separate and independent—are members of an association by means of which they cooperate under the so-called 'Open Competition Plan.' Their mills—about 470 in number

* See page 176, *The Dissenting Opinions of Mr. Justice Holmes.*

[89]

—are located in eighteen States. Their aggregate production is about thirty percent of the total production of hardwood in the United States. The question presented for our decision is whether the Open Competition Plan, either inherently or as practiced by these concerns, violates the Sherman Law. The plan provides for cooperation in collecting and distributing information concerning the business of members and generally in regard to the trade. That in adopting the Plan the members formed a combination in trade is clear. Cooperation implies combination. And this combination confessedly relates to interstate trade. It is also clear that a plan for cooperation, although itself innocent, may be made an instrument by which illegal restraint is practiced. But the decree below should, in my opinion, be reversed, because the Plan is not inherently a restraint of trade, and the record is barren of evidence to support a finding that it has been used, or was intended to be used, as an instrument to restrain trade.

"Restraint of trade may be exerted upon rivals; upon buyers or upon sellers; upon employers or upon employed. Restraint may be exerted through force or fraud or agreement. It may be exerted through moral or through legal obligations; through fear or through hope. It may exist, although it is not manifested in any overt act, and even though there is no intent to restrain. Words of advice, seemingly innocent and perhaps benevolent, may restrain, when uttered under circumstances that make advice equivalent to command. For the essence of restraint is power; and power may arise merely out of position. Wherever a dominant position has been attained, restraint necessarily arises. And when dominance is attained, or is sought, through combination—however good the motives or the manners of those participating—the Sherman Law is violated; provided, of course, that the restraint be what is called unreasonable.

"In the case before us there was clearly no coercion. There

is no claim that a monopoly was sought or created. There is
no claim that a division of territory was planned or secured.
There is no claim that uniform prices were established or desired. There is no claim that by agreement, force, or fraud,
any producer, dealer, or consumer was to be or has in fact been
controlled or coerced. The Plan is a voluntary system for collecting from these independent concerns detailed information
concerning the business operations of each, and its opinions as
to trade conditions, prospects, and policy, and of collating, in-
terpreting, and distributing the data so received among the
members of the Association and others. No information gathered under the Plan was kept secret from any producer, any
buyer, or the public. Ever since its inception in 1917, a copy
of every report made and of every market letter published
has been filed with the Department of Justice, and with the
Federal Trade Commission. The district meetings were open
to the public. Dealers and consumers were invited to participate in the discussions, and to some extent have done so.

"It is claimed that the purpose of the Open Competition
Plan was to lessen competition. Competition among members
was contemplated and was in vigorous operation. The Sherman Law does not prohibit every lessening of competition;
and it certainly does not command that competition shall be
pursued blindly, that business rivals shall remain ignorant of
trade facts, or be denied aid in weighing their significance. It
is lawful to regulate competition in some degree. *Chicago
Board of Trade* v. *United States*, 246 U. S. 231. But it was
neither the aim of the Plan, nor the practice under it, to regulate competition in any way. Its purpose was to make rational
competition possible, by supplying data not otherwise available, and without which most of those engaged in the trade
would be unable to trade intelligently.

"The hardwood lumber mills are widely scattered. The
principal area of production is the Southern States. But there

are mills in Minnesota, New York, New England, and the Middle States. Most plants are located near the sources of supply, isolated, remote from the larger cities and from the principal markets. No official, or other public, means have been established for collecting from these mills and from dealers data as to current production, stocks on hand, and market prices. Concerning grain, cotton, coal, and oil, the Government collects and publishes regularly, at frequent intervals, current information on production, consumption, and stocks on hand; and Boards of Trade furnish freely to the public details of current market prices of those commodities, the volume of sales, and even individual sales, as recorded in daily transactions. Persons interested in such commodities are enabled through this information to deal with one another on an equal footing. The absence of such information in the hardwood lumber trade enables dealers in the large centers more readily to secure advantage over the isolated producer. And the large concerns, which are able to establish their own bureaus of statistics, secure an advantage over smaller concerns. Surely it is not against the public interest to distribute knowledge of trade facts, however detailed. Nor are the other features of the Plan, the market letters and the regional conferences, an unreasonable interference with freedom in trade. Intelligent conduct of business implies, not only knowledge of trade facts, but an understanding of them. To this understanding editorial comment and free discussion of those engaged in the business and by others interested are aids. Opinions expressed may be unsound; predictions may be unfounded; but there is nothing in the Sherman Law which should limit freedom of discussion, even among traders.

"It is insisted that there was a purpose to curtail production. No evidence of any such purpose was introduced. There was at no time uniformity in the percentage of production to capacity. On the contrary, the evidence is uncontradicted that the high prices induced strenuous efforts to increase production. Weather and labor conditions had made production difficult. Tractors were purchased at great cost to get the logs out of the forests which excessive rains had rendered inaccessible to the usual methods of transport. The current sales of new machinery to hardwood lumber mills were on an unprecedented scale. Where equipment and supply of logs permitted, mills were run at night to overcome the restrictions upon production which the bad weather had imposed. There were, it is true, from time to time, warnings in the 'Market Letters' and otherwise, against overproduction—warnings which seem not to have been heeded. But surely Congress did not intend by the Sherman Act to prohibit self-restraint—and it was for self-restraint that the only appeal was made. The purpose of the warnings was to induce mill owners to curb their greed— lest both they and others suffer from the crushing evils of overproduction. Such warning or advice, whether given by individuals or the representatives of an association, presents no evidence of illegality.

"It is urged that this was a concerted effort to enhance prices. There was at no time uniformity in prices. So far as appears, every mill charged for its product as much as it could get. There is evidence that the hardwood mills expected, by adopting the Plan, to earn more in profits, and to do so, at least in part, by getting higher prices for their product. It may be that the distribution of the trade data, the editorial comment, and the conferences enabled the producers to obtain, on the average, higher prices than would otherwise have been possible. But there is nothing in the Sherman Law to indicate that Congress intended to condemn cooperative action in the exchange of information, merely because prophecy resulting from comment on the data collected may lead, for a period, to higher market prices. Congress assumed that the desire to acquire and to enjoy property is the safest and most promising

[93]

basis for society, and to that end it sought, among other things, to protect the pursuit of business for private profit. Its purpose, obviously, was not to prevent the making of profits, or to counteract the operation of the law of supply and demand. Its purpose was merely to prevent restraint. The illegality of a combination under the Sherman Law lies not in its effect upon the price level, but in the coercion thereby effected. It is the limitation of freedom, by agreements which narrow a market . . . or by organized boycott . . . or by the coercive power of rebates, which constitutes unlawful restraint.

"The cooperation which is incident to this Plan does not suppress competition. On the contrary, it tends to promote all in competition which is desirable. By substituting knowledge for ignorance, rumor, guess, and suspicion, it tends also to substitute research and reasoning for gambling and piracy, without closing the door to adventure, or lessening the value of prophetic wisdom. In making such knowledge available to the smallest concern, it creates among producers equality of opportunity. In making it available, also, to purchasers and the general public, it does all that can actually be done to protect the community from extortion. If, as is alleged, the Plan tends to substitute stability in prices for violent fluctuations, its influence, in this respect, is not against the public interest. The evidence in this case, far from establishing an illegal restraint of trade, presents, in my opinion, an instance of commendable effort by concerns engaged in a chaotic industry to make possible its intelligent conduct under competitive conditions.

"The refusal to permit a multitude of small rivals to cooperate, as they have done here, in order to protect themselves and the public from the chaos and havoc wrought in their trade by ignorance, may result in suppressing competition in the hardwood industry. These keen business rivals, who sought through cooperative exchange of trade information to create conditions under which alone rational competition is possible,

[94]

produce in the aggregate about one-third of the hardwood lumber of the country. This Court held in *United States* v. *U. S. Steel Corporation*, 251. U. S. 417, that it was not unlawful to vest in a single corporation control of fifty percent of the steel industry of the country; and in *United States* v. *United Shoe Machinery Co.*, 247 U. S. 32, the Court held that it was not unlawful to vest in a single corporation control of practically the whole shoe machinery industry. May not these hardwood lumber concerns, frustrated in their efforts to rationalize competition, be led to enter the inviting field of consolidation? And, if they do, may not another huge trust, with highly centralized control over vast resources, natural, manufacturing, and financial, become so powerful as to dominate competitors, wholesalers, retailers, consumers, employees, and, in large measure, the community?"

American Column & Lumber Co., et al. v. United States,
257 U. S. 377, 413

Protection from Short Weight

(Dissenting Opinion, *Jay Burns Baking Co.* v. *Bryan*, 1924)

A NEBRASKA LAW ATTEMPTED TO PREVENT DECEPTION IN THE SALE of bread by requiring that every loaf made or sold in the State be of a standard weight—one-half pound, one pound, a pound and a half, or an exact multiple of a pound. A tolerance of an additional two ounces per pound was allowed, but the sale of loaves which exceeded the standard by more than this tolerance, as well as those below the standard, was prohibited. The weight requirements applied for twenty-four hours after baking.

On a suit to enjoin the enforcement of this act, the Supreme Court, speaking through Mr. Justice Butler, held that it violated the due process clause of the Fourteenth Amendment by subjecting "bakers and sellers of bread to restrictions which are essentially unreasonable and arbitrary." The grounds on which this conclusion was reached are stated as well as attacked by Mr. Justice Brandeis (with whom Mr. Justice Holmes concurred).

"THE PURPOSE of the Nebraska standard-weight bread law is to protect buyers from short weights and honest bakers from unfair competition. It provides for a few standard-size loaves, which are designated by weight, and prohibits, as to each size, the baking or selling of a loaf which weighs either less or more than the prescribed weight. *Schmidinger* v. *Chicago*, 226 U. S. 578, settled that the business of making and selling bread is a permissible subject for regulation, that the prevention of short weights is a proper end of regulation, that the fixing of standard sizes and weights of loaves is an appropriate means to

[96]

that end, and that prevalent marketing frauds make the enactment of some such protective legislation permissible. The ordinance there upheld, besides defining the standard-weight loaf, required that every loaf should bear a label stating the weight, and to sell a loaf weighing less than the weight stated in the label was made a misdemeanor.

"The Nebraska regulation is in four respects less stringent than the ordinance upheld in the *Schmidinger Case:* (1) It provides for a tolerance; that is, it permits a deviation from the standard weight of not more than two ounces in a pound, provided that the prescribed standard weight shall be determined by averaging the weights of not less than twenty-five loaves of any one unit. (2) The prescribed weight applies for only twenty-four hours after the baking. (3) The weight is to be ascertained by weighing on the premises where the bread is baked. (4) No label stating the weight is required to be affixed to the loaf; that is, as a representation of the weight, the familiar size of the loaf is substituted for the label. On the other hand, the Nebraska requirement is more stringent than the Chicago ordinance, in that it prohibits making and selling loaves which exceed the prescribed weight by more than the tolerance. This prohibition of excess weights is held to deny due process of law to bakers and sellers of bread. In plain English, the prohibition is declared to be a measure so arbitrary or whimsical that no body of legislators, acting reasonably, could have imposed it. In reaching this conclusion, the Court finds specifically that this prohibition 'is not necessary for the protection of purchasers against imposition and fraud by short weights,' that it 'is not calculated to effectuate that purpose,' and that the practical difficulties of compliance with the limitation are so great that the provision 'subjects bakers and sellers of bread to restrictions which are essentially unreasonable and arbitrary.'

"To bake a loaf of any size other than the standard is made

[97]

a misdemeanor. Why baking a loaf which weighs less than the standard size should be made a crime is obvious. Such a loaf is a handy instrument of fraud. Why it should be a crime to bake one which weighs more than the standard is not obvious. The reason given is that such a loaf, also, is a handy instrument of fraud. In order that the buyer may be afforded protection, the difference between the standard sizes must be so large as to be evident and conspicuous. The buyer has usually in mind the difference in appearance between a one-pound loaf and a pound and a half loaf, so that it is difficult for the dealer to palm off the former for the latter. But a loaf weighing one pound and five ounces may look so much like the buyer's memory of the pound and a half loaf that the dealer may effectuate the fraud by delivering the former. The prohibition of excess weight is imposed in order to prevent a loaf of one standard size from being increased so much that it can readily be sold for a loaf of a larger standard size.

"With the wisdom of the legislation we have, of course, no concern. But, under the due process clause as construed, we must determine whether the prohibition of excess weights can reasonably be deemed necessary, whether the prohibition can reasonably be deemed an appropriate means of preventing short weights and incidental unfair practices, and whether compliance with the limitation prescribed can reasonably be deemed practicable. The determination of these questions involves an inquiry into facts. Unless we know the facts on which the legislators may have acted, we cannot properly decide whether they were (or whether their measures are) unreasonable, arbitrary, or capricious. Knowledge is essential to understanding, and understanding should precede judging. Sometimes, if we would guide by the light of reason, we must let our minds be bold. But, in this case, we have merely to acquaint ourselves with the art of bread-making and the usages of the trade, with the devices by which buyers of bread are imposed upon and honest bakers or dealers are subjected by their dishonest fellows to unfair competition, with the problems which have confronted public officials charged with the enforcement of the laws prohibiting short weights, and with their experience in administering those laws.

"*First.* Why did legislators, bent only on preventing short weights, prohibit also excessive weights? It was not from caprice or love of symmetry. It was because experience had taught consumers, honest dealers, and public officials charged with the duty of enforcing laws concerning weights and measures that, if short weights were to be prevented, the prohibition of excessive weights was an administrative necessity. Similar experience had led to the enactment of a like prohibition of excess quantities in laws designed to prevent defrauding, by short measure, purchasers of many other articles. It was similar experience which had led those seeking to prevent the sale of intoxicating liquor to enact the law which prohibits the sale of malt liquor, although not containing any alcohol (sustained in *Purity Extract Co.* v. *Lynch*, 226 U. S. 192), and that which prohibits the sale of liquor containing more than one-half of one percent of alcohol (sustained in *Ruppert* v. *Caffey*, 251 U. S. 264). . . .

"In January, 1858, the late corporation of Washington adopted an ordinance fixing a standard-weight loaf, and establishing an excess tolerance. The standard-weight bread ordinance adopted by Chicago in 1908 and sustained in the *Schmidinger Case* is said to have been the first standard-weight bread law in the United States enacted in this century. Prior thereto many different kinds of legislation had been tried in the several States and cities with a view to preventing short weights. Experience had shown the inefficacy of those preventive measures. Experience under the Chicago ordinance indicated the value of introducing the standard-weight loaf; but it proved, also, that the absence of a provision prohibiting excess weights seriously impaired the efficacy of the ordinance. When in 1917 the United States Food Administration was established, pursuant to the Lever Act (Aug. 10, 1917, c. 53, 40 Stat. 276) the business of baking came under its supervision and control; and provision was made for licensing substantially all bakers. The protection of buyers of bread against the fraud of short weights was deemed essential. After an investigation which occupied three months, the Food Administration issued the regulations by which licensees were to be governed. No standard-weight bread statute had then been enacted in any State. The regulations adopted established standard-weight loaves, prohibited the sale of loaves other than of the standard weights, and limited the excess weight to not more than one ounce to the pound. This provision remained in force unchanged until the licensing system was abrogated on December 19, 1918 (after the Armistice).

"The efficacy of the prohibition of excess weights as a means of preventing short weights having been demonstrated by experience during the period of Food Administration control, a widespread demand arose for legislative action in the several States to continue the protection which had been thus afforded. Dissatisfaction with the old methods of regulation was expressed in a number of States. During the years 1919 to 1923, standard-weight bread laws, containing the prohibition of excess weights, were enacted in twelve States. Similar bills were introduced in others. Congress enacted such a law for the District of Columbia. Hawaii and Porto Rico did likewise. The National Conference on Weights and Measures indorsed a similar provision. A bill embodying the same principles, applicable to sales of bread in interstate commerce, prepared by the Department of Agriculture and the Department of Commerce, was introduced in 1923 and is now pending. At the congressional hearings thereon, it was shown that the provision against excess weights is deemed necessary by a large majority of the bakers, as well as by consumers and by local public officials charged with the duty of preventing short weights. In Nebraska the demand for the legislation under review was general and persistent. It was enacted after a prolonged public discussion carried on throughout the State as well as in the Legislature. Can it be said, in view of these facts, that the legislators had not reasonable cause to believe that the prohibition of excess weights was necessary in order to protect buyers of bread from imposition and honest dealers from unfair competition?

"*Second*. Is the prohibition of excess weights calculated to effectuate the purpose of the Act? In other words, is it a provision which can reasonably be expected to aid in the enforcement of the prohibition of short weights? That it has proved elsewhere an important aid is shown by abundant evidence of the highest quality. It is shown by the fact that the demand for the legislation arose after observation of its efficacy during the period of Food Administration control. It is shown by the experience of the several communities in which the provision has since been in operation: Chicago, California, Ohio, Indiana, and the District of Columbia. The value of the prohibition is shown, also, by the fact that after extensive application and trial it has been indorsed by the National Conference on Weights and Measures and is included in the proposed 'Federal Bread Law.' Can it be said, in view of these facts, that the Legislature of Nebraska had no reason to believe that this provision is calculated to effectuate the purpose of the standard-weight bread legislation?

"*Third*. Does the prohibition of excess weight impose unreasonable burdens upon the business of making and selling bread? In other words, would compliance involve bakers in heavy costs, or necessitate the employment of persons of greater skill than are ordinarily available? Or would the probability of unintentional transgression be so great as unreason-

[101]

ably to expose those engaged in the business to the danger of criminal prosecution? Facts established by widespread and varied experience of the bakers under laws containing a similar provision, and the extensive investigation and experiments of competent scientists, seem to compel a negative answer to each of these questions. But we need not go so far. There is certainly reason to believe that the provision does not subject the baker to an appreciable cost; that it does not require a higher degree of skill than is commonly available to bakery concerns; and that it does not expose honest bakers to the danger of criminal proceedings. As to these matters, also, the experience gained during the period of Food Administration control, and since then in the several States, is persuasive. For under the Food Administration, and in most of the States, the business was successfully conducted under provisions for tolerances which were far more stringent than that enacted in Nebraska. In the Food Administration regulation, and in most of the statutes, the tolerance was one ounce in the pound. In Nebraska it is two. In some States the weight is taken of the individual loaf. In Nebraska it is the average of at least twenty-five loaves. In some States in which the average weight is taken, it is computed on a less number of loaves than twenty-five. In some, where an average of twenty-five is taken, the tolerance is smaller. Moreover, even if it were true that the varying evaporation made compliance with the law difficult, a sufficiently stable weight can, confessedly, be secured by the use of oil paper wrapping (now required in several States for sanitary reasons), which can be inexpensively supplied. Furthermore, as bakers are left free to charge for their bread such price as they choose, enhanced cost of conducting the business would not deprive them of property without due process of law. Can it be said, in view of these facts, that the Legislature of Nebraska had no reason to believe that the excess weight provision would not unduly burden the business of making and selling bread? Much evidence referred to by me is not in the record. Nor could it have been included. It is the history of the experience gained under similar legislation, and the results of scientific experiments made since the entry of the judgment below. Of such events in our history, whether occurring before or after the enactment of the statute or of the entry of the judgment, the Court should acquire knowledge, and must, in my opinion, take judicial notice, whenever required to perform the delicate judicial task here involved. Compare *Muller* v. *Oregon,* 208 U. S. 412, 419, 420 [See page 337]; *Dorchy* v. *Kansas,* 264 U. S. 186. The evidence contained in the record in this case is, however, ample to sustain the validity of the statute. There is in the record some evidence in conflict with it. The Legislature and the lower court have, doubtless, considered that. But with this conflicting evidence we have no concern. It is not our province to weigh evidence. Put at its highest, our function is to determine, in the light of all facts which may enrich our knowledge and enlarge our understanding, whether the measure, enacted in the exercise of an unquestioned police power and of a character inherently unobjectionable, transcends the bounds of reason; that is, whether the provision as applied is so clearly arbitrary or capricious that legislators acting reasonably could not have believed it to be necessary or appropriate for the public welfare.

"To decide, as a fact, that the prohibition of excess weights 'is not necessary for the protection of the purchasers against imposition and fraud by short weights,' that it 'is not calculated to effectuate that purpose,' and that it 'subjects bakers and sellers of bread' to heavy burdens, is, in my opinion, an exercise of the powers of a super-Legislature—not the performance of the constitutional function of judicial review."

Jay Burns Baking Co., et al. v. *Bryan*
264 U. S. 504, 517

Farmers' Cooperative Associations

(Dissenting Opinion, *Frost* v. *Corporation Commission*, 1929)

COTTON GINS WERE DECLARED TO BE PUBLIC UTILITIES BY AN Oklahoma statute which provided that no gin should be operated without a license, and that to secure such a license there must be a satisfactory showing of public necessity. A later amendment permitted the licensing (without such a showing) of gins to be run cooperatively. Frost, the operator of a private gin, sued to enjoin the Corporation Commission from granting a license to a cooperative association, claiming that there was no public necessity for the additional gin and that the provision exempting the association from the requirement that such need be shown denied him the equal protection of the laws, in violation of the Fourteenth Amendment.

The Supreme Court, reversing the District Court, held that the injunction should be granted. Mr. Justice Sutherland, for the majority, said that if the cooperative in question were of the non-stock type (organized under a 1917 law) the classification might be upheld. But in granting to a cooperative organized as a stock corporation (under a 1919 law) and doing business with the general public for profit a privilege that was denied to an individual operator, the statute established a classification which "is essentially arbitrary, because based upon no real or substantial differences having reasonable relation to the subject dealt with by the legislation."

Justices Holmes and Stone concurred in Mr. Justice Brandeis' dissent:

"UNDER §3714 of Oklahoma Compiled Statutes 1921, as amended by c. 109 of the Laws of 1925, Frost secured from the Corporation Commission a license to operate a cotton gin

[104]

in the city of Durant. Later, the Durant Cooperative Gin Company applied to the Commission under that statute for a license to operate a gin in the same city. In support of its application, it presented a certificate of organization under chapter 147 of the Laws of 1919 entitled 'An Act providing for the organization and regulation of cooperative corporations' (Oklahoma Compiled Statutes 1921, §§5637-5652), and a petition signed by one hundred citizens and taxpayers of that community requesting that the license be issued. Frost objected to the granting of a license, on the ground that there was no necessity for an additional gin in that city. The Commission ruled that, upon the showing made, it was obliged by §3714 as so amended to issue a license, without hearing evidence as to necessity; and indicated its purpose to issue the license. Thereupon, Frost brought this suit under §266 of the Judicial Code against the Commission, the Attorney General, and the Durant Company to enjoin granting the license. A restraining order issued upon the filing of the bill.

"The case was first heard by three judges upon application for an interlocutory injunction and upon defendants' motion to dismiss. Frost contended that his license had conferred a franchise; that from it there arose in him the property right to be protected against further local competition, unless existing ginning facilities were inadequate; that in the absence of a showing of necessity competition by the Durant Company would be illegal; and that to issue a license which authorized such competition would take Frost's property without due process of law and deny to him the equal protection of the law. The District Court denied both the injunction and the motion to dismiss; and it dissolved the restraining order. Upon direct appeal by Frost, this Court affirmed the interlocutory decree *per curiam* in *Frost* v. *Corporation Commission*, 274 U. S. 719, on the authority of *Chicago Great Western Ry. Co.* v. *Kendall*, 266 U. S. 94, 100. Thereupon, the facts being stipulated, the

[105]

case was submitted in the District Court on final hearing to the same judges; and a decree was entered dismissing the bill. . . . This appeal presents the same questions which were argued on the appeal from the interlocutory decree.

"Under the Oklahoma Act of 1907 cotton gins were held subject to regulation by the Corporation Commission. In 1915, the Legislature declared them public utilities and restriction of competition was introduced by prohibiting operation of a gin without a license from the Commission. That statute required that a license issue for proper gins already established, but directed that none should issue for a new gin in any community already adequately supplied, except upon 'the presentation of a petition signed by not less than fifty farmer petitioners of the immediate vicinity.' . . . Chapter 191 of the Session Laws of 1923 struck out of §3714 the provision referring to farmers. But in 1925 there was inserted in lieu thereof the proviso 'that on the presentation of a petition for the establishment of a gin to be run cooperatively, signed by one hundred (100) citizens and taxpayers of the community where the gin is to be located, the Corporation Commission shall issue a license for said gin.' . . . In 1926, the Supreme Court of Oklahoma held in *Choctaw Cotton Oil Co.* v. *Corporation Commission,* 121 Okl. 51, 52, that a corporation organized under chapter 147 of the Laws of 1919 was run cooperatively within the meaning of §3714 as so amended.

"The attack upon the statute is rested mainly upon the contention that by requiring issuance of a license to so-called cooperative corporations organized under the law of 1919, the statute as amended in 1925 creates an arbitrary classification. The classification is said to be arbitrary, because the differences between such concerns and commercial corporations or individuals engaged in the same business are in this connection not material. The contention rests, I think, upon misapprehensions of fact. The differences are vital; and the classification is a reasonable one. Before stating why I think so, other grounds for affirming the judgment should be mentioned.

"*First.* The bill alleges, and the parties have stipulated, that Frost was licensed under §3714 of the Compiled Statutes as amended by the Act of 1925. The stipulation does not show that prior to the amendment he held any license. His alleged property right to conditional immunity from competition rests wholly on the statute now challenged. It is settled that one cannot in the same proceeding both rely upon a statute and assail it. . . . This established rule requires affirmance of the judgment below.

"*Second.* Frost claims that to grant a license to the Durant Company without a showing of public necessity would involve taking his property without due process. The only property which he asserts would be so taken is the alleged right to be immune from the competition of persons operating without a valid license. But for the statute, he would obviously be subject to competition from anyone. Whether the license issued to him under §3714 conferred upon him the property right claimed is a question of statutory construction—and thus, ordinarily, a question of State law. 'Whether State statutes shall be construed one way or another is a State question, the final decision of which rests with the courts of the State.' (*Hebert* v. *Louisiana,* 272 U. S. 312, 316.) In the absence of a decision of the question by the highest court of the State, this Court would be obliged to construe the statute; and in doing so it might be aided by consideration of the decisions of courts of other States dealing with like statutes. But the Supreme Court of Oklahoma has decided the precise question in *Choctaw Cotton Oil Co.* v. *Corporation Commission,* 121 Okl. 51, 52. It held that a license under §3714 does not confer the property right claimed, saying: 'What property rights are taken from petitioners by licensing another gin, under the foregoing proviso? It does not disturb the property of petitioners, nor prevent the free operation of their gins. The only right which could be affected by such license is the right of petitioners to operate their gin without competition, a right which is not secured to them either by the State or Federal Constitution, hence the contention as to taking their property without due process of law cannot be sustained.' As no property right of Frost is invaded—his suit must fail, however objectionable the statute may be.

"*Third.* Frost claims that to issue a license to the Durant Company without a showing of necessity would violate the equality clause. Whether the license was issued to Frost upon a showing of necessity does not appear. The mere granting of a license to the Durant Company later on different, and perhaps easier, terms would not violate Frost's constitutional right to equality, since he has already secured his license under the statute as written. The fact that someone else similarly situated may hereafter be refused a license, and would be thereby discriminated against, is obviously not of legal significance here. . . .

"*Fourth.* Frost claims on another ground that his constitutional rights have been violated. He says that what the statute and the Supreme Court of Oklahoma call a license is in law a franchise; that a franchise is a contract; that where a constitutional question is raised this Court must determine for itself what the terms of a contract are; and that this franchise should be construed as conferring the right to the conditional immunity from competition which he claims. None of the cases cited lend support to the contention that the license here issued is a franchise. They hold merely that subordinate political bodies, as well as a legislature, may grant franchises; and that violations of franchise rights are remediable, whoever the transgressor. Moreover, the limited immunity from competition claimed as an incident of the license was obviously terminable at any moment. . . . It was within the power of the Legislature, at any time after the granting of Frost's license, to abrogate the requirement of a certificate of necessity, thus opening the business to the competition of all comers. It is difficult to see how the lesser enlargement of the possibilities of competition by a license granted under the 1925 proviso could operate as a denial of constitutional rights.

"It must also be borne in mind that a franchise to operate a public utility is not like the general right to engage in a lawful business, part of the liberty of the citizen; that it is a special privilege which does not belong to citizens generally; that the State may, in the exercise of its police power, make that a franchise or special privilege which at common law was a business open to all; that a special privilege is conferred by the State upon selected persons; that it is of the essence of a special privilege that the franchise may be granted or withheld at the pleasure of the State; that it may be granted to corporations only, thus excluding all individuals; and that the Federal Constitution imposes no limits upon the State's discretion in this respect. In *New Orleans Gas Co.* v. *Louisiana Light Co.*, 115 U. S. 650, the plaintiff, claiming an exclusive franchise, sought to enjoin the competition of the defendant. The Court said, (p. 659), ' "The right to operate gas-works, and to illuminate a city, is not an ancient or usual occupation of citizens generally. No one has the right to*** carry on the business of lighting the streets*** without special authority from the sovereign. It is a franchise belonging to the State, and, in the exercise of the police power, the State could carry on the business itself or select one or several agents to do so." ' The demurrer to the bill was dismissed. In *New Orleans Water-Works Co.* v. *Rivers*, 115 U. S. 674, on similar facts in deciding for the plaintiff, the Court said (p. 682), 'The restriction, imposed by the contract upon the use by others than plaintiff of the public streets and ways, for such purposes, is not one of which the appellee can complain. He was not thereby restrained of any freedom or liberty he had before.***' One who would strike down a statute must show not only that he is affected by it, but that as applied to him, the statute exceeds the power of the State. This rule, acted upon as early as *Austin* v. *The Aldermen*, 7 Wall. 694, and definitely stated in *Supervisors* v. *Stanley*, 105 U. S. 305, 314, has been consistently followed since that time.

"*Fifth*. Frost's claim that the Act of 1925 discriminates unjustifiably is not sound. The claim rests wholly on the fact that individuals and ordinary corporations must show inadequacy of existing facilities, while cooperatives organized under the Act of 1919 may secure a license without making such a showing, if the application is supported by a petition of one hundred persons who are citizens and taxpayers in the community. It is settled that to provide specifically for peculiar needs of farmers or producers is a reasonable basis of classification. . . . And it is conceded that the classification made by the Act of 1925 would be reasonable if it had been limited to cooperatives organized under chapter 22 of the Laws of 1917. Thus the contention that the classification is arbitrary is directed only to cooperatives organized under the law of 1919. It rests upon two erroneous assumptions: (1) That cooperatives organized under the law of 1919 are substantially unlike those organized under chapter 22 of the Laws of 1917; and (2) that there are between cooperative corporations under the law of 1919 and commercial corporations no substantial differences having reasonable relation to the subject dealt with by the gin legislation.

"The assertion is that cooperatives organized under the law of 1919, being stock companies, do business with the general public for the sole purpose of making money, as do individual or other corporate competitors; whereas cooperatives organized under the law of 1917 are 'for mutual help, without capital stock, not conducted for profit, and restricted to the business of their own members.' The fact is that these two types of cooperative corporations—the stock and the non-stock—differ from one another only in a few details, which are without significance in this connection; that both are instrumentalities commonly employed to promote and effect cooperation among farmers; that the two serve the same purpose; and that both differ vitally from commercial corporations. The farmers seek through both to secure a more efficient system of production and distribution and a more equitable allocation of benefits. But this is not their only purpose. Besides promoting the financial advantage of the participating farmers, they seek through cooperation to socialize their interests—to require an equitable assumption of responsibilities while assuring an equitable distribution of benefits. Their aim is economic democracy on lines of liberty, equality, and fraternity. To accomplish these objectives, both types of cooperative corporations provide for excluding capitalist control. As means to this end, both provide for restriction of voting privileges, for curtailment of return on capital and for distribution of gains or savings through patronage dividends or equivalent devices.

"In order to insure economic democracy, the Oklahoma Act of 1919 prevents any person from becoming a shareholder without the consent of the board of directors. It limits the amount of stock which one person may hold to $500. And it limits the voting power of a shareholder to one vote. Thus, in the Durant Company, the holder of a single share of the par value of $10 has as much voting power as the holder of fifty shares. The Act further discourages entrance of mere capitalists into the cooperative by provisions which permit five percent of the profits to be set aside for educational purposes; which require ten percent of the profits to be set aside as a reserve fund, until such fund shall equal at least fifty percent of the capital stock; which limit the annual dividends on stock to eight percent; and which require that the rest of the year's profits be distributed as patronage dividends to members, except so far as the directors may apportion them to non-members.

"The provisions for the exclusion of capitalist control of the non-stock type of cooperative organized under the Oklahoma Act of 1917 do not differ materially in character from those in the 1919 Act. The non-stock cooperative also may reject applicants for membership; and no member may have more than one vote. This type of cooperative is called a non-profit organization; but the term is merely one of art, indicating the manner in which the financial advantage is distributed. This type also is organized and conducted for the financial benefit of its members and requires capital with which to conduct its business. In the stock type the capital is obtained by the issue of capital stock, and members are not subjected to personal liability for the corporation's business obligations. In the non-stock type the capital is obtained partly from membership fees, partly through dues or assessments and partly through loans from members or others. And for fixed capital it substitutes in part personal liability of members for the corporation's obligations. In the stock type there are *eo nomine* dividends on capital and patronage dividends. In the non-stock type the financial benefit is distributed by way of interest on loans and refunds of fees, dues and assessments. And all funds acquired through the cooperative's operations, which are in excess of the amount desirable for a 'working fund,' are to be distributed as refunds of fees, dues, and assessments. Both Acts allow business to be done for non-members; and though the non-stock association may, it is not required, to impose obligations on the non-member for the liability of the association. Thus, for the purposes here relevant, there is no essential difference between the two types of cooperatives.

"The Oklahoma law of 1919 follows closely in its provisions the legislation enacted earlier in other States with a view to furthering farmers' cooperation. The first emergence of any settled policy as to the means to be employed for effecting cooperation among farmers in the United States came in 1875 when, at the annual convention of the National Grange of the Patrons of Husbandry, recommendations were formally adopted indorsing 'Rochdale principles,' and a form of rules for the guidance of prospective organizers was promulgated. These provided for stock companies with shares of five dollars each; that no member be allowed to hold more than 100 shares; that ownership of a single share shall constitute the holder a member of the association; that only eight percent 'interest' shall be paid on the capital; that the balance of the profits shall go 'either to increase the capital or business of the association, or for any educational or provident purposes authorized by the association,' or be distributed as patronage dividends; and that the patronage dividends be distributed among customers, except that non-members should receive only one-half the proportion of members.

"The need of laws framed specifically for incorporating farmers' cooperatives being recognized, Massachusetts enacted in 1866 the necessary legislation by a general law which differed materially from that under which commercial organizations were formed. The statute provided for cooperatives having capital stock. Before 1900 ten other States enacted laws of like character. After 1900 many such statutes were passed. Now, only two States lack laws making specific provision for the incorporation of farmers' cooperatives. Thirty-three States, at least, have enacted laws providing for the formation of cooperative associations of the stock type. All of them permit a fixed dividend on capital stock, the doing of business for non-members, and the distribution of patronage dividends. Some of them, recognizing the need for elasticity, impose the

[113]

single requirement that earnings be apportioned in part on a patronage basis, and leave all other provisions for organization and distribution of profits to the by-laws.

"Farmers' cooperative incorporation laws of the non-stock type are of much more recent origin, and are fewer in number. The earliest law of this character was the crude measure enacted in California in 1895. Statutes of that type have been passed in about sixteen States; but ten of these have also laws of the stock type. The enactment of State laws for the incorporation of non-stock cooperatives and their extensive use in the co-operative marketing of commodities, are due largely to the fact that, prior to 1922, the Clayton Act (c. 232, §6) limited to non-stock cooperatives the right to make a class of agreements with members which prior thereto would have been void as in restraint of trade. . . . Nearly one-half of the existing laws of the non-stock type were enacted between 1914 and 1922. This limitation in the Clayton Act proved to be unwise. By the Capper-Volstead Act of February 18, 1922, c. 57, §1, Congress recognizing the substantial identity of the two classes of cooperatives, extended the same right to stock cooperatives. The terms of this legislation are significant:

'That persons engaged in the production of agricultural products as farmers, planters, ranchmen, dairymen, nut or fruit growers may act together in associations, corporate or otherwise, with or without capital stock in collectively processing, preparing for market, handling, and marketing in interstate and foreign commerce, such products of persons so engaged. Such associations may have marketing agencies in common; and such associations and their members may make the necessary contracts and agreements to effect such purposes: Provided, however, that such associations are operated for the mutual benefit of the members thereof, as such producers, and conform to one or both of the following requirements:

'*First*. That no member of the association is allowed more than one vote because of the amount of stock or membership capital he may own therein, or,

'*Second*. That the association does not pay dividends on stock or membership capital in excess of eight per centum per annum.

'And in any case to the following:

'*Third*. That the association shall not deal in the products of non-members to an amount greater in value than such as are handled by it for members.'

"Congress recognized the identity of the two classes of cooperatives, and the distinction between agricultural stock cooperative corporations and ordinary business corporations, also, by providing in the Revenue Act of 1926, c. 27, pt. III, §231, that exemption from the income tax was not to be denied 'any such [cooperative] association because it has capital stock, if the dividend rate of such stock is fixed at not to exceed the legal rate of interest in the State of incorporation or eight per centum per annum, whichever is greater,*** and if substantially all such stock*** is owned by producers;*** nor shall exemption be denied any such association because there is accumulated and maintained by it a reserve.*** Such an association may market the products of non-members in an amount the value of which does not exceed the value of the products marketed for members.' This exemption was continued in the Revenue Act of 1928, c. 852, §103.

"More than two-thirds of all farmers' cooperatives in the United States are organized under the stock type laws. In 1925 there were 10,147 reporting organizations. Of these 68.7 percent were stock associations. In leading States the percentage was larger. In Wisconsin the percentage was 80; in North

Dakota 87; in Nebraska 91.3; and in Kansas 92. Of the farmers' cooperatives existing in Oklahoma in 1925, 87.6 per cent were stock associations. The great cooperative systems of England, Scotland, and Canada were developed and are now operated by organizations of the stock type. The non-stock type of cooperative is not adapted to enterprises, which like gins require large investment in plant, and hence considerable fixed capital. For this reason it was a common practice for marketing cooperatives, which had been organized as non-stock cooperatives in order to comply with the requirements of the Clayton Act above described, to form a subsidiary cooperative corporation with capital stock to carry on the incidental business of warehousing or processing which requires a large investment in plant. And the fact that even the marketing of some products may be better served by the stock type of cooperative organizations is so widely recognized that most of the marketing acts provide that associations formed thereunder may organize either with or without capital stock.

"Experience has demonstrated, also, that doing business for non-members is usually deemed essential to the success of a cooperative. More than five-sixths of all the farmers' cooperative associations in the United States do business for non-members. In 1925, 86.3 percent of the reporting organizations·did so. In leading States the percentage was even larger. In Wisconsin the percentage was 89; in Missouri 93.2; in Minnesota 94.1; in Nebraska 95.8; in Kansas 96.5; in North Dakota 97. In Oklahoma 92 percent of all cooperatives did business for non-members. Of the cotton cooperatives in the United States 93.9 percent did business for non-members. In Texas, where cooperative ginning has received successful trial, all the cotton cooperatives perform service for non-members. In Oklahoma, also, all of the cotton cooperatives reporting do business for non-members.

"That no one plan of organization is to be labeled as truly

cooperative to the exclusion of others was recognized by Congress in connection with cooperative banks and building loan associations. . . . With the expansion of agricultural cooperation it has been recognized repeatedly. Congress gave its sanction to the stock type of cooperative by the Capper-Volstead Act and also by specifically exempting stock as well as non-stock cooperatives from income taxes. State Legislatures recognized the fundamental similarity of the two types of cooperation by unifying their laws so as to have a single statute under which either type of cooperative might organize. And experts in the Department of Agriculture, charged with disseminating information to farmers and Legislatures, have warned against any crystallization of the cooperative plan so as to exclude any type of cooperation.

"That in Oklahoma a law authorizing incorporation on the stock plan was essential to the development of cooperation among farmers has been demonstrated by the history of the movement in that State. Prior to 1917 there was no statute which specifically authorized the incorporation of cooperatives. In that year the non-stock law above referred to was enacted. Two years passed, and only three cooperatives availed themselves of the provisions of that Act. Then persons familiar with the farmers' problems in Oklahoma secured the passage of the law of 1919, providing for the incorporation of cooperatives with capital stock. Within the next five years 202 cooperatives were formed under it; and since then 139 more. In the twelve years since 1917 only sixty non-stock cooperatives have been organized; most of them since 1923, when through an amendatory statute this type was made to offer special advantages for cooperative marketing. Thus over 82 percent of all cooperatives in Oklahoma are organized under the 1919 stock Act. One hundred and one Oklahoma cooperative cotton gins have been organized under the 1919 stock law; not a single one under the 1917 non-stock law. To deny the cooperative character of the 1919 Act is to deny the cooperative character, not only of the gins in Oklahoma, which farmers have organized and operated for their mutual benefit, but also that of most other cooperatives within the State, which have been organized under its statutes in harmony with the legislation of Congress and pursuant to instructions from the United States Department of Agriculture. A denial of cooperative character to the stock cooperatives is inconsistent also with the history of the movement in other States and countries. For the stock type of cooperative is not only the older form, but is the type more widely used among English-speaking peoples.

"There remain to be considered other circumstances leading to the passage of the statute here challenged. As was said in *Lindsley v. Natural Carbonic Gas Co.*, 220 U. S. 61, 78: 'When the classification in such a law is called in question, if any state of facts reasonably can be conceived that would sustain it, the existence of that state of facts at the time the law was enacted must be assumed'. Here that presumption is reinforced by facts which have been called to our attention. That evils exist in cotton ginning which are subject to drastic legislative regulation has recently been recognized by this Court. . . . The specific evils existing in Oklahoma which the statute here assailed was enacted to correct the charging of extortionate prices to the farmer for inferior ginning service and the control secured of the cotton seed. These conditions are partly attributable to the fact that a large percentage of the ordinary commercial gins in Oklahoma are controlled by cotton-seed oil mills, which make their service as ginners incidental to that as crushers of seed, and are thereby enabled to secure the seed at less than its value. That such control of gins may lead to excessive prices for the ginning service was recognized in the *Crescent Oil Case*. [257 U. S. 129.] The fact that, despite the regulatory provisions of the Public Service Law, a public utility is permitted to earn huge profits indicates that something more than rate regulation may be needed for the protection of farmers. Certainly it cannot be said that the Legislature could not reasonably believe that cooperative ginning might afford a corrective for rates believed to be extortionate."

Frost v. *Corporation Commission*
of State of Oklahoma, et al.
278 U. S. 515, 528

III. Public Utility Economics

Valuation and Returns

(Opinion of the Court, *Galveston Electric Co.*
v. *City of Galveston,* 1922.)

"THE street railway system of Galveston was started as a horse-car line in 1881. It was electrified about 1890; and after the hurricane of 1900 was largely rebuilt. Upon sale on fore-closure the railway passed in 1901 to a new company; and in 1905 it was purchased by the Galveston Electric Company, which supplies to the inhabitants of the city also electric light and power. At no time has the full fare on the railway been more than five cents—except during the period of eight months, from October 1, 1918, to June 5, 1919, when six cents was charged. This higher fare was authorized by ordinance of the municipal Board of Commissioners, which possesses regu-latory powers; and on June 5, 1919, the same Board reduced the maximum fare to five cents. The latter ordinance was passed after a hearing and a finding by the Board that with the reduced rate the company would continue to earn a fair return. Under the 1919 ordinance the company operated for eleven months. Then it brought this suit, in the Federal court for Southern Texas, to enjoin its enforcement. The company contends that the fare prescribed is confiscatory in violation of the Fourteenth Amendment; the city, that it is sufficient to yield a return of eight percent on the value of the property used in the public service.

"A temporary injunction having been denied, the court appointed a master to take the evidence and make advisory findings. There was substantially no dispute concerning the facts past or present. It was assumed, in view of then prevailing money rates, that eight percent was a fair return upon money invested in the business. The experts agreed on what they called the estimated undepreciated cost of reproduction on the historical basis; that is, what the property ought to have cost on the basis of prices prevailing at the time the system and its various units were constructed. They agreed also on the amount of gross revenue, and on the expenditures made in operation and for taxes, except as hereinafter stated. The differences between the parties resulted mainly, either from differences in prophecy as to the future trend of prices or from differences in legal opinion as to the elements to be considered in determining whether a fair return would be earned. These differences affected both the base value and the amount to be deemed net revenues. The master, who heard the case in October, 1920, and filed his report in November, made findings in which he advised that the fare was confiscatory. The District Judge, who heard the case in January, 1921, found a much smaller base value and much larger net revenues; stated that he did not deem it necessary to determine whether the ordinance will 'produce eight percent, or a little more or a little short of it'; decided that he was 'not satisfied that the ordinance produces a return so plainly inadequate as to justify this court in interfering with the action of the municipality in the exercise of its rate-making function'; and in March, 1921, entered a decree dismissing the bill without prejudice. In April he denied a petition for rehearing. . . . The case comes here on appeal under §238 of the Judicial Code.

"The undepreciated reproduction cost on the historical basis—which seems to be substantially equivalent to what is often termed the prudent investment—was agreed to be $1,715,825. The parties failed to agree in their estimates of the depreciation accrued up to 1921. The master estimated that,

based on the 1913 price level, it was $390,000; and this esti-
mate the court accepted. Thus measured, the value of the
property, less depreciation, was $1,325,825. The court found
that the net earnings under the five-cent fare for the year ending June 30, 1920, had been $90,159, and for the year ending
December 31, 1920, $109,286, and estimated that for the
year ending June 30, 1921, it would be at least $111,285.
The return so found for the year ending June 30, 1920, is
6.8 percent of $1,325,825; for the calendar year 1920, 8.2
percent, and for the year ending June 30, 1921, 8.4 percent.
The master made calculations only for the year ending June
30, 1920, and, mainly because he allowed an amount for
maintenance and depreciation equal to nearly 18 percent of
the prudent investment for the depreciable property (less accrued depreciation), found the net earnings to be only $50,-
249.60. This sum is 3.8 percent on the prudent investment
value, less depreciation. But neither the District Judge nor
the master reached his conclusion as to net return by a calculation as simple as that indicated above.

"*First.* As the base value of the property, master and court
took—instead of the prudent investment value—the estimated
cost of reproduction at a later time less depreciation; and in
estimating reproduction cost both refused to use as a basis the
prices actually prevailing at the time of the hearings. These
had risen 110 percent above those of 1913. The basis for calculating reproduction cost adopted by all was prophecy as to
the future general price level of commodities, labor, and money.
This predicted level, which they assumed would be stable for an
indefinite period, they called the new plateau of prices. As to
the height of this prophesied plateau there was naturally wide
divergence of opinion. The company's expert prophesied that
the level would be sixty to seventy percent above 1913 prices;
the master that an increase of 33 1/3 percent would prove
fair; and the court accepted the master's prophecy of 33 1/3 per-

cent. Thus both master and court assumed a reproduction cost, after deducting accrued depreciation, of about $1,625,000. On this sum the net earning found by the court yielded—after deducting a four percent depreciation annuity on property subject to depreciation, a maintenance charge, and a charge for taxes, other than the Federal income tax—a net return of 5½ percent for the fiscal year ending June 30, 1920, of 6.7 percent for the calendar year 1920, and the promise of more for the fiscal year ending June 30, 1921. But to fix base value the master added, and the court disallowed, items aggregating nearly $600,000, which must now be considered.

"The most important of these items is $520,000 for 'development cost.' The item is called by the master also 'going concern value or values of plant in successful operation.' He could not have meant by this to cover the cost of establishing the system as a physically going concern, for the cost of converting the inert railway plant into an operating system is covered in the agreed historical value by items aggregating $202,000. These included, besides engineering, supervision, interest, taxes, law expenses, injuries and damages during construction, the sum of $73,281 for the expenses of organization and business management. The going concern value for which the master makes allowance is the cost of developing the operating railway system into a financially successful concern. The only evidence offered, or relied upon, to support his finding is a capitalization of the net balance of alleged past deficits in accordance with what was said to be the Wisconsin rule. . . . The experts calculated this sum in various ways. One estimate placed the development cost at $2,000,000; a more moderate estimate by the company's expert was $575,300; and the city's expert made a calculation by which he estimated this so-called cost at $212,452.

"If the rule were that a prescribed rate is to be held confiscatory in case net earnings are not sufficient to yield eight percent on the amount prudently invested in the business, there might be propriety in counting as part of the investment such amount, if any, as was necessarily expended at the start in overcoming initial difficulties incident to operation and securing patronage. But no evidence of any such expenditure was introduced; and the claim of the company does not proceed upon that basis. What was presented by the witnesses are studies, on various theories, of what past deficiencies in net income would aggregate, if four percent were allowed as a depreciation annuity and eight percent compound interest were charged annually on the value of the property used. These calculations covered, on one basis, the period of thirty-nine years since the original horse-car line was built; on another, the period of fifteen years since the appellant purchased the property as a going concern. If net deficits so estimated were made a factor in the rate base, recognition of eight percent as a fair return on the continuing investment would imply substantially a guaranty by the community that the investor will net on his investment ultimately a return of eight percent yearly, with interest compounded on deferred payments; provided only that the traffic will in course of time bear a rate high enough to produce that amount.

"The fact that a utility may reach financial success only in time or not at all, is a reason for allowing a liberal return on the money invested in the enterprise; but it does not make past losses an element to be considered in deciding what the base value is and whether the rate is confiscatory. A company which has failed to secure from year to year sufficient earnings to keep the investment unimpaired and to pay a fair return, whether its failure was the result of imprudence in engaging in the enterprise or of errors in management, or of omission to exact proper prices for its output, cannot erect out of past deficits a legal basis for holding confiscatory for the future, rates which would, on the basis of present reproduction value, otherwise be compensatory. . . .

"Nor is there evidence in the record to justify the master's finding that a business brought to successful operation 'should have a going concern value at least equal to one-third of its physical properties.' Past losses obviously do not tend to prove present values. The fact that a sometime losing business becomes profitable eventually through growth of the community or more efficient management, tends to prove merely that the adventure was not wholly misconceived. It is doubtless true, as the master indicated, that a prospective purchaser of the Galveston system would be willing to pay more for it with a record of annual losses overcome, than he would if the losses had continued. But would not the property be, at least, as valuable if the past had presented a record of continuous successes? And shall the base value be deemed less in law if there was no development cost, because success was instant and continuous? Or, if the success had been so great that, besides paying an annual return at the rate of eight percent, a large surplus had been accumulated, could the city insist that the base value be reduced by the amount of the surplus? . . .

"In determining the value of a business as between buyer and seller, the good will and earning power due to effective organization are often more important elements than tangible property. Where the public acquires the business, compensation must be made for these, at least under some circumstances. . . . And they, like past losses, should be considered in determining whether a rate charged by a public utility is reasonable. . . . But in determining whether a rate is confiscatory, good will and franchise value were excluded from the base value in *Cedar Rapids Gas Co.* v. *Cedar Rapids*, 223 U. S. 655, 669, and *Des Moines Gas Co.* v. *Des Moines*, 238 U. S. 153, 169; and the expressions in *Denver* v. *Denver Union Water Co.*, 246

U. S. 178, 184, 191, and in *Lincoln Gas Co.* v. *Lincoln,* 250 U. S. 256, 267, are not to be taken as modifying in any respect the rule there declared. Going concern value and development cost, in the sense in which the master used these terms, are not to be included in the base value for the purpose of determining whether a rate is confiscatory.

"The other item included by the master in determining base value, but disallowed by the court, is $67,078 for brokerage fees. There is no evidence that any sum was in fact paid as brokerage, and there was included, as above shown, the sum of $73,281 for organization and business management in calculating the historical reproduction cost. The finding of the master rests upon testimony that bankers customarily get, in some form, compensation equal to four percent on the money procured by them for such enterprises. But compensation for bankers' services is often paid in the lessened price at which they take the company's securities, and is thus represented in the higher rate of interest or dividend paid on the money actually received by the company as capital. The reason given by the master for including the allowance for an assumed brokerage fee, is that a brokerage fee is 'a normal incident of large industrial investments and has not been amortized,' since 'the record shows that the plant has been operated at a loss.' If base value were to be fixed by the money expended, brokerage fees actually paid might with propriety be included, as are taxes paid pending construction. But as the base value considered is the present value, that value must be measured by money, and the customary cost of obtaining the money is immaterial. We cannot say that the court erred in refusing to include in base value an allowance for hypothetical broker's fees.

"The appellants insisted also that the base value should be raised by assuming that the future plateau of prices would be sixty to seventy percent above the historical reproduction value instead of 33 1/3 percent as the master and the court assumed. The appellee insisted, on the other hand, that an item of $142,281 for grade raising included by master and court in the historical cost should be eliminated. We cannot say that there was error in overruling these contentions.

"*Second.* Concerning deductions to be made from gross revenue in order to determine net earnings, the court differed from the master in regard both to the yearly charge for maintenance and to the depreciation annuity. It appeared that in the fifteen years since appellant acquired the system in 1905, the average annual expenditure for maintenance had been $42,771; that during the war the property had been admittedly under-maintained; that the expenditure was $64,108 in the calendar year 1919, $80,322 in the fiscal year ending June 30, 1920, and $90,861.28 in the calendar year 1920. The court estimated the proper charge for current maintenance at $70,000, and allowed, in addition, a depreciation annuity of $45,245 (that is, four percent on property subject to depreciation) to provide a fund out of which annual replacements and renewals could be made. Thus the court allowed for the year's depreciation and maintenance $115,245, which is nearly fourteen percent of the historical reproduction value, and about ten percent of the assumed reproduction cost, of the depreciable part of the system. The master allowed $147,146.40 for maintenance and depreciation during the year ending June 30, 1920. This larger figure was arrived at partly by charging as cost of maintenance the full $80,322 expended during that year, and partly by including as depreciable property expenditures for overhead items which the court excluded. The proper annual charge for maintenance is the amount normally required for that purpose during the period; it is not necessarily the amount actually expended within the year. Many items included in the overhead cost of original construction may properly be excluded in calculating the amount of depreciation

[130]

annuity. We cannot say that the court erred in limiting the year's maintenance to an aggregate of $115,245.

"The company asked to have allowed as a further charge $29,500 a year on account of what it called deferred maintenance. The contention is that during the war and two years following, the company had deferred maintenance, pursuant to a policy established at the express request of the Government, to the end that material and labor might be released for war purposes; that to make good this deferred maintenance would cost $197,000; and that in order to amortize this amount an annual allowance from earnings of $29,500 should be made for five years. This is an attempt, in another form, to capitalize alleged past losses; and the request was properly refused both by the master and the court.

"*Third.* The remaining item as to which the master and the court differed relates to the income tax. The company assigns as error that the master allowed, but the court disallowed, as a part of the operating expenses for the year ending June 30, 1920, the sum of $16,254 paid by the company during that year for Federal income taxes. The tax referred to is presumably that imposed by Act Feb. 24, 1919, c. 18, §§230-238, 40 Stat. 1057, 1075-1080, which for any year after 1918 is ten percent of the net income. In calculating whether the five-cent fare will yield a proper return, it is necessary to deduct from gross revenue the expenses and charges; and all taxes which would be payable if a fair return were earned are appropriate deductions. There is no difference in this respect between State and Federal taxes or between income taxes and others. But the fact that it is the Federal corporate income tax for which deduction is made, must be taken into consideration in determining what rate of return shall be deemed fair. For under §216 the stockholder does not include in the income on which the normal Federal tax is payable dividends received

[131]

from the corporation. This tax exemption is therefore, in effect, part of the return on the investment.

"It is thus clear that both in the year ending June 30, 1920, and in the calendar year 1920, the net earnings of the system were less than eight percent of its value, whether the value be estimated on the basis of prudent investment or on the basis of the reproduction cost actually adopted. When the court rendered its decision the ordinance had been tested for more than a year and a half—a period ample in ordinary times to test the current effect of the rate prescribed and to indicate its probable effect in the near future. The times here involved were, however, in a high degree abnormal. It did not follow that, because the system had earned less than eight percent in 1919 and in 1920, that it would earn less than eight percent in 1921. A rate ordinance invalid when adopted may later become valid, just as an ordinance valid when made may become invalid by change in conditions. . . .

"The District Judge was obliged to form an opinion as to the probable net earnings in the future. All relevant facts, except as stated, and all applicable arguments were fully and clearly presented by the parties and were carefully considered by the court. Although the District Judge treated the master's report as advisory merely, he passed upon the numerous exceptions taken to the master's findings in order to indicate his view on the precise points raised. He allowed some exceptions and disallowed others. Upon petition for rehearing further careful consideration was given to the case. Views expressed in the first opinion on some matters were modified; but these changes did not call for any change in the decree. The District Judge had before him some evidence not before the master; for the company's expert was recalled and testified both to the result of operations of later months in which there was a large increase in travel and to the heavy decline in prices which occurred after October. Concerning actual facts there was substantially no controversy. On the elements to be considered in determining whether the rate would be confiscatory no error was made which could substantially affect the result. His determination whether the prescribed rate would be confiscatory was necessarily based largely on a prophecy, for normal conditions had not been restored. He found that gross revenues were steadily increasing; and that they were larger under the five-cent fare than they had been during the preceding year when the six-cent rate was in effect. He was convinced that operating costs would decrease largely during the year. His two opinions show that every element upon which his prophecy should be based received careful consideration. We cannot say that the evidence compelled a conviction that the rate would prove inadequate. . . .

"The occasion for the suit was solely the extraordinary rise in prices incident to the war. There was no suggestion that the action of the board evidenced hostility to the utility, or that the board was arbitrary or hasty. It had been theretofore considerate of the company's rights and needs. When prices rose rapidly in 1918, it raised the fare limit to six cents, although the franchise ordinance prescribed the five-cent fare. And this was before our decision in *San Antonio* v. *San Antonio Public Service Co.*, 255 U. S. 547. Its reduction of the fare by ordinance of June 5, 1919, was made after hearing and was doubtless due to the conviction, shared by many, that, with the cessation of hostilities and the negotiation of the Peace Treaty, prices and operating cost would fall abruptly. This prophecy, if such there was, proved false. But nearly three years have elapsed since the board adopted the ordinance; and more than a year since entry of the decree below. We know judicially that the period has, in general, been one of continuous price recession, and that the current rates of return on capital are much lower than they then were. But we cannot know to what extent the important changes occurring have

[133]

affected either gross revenues or the net return. There is no reason to believe that the board would not give full and fair consideration to a proposed change in rate if application were now made to it. And the District Judge stated in his opinion (272 Fed. 147) that the decree to be entered would be vacated or amended in case it should later appear that the regulating board declined such adjustment of rates as the actual experience of the utility might show it entitled to; and the decree was thereupon entered without prejudice.

"The District Judge refused a temporary injunction and did not exact a bond. Hence the only relief we can grant is such as operates *in futuro*. . . . An injunction should not issue now, unless conditions are such that the prescribed rate is confiscatory. As by the reservation in the decree appellant may secure protection against the ordinance if under existing conditions the five-cent rate appears to be inadequate, the decree should be affirmed. . . .

Decree affirmed."

Galveston Electric Co.
v. *City of Galveston, et al.*
258 U. S. 388

The Prudent Investment Principle

(Concurring Opinion, *Southwestern Bell*
v. *Public Service Commission*, 1923)

THE COURT REVERSED A JUDGMENT OF THE SUPREME COURT OF
Missouri upholding an order of its Public Service Commission to reduce
certain telephone rates. These rates had been advanced by the Postmaster General during the period of Federal control (August 1, 1918,
to August 1, 1919). Mr. Justice McReynolds delivered the opinion
of the Court, which determined a fair return by a method from which
Mr. Justice Brandeis differed. Brandeis said (Holmes concurring):

"I CONCUR in the judgment of reversal. But I do so on the
ground that the order of the State Commission prevents the
utility from earning a fair return on the amount prudently invested in it. (The term 'prudent investment' is not used in a
critical sense. There should not be excluded, from the finding
of the base, investments which, under ordinary circumstances,
would be deemed reasonable. The term is applied for the purpose of excluding what might be found to be dishonest or
obviously wasteful or imprudent expenditures. Every investment may be assumed to have been made in the exercise of
reasonable judgment, unless the contrary is shown.) Thus, I
differ fundamentally from my brethren concerning the rule to
be applied in determining whether a prescribed rate is confiscatory. The Court, adhering to the so-called rule of *Smyth*
v. *Ames*, 169 U. S. 466, and further defining it, declares that
what is termed value must be ascertained by giving weight,

[135]

among other things, to estimates of what it would cost to reproduce the property at the time of the rate hearing.

"The so-called rule of *Smyth* v. *Ames* is, in my opinion, legally and economically unsound. The thing devoted by the investor to the public use is not specific property, tangible and intangible, but capital embarked in the enterprise. Upon the capital so invested the Federal Constitution guarantees to the utility the opportunity to earn a fair return. (Except that rates may, in no event, be prohibitive, exorbitant, or unduly burdensome to the public. . . .) Thus it sets the limit to the power of the State to regulate rates. The Constitution does not guarantee to the utility the opportunity to earn a return on the value of all items of property used by the utility or of any of them. The several items of property constituting the utility, taken singly, and freed from the public use, may conceivably have an aggregate value greater than if the items are used in combination. The owner is at liberty, in the absence of controlling statutory provision, to withdraw his property from the public service, and, if he does so, may obtain for it exchange value. . . . But, so long as the specific items of property are employed by the utility, their exchange value is not of legal significance.

"The investor agrees, by embarking capital in a utility, that its charges to the public shall be reasonable. His company is the substitute for the State in the performance of the public service, thus becoming a public servant. The compensation which the Constitution guarantees an opportunity to earn is the reasonable cost of conducting the business. Cost includes, not only operating expenses, but also capital charges. Capital charges cover allowance, by way of interest, for the use of the capital, whatever the nature of the security issued therefor, the allowance for risk incurred, and enough more to attract capital. The reasonable rate to be prescribed by a commission may allow an efficiently managed utility much more. But a

[136]

rate is constitutionally compensatory, if it allows to the utility the opportunity to earn the cost of the service as thus defined.

"To decide whether a proposed rate is confiscatory the tribunal must determine both what sum would be earned under it and whether that sum would be a fair return. The decision involves ordinarily the making of four subsidiary ones:

"(1) What the gross earnings from operating the utility under the rate in controversy would be. (A prediction.)

"(2) What the operating expenses and charges, while so operating, would be. (A prediction.)

"(3) The rate base; that is, what the amount is on which a return should be earned. (Under *Smyth* v. *Ames*, an opinion, largely.)

"(4) What rate of return should be deemed fair. (An opinion, largely.)

"A decision that a rate is confiscatory (or compensatory) is thus the resultant of four subsidiary determinations. Each of the four involves forming a judgment, as distinguished from ascertaining facts; and as to each factor there is usually room for difference in judgment. But the first two factors do not ordinarily present serious difficulties. The doubts and uncertainties incident to prophecy, which affect them, can often be resolved by a test period; and meanwhile protection may be afforded by giving a bond. . . . The doubts and uncertainties incident to the last two factors can be eliminated, or lessened, only by redefining the rate base, called value, and the measure of fairness in return, now applied under the rule of *Smyth* v. *Ames*. The experience of the twenty-five years since that case was decided has demonstrated that the rule there enunciated is delusive. In the attempt to apply it insuperable obstacles have been encountered. It has failed to afford adequate protection either to capital or to the public. It leaves open the door to grave injustice. To give to capital embarked in public utilities the protection guaranteed by the Constitution, and to secure for the public reasonable rates, it is essential that the rate base be definite, stable, and readily ascertainable, and that the percentage to be earned on the rate base be measured by the cost, or charge, of the capital employed in the enterprise. It is consistent with the Federal Constitution for this Court now to lay down a rule which will establish such a rate base and such a measure of the rate of return deemed fair. In my opinion, it should do so.

"The rule of *Smyth* v. *Ames* sets the laborious and baffling task of finding the present value of the utility. It is impossible to find an exchange value for a utility, since utilities, unlike merchandise or land, are not commonly bought and sold in the market. Nor can the present value of the utility be determined by capitalizing its net earnings, since the earnings are determined, in large measure, by the rate which the company will be permitted to charge, and thus the vicious circle would be encountered. So, under the rule of *Smyth* v. *Ames*, it is usually sought to prove the present value of a utility by ascertaining what it actually cost to construct and install it, or by estimating what it should have cost, or by estimating what it would cost to reproduce or to replace it. To this end an enumeration is made of the component elements of the utility, tangible and intangible; then the actual, or the proper, cost of producing, or of reproducing, each part is sought; and finally it is estimated how much less than the new each part, or the whole, is worth. That is, the depreciation is estimated. Obviously each step in the process of estimating the cost of reproduction, or replacement, involves forming an opinion, or exercising judgment, as distinguished from merely ascertaining facts. And this is true, also, of each step in the process of estimating how much less the existing plant is worth than if it were new. There is another potent reason why, under the rule of *Smyth* v. *Ames*, the room for difference of opinion is so wide. The rule does not measure the present value either by what the utility cost to produce, or

by what it should have cost, or by what it would cost to reproduce, or to replace it. Under that rule the tribunal is directed,
in forming its judgment, to take into consideration all those
and also, other elements, called relevant facts.

"Obviously, 'value' cannot be a composite of all these elements. Nor can it be arrived at on all these bases. They are very
different, and must, when applied in a particular case, lead to
widely different results. The rule of *Smyth* v. *Ames*, as interpreted and applied, means merely that all must be considered.
What, if any, weight shall be given to any one, must practically
rest in the judicial discretion of the tribunal which makes the
determination. Whether a desired result is reached may depend
upon how any one of many elements is treated. It is true that
the decision is usually rested largely upon records of financial
transactions, on statistics and calculations. But as stated in *Louisville* v. *Cumberland Telegraph & Telephone Co.*, 225 U. S.
430, 436, 'every figure*** that we have set down with delusive
exactness' is 'speculative.' [Opinion by Holmes.]

"The efforts of courts to control commissions' findings of
value have largely failed. The reason lies in the character of the
rule declared in *Smyth* v. *Ames*. The rule there stated was to
be applied solely as a means of determining whether rates already prescribed by the Legislature were confiscatory. It was to
be applied judicially after the rate had been made, and by a
court which had had no part in making the rate. When applied
under such circumstances, the rule, although cumbersome, may
occasionally be effective in destroying an obstruction to justice,
as the action of a court is, when it sets aside the verdict of a
jury. But the commissions undertook to make the rule their
standard for constructive action. They used it as a guide for
making and approving rates, and the tendency developed to fix
as reasonable the rate which is not so low as to be confiscatory.
(This, it appears, was the purpose of the board in *Galveston
Electric Co.* v. *City of Galveston* [*supra*].) Thus the rule which

[139]

assumes that rates of utilities will ordinarily be higher than the minimum required by the Constitution has, by the practice of the commissions, eliminated the margin between a reasonable rate and a merely compensatory rate, and, in the process of rate-making, effective judicial review is very often rendered impossible. The result, inherent in the rule itself, is arbitrary action on the part of the rate-regulating body; for the rule not only fails to furnish any applicable standard of judgment, but directs consideration of so many elements that almost any result may be justified.

"The adoption of present value of the utility's property, as the rate base, was urged in 1893 on behalf of the community, and it was adopted by the courts, largely, as a protection against inflated claims, based on what were then deemed inflated prices of the past. See argument in *Smyth* v. *Ames*, 169 U. S. 456, 479, 480 [and three other cases cited]. Reproduction cost, as the measure, or as evidence, of present value, was also pressed then by representatives of the public, who sought to justify legislative reductions of railroad rates. The long depression which followed the panic of 1893 had brought prices to the lowest level reached in the Nineteenth Century. Insistence upon reproduction cost was the shippers' protest against burdens believed to have resulted from watered stocks, reckless financing, and unconscionable construction contracts. Those were the days before State legislation prohibited the issue of public utility securities without authorization from State officials, before accounting was prescribed and supervised, when outstanding bonds and stocks were hardly an indication of the amount of capital embarked in the enterprise, when depreciation accounts were unknown, and when book values, or property accounts, furnished no trustworthy evidence either of cost or of real value. Estimates of reproduction cost were then offered, largely as a means, either of supplying lacks in the proof of actual cost and investment, or of testing the creditability of evidence adduced, or of showing that the cost of installation had been wasteful. For these purposes evidence of the cost of reproduction is obviously appropriate.

"At first reproduction cost was welcomed by commissions as evidence of present value. Perhaps it was because the estimates then indicated values lower than the actual cost of installation; for, even after the price level had begun to rise, improved machinery and new devices tended for some years to reduce construction costs. Evidence of reproduction costs was certainly welcomed, because it seemed to offer a reliable means for performing the difficult task of fixing, in obedience to *Smyth* v. *Ames,* the value of a new species of property to which the old tests—selling price or net earnings—were not applicable. The engineer spoke in figures—a language implying certitude. His estimates seemed to be free of the infirmities which had stamped as untrustworthy the opinion evidence of experts common in condemnation cases. Thus, for some time, replacement cost, on the basis of prices prevailing at the date of the valuation, was often adopted by State commissions as the standard for fixing the rate base. But gradually it came to be realized that the definiteness of the engineer's calculations was delusive, that they rested upon shifting theories, and that their estimates varied so widely as to intensify, rather than to allay, doubts. When the price levels had risen largely, and estimates of replacement cost indicated values much greater than the actual cost of installation, many commissions refused to consider valuable what one declared to be assumptions based on things that never happened and estimates requiring the projection of the engineer's imagination into the future and methods of construction and installation that have never been and never will be adopted by sane men. Finally the great fluctuation in price levels incident to the World War led to the transfusion of the engineer's estimate of cost with the economist's prophecies concerning the future price plateaus. Then the view that these

[141]

estimates were not to be trusted as evidence of present value was frequently expressed, and State utility commissions, while admitting the evidence in obedience to *Smyth* v. *Ames*, failed, in ever-increasing numbers, to pay heed to it in fixing the rate base. The conviction is widespread that a sound conclusion as to the actual value of a utility is not to be reached by a meticulous study of conflicting estimates of the cost of reproducing new the congeries of old machinery and equipment, called the plant, and the still more fanciful estimates concerning the value of the intangible elements of an established business. Many commissions, like that of Massachusetts, have declared recently that 'capital honestly and prudently invested must, under normal conditions, be taken as the controlling factor in fixing the basis for computing fair and reasonable rates.'

"To require that reproduction cost at the date of the rate hearing be given weight in fixing the rate base may subject investors to heavy losses when the high war and post-war price levels pass and the price trend is again downward. The aggregate of the investments which have already been made at high costs since 1914, and of those which will be made before prices and costs can fall heavily, may soon exceed by far the depreciated value of all the public utility investments made theretofore at relatively low cost. For it must be borne in mind that depreciation is an annual charge. That accrued on plants constructed in the long years prior to 1914 is much larger than that accruing on the properties installed in the shorter period since.

"That part of the rule of *Smyth* v. *Ames* which fixes the rate of return deemed fair at the percentage customarily paid on similar investments at the time of the rate hearing also exposes the investor and the public to danger of serious injustice. If the replacement-cost measure of value and the prevailing-rate measure of fairness of return should be applied, a company which raised, in 1920, for additions to plant, $1,000,-000 on a nine percent basis, by a stock issue, or by long-term bond issue, may find a decade later that the value of the plant (disregarding depreciation) is only $600,000, and that the fair return on money then invested in such enterprise is only six percent. Under the test of a compensatory rate, urged in reliance upon *Smyth* v. *Ames*, a prescribed rate would not be confiscatory, if it appeared that the utility could earn under it $36,000 a year; whereas $90,000 would be required to earn the capital charges. On the other hand, if a plant had been built in times of low costs, at $1,000,000 and the capital had been raised to the extent of $750,000 by an issue of five percent thirty-year bonds and to the extent of $250,000 by stock at par, and ten years later the price level was seventy-five percent higher and the interest rates eight percent, it would be a fantastic result to hold that a rate was confiscatory unless it yielded eight percent on the then reproduction cost of $1,750,000; for that would yield an income of $140,000, which would give the bondholders $37,500, and to the holders of the $250,000 stock $102,500, a return of forty-one percent per annum. Money required to establish in 1920 many necessary plants has cost the utility ten percent on thirty-year bonds. These long-time securities, issued to raise needed capital, will in 1930 and thereafter continue to bear the extra high rates of interest, which it was necessary to offer in 1920 in order to secure the required capital. The prevailing rate for such investments may in 1930 be only seven percent, or indeed six percent, as it was found to be in 1904, in *Stanislaus County* v. *San Joaquin Co.*, 192 U. S. 201; in 1909 in *Knoxville* v. *Knoxville Water Co.*, 212 U. S. 1, and in 1912 in *Cedar Rapids Gas Co.*, v. *Cedar Rapids*, 223 U. S. 655, 670. A rule which limits the guaranteed rate of return on utility investments to that which may prevail at the time of the rate hearing may fall far short of the capital charge then resting upon the company.

"In essence, there is no difference between the capital charge and operating expenses, depreciation, and taxes. Each is a part of the current cost of supplying the service, and each should be met from current income. When the capital charges are for interest on the floating debt paid at the current rate, this is readily seen. But it is no less true of a legal obligation to pay interest on long-term bonds, entered into years before the rate hearing and to continue for years thereafter; and it is true, also, of the economic obligation to pay dividends on stock, preferred or common. The necessary cost, and hence the capital charge, of the money embarked recently in utilities, and of that which may be invested in the near future, may be more, as it may be less, than the prevailing rate of return required to induce capital to enter upon like enterprises at the time of a rate hearing ten years hence. To fix the return by the rate which happens to prevail at such future day, opens the door to great hardships. Where the financing has been proper, the cost to the utility of the capital, required to construct, equip, and operate its plant, should measure the rate of return which the Constitution guarantees opportunity to earn.

"The adoption of the amount prudently invested as the rate base and the amount of the capital charge as the measure of the rate of return would give definiteness to these two factors involved in rate controversies which are now shifting and treacherous, and which render the proceedings peculiarly burdensome and largely futile. Such measures offer a basis for decision which is certain and stable. The rate base would be ascertained as a fact, not determined as matter of opinion. It would not fluctuate with the market price of labor, or materials, or money. It would not change with hard times or shifting populations. It would not be distorted by the fickle and varying judgments of appraisers, commissions, or courts. It would, when once made in respect to any utility, be fixed, for all times, subject only to increases to represent additions to plant, after allowance for the depreciation included in the annual operating charges. The wild uncertainties of the present method of fixing the rate base under the so-called rule of *Smyth* v. *Ames* would be avoided, and likewise the fluctuations which introduce into the enterprise unnecessary elements of speculation, create useless expense, and impose upon the public a heavy, unnecessary burden.

"In speculative enterprises the capital cost of money is always high—partly because the risks involved must be covered; partly because speculative enterprises appeal only to the relatively small number of investors who are unwilling to accept a low return on their capital. It is to the interest both of the utility and of the community that the capital be obtained at as low a cost as possible. About seventy-five percent of the capital invested in utilities is represented by bonds. He who buys bonds seeks primarily safety. If he can obtain it, he is content with a low rate of interest. Through a fluctuating rate base the bondholder can only lose. He can receive no benefit from a rule which increases the rate base as the price level rises; for his return, expressed in dollars, would be the same, whatever the income of the company. That the stockholder does not in fact receive an increased return in time of rapidly rising prices under the rule of *Smyth* v. *Ames*, as applied, the financial record of the last six years demonstrates. But the burden upon the community is heavy, because the risk makes the capital cost high.

"The expense and loss now incident to recurrent rate controversies is also very large. The most serious vice of the present rule for fixing the rate base is not the existing uncertainty, but that the method does not lead to certainty. Under it, the value for rate-making purposes must ever be an unstable factor. Instability is a standing menace of renewed controversy. The direct expense to the utility of maintaining an army of experts and of counsel is appalling. The indirect cost is far greater. The attention of officials high and low is, necessarily, diverted from the constructive tasks of efficient operation and of development. The public relations of the utility to the community are apt to become more and more strained, and a victory for the utility

[145]

may in the end prove more disastrous than defeat would have been. The community defeated, but unconvinced, remembers, and may refuse aid when the community has occasion later to require its consent or cooperation in the conduct and development of its enterprise. Controversy with utilities is obviously injurious, also, to the public interest. The prime needs of the community are that facilities be ample and that rates be as low and as stable as possible. The community can get cheap service from private companies, only through cheap capital. It can get efficient service only if managers of the utility are free to devote themselves to problems of operation and of development. It can get ample service through private companies only if investors may be assured of receiving continuously a fair return upon the investment.

"What is now termed prudent investment is, in essence, the same thing as that which the Court has always sought to protect in using the term present value. Twenty-five years ago, when *Smyth* v. *Ames* was decided, it was impossible to ascertain with accuracy, in respect to most of the utilities, in most of the States in which rate controversies arose, what it cost in money to establish the utility; or what the money cost with which the utility was established; or what income had been earned by it; or how the income had been expended. It was, therefore, not feasible, then, to adopt, as the rate base, the amount properly invested or, as the rate of fair return, the amount of the capital charge. Now the situation is fundamentally different. These amounts are, now, readily ascertainable in respect to a large and rapidly increasing proportion of the utilities. The change in this respect is due to the enlargement, meanwhile, of the powers and functions of State utility commissions. The issue of securities is now, and for many years has been, under the control of commissions, in the leading States. Hence the amount of capital raised (since the conferring of these powers) and its cost are definitely known, through current supervision and prescribed accounts, supplemented by inspection of the commission's engineering force. Like knowledge concerning the investment of that part of the capital raised and expended before these broad functions were exercised by the utility commissions has been secured, in many cases, through investigations undertaken later, in connection with the issue of new securities or the regulation of rates. The amount and disposition of current earnings of all the companies are also known. It is, therefore, feasible now to adopt as the measure of a compensatory rate, the annual cost, or charge, of the capital prudently invested in the utility. And, hence, it should be done.

"Value is a word of many meanings. That with which commissions and courts in these proceedings are concerned, in so-called confiscation cases, is a special value for rate-making purposes, not exchange value. This is illustrated by our decisions which deal with the elements to be included in fixing the rate base. . . . Good will and franchise value were excluded from the rate base in determining whether the prescribed charges of the public utility were confiscatory. . . . The cost of developing the business as a financially successful concern was excluded from the rate base. . . . The fact that the street had been paved (and hence the reproduction cost of laying gas mains greatly increased) was not allowed as an element of value. . . . But, obviously, good will and franchise are important elements when exchange value is involved; and where the community acquires a public utility by purchase or condemnation, compensation must be made for its good will and earning power, at least under some circumstances. . . . Likewise, as between buyer and seller, the good will and earning power due to effective organization are often more important elements than tangible property. These cases would seem to require rejection of a rule which measured the rate base by cost of reproduction or by value in its ordinary sense.

"The rule by which the utilities are seeking to measure the return is, in essence, reproduction cost of the utility or prudent investment, whichever is the higher. This is indicated by the instructions contained in the Special Report on Valuation of Public Utilities, made to the American Society of Civil Engineers, October 28, 1916, *Proceedings*, vol. 42. [Justice Brandeis makes a quotation from the report, bringing out this point.]

"If the aim were to ascertain the value (in its ordinary sense) of the utility property, the enquiry would be, not what it would cost to reproduce the identical property, but what it would cost to establish a plant which could render the service, or in other words, at what cost could an equally efficient substitute be then produced. Surely the cost of an equally efficient substitute must be the maximum of the rate base, if prudent investment be rejected as the measure. The utilities seem to claim that the constitutional protection against confiscation guarantees them a return both upon unearned increment and upon the cost of property rendered valueless by obsolescence."

State of Missouri ex rel. Southwestern Bell Telephone Co.
v. Public Service Commission of Missouri, et al.
262 U. S. 276, 289

The O'Fallon Case

(Dissenting Opinion, *St. Louis & O'Fallon Ry. Co.*
v. *United States*, 1929)

UNDER THE TRANSPORTATION ACT OF 1920, THE INTERSTATE COM-
merce Commission is authorized to order carriers earning an income in
excess of six percent of their property valuation to place one-half of
that excess in a reserve fund and to pay over the other half to the
Commission, to be applied for the benefit of the weaker roads. Such an
order was issued to the St. Louis & O'Fallon Railway Company, which
denied that it had any excess.

Congress had directed, in paragraph 4, §15a, of the Transportation
Act, that the Commission "shall give due consideration to all the elements of value recognized by the law of the land for rate-making
purposes, and shall give to the property investment account of the
carriers only that consideration which under such law it is entitled to
in establishing values for rate-making purposes."

The question presented to the Court was whether the method of
valuation applied by the Commission complied with this provision. The
Commission itself was divided on the weight required to be given to
reproduction cost. A majority of the Court sided with the minority of
the Commission, Mr. Justice McReynolds writing the opinion.

The conflicting views are set out in Justice Brandeis' exhaustive
dissenting opinion (in which Holmes and Stone, JJ., concurred):

"THE MAIN question for consideration is that of statutory
construction. By Transportation Act, 1920, February 28,
1920, c. 91, §15a, 41 Stat. 456, 488, Congress delegated to
the Interstate Commerce Commission the duty to establish and

[149]

maintain rates which will yield 'a fair return upon the aggregate value of the railway property' of the United States. By paragraph 4 thereof it directs that in ascertaining value the Commission shall 'give due consideration to all the elements of value recognized by the law of the land for rate-making purposes,' and shall 'give to the property investment account * * * only that consideration which under such law it is entitled to in establishing value for rate-making purposes.' The report of the Commission, which accompanies the order challenged, declares: 'In the methods of valuation which we have followed in this proceeding we have endeavored to give heed to this direction [that contained in paragraph 4]. * * * ' (*Excess Income of St. Louis & O'Fallon Ry. Co.*, 124 I. C. C. 3, 19.) Speaking for the dissenting members, Mr. Commissioner Hall said: 'If the law needs change, let those who made it change it. Our duty is to apply the law as it stands.' (Pp. 63, 64.) And Mr. Commissioner Atchison added: 'If we anticipate grave results will follow, our responsibility will be fully met if we suggest to the Congress, under our statutory powers to recommend new legislation to that body, the enactment of a rule for rate-making under the commerce clause which will have no such unfavorable effects.' (Page 64.)

"Section 15a makes no specific reference either to the original cost of the property, or to prudent investment, or to current reproduction cost, or to the then existing price level. Section 19a—the valuation provisions of the Act of 1913—to which §15a refers, directs the Commission to report, among other things, 'in detail as to each piece of property, * * * the original cost to date, the cost of reproduction new, the cost of reproduction less depreciation'; and also 'other values, and elements of value.' After the enactment of §15a and before entry of the order challenged, it was held in *Southwestern Bell Telephone Co.* v. *Public Service Commission*, [see page 135], a case arising under a State law, that the rate base on which a public utility is constitutionally entitled to earn a fair return is the then actual value of the property used and useful in the business, not the original cost or the amount prudently invested in the enterprise. The Government concedes that current reproduction cost is admissible as evidence to show present value under §15a. The carrier concedes now that neither Congress nor the common law made current reproduction cost the measure of value. The question on which the Commission divided is this: Did Congress require the Commission, when acting under §15a, to give, in all cases and in respect to all property, some, if not controlling, effect to evidence establishing the estimated current cost of reproduction? Or did Congress intend to leave to the Commission the authority to determine, as in passing upon other controverted issues of fact, what weight, if any, it should give to that evidence?

"The O'Fallon contends, among other things, that the order is confiscatory. The claim is that the order left to the company a return of only 4.35 percent upon the value ascertained in accordance with the rule declared in the *Southwestern Bell Case* and *McCardle* v. *Indianapolis Water Co.*, 272 U. S. 400. If this were true, it would be immaterial whether Congress purported to authorize the course pursued by the Commission. But the fact is that in each of the recapture periods the earnings were so large as to leave, after making the required payments to the Commission, about eight percent on what the carrier alleged was the fair value of the property. The O'Fallon argues that, since the statute and the order required it to hold as a reserve one-half of the excess over six percent, it is deprived of that property. This is not true. The requirement that one-half of the earnings in excess of six percent shall be retained by the carrier until the reserve equals five percent of the value of the railroad does not deprive the carrier of any property. It merely regulates the use thereof.

. . . The provision is one designed to secure financial stability and is similar to those prescribing sinking funds, depreciation, and other appropriate accounts. Congress may regulate the use of railroad property so as to ensure financial as well as physical stability. Both are essential to the safety and the service of the public. In *Dayton-Goose Creek Ry. Co.* v. *United States,* 263 U. S. 456, 486, where the facts were in this respect identical with those in the case at bar, the constitutional validity of the order was sustained. If the failure to give to the evidence of current reproduction costs the effect claimed for it by the O'Fallon was error, it is not because the carrier's constitutional rights have been invaded, but because the Commission failed to observe a rule prescribed by Congress for determining the amounts to be recaptured and preserved.

"The claim of the O'Fallon is in substance that, since construction costs were higher during the recapture periods than in 1914, the order should be set aside, because the Commission failed to find that the existing structural property and equipment which had been acquired before June 30, 1914, was worth more than it had been then. (The complaint concerns all the structural property and equipment acquired before June 30, 1919. But, as nearly all of this had been installed before July 1, 1914, the discussion is limited to the property acquired before June 30, 1914—the valuation being made on the basis of construction costs as of that date.) The Commission undertook, as will be shown, to find present actual value, and, in so doing, both to follow the direction of Congress and to apply the rule declared in the *Southwestern Bell Case.* It is true that this Court there declared that current reconstruction cost is an element of actual value, and that Congress directed the Commission 'to give due consideration to all the elements of value recognized by the law of the land for rate-making purposes.' But while the Act required the Commission to consider all such evidence, neither Congress nor this Court required it to give evidence of reconstruction cost a mechanical effect or artificial weight. They left untrammeled its duty to give all relevant evidence such probative force as, in its judgment, the evidence inherently possesses. The Commission concluded that in respect to the evidence of reproduction costs the differences between the *Southwestern Bell Case* and that at bar were such as to lead to different results in the two cases. It did so mainly because 'in the administration of the valuation and recapture provisions,' ascertainment of value 'is affected by a vast variety of considerations that either do not enter into, or are less easily perceived in, problems incident to the regulation of local public utilities.' (Page 27.) In my opinion, the conclusions of the Commission are well founded. To make clear the reasons, requires consideration of the function of the Commission in applying §15a and of the problems with which it is confronted.

"*First.* The Commission is a fact-finding body. The question whether it must give to confessedly relevant facts evidential effect is solely one of adjective law. Statutes have sometimes limited the weight or effect of evidence. They have often created rebuttable presumptions and have shifted the burden of proof. But no instance has been found where under our law a fact-finding body has been required to give to evidence an effect which it does not inherently possess. Proof implies persuasion. To compel the human mind to infer in any respect that which observation and logic tells us is not true interferes with the process of reasoning of the fact-finding body. It would be a departure from the unbroken practice to require an artificial legal conviction where no real conviction exists.

"An arbitrary disregard by the Commission of the probative effect of evidence would, of course, be ground for setting aside an order, as this would be an abuse of discretion. Orders have been set aside because entered without evidence; or because matters of fact had been considered which were not in the record; or because the Commission excluded from consideration facts and circumstances which ought to have been considered; or because it took into consideration facts which could not legally influence its judgment. But no case has been found in which this Court has set aside an order on the ground that the Commission failed to give effect to evidence which seemed to the Court to be of probative force, or on the ground that the Commission had drawn from the evidence an inference or conclusion deemed by the Court to be erroneous. On the contrary, findings of the Commission involving the appreciation or effect of evidence have been treated with the deference due to those of a tribunal 'informed by experience' and 'appointed by law' to deal with an intricate subject. . . . Unless, therefore, Congress required the Commission, not only to consider evidence of reconstruction cost in ascertaining values for rate-making purposes under §15a, but also to give, in all cases and in respect to all property, some weight to evidence of enhanced reconstruction cost, even if that evidence was not inherently persuasive, the Commission was clearly authorized to determine for itself to what extent, if any, weight should be given to the evidence; and its findings should not be disturbed by the Court, unless it appears that there was an abuse of discretion.

"*Second.* While current reproduction cost may be said to be an element in the present value of property, in the sense that it is 'evidence properly to be considered in the ascertainment of value' (*Standard Oil Co.* v. *Southern Pacific Co.,* 268 U. S. 146, 156), it is clear that current cost of reproduction higher than the original cost does not necessarily tend to prove a present higher value. Often the fact of higher reconstruction cost is without any influence on present values. It is common knowledge that the current market value of many office buildings and residences constructed prior to the World War have failed to reflect the greatly increased building costs of recent years, although the need of new buildings of like character was being demonstrated by the large volume of construction at the higher price level. Many railroads built before the World War have never been worth as much as their original cost, because the high construction cost combined with adverse operating conditions and limited traffic have at all times prevented their earning, despite reasonable rates, a fair return on the original cost. The Puget Sound extension of the Chicago, Milwaukee and St. Paul is a notable example. Many branches, and indeed whole lines of railroad, have been scrapped since 1920. Abandonment of 2,439 miles of railroad was authorized under paragraph 18 of §1 of the Interstate Commerce Act between 1920 and 1925, and in the three following years 2,010 miles more. These properties had, in the main, become valueless for transportation, either because traffic ceased to be available, or because competitive means of transportation precluded the establishment of remunerative rail rates. Obviously, no one would contend that their actual value just before abandonment was what it originally cost to construct them or what it would then have to cost to reconstruct them.

"*Third*. The terms of §15a and its legislative history preclude the assumption that Congress intended by paragraph 4 to deny to the Commission in respect to evidence of reconstruction cost the discretion commonly exercised in determining what weight, if any, shall be given to an evidential fact. In 1920, no fact was more prominent in the mind of the public and of Congress than that the cost of living was far greater than that prevailing when the existing railroads were built. But neither in Transportation Act 1920, nor in any committee report, is there even a suggestion that the Commission would be required to give to that fact any effect in ascertaining values for rate-making purposes under §15a. If it had been the intention of Congress to compel the Commission to increase values for rate-making purposes because the price level had

[155]

risen, it would naturally have incorporated such a direction in the paragraph. On the other hand, the committee reports and the debates show that the opinion was quite commonly held that the actual values were less than the property investment account appearing on the books of the carriers; and the proposal made by the railroads that the investment account be accepted as the measure of value was resisted as being excessive. The property investment account in 1920 was about nineteen billions of dollars. The then reproduction cost of the railroads, applying index figures to estimated actual cost, was over forty billions. It is inconceivable that Congress, after rejecting property investment account as excessive, intended by §15a to make mandatory on the Commission the consideration of elements which would give a valuation double that which had been rejected. The insertion in §15a of the provision that the Commission 'shall give to the property investment account of the carriers only that consideration which under law it is entitled to in establishing values for rate-making purposes' and the rejection of other proposed measures of value, show that Congress intended not to impose restrictions upon the discretion of the Commission.

"Congress did intend to provide a return on the existing railroad property which should be only slightly more than that which had been enjoyed during the six preceding years. To have required that the then price level be reflected in the values to be fixed under §15a would have resulted in a rate base of double the property investment account of the carriers; for the cost of living was then about double pre-war prices. The prescribed fair return applied to such a rate base would have produced more than double the average net earnings from operation of the several properties during the three years preceding Federal control; more than double the amount which the carriers agreed to accept under the Federal Control Act, March 21, 1918, c. 25, §1, 40 Stat. 451, as fair compensation for the use of their property; more than double the guaranty provided by Transportation Act 1920, §209, for the six months' period after the surrender of control. The sum which the railroads had thus earned net in those six years equalled 5.2 percent on the property investment account, as carried on their books.

"In making provision for a fair return, the main purpose was not to increase the earnings of capital already invested in railroads, but to attract the new capital needed for improvement or extension of facilities. This was to be accomplished by raising the rate of return from 5.2 percent to 5.5 percent. [The opinion quotes from Senate Reports, No. 304, Vol. 1, Sixty-sixth Congress, 1st Session.]

"Either increase in the rate of return or increase of the base on which that return is measured would have served to adjust compensation to higher price levels. The adoption by Congress of the increase in the return, as the means of compensating for the decreased purchasing power of the dollar, precludes the assumption that it intended that the valuation should reflect that lessened purchasing power. By explicitly choosing the former Congress implicitly rejected the latter. For to have allowed an increase in both would have gone beyond adjusting earnings to increased costs and have made this increase a mere pretext for allowing unwarranted profits to the railroads. The proceedings which led to the passage of the Act make it clear that Congress intended no such result.

"*Fourth*. The declared purpose of Congress in enacting §15a was the maintenance of an adequate national system of railway transportation, capable of providing the best possible service to the public at the lowest cost consistent with full justice to the private owners. Following the course consistently pursued by this Court in applying other provisions of the Interstate Commerce Act (*Texas & Pacific Ry. Co.* v. *Interstate Commerce Commission*, 162 U. S. 197, 211, 219; *New England*

Divisions Case, 261 U. S. 184, 189, 190; *Dayton-Goose Creek
Ry. Co.* v. *United States,* 263 U. S. 456, 478), the Commission construed §15a in the light of the declared purpose of
Congress and of the economic factors involved. From its wide
knowledge of actual conditions and its practical experience in
rate making, it concluded that to give effect to enhanced reproduction costs would defeat that purpose. (Page 27.)

"It knew that the value for rate-making purposes could
not be more than that sum on which a fair return could be
earned by legal rates, and that the earnings were limited both
by the commercial prohibition of rates higher than the traffic
would bear and the legal prohibition of rates higher than are
just and reasonable. It knew that a rate base fluctuating with
changes in the level of general prices would imperil industry
and commerce. It knew that the adoption of a fluctuating rate
base would not, as is claimed, do justice to those pre-war investors in railroad securities who were suffering from the
lessened value of the dollar, since the great majority of the
railroad securities are represented by long-term bonds or the
guaranteed stocks of leased lines which bear a fixed return,
and that only the stockholders could gain through the greater
earnings required to satisfy the higher rate base. It recognized
that an adequate national system of railways, so long as it is
privately owned, cannot be provided and maintained without a
continuous inflow of capital; that, 'obviously, also, such an
inflow can only be assured by treatment of capital already
invested which will invite and encourage further investment'
(page 30); and that as was said in *Dayton-Goose Creek Ry.
Co.* v. *United States:* 'By investment in a business dedicated
to the public service the owner must recognize that, as compared with investment in private business, he cannot expect
either high or speculative dividends but that his obligation
limits him to only fair or reasonable profit'.

"The conviction that there would in time be a fall in the

price level was generally held. As a fluctuating rate base would thus directly imperil industry and commerce and investments made at relatively high price levels during and since the World War, would tend to increase the cost of new money required to supply adequate service to the public, and would discourage such investment, the Commission concluded that Congress could not have intended to require it to measure the value or rate base by reproduction cost, since this would produce a result contrary to its declared purpose. And, as confirming its construction of §15a, the Commission showed that, with the stable rate base which it had accepted as the basis for administering the Act, the aim of Congress to establish an adequate national system had been attained. It pointed out that:

> 'During the period 1920-1926, inclusive, the investment in railroad property increased by four billions of dollars. A substantial part of this money was derived from income, but much of it was obtained by the sale of new securities. The market for railroad securities since the passage of the Transportation Act 1920 has steadily improved and the general trend of interest rates has been downward. The credit of the railroads in general is now excellent. ***' (Page 33.)

"*Fifth.* Other considerations confirm the construction given by the Commission to the phrase 'value for rate-making purposes' as used in §15a. In condemnation proceedings the owner recovers what he has lost by the taking of the property, and such loss must be determined, 'not merely with reference to the uses to which it is at the time applied, but with reference to the uses to which it is plainly adapted' . . . But the actual value of a railroad—its value for rate-making purposes under §15a—may be less than its condemnation value. As was said in *Southern Ry. Co.* v. *Kentucky*, 274 U. S. 76, 81-82, a case involving State taxation:

[159]

'The value of the physical elements of a railroad—whether that value be deemed actual cost, cost of reproduction new, cost of reproduction less depreciation or some other figure—is not the sole measure or guide to its value in operation. *Smyth* v. *Ames*, 169, U. S. 466, 547. Much weight is to be given to present and prospective earning capacity at rates that are reasonable, having regard to traffic available and competitive and other conditions prevailing in the territory served.'

"Value has been defined as the ability to command the price. Railroad property is valuable as such only if, and so far as, used. If rates are too high, the traffic will not move. Hence the value or rate base is necessarily dependent, in the first place, upon the commercial ability of the property to command the rates which will yield a return in excess of operating expenses and taxes; and such value cannot be higher than the sum on which, with the available traffic, the fair return fixed under §15a can be earned. Persistent depression of rates or lessening volume of traffic, from whatever cause arising, ordinarily tends to lower actual values of railroad properties. It follows that, since the Commission is required by the rule of *Smyth* v. *Ames,* reaffirmed in the *Southwestern Bell Case,* to determine the rate base under §15a by actual value as distinguished from prudent investment, it must, in making the finding, consider the effect upon value of both the commercial and the legal limitations upon rates, and, among other things, the effect of competition upon the volume of traffic.

"Recent experience affords striking examples of commercial limitations upon rates. In *Ex parte* 74, *Increased Rates,* 1920, 58 I. C. C. 220, the Commission sought to establish rates which would yield six percent upon the aggregate values of the railroads in the several groups. The carriers claimed as the aggregate value $20,040,572,611—that amount being carried on their books as the cost of road and equipment. The Commission fixed the value about five percent lower— $18,900,000,000. In order to produce on that sum net earnings equal to six percent, it increased freight rates, in the eastern group, forty percent over the then existing rates; in the southern group, twenty-five percent; in the western group, thirty-five percent; and, in the mountain-Pacific group, twenty-five percent. As a result of these increases, the average gross revenue per ton-mile in 1921 was in the eastern district 96.1 percent greater than for the fiscal year ended June 30, 1914; in the southern, 61.4; in the western, 59.3; and in the United States as a whole, 76.2. (*Reduced Rates*, 1922, 68 I. C. C. 676, 702.) Passenger rates were subjected by the order in *Ex parte* 74 to a flat increase of twenty percent, and surcharges were added. (Page 242 of 58 I. C. C.)

"On a larger number of basic commodities, which were among the most important articles of commerce, the rates proved to be higher than the traffic would bear. Reductions became imperative. Within a year after the entry of that order, many applications for reductions were made to the Commission, not only by shippers, but also by the carriers themselves. It was estimated that the reductions in freight rates made by the carriers prior to March 15, 1922, would aggregate for that year $186,700,000, and would lower the general rate level nearly five percent. On some important articles of traffic the entire increase made by *Ex parte* 74 was canceled. Further reductions were then ordered by *Reduced Rates*, 1922, 68 I. C. C. 676, pages 732, 733, the Commission saying:

'High rates do not necessarily mean high revenues, for, if the public cannot or will not ship in normal volume, less revenue may result than from lower rates. Shippers almost unanimously contend, and many representatives of the carriers agree, that "freight rates are too high and must come down." This indicates that transportation charges have mounted to a point where they are impeding the free flow of commerce and thus tending to defeat the purpose for which they were established, that of producing revenues which would enable the carriers "to provide the people of the United States with adequate transportation." '

Further reductions made in the year 1923 are said to have again lowered freight rates five percent. The effect of the several reductions made in the rates authorized by *Ex parte* 74 is said to have lowered by $800,000,000 the freight charges otherwise payable on the traffic carried during the eighteen months ending December 31, 1923. Each year since has witnessed a further lowering in the revenue per ton-mile and per passenger-mile.

"This constant lowering of the weighted average of rates since 1920 must have been due to causes other than desire on the part of the Commission. Its aim was to adjust rates so that they would yield the prescribed return. But, for the period from 1920 to 1927, inclusive, there was only one year in which the railroads of the United States as a whole, despite general prosperity and greater efficiency, earned on the value found in *Ex parte* 74 brought down to date, the full average return prescribed as fair under §15a. The Commission repeatedly refused to permit carriers to make reductions, because the reduction would lower the revenues sought to be provided under §15a. On the other hand, carriers, although earning less than the fair return prescribed under §15a, have often voluntarily reduced rates. The lowering of rates was probably due in large measure to the influence of competing means of transportation.

"*Sixth.* Since 1914 the railroads have been obliged, to an ever-increasing extent, to compete with water lines and with motors. This competition has been fostered by the Government through the Panama Canal Act, through intracoastal waterways acts, through the inland waterways acts, through the development of coastwise shipping by means of harbor improvements, and through Federal aid in the construction of highways. There has also been increased competition by pipe lines. Competition from other means of transportation has tended to arrest the normal increase in the volume of rail traffic; and, as to some traffic, it has actually produced a reduction in both the volume and the rates. It has resulted in a general shrinkage in the passenger business; in some regions, in a lessening of the carload freight; and, in many, in a reduction of the volume of the less-than-carload freight.

"The influence of water competition on rates is strikingly illustrated by the effect of the Panama Canal on transcontinental freight rates. In order to meet this water competition, carriers have repeatedly asked leave to make sweeping reductions. Rates voluntarily established by the rail carriers are lower now, on some articles of traffic, than they were in 1914. On others they are only a little higher. The influence of competition by the inland waterways on the volume of rail traffic is illustrated in the effect which improvement of the Ohio River and its tributaries has had in the Pittsburg district. The rail tonnage in 1927 was materially less than in 1914, while the water tonnage more than doubled. The influence of barge lines in reducing or holding down rail rates is illustrated by the rail rates in competition with those of the barge lines on the Ohio, the Mississippi, and the Warrior Rivers. The widespread effect of competition by motor-truck in lowering both the rates and the volume of rail traffic is obvious. Not obvious, but indisputable, has been the effect of the potential competition of pipe lines shown by reductions in oil rates caused by the threat of competing pipe lines.

"Moreover, rates which are not so high as to prevent commercially the movement of traffic are often required to be lowered because they conflict with some statutory provision. Thus Congress compels reduction of rates which discriminate unjustly against individuals, localities, articles of traffic, or other carriers. Perhaps the most striking instance of the limitation by law of rates which the traffic would bear commercially is furnished by cases under the long and short haul clause. By that clause a rail carrier is often obliged (unless relieved by order of the Commission) to elect between suffering practically a total loss of existing traffic between competitive points or suffering a loss in existing revenues by reducing rates at both the competitive points and intermediate non-competitive points. The effect of this limitation upon rates, and hence upon the actual value of railroads, has become very great. Its influence has grown steadily with the growth of competition by water and motor, with the growth in the size of the individual railroad system, with the growth in the dependence of railroads for their revenues upon long-haul freight traffic and with the growing length of the average haul. It has become so important for rail carriers to hold a share of the long-haul freight traffic at competitive points, that the long and short haul clause, if not relieved from, results in the carriers' giving, in large measure, to the intermediate non-competitive points which otherwise would be subject to monopoly exactions, the full benefit of that lowering of rates required to meet the competition. The many applications for reductions made in petitions for relief from the operation of the long and short haul clause illustrate the influence of rail, as well as of water and motor, competition in thus depressing rates. Congress has by that clause limited values for rate-making purposes under §15a, almost as effectively as by its promotion of competitive means of transportation.

"*Seventh.* In requiring that the value be ascertained for rate-making purposes, Congress imposed upon the rate base as defined in *Smyth* v. *Ames,* still another limitation which is far-reaching in its operation. By declaring in §15a that the Commission shall, 'in the exercise of its power to prescribe just and reasonable rates' so adjust them that upon the value a fair return may be earned 'under honest, efficient, and economical management' Congress made efficiency of the plant an element or test of value. Efficiency and economy imply employment of the right instrument and material as well as their use in the right manner. To use a machine, after a much better and more economical one has become available, is as inefficient as to use two men to operate an efficient machine when the work could be performed equally well by one at half the labor cost. Such an instrument of transportation, although originally well conceived and remunerative, should, like machines used in manufacturing, be scrapped when it becomes wasteful.

"Independently of any statute, it is now recognized that, when in confiscation cases it is sought to prove actual value by evidence of reproduction cost, the evidence must be directed to the present cost of installing such a plant as would be required to supply the same service. For valuation of public utilities by reproduction cost implies that 'the rates permitted should be high enough to allow a reasonable percent of return on the money that would now be required to construct a plant capable of rendering the desired service,' and does not mean 'that the plant should be valued at what would now be needed to duplicate the plant precisely.' Proof of value by evidence of reproduction cost presupposes that a plant like that being valued would then be constructed. To the extent that a railroad employs instruments which are inconsistent with efficiency, the plant would not be constructed; and, because of the inefficient part, the railroad is obviously not then worth the cost of reconstructing the identical plant. While a part often has some service value, although not efficient according to the existing

[165]

standard, its use may involve such heavy, unnecessary operating expense as to render it valueless for rate-making purposes under §15a. The Commission, when requested to consider evidence of reproduction cost, must therefore examine the value of every part of the plant, and that of the whole plant, as compared with the value of a modern, efficient plant. Upon such consideration the Commission may conclude that the railroad is so largely obsolete in construction and equipment as to render evidence of the reproduction cost of the identical plant of no probative force whatsoever. The duty so to deal with the evidence seems to flow necessarily from the rejection by the Court of prudent investment as the measure of value, and the adoption, instead, of the actual value of the property at the time of the rate hearing as the governing rule of substantive law.

"The physical deterioration of a railroad plant through wear and tear may be very small as compared with a plant new, while its functional deterioration may be very large as compared with a modern efficient plant. This lessening of service value may be due to any one of several causes. It may, in the first place, be due to causes wholly external. Freight terminals, originally well conceived as wisely located in the heart of a city, may have become valueless for rate-making purposes under §15a, because through growth of the city the expense of operating therein has become so high, or the inescapable costs of eliminating grade crossings so large, that efficient management requires immediate abandonment of the terminals. And, even if the cost of continuing operation there is not so high as to require abandonment, the property may have for rate-making purposes a value far below its market value. . . .

"The lessening of the service value of a part of the railroad plant may flow from changes in the volume or character of its traffic. For economy and efficiency are obviously to be determined with reference to the business of the carrier then being done and about to be done. A station warehouse for less-than-carload freight may have become valueless for rate-making purposes, because, through motor competition, the railroad had lost substantially all its less-than-carload business at that point. Large reductions in the value of passenger stations and equipment may have resulted from decline in the passenger traffic. Branch lines may lose all their service value so that they should be abandoned because motor transportation has become more efficient. On the other hand, the traffic may have grown so much as to render inefficient a part of a line originally wisely constructed with heavy grades or curves. In that event economy and efficiency will demand elimination of the grades and curves and may even require the building of tunnels or a cut-off. In so far as such a condition exists, the railroad would obviously not be reconstructed with the heavy grades and curves; and, when considering the reconstruction cost of the whole property, that part of the line must be given merely scrap value. . . .

"Perhaps the most common cause of the lessening of service value of parts of railroad plants originally well conceived and still in good physical condition is the progress in the art of rail transportation. Science and invention have wrought since June 30, 1914, such extraordinary improvements in the types of automobiles and aëroplanes that no one would contend that the present service value of such machines should be ascertained by inquiring what their original cost was or what their reproduction cost would be. The progress since June 30, 1914, in the art of transportation by railroad has been less spectacular; but the art has been far from stagnant. In railroading, as in other fields of business, the great rise in the cost of labor and of supplies, and the need of better service, have stimulated, not only inventions, but also their utilization. Through technological advances, instruments of transportation with largely increased efficiency and economy have developed. The price of lower operating costs is the scrapping of those parts of the plant which progress in the art renders obsolete. The present greatly increased efficiency of the railroads as compared with 1920, their greatly improved credit, and their present prosperity, are, in large measure, due to the advances made toward introducing the improved instruments of rail transportation which have become available. Obviously much remains to be done.

"The extent of this technological progress may be illustrated by the modern locomotive. The development of the superheater, the mechanical stoker, the booster, and other devices, the increase in the size of the boiler, and other radical changes in size, weight, and design have resulted in the production of engines which are recognized by railway experts as having set such an entirely new standard of efficiency in fuel consumption, in tractive power, and in speed as to render wasteful, under many conditions, the use of older locomotives, no matter how good their condition. Statistics as to actual performances of the locomotive of today, as compared with that built but a few years ago, graphically illustrate this great advance in efficiency.

"Its economies are compelling. But important changes in roadway and equipment are conditions of its effective use. Heavier locomotives make greater demands on the road structures which carry them. To obviate large maintenance expenses attendant upon frequent repair and replacement the roadway must be made more durable. To this end rails of heavier section, and of increased length are adopted. Anticreepers are freely used to prevent rail movement. Larger ties are selected; and they are treated to prevent deterioration. Ballast is made deeper and heavier, and of gravel or stone rather than of cinders. Bridges are of stronger construction. And, to facilitate the movement of traffic, watering stations and automatic signals of improved design are introduced. Moreover, the effective employment of the modern locomotive involves ordinarily the use of larger cars of steel construction, displacing the wooden car of small capacity with which so many of the railroads were equipped in 1914. Engine terminals and carshops built prior to 1914 are, in many cases, inadequate for the efficient and economical handling, housing, and repairing of the modern locomotives and cars, and must be replaced to prevent curtailment of the productive capacity of the rolling stock by needless idle hours while awaiting service or repair. And the waste incident to the use of shop tools and machinery long since rendered obsolete by progress in the art must be stopped.

"Thus, the efficient post-war railroad plant differs widely even from the efficient one of 1914. That during the recapture period here in question the plants of most of the railroads of the United States built before the war were lacking in improved instruments of transportation made available by recent progress in the art is of common knowledge. That this is true even today of many of the railroads will not be denied. To the extent that there is inefficiency in plant, there was and is functional depreciation, lessening actual value. That this functional depreciation, arising through external changes, through competitive means of transportation, and through progress in the art of transportation may, in respect to a particular railroad, have become so large as to more than counterbalance that increase in its value which would otherwise flow from the rise in the price level since 1914, seems clear.

"It may be urged that the continued use of the inefficient plant, and the repairing rather than replacement of its antiquated parts, has been due to lack of capital and insufficient revenues. Such an excuse for failing to install the improved plant might have been conclusive if prudent investment had been accepted as the measure of value. But the fact that the management may have been wholly free from blame in continuing to use the inefficient parts obviously does not add to their actual value. The actual value of an existing plant, and the difference between its value and the present cost of constructing a modern efficient plant which will render the service, is precisely the same whether the continued use of the obsolete part was due to lack of capital, or to lack of good judgment, or to somnolence on the part of the management. As was said in *Board of Commissioners* v. *New York Telephone Co.*, 271 U. S. 23, 32: 'Customers pay for service, not for the property used to render it.' Only the then service value of the property is of legal significance under the rule of *Smyth* v. *Ames*.

"It may also be urged that such functional depreciation of the railroad plant since 1914 is allowed for in the depreciation customarily estimated by the Commission. But this is not true. Functional depreciation prior to June 30, 1914, was included when valuing as of that date the then property of the railroads. But the instructions of the Commission provided that functional depreciation arising after that date should not be considered unless 'imminent.' And the Commission made clear that it did not intend by the term to include functional depreciation of the character described above arising from external causes, from the competition of new methods of transportation, from the extraordinary urban growth, from the need of new economies arising from the largely increased labor and fuel costs, and from other incidents of the war and post-war developments in industry and transportation. . . .

"If weight is to be given to reproduction cost in making the valuation of any railroad for rate-making purposes, under §19a and §15a, there must be a determination of the functional depreciation of the individual plant as compared with a modern, efficient plant adequate to perform the same service. To make such a determination for any railroad involves a detailed inquiry into the character and condition of all those parts of the plant which may have reduced functional value because of the post-war changes affecting transportation above referred to, and also into the character and the volume of the carrier's business. For the efficient plant means that plant which is economical and efficient for the particular carrier in view of the peculiar requirements and possibilities of its own business. To make such a determination justly, the Commission must have the data on which a competent and vigilant management would insist when required to pass upon the advisability of making capital expenditures. And the Commission would be obliged to give them the same careful consideration. The determination of the extent of functional depreciation is thus a very serious task—a task far more serious than that of determining merely physical depreciation.

"To make such a determination of functional depreciation annually for each of the railroads of the United States would be a stupendous task, involving perhaps prohibitive expense. To make the necessary decisions promptly would seem impossible, among other reasons, because railroad valuation is but a small part of the many duties of the Commission. On the other hand, to adjust rates so as to render a fair return, and to provide through the recapture provision funds in aid of the weaker railroad, are tasks which Congress deemed urgent; and which must be promptly performed if its purpose is to be achieved. Obviously Congress intended that in making the necessary valuations under §15a a method should be pursued by which the task which is imposed upon the Commission could be performed. . . . Recognizing this, the Commission construed §15a as it had paragraph (f) of §19a; that is, as permitting the Commission to make a basic valuation as of some general date (June 30, 1914 was selected); and, unless some good reason to the contrary appeared, to find the value for any year thereafter by adding to or subtracting from the 1914 value the net increases or decreases in the investment in property devoted to transportation service as determined from the carrier's annual returns with due regard to the element of depreciation.

"*Eighth*. The significance, in connection with current reproduction costs, of the requirement in §15a that value be ascertained 'for rate-making purposes' as there defined becomes apparent when the position of railroads, in this respect, is compared with that of most local utilities enjoying a monopoly of a necessary of life. The fundamental question in the *Southwestern Bell Case* was one of substantive constitutional law, namely: Is the rate base on which the Constitution guarantees to a public utility the right to earn a fair return the actual value of the property at the time of the rate hearing, or is it the cost or capital prudently invested in the enterprise? The Court decided that the rate base is the actual value at the time of the rate hearing. That proposition of substantive law the Commission undertook to apply to the facts presented in the case at bar. Recognizing that evidence of increased reconstruction costs is admissible for the purpose of showing an actual value greater than the original cost or the prudent investment, it found in respect to some of the carrier's property that the evidence of enhanced reconstruction cost was persuasive of higher present value. As to the rest of the property, it held that the evidence was neither adequate nor persuasive.

"Of both railroads and the local utility it is true, under the rule of substantive law adopted in the *Southwestern Bell Case,* that value is the sum on which a fair return can be earned consistently with the laws of trade and legal enactments. But the operative scope upon railroads of the limitations so imposed upon the rates, and hence upon values, is much greater than in the case of local utilities. Rail rates are being constantly curbed by the competition of markets and of rival means of transportation. Rail rates are curbed also by the influence of high rates upon the desires of individuals. The public can, to a considerable extent, do without rail service. If the rates are excessive, traffic falls off. Thus when passenger rates are too high, travel is either curtailed or people employ other means of transportation. But the service rendered by a local water company in a populous city is practically indispensable to every inhabitant. There can be no substitute for water, and to escape taking the service is practically impossible; for an alternative means of supply is rarely available. Even the common business incentive of establishing low prices in order to induce an enlarged volume of sales is absent, since the volume of the business done by a water company will not be appreciably affected by a raising or lowering of the rates, except in so far as water in quantity is used for manufacturing purposes. In other words, the commercial limitation upon rates—what the traffic will bear —is to a large extent absent in the case of such a local monopoly. The city water user must submit to such rates as the utility chooses to impose, unless they are curbed by legislative enactment.

"The legal limitations upon rates (so potent in the case of railroads) are, in the main, inoperative in the case of such a water company. Rail rates are sometimes held illegal because the exaction is greater than the value of the service to the shipper. There is in fact no corresponding limitation upon water rates. The charge is so small, as compared with the inconvenience which would be suffered in doing without the service, that the worth to the water taker could rarely be doubted. The prohibition of discrimination against persons, places, or articles of commerce which so frequently interferes to prevent railroads from charging higher rates, although the traffic would easily bear them, affords no protection to city water users, and seldom causes a loss of revenue to the water company. There is in respect to the water rates no prohibition comparable to that embodied in the long and short haul clause, which has an important effect in limiting rail rates. Hence, under the rule of substantive law declared in the *Southwestern Bell Case*, practically the only limitation imposed upon water rates is the denial to the utility of rates which will yield an excessive return upon the actual value of the property. In applying that rule of substantive law, the then actual cost of reproducing the plant would (assuming it to be efficient) commonly be persuasive evidence of its actual value, as the current cost of reproducing the vessel was held to be in *Standard Oil Co.* v. *Southern Pacific Co.*, 268 U. S. 146, 156.

"It is true that, in the *Southwestern Bell Case*, the Court passed also upon a subsidiary question—the weight and effect of the evidence of reconstruction cost. But the question of adjective law arose upon a record very different from that in the case at bar; and the action of the Commission here is entirely consistent with that decision. In the *Southwestern Bell Case* direct testimony as to the then value of the property was introduced. The efficiency of the plant was unquestioned. Witnesses had testified both to the actual cost of constructing identical property at that time, and that the specific property under consideration was worth at least twenty-five percent more than the estimate of the State Commission. The Court believed those witnesses. Concluding that this direct and uncontradicted evidence had been ignored by the State Commission because of error as to the governing rule of substantive law, this Court set aside the rate order as confiscatory, saying: 'We think the proof shows that for the purposes of the present case, the valuation should be at least $25,000,000.' (262 U. S. 276, 288.)

"The action of the Commission in the case at bar was consistent also with *McCardle* v. *Indianapolis Water Co.*, 272 U. S. 400, and *Bluefield Water Works Co.* v. *Public Service Commission*, 262 U. S. 679. Each of these water companies enjoyed a local monopoly of an indispensable service. In order to provide a substitute, the community would have either to take the utility's property by eminent domain; or, if it was free to do so, build a competing plant. There was practically no commercial limitation upon the earning power of these water companies except the extent of the local market, and practically no legal limitation except the requirement that the rates charged should not be so high as to yield an excessive return upon the actual value of the utility's property. The current cost of constructing, then, a plant substantially like the utility's (assuming it to be efficient) would be persuasive evidence of its actual value. For upon that issue, concerning a local water monopoly, the inquiry would naturally be: How much would it cost the community to substitute for the private monopoly a publicly owned plant? But evidence of the cost of reconstructing a railroad built before 1914 might, for the reasons stated above, be no indication whatever of its post-war value for rate-making purposes under §15a. And where, as in the case at bar, the probative force of the evidence may be considered free from any question of confiscation, the rule declared in *Ohio Valley Water Co.* v. *Ben Avon*, 253 U. S. 287, which requires in confiscation cases a judicial determination on the weight of the evidence, does not apply.

"*Ninth.* A further question of construction requires consideration. It is suggested that, even if the Commission is not required to give effect to the higher price level when finding values for rate-making purposes under §15a, it must do so when fixing the amount of the excess income to be recaptured from a particular railroad under paragraphs 6 to 18. The language of the section affords a short answer to that contention. The valuation prescribed in paragraph 4 is declared to be 'for the purposes of this section'—that is, for recapture purposes as well as for rate making. And paragraph 6, which provides for the recapture, declares: 'The value of such railway property shall be determined by the Commission in the manner provided in paragraph 4.'

"The recapture of excess earnings and the establishment of reserves are a part of the process of establishing such rates

'. . . that carriers as a whole (or as a whole in each of such rate groups of territories as the Commission may from time to time designate) will, under honest, efficient and economical management,*** earn an aggregate annual net railway operating income equal, as nearly as may be, to a fair return upon the aggregate value of the railway property of such carriers held for and used in the service of transportation.' (Paragraph 2.)

"The recapture and reserve are the readjustment made necessary—

'inasmuch as it is impossible (without regulation and control in the interest of the commerce of the United States considered as a whole) to establish uniform rates upon competitive traffic which will adequately sustain all the carriers which are engaged in such traffic and which are indispensable to the communities to which they render the service of transportation, without enabling some of such carriers to receive a net railway operating income substantially and unreasonably in excess of a fair return upon the value of their railway property held for and used in the service of transportation, it is hereby declared that any carrier which receives such an income so in excess of a fair return, shall hold such part of the excess, as hereinafter prescribed, as trustee for, and shall pay it to, the United States.' (Paragraph 5.)

"Thus, the direction in the order here challenged to pay or reserve the excess over six percent of the amounts earned from 1920 to 1923 by rates established pursuant to *Ex parte 74, Increased Rates*, 1920, 58 I. C. C. 220, is merely a readjustment of those rates.

[176]

"*Tenth.* The question remains, whether the Commission, in valuing the structural property acquired before June 30, 1914, abused its discretion by declining to give effect to the evidence of enhanced reconstruction cost. The O'Fallon insists that the Commission, in fact, adopted a mathematical formula; that it declined to determine the present value of the carrier's property in accordance with 'the flexible and rational rule of *Smyth* v. *Ames,* under which value is a matter of judgment to be determined by a consideration of all relevant facts and circumstances'; that it erected 'an arbitrary standard of its own based on no relevant facts'; that, if it had given consideration to all relevant facts and circumstances, including as one its cost of reproduction at current prices, 'the value found must have been substantially higher'; and that its primary purpose was to determine the amount of the investment in the carrier's property. In short, the O'Fallon asserts that the Commission refused to find actual value, and, instead, found the prudent investment.

"In support of this assertion, the O'Fallon points to the statement in the report that 'the value of the property of railroads for rate-making purposes*** approaches more nearly the reasonable and necessary investment in property than the cost of reproducing it at a particular time.' (Page 41.) The statement just quoted does not mean that the Commission accepted prudent investment as a measure of value. It means merely that the Commission deemed the estimated original cost a better indication of actual value than the estimated reconstruction cost. While this Court declared in the *Southwestern Bell Case* that prudent investment is not to be taken as the measure of value, it has never held that the prudent investment may not be accepted as evidence of value, or that a finding of value is necessarily erroneous if it happens to be more nearly coincident with what may be supposed to have been the cost of the property than with its estimated reproduction cost.

[177]

The single-sum values found by the Commission do not coincide either with the estimated prudent investment or with the estimated reconstruction cost. They are much nearer the estimated original cost of the property than they are to its estimated reproduction cost. But the values found do not conform to any formula.

"The general method pursued by the Commission in reaching its conclusion closely resembles that approved by the Court in *Georgia Ry. & Power Co.* v. *Railroad Commission,* 262 U. S. 625, 629, 630. It appeared that the O'Fallon Railroad had been constructed long prior to June 30, 1914. The Commission had before it 'the cost of reproduction new of the structural portion of this property estimated on the basis of our 1914 unit prices, coupled with the knowledge that costs of reproduction so arrived at were not greatly different from the original costs.' As bearing upon the value of those parts of the railroad's property which were added or replaced later, the Commission had the actual cost. As bearing upon the then value of the railroad land, it had current values of adjacent lands. It had evidence concerning the railroad and the character and volume of its traffic, the working capital, revenues, and expenses. It had evidence of increased price levels after 1914 and estimates of current reproduction costs during the recapture periods.

"The carrier insisted that physically the property had appreciated more than it had depreciated, and urged the Commission to take as the basic measure of value the 'cost of reproduction new at current prices to the exclusion of everything else, or at least of everything that might tend to a lower value.' (124 I. C. C. 28.) This the Commission declined to do. It gave full effect to increased current market values in determining the value of the land. It gave to the additions and betterments made after June 30, 1914, a value approximating their cost less physical depreciation. But, in respect to structural property and equipment acquired before June 30, 1914, it declined to give weight to the evidence introduced to show current reproduction costs greater than those of 1914. It concluded, despite the estimates of higher reconstruction costs, that, except for the additions, the actual value of this part of the O'Fallon Railroad had not increased; and it found the single-sum value for rate-making purposes in 1920 to be $856,065; in 1921, $875,360; in 1922, $978,874; in 1923, $978,246.

"The Commission recognized, as stated in *Minnesota Rate Cases*, 230 U. S. 352, 434, that the determination of value is 'not a matter of formulas, but there must be a reasonable judgment having its basis in a proper consideration of all relevant facts.' . . . It states that 'it considered and weighed carefully, in the light of its own knowledge and experience, each fact, circumstance and condition called to its attention on behalf of the carrier' as well as the evidence otherwise introduced; and that 'from this accumulation of information we have formed our judgment as to the fair basic single-sum values, not by the use of any formula but after consideration of all relevant facts.' The report makes clear that its finding was the result of an exercise of judgment upon all the evidence; that the Commission accorded to the evidence of reconstruction cost all the probative force to which it deemed that evidence entitled on the issue of actual value; and that it considered, as bearing upon value, not only the probable cost and the estimated reproduction cost, but also 'descriptions of the carrier, of its traffic, of the territory in which it operates, its history, and summaries of the results of its operation.' (Page 25.)

"The difficulties by which the Commission was confronted when requested to apply the evidence of reproduction cost can hardly be exaggerated. In the first place, the evidence was of such character that it did not satisfactorily establish what would have been the current cost of reproduction during the recapture periods. During the years here in question there was practically no construction of new lines. Thus, the current cost of reproduction for those years had to be obtained by using index figures as the basis for a guess as to what it would cost to build then the identical railroad. To give to such figures effect as proving what it would then have cost to reproduce the O'Fallon Railroad, it must be assumed that there had not been introduced since June 30, 1914, new cost-saving methods of construction which would overcome, in whole or in part, the effect of the higher price level upon the cost of reproducing the identical property. This, in view of its experience, the Commission properly declined to do. In the second place, there was a lack of evidence to show to what extent, if any, higher reconstruction cost, in the several recapture periods, implied a value higher than that theretofore prevailing. The Commission believed that it could act only on proof; that it was not required or permitted to base findings on conjecture; and that to assign, under the circumstances, any weight to the evidence of reconstruction cost would be mere conjecture.

"Moreover, the Commission had, through its valuation department, special knowledge of the property of this carrier. It had acquired necessarily in the performance of its many duties the general knowledge, already referred to, concerning the changes in transportation conditions and of the advances in the art; and it knew how great was their effect upon the actual values of railroad property. The value of the O'Fallon Railway not having been finally ascertained under §19a, it was obliged by paragraph 4 to utilize 'the results of its investigation under §19a of this Act in so far as deemed by it available.' The evidence introduced in the recapture proceedings showed, among other things, that of the five locomotives in the O'Fallon's service December 31, 1920, one had been built as early as 1874, and that their average age was 20.8 years; also that the aggregate outlays for additions and betterments in the railroad, less small retirements, had in eleven years been only $98,148.25. The O'Fallon did not introduce any evidence bearing upon functional depreciation of the property. The Commission may reasonably have concluded that, even if there had been introduced persuasive evidence that the cost, during the recapture periods, of reproducing new the identical plant approximated the rise in the general price level, still the actual value of the O'Fallon Railway, as it existed June 30, 1914, had not increased, because the functional depreciation plus the physical depreciation since that date counterbalanced fully what otherwise might have been the higher value of the plant.

"The O'Fallon urged that its large net earnings during the recapture periods and earlier fully established a higher value, independently of the evidence of reproduction cost. This contention ignores the peculiar character of the property. The railroad, which is owned by the Adolphus Busch estate and family and lies wholly in Illinois, operates about nine miles of main line from two coal mines, also owned by the Busch estate and family, to the tracks of the Terminal Company in East St. Louis. There are twelve miles of yardage tracks, located largely at the Busch mines. While the railroad is legally a common carrier, it is actually an industrial railroad. Ninety-nine percent of its revenues are derived directly from the carriage of coal; and, of the remaining one percent, about half appears to come from a payment of $300 a month made by the Busch Coal Company for carrying its miners to and from its mines. Besides the coal from the Busch mines, there is a substantial but diminishing amount carried under a long-time contract from two mines located on an electric road, the East St. Louis & Suburban Railway, which crosses the O'Fallon. This coal it carries from the junction to East St. Louis. . . . Obviously the value of this railroad property is wholly dependent upon the operation of the mines.

"How long the four mines will continue to be operated

was and still is entirely uncertain. Their product is subject to the competition of 221 other bituminous coal mines in Illinois. These, which are all located on other railroads, enjoy low rates to St. Louis. . . . The vicissitudes of coal mining, the diminishing use of coal since the war because of increased fuel efficiency, the competition of oil as fuel, and the growing use of hydro-electric power are matters of common knowledge, as are the diminishing operations during recent years of the Illinois coal mines as compared with the mines in non-union territory. Moreover, the decline in the volume of traffic, the reduction in coal rates made by *Reduced Rates*, 1922, 68 I. C. C. 676, and the growing expenses of the carrier due to increased payroll, were put in evidence by it. In view of these facts, the Commission was clearly justified in refusing to find that the railroad had a higher value than in 1914, although the net earning as reported showed a return for the earlier period averaging 7½ percent upon the amount claimed as reproduction cost.

"This Court has no concern with the correctness of the Commission's reasoning on the evidence in making its findings of fact, since it applied the rules of substantive law prescribed by Congress and reached its findings of actual value by the exercise of its judgment upon all the evidence, including enhanced construction costs. . . . We must bear in mind that here we are not dealing with a question of confiscation; that we are dealing, as was pointed out in *Smyth* v. *Ames*, with a legislative question which can 'be more easily determined by a commission composed of persons whose special skill, observation and experience qualifies them to so handle great problems of transportation as to do justice both to the public and to those whose money has been used to construct and maintain highways for the convenience and benefit of the people.' "

St. Louis & O'Fallon Ry. Co., et al. v. *United States*
279 U. S. 461, 488

[182]

Franchises as Rate Contracts

(Dissenting Opinion, *Railroad Commission* v. *Los Angeles Ry.*, 1929)

A LOS ANGELES STREET RAILWAY COMPANY, OPERATING A SERIES OF lines under city franchises, petitioned the Railroad Commission of the State for an increase in its basic rate of fare. The Commission twice entertained jurisdiction, but the only order it issued was a denial of any increase on the ground that the existing rate was reasonable. Thereupon the company brought suit in a Federal District Court to enjoin the Commission from interfering with its proposed increase on the ground that the existing rates were confiscatory and that their enforcement violated the due process clause of the Fourteenth Amendment.

The city admitted that the rates would be confiscatory if the company were under no contractual duty to maintain them, but argued that the company, in accepting the franchises, contracted to maintain a five-cent fare. The District Court granted the injunction and the city appealed.

Mr. Justice Butler delivered the majority opinion, affirming the decision of the lower court. He held that the company was under no contractual duty to maintain a five-cent fare because the city's charter did not empower it to enter into rate contracts admittedly dependent upon State authorization for their validity. Moreover, even if the contracts were authorized, the city acted only as agent of the State, which had abrogated the contracts when its Commission twice assumed jurisdiction of the company's application.

Holmes, Brandeis, and Stone, JJ., dissented. Brandeis wrote:

T HE Railway claims that the Commission's refusal to authorize a fare higher than five cents confiscates its property. The City and the Commission do not insist here that the five-

[183]

cent fare is compensatory; and they concede that, since 1915, the latter has had jurisdiction to authorize a higher fare. They defend solely on the ground that the Railway bound itself by contracts not to charge more; that these contract provisions are still in force, except as modified by the act of 1915 empowering the Commission to authorize changes in the rate; that an alleged error of the Commission in refusing authority to charge more can be corrected only by proceedings brought in the Supreme Court of the State to compel the Commission to do its duty; and that the lower court's finding that the rate is noncompensatory is therefore immaterial.

"The District Court recognized that such contracts, if existing, would be a complete defense to this suit; expressed a strong doubt whether the city ever had the power to contract concerning the rate of fare, and, declining to pass upon that question, granted the relief prayed for solely on the ground that any such contract right which existed had been abrogated. . . .

"The franchises under which the Railway is operating are confessedly contracts. The words used concerning the rate of fare are apt ones to express contractual obligations. The Railway contends, however, that the fare provisions were not intended to be contracts, and that, if they were so intended, they were not binding, because neither the city nor the county had the power to contract as to the rate of fare. It insists, further, that if the fare provisions were originally binding as contracts, they were abrogated in 1921 or 1928 by action of the Commission.

"*First.* Most of the franchises were granted before the State had vested in the Commission power to regulate street railway rates or had expressly reserved to itself, otherwise, the power to change rates theretofore fixed by ordinance. This power of regulation was first expressly conferred upon the Commission in 1915, by amendments to §§13, 27, and 63 of the Public Utilities Act (Stats. 1915, p. 115) made pursuant to an amendment of §23 of Article XII of the California Constitution adopted November 3, 1914. These enactments did not purport to abrogate any existing contract. Nor did they purport to take from the city or from the county any power theretofore possessed to make a contract concerning the rate of fare. Their effect was merely to make any such contract, whether theretofore or thereafter entered into, subject to change by the Commission. Unless and until so changed, a contractual fare fixed by franchise remains in full force. . . . Consequently, it is not here claimed that these enactments alone abrogated the alleged contracts as to rate of fare.

"*Second*. The Railway contends, however, that the Commission abrogated the fare contracts by its action taken in 1921 pursuant to this legislation. The facts are these. In 1918 the Railway asked the Commission to make an investigation of its service and its financial condition and for an order enabling it to so operate its system that the income would be sufficient to pay the cost of the service. In that application the Railway expressly disclaimed any desire to increase its rate of fare, but about two years later it made a supplemental application for leave to do so. On May 31, 1921, the Commission made a report in which it declared that 'an increase in the fare in some form' should be granted, and that the Railway be authorized 'to file with the Commission and put into effect within thirty (30) days from the date of this order a schedule of rates increasing the present basic five-cent fare to six cents,' ten tickets for 50 cents. The Railway did not file a schedule of fares. Instead, it moved for a rehearing. That motion was promptly set down for hearing by the Commission, but was never heard; for the Railway asked, first, for an adjournment, then that its motion be striken from the calendar, and, finally, that an order be entered setting aside the decision made and dismissing the entire proceeding, including the application for increase of fare.

[185]

"This request of the Railway was granted, the order of dismissal reciting that the authorization to increase the fare had 'been suspended by virtue of the pendency of a petition for rehearing,' as the statutes provided. . . . Obviously this action taken in 1921 cannot be deemed an abrogation or modification of any existing fare provision of the franchises, unless it be held that mere entry by the Commission upon an inquiry as to the rate of fare, as commanded by the statute, has that effect. Reason and authority are to the contrary.

"*Third.* Nor did the action taken by the Commission in 1928, in the proceedings now under review, abrogate any existing fare provision. There also the Commission took jurisdiction, as it was by the statute authorized to do. It refused to authorize a higher fare, because it concluded that for the past five years the Railway had been earning an average annual return of 7.1 percent; that it was not being efficiently operated; that the management had failed to introduce certain economies previously recommended which would have increased its net earnings; and that for these reasons the existing five-cent fare was just and reasonable. The Commission may have erred in its judgment, but it is clear that it did not change the rate of fare. In *Georgia Ry. & Power Co.* v. *Decatur*, 262 U. S. 432, 439, it was held that the assumption of jurisdiction by the Commission to the extent of affirmatively ordering the continuance of existing transfer privileges did not effect an abrogation of an existing contract provision relating thereto, since such action did not conflict with the terms of the contract. . . . In *Denney* v. *Pacific Telephone Co.*, 276 U. S. 97, the Commission had previously granted an increase in fare of which the company had availed itself.

"Assuming that the Railway was bound by contract to maintain a five-cent fare, it could be relieved from its obligation only by the Commission. Had the Commission authorized an increase in fare, it would still be questionable whether the contract would have been thereby abrogated or only modified by making the Railway's obligation less onerous. Surely the Commission's refusal to grant any help, because in its opinion none is needed, cannot have the anomalous effect of entirely relieving the Railway of its obligation.

"*Fourth.* If the District Court erred in holding that the action taken in 1921 or 1928 had the effect of abrogating any existing contract, there must be a determination whether such contracts did exist, in fact and law. It was assumed by the District Court and by counsel in this Court that, if the city lacked the power to bind itself contractually by the fare provisions, the Railway could not be bound thereby. This conclusion is not commanded by logic or by the law of contracts. Lack of power in the municipality to bind itself is a factor to be considered in determining whether the parties intended to enter into a contract. But, if they did, the Railway's promise need not fail for lack of mutuality. The law does not require that a particular contractual obligation must be supported by a corresponding counter obligation. It is conceded that the city possessed the power to enter into the franchise contract. The contention is merely that it could not surrender its power to regulate rates. But there is nothing in the fare provisions to indicate that the city attempted to do that. These provisions in terms bind only the Railway. The Railway unquestionably had power to agree to charge a fixed fare. The grant of the franchise is sufficient consideration, if so intended, for any number of contractual obligations which the Railway may have chosen to assume. In *Southern Iowa Electric Co.* v. *Chariton,* 255 U. S. 539, a case coming from Iowa, it was held, following Iowa decisions, that, since the city lacked power to bind itself, there was no contract. And there is a statement to that effect in *San Antonio* v. *San Antonio Public Service Co.,* 255

U. S. 547, 556. But in *Southern Utilities Co.* v. *Palatka,* 268 U. S. 232, 233, the question was expressly left open. Obviously that is a matter of State law on which the decisions of this Court are not controlling.

"*Fifth.* If it be true that the Railway is not bound by the fare provisions, unless the city had power to bind itself in that respect, it is necessary to determine whether the city had that power and whether the parties did in fact contract as to the rate of fare. Whether the city had the power is, of course, a question of State law. In California, the Constitution and the statutes leave the question in doubt. Counsel agree that there is no decision in any court of the State directly in point. They reason from policy and analogy. In support of their several contentions they cite, in the aggregate, 30 decisions of the California courts, 15 statutes of the State, besides three provisions of its Code and seven provisions of its Constitution. The decisions referred to occupy 308 pages of the official reports; the sections of the Constitution, Code and statutes, 173 pages. Moreover, the 102 franchises here involved were granted at many different times between 1886 and 1927. And during that long period there have been amendments both of relevant statutes and of the Constitution. The city or the county may have had the power to contract as to the rate of fare at one time and not at another. If it is held that the city or the county ever had the power to contract as to rate of fare, it will be necessary to examine the 102 franchises to see whether the power was exercised. It may then be that some of the franchises contain valid fare contracts, while others do not. In that event, the relief to be granted will involve passing also on matters of detail.

"In my opinion, these questions of statutory construction, and all matters of detail, should, in the first instance, be decided by the trial court. To that end, the judgment of the District Court should be vacated and the case remanded for further proceedings, without costs to either party in this Court. Pending the decision of the trial court, an interlocutory injunction should issue. . . . It is a serious task for us to construe and apply the written law of California. . . . To 'one brought up within it, varying emphasis, tacit assumptions, unwritten practices, a thousand influences gained only from life, may give to the different parts wholly new values that logic and grammar never could have gotten from the books.' (*Diaz v. Gonzalez*, 261 U. S. 102, 106.) This Court is not particularly fitted for that work. We may properly postpone the irksome burden of examining the many relevant State statutes and decisions until we shall have had the aid which would be afforded by a thorough consideration of them by the judges of the District Court, who are presumably more familiar with the law of California than we are. The practice is one frequently followed by this Court.

"In the case at bar, there are persuasive reasons for adopting the course suggested. The subject-matter of this litigation is local to California. The parties are all citizens of that State and creatures of its Legislature. Since the Railway denies that there ever was a valid contract governing the rate and asserts that, if any such existed they have been abrogated, the contract clause of the Federal Constitution is not involved. The alleged existence of contracts concerning the rate of fare presents the fundamental issue of the case. Whether such contracts exist, or ever existed, depends wholly upon the construction to be given to laws of the State. Upon these questions, the decision of the Supreme Court of California would presumably have been accepted by this Court, if the case had come here on appeal from it. . . .

"The constitutional claim of confiscation gave jurisdiction to the District Court. We may be required, therefore, to pass, at some time, upon these questions of State law. And we may do so now. But the special province of this Court is the Federal law. The construction and application of the Constitution of the United States and of the legislation of Congress is its most important function. In order to give adequate consideration to the adjudication of great issues of government, it must, so far as possible, lessen the burden incident to the disposition of cases which come here for review."

Railroad Commission of California, et al.
v. Los Angeles Railway Corporation
280 U. S. 145, 158

How to Ascertain Depreciation

(Dissenting Opinion, *United Rys.* v. *West*, 1930)

A BALTIMORE STREET RAILWAY COMPANY CLAIMED THAT A RATE OF fare, set to yield a return of 6.26 percent on the valuation of its property, was confiscatory, and so conflicted with the due process clause. On appeal from the Maryland Court of Appeals, the Supreme Court held that the company should be allowed to charge the rates for which it had applied, which were calculated to produce a return of 7.44 percent. In the light of conditions shown to exist, Mr. Justice Sutherland said, no lower rate of return would permit the company to pay reasonable dividends and have the balance for its surplus account which is required by sound business management.

In ascertaining the company's net return, one item which is subtracted from its gross income is an annual allowance for the depreciation of its physical property. The State courts had held that the basis on which this allowance is calculated should be the present value of the company's depreciable property, and not its cost. This, the Court found, was "plainly right". "It is the settled rule of this Court that the rate base is present value, and it would be wholly illogical to adopt a different rule for depreciation."

Holmes, Brandeis, and Stone, JJ., again dissented. Brandeis wrote:

"ACTING under the direction of the Court of Appeals (*Public Service Commission* v. *United Railways & Electric Co.*, 155 Md. 572) the Commission entered, on November 28, 1928, an order permitting the Railways to increase its rate of fare to ten cents cash, four tokens for thirty-five cents. That order was sustained in *United Railways & Electric Co.*, v. *West*, 157

[191]

Md. 70, and the Railways has appealed to this Court. The claim is that the order confiscates its property because the fare fixed will yield, according to the estimates, no more than 6.26 percent upon the assumed value. There are several reasons why I think the order should be held valid.

"A net return of 6.26 percent upon the present value of the property of a street railway enjoying a monopoly in one of the oldest, largest, and richest cities on the Atlantic Seaboard would seem to be compensatory. Moreover, the estimated return is in fact much larger, if the rules which I deem applicable are followed. It is 6.70 percent if, in valuing the rate base, the prevailing rule which eliminates franchises from a rate base is applied. And it is 7.78 percent if also, in lieu of the deduction for depreciation ordered by the Court of Appeals, the amount is fixed, either by the method of an annual depreciation charge computed according to the rules commonly applied in business, or by some alternative method, at the sum which the long experience of this railway proves to have been adequate for it.

"*First.* The value of the plant adopted by the Commission as the rate base was fixed by it at $75,000,000 in a separate valuation case, decided on March 9, 1926, modified, pursuant to directions of the Court of Appeals, on February 1, 1928, and not before us for review. . . . Included in this total is $5,000,000 representing the value placed upon the Railways' so-called 'easements.' If they are excluded, the estimated yield found by the Commission would be increased by .44 percent; that is, the net earnings, estimated at $4,691,606 would yield, on a $70,000,000 rate base, 6.70 percent. The people's counsel contended that, since these 'easements' are merely the privileges gratuitously granted to the Railways by various county and municipal franchises to lay tracks and operate street cars on the public highways, they should be excluded from the rate base when considering whether the order is confiscatory in violation of the Federal Constitution. This alleged error of

Federal law in the valuation may be considered on this appeal; for the rate allowed by the Commission is attacked on the assumption that the return on the property is only 6.26 percent. . . .

"Where a rate order is alleged to be void under the Federal Constitution because confiscatory, the question whether a specific class of property should be included in the rate base is to be determined not by the State law, but by the Federal law. Whether the return is sufficient under the State law is a question which does not concern us. We are concerned solely with the adequacy or inadequacy of the return under the guaranties of the Federal law. In determining whether a prescribed rate is confiscatory under the Federal Constitution, franchises are not to be included in valuing the plant, except for such amounts as were actually paid to the State, or a political subdivision thereof, as consideration for the grant. . . . Franchises to lay pipes or tracks in the public streets, like franchises to conduct the business as a corporation, are not donations to a utility of property by the use of which profit may be made. They are privileges granted to utilities to enable them to employ their property in the public service and make profit out of such use of that property. As stated in the New Hampshire statute, 'all such franchises, rights and privileges being granted in the public interest only' are 'not justly subject to capitalization against the public.'

"Had the 'easements' been called franchises, it is probable that no value would have been ascribed to them for rate-making purposes. For the Maryland Public Utilities Law, in common with the statutes of many States, forbids the capitalization of franchises. But calling these privileges 'easements' does not differentiate them for rate purposes from ordinary corporate franchises, when applying the Federal Constitution. In none of the cases excluding franchises from plant value was any distinction made, in this respect, between ordinary corporate franchises and franchises to use the public streets, although many of the cases involved privileges of the latter type. The Court of Appeals and the Commission were influenced by the fact that the so-called 'easements' were taxed. This fact does not justify including them in the rate base. Corporate franchises are frequently taxed, and, although taxed, are not valued for rate purposes. . . . The 'easements' differ from ordinary franchises only in the technicality that, under the law of Maryland, the right to use the streets is, for taxation purposes, real property, whereas ordinary franchises are personal property.

"*Second.* The amount which the Commission fixed, in its original report, as the appropriate depreciation charge was $883,544. That sum is five percent of the estimated gross revenues. Referring to the method of arriving at the amount of the charge the Commission there said:

'The Commission believes that it might be more logical to base the annual allowance for depreciation upon the cost of depreciable property, rather than upon gross revenues. The relation between gross revenues and depreciation is remote and indirect while there is a direct relation between the cost of a piece of property and the amount that ought to be set aside for its consumption by use. However, the allowance which this Commission has made for depreciation, five percent of the gross revenues, has provided fairly well for current depreciation and retirements.*** Moreover, there is a broad twilight zone between depreciation and maintenance, and it may well be (and without any impropriety) that the maintenance account has been used to a certain extent to provide for depreciation.*** Any increase in the gross revenues resulting from an increase in fares would increase the amounts that would be set aside for depreciation and maintenance.'

Without deciding that this allowance was inadequate, the Court of Appeals held that, as a matter of law, the depreciation charge should be based upon the then value of the depreciable property as distinguished from its cost; and directed the Commission to revise its estimates accordingly. Pursuant to that direction, the Commission added, in its supplemental report, $755,116 to the depreciation charge. The addition was, I think, ordered by the Court of Appeals under a misapprehension of the nature and function of the depreciation charge. And, in considering the adequacy of the return under the Federal Constitution, the estimate of the net earnings should accordingly be increased by $755,116, which, on the rate base of $70,000,000, would add 1.08 percent to the estimated return.

"That the Court of Appeals erred in its decision becomes clear when the nature and purpose of the depreciation charge are analyzed and the methods of determining its proper amount are considered. The annual account of a street railway, or other business, is designed to show the profit or loss, and to acquaint those interested with the condition of the business. To be true, the account must reflect all the operating expenses incurred within the accounting period. One of these is the wearing out of the plant. Minor parts, which have short lives and are consumed wholly within the year, are replaced as a part of current repairs. Larger plant units, unlike supplies, do not wear out within a single accounting period. They have varying service lives, some remaining useful for many years. Experience teaches that at the end of some period of time most of these units, too, will wear out physically or cease to be useful in the service. If the initial outlay for such units is entirely disregarded, the annual account will not reflect the true results of operation and the initial investment may be lost. If, on the other hand, this original expense is treated as part of the operating expenses of the year in which the plant unit was purchased, or was retired or replaced, the account again will not reflect the true results of operation. For operations in one year will then be burdened with an expense which is properly chargeable against a much longer period of use. Therefore, in ascertaining the profits of a year, it is generally deemed necessary to apportion to the operations of that year a part of the total expense incident to the wearing out of plant. This apportionment is commonly made by means of a depreciation charge.

"It is urged by the Railways that if the base used in determining what is a fair return on the use of its property is the present value, then logically the base to be used in determining the depreciation charge—a charge for the consumption of plant in service—must also be the present value of the property consumed. Much that I said about valuation in *Southwestern Bell Tel. Co.* v. *Pub. Serv. Comm.* [See page 135] and the *St. Louis & O'Fallon Ry. Co.* v. *United States* [See page 149] applies to the depreciation charge. But acceptance of the doctrine of *Smyth* v. *Ames* does not require that the depreciation charge be based on present value of plant; for an annual depreciation charge is not a measure of the actual consumption of plant during the year. No such measure has yet been invented. There is no regularity in the development of depreciation. It does not proceed in accordance with any mathematical law. There is nothing in business experience or in the training of experts, which enables man to say to what extent service life will be impaired by the operations of a single year, or of a series of years less than the service life.

"Where a plant intended, like a street railway, for continuing operation is maintained at a constant level of efficiency, it is rarely possible to determine definitely whether or not its service life has in fact lessened within a particular year. The life expectancy of a plant, like that of an individual, may be in fact greater, because of unusual repairs or other causes, at

[196]

the end of a particular year than it was at the beginning. And even where it is known that there has been some lessening of service life within the year it is never possible to determine with accuracy what percentage of the unit's service life has, in fact, been so consumed. Nor is it essential to the aim of the charge that this fact should be known. The main purpose of the charge is that irrespective of the rate of depreciation there shall be produced, through annual contributions, by the end of the service life of the depreciable plant, an amount equal to the total net expense of its retirement. To that end it is necessary only that some reasonable plan of distribution be adopted. Since it is impossible to ascertain what percentage of the service life is consumed in any year, it is either assumed that depreciation proceeds at some average rate (thus accepting the approximation to fact customarily obtained through the process of averaging) or the annual charge is fixed without any regard to the rate of depreciation.

"The depreciation charge is an allowance made pursuant to a plan of distribution of the total net expense of plant retirement. It is a bookkeeping device introduced in the exercise of practical judgment to serve three purposes. It preserves the integrity of the investment. . . . It serves to distribute equitably throughout the several years of service life the only expense of plant retirement which is capable of reasonable ascertainment—the known cost less the estimated salvage value. And it enables those interested, through applying that plan of distribution, to ascertain, as nearly as is possible, the actual financial results of the year's operation. Many methods of calculating the amount of the allowance are used. The charges to operating expenses in the several years and in the aggregate vary according to the method adopted. But under none of these methods of fixing the depreciation charge is an attempt made to determine the percentage of actual consumption of plant falling within a particular

[197]

year or within any period of years less than the service life.

"*Third.* The business device known as the depreciation charge appears not to have been widely adopted in America until after the beginning of this century. Its use is still stoutly resisted by many concerns. Wherever adopted, the depreciation charge is based on the original cost of the plant to the owner. When the great changes in price levels incident to the World War led some to question the wisdom of the practice of basing the charge on original cost, the Chamber of Commerce of the United States warned business men against the fallacy of departing from the accepted basis. And that warning has been recently repeated. [Justice Brandeis quotes from Pamphlet No. 512 (May, 1929) of the Chamber of Commerce of the United States to the effect that consumers should pay for expired, not anticipated, costs. *'Charge depreciation upon actual cost less any salvage.'*]

"Such is today, and ever has been, the practice of public accountants. Their statements are prepared in accordance with principles of accounting which are well established, generally accepted, and uniformly applied. By those accustomed to read the language of accounting a depreciation charge is understood as meaning the appropriate contribution for that year to the amount required to make good the cost of the plant which ultimately must be retired. On that basis, public accountants certify to investors and bankers the results of operation, whether of public utilities or of manufacturing or mercantile concerns. Corporate securities are issued, bought, and sold, and vast loans are made daily, in reliance upon statements so prepared. The compelling logic of facts which led business men to introduce a depreciation charge has led them to continue to base it on the original cost of the plant despite the great changes in the price level incident to the World War. Basing the depreciation charge on cost is a rule prescribed or recommended by those associations of business men who have had occasion since the World War to consider the subject.

"Business men naturally took the plant at cost, as that is how they treat other articles consumed in operation. The plant, undepreciated, is commonly carried on the books at cost; and it is required at cost. The net profit or loss of a business transaction is commonly ascertained by deducting from the gross receipts the expenditures incurred in producing them. Business men realized fully that the requirements for replacement might be more or less than the original cost. But they realized also that to attempt to make the depreciation account reflect economic conditions and changes would entail entry upon new fields of conjecture and prophecy which would defeat its purposes. For there is no basis in experience which can justify predicting whether replacement, removal or substitution falling in some future year will cost more or less than it would at present, or more or less than the unit cost when it was acquired.

"The business men's practice of using a depreciation charge based on the original cost of the plant in determining the profits or losses of a particular year has abundant official sanction and encouragement. The practice was prescribed by the Interstate Commerce Commission in 1907, when, in cooperation with the Association of American Railway Accounting Officers, it drafted the rule, which is still in force, requiring steam railroads to make an annual depreciation charge on equipment. It has been consistently applied by the Federal Government in assessing taxes on net income and corporate profits, and by the tax officials of the several States for determining the net profits or income of individuals and corporations. Since 1911 it has been applied by the United States Bureau of Census. Since 1915 it has been recommended by the Department of Agriculture. Since 1917, by the Bureau of Mines. In 1916 it was adopted by the Federal Trade Commission in recommendations concerning depreciation issued to manufacturers. In 1917 it was prescribed by the United States Fuel Administration and by the War Ordnance Department. In 1918, by the Air Craft Production Board. In 1921 it was prescribed by the Federal Power Commission; and it is continued in the revised rules of 1928. In 1923 it was adopted by the depreciation section of the Interstate Commerce Commission in the report of tentative conclusions concerning depreciation charges submitted to the steam railroads, telephone companies, and carriers by water, pursuant to paragraph 5 of §20 of the Interstate Commerce Act, as amended by Transportation Act 1920. On November 2, 1926, it was prescribed by the Commission in *Telephone and Railroad Depreciation Charges*, 118 I. C. C. 295. A depreciation charge based on original cost has been uniformly applied by the public utility commissions of the several States when determining net income, past or expected, for rate-making purposes.

"*Fourth.* In 1927 the business men's practice of basing the depreciation charge on cost was applied by this Court in *United States v. Ludey,* 274 U. S. 295, 300, 301, a Federal income tax case, saying: 'The amount of the allowance for depreciation is the sum which should be set aside for the taxable year, in order that, at the end of the useful life of the plant in the business, the aggregate of the sums set aside will (with salvage value) suffice to provide an amount equal to the original cost'. [The decision in *United States* v. *Ludey* was rendered by Justice Brandeis.] (The Railways must hereafter assume the anomalous position of classing the additional $755,116 as an operating expense in its report to the Commission, and as part of its net income in its income tax returns.)

"I know of nothing in the Federal Constitution, or in the decisions of this Court, which should lead us to reject in determining net profits, the rule sanctioned by the universal practice of business men and governmental departments. For, whether the expense in plant consumption can be more nearly approximated by using a depreciation charge based on original cost or by one based upon fluctuating present values is a problem to be solved, not by legal reasoning, but by the exercise of practical judgment based on facts and business experience. The practice of using an annual depreciation charge based on original cost when determining for purposes of investment, taxation, or regulation, the net profits of a business or the return upon property was not adopted in ignorance of the rule of *Smyth* v. *Ames*. That decision, rendered in 1898, antedates the general employment of public accountants, and also antedates the general introduction here of the practice of making a depreciation charge. The decision of the Court of Appeals of Maryland here under review, as well as *State ex rel. Hopkins* v. *Southwestern Bell Telephone Co.*, 115 Kan. 236, and *Michigan Public Utilities Commission* v. *Michigan State Telephone Co.*, 228 Mich. 658, were all decided after this Court reaffirmed the rule of *Smyth* v. *Ames* in *Southwestern Bell Telephone Co.* v. *Public Service Commission* [See page 135.] But since this decision, as before, the Bell Telephone Companies have persisted in basing their depreciation charges upon the original cost of the depreciable property. . . . And they have insisted that the order of the Interstate Commerce Commission requiring a depreciation charge, 118 I. C. C. 295, should be so framed as to permit the continuance of that accounting practice. The protest of the railroads, in that proceeding, against basing the charge on cost was made for the first time in 1927, in their petitions for a rehearing. And this protest came only from those who insist that no depreciation charge whatsoever shall be made.

"To use a depreciation charge as the measure of the year's consumption of plant, and at the same time reject original cost as the basis of the charge, is inadmissible. It is a perversion of this business device. No method for the ascertainment of the amount of the charge yet invented is workable if fluctuating present values be taken as the basis. Every known method contemplates, and is dependent upon, the accumulation or credit of a fixed amount in a given number of years. The distribution of plant expense expressed in the depreciation charge is justified by the approximation to the fact as to the year's plant consumption which is obtained by applying the doctrine of averages. But if fluctuating present values are substituted for original cost there is no stable base to which the process of averaging can be applied. For thereby the only stable factor involved in fixing a depreciation charge would be eliminated. Each year the present value may be different. The cost of replacement at the termination of the service life of the several units or of the composite life cannot be foretold. To use as a measure of the year's consumption of plant a depreciation charge based on fluctuating present values substitutes conjecture for experience. Such a system would require the consumer of today to pay for an assumed operating expense which has never been incurred and which may never arise.

"The depreciation charge is frequently likened to the annual premium in legal reserve life insurance. The life insurance premium is calculated on an agreed value of the human life—comparable to the known cost of plant—not on a fluctuating value, unknown and unknowable. The field of life insurance presented a problem comparable to that here involved. Despite the large experience embodied in the standard mortality tables and the relative simplicity of the problem there presented, the actual mortality was found to vary so widely from that for which the premiums had provided, that their rate was found to work serious injustice either to the insurer or to the insured. The transaction resulted sometimes in bankruptcy of the insurer; sometimes in his securing profits which were extortionate; and rarely, in his receiving only the intended fair compensation for the service rendered. Because every attempt to approximate more nearly the amount of premium required proved futile, justice was sought and found in the system of strictly mutual insurance. Under that system the premium charged is made clearly ample; and the part which proves not to have been needed enures in some sort of benefit to him who paid it.

"Similarly, if, instead of applying the rule of *Smyth* v. *Ames*, the rate base of a utility were fixed at the amount prudently invested, the inevitable errors incident to estimated service life and net expense in plant consumption could never result in injustice either to the utility or to the community. For, if the amount set aside for depreciation proved inadequate and investment of new capital became necessary, the utility would be permitted to earn a return on the new capital. And if the amount set aside for depreciation proved to be excessive, the income from the surplus reserve would operate as a credit to reduce the capital charge which the rates must earn. If the Railways should ever suffer injustice from adopting cost of plant as the basis for calculating the depreciation charge, it will be an unavoidable incident of applying in valuation the rule of *Smyth* v. *Ames*. This risk, if it exists, cannot be escaped by basing the charge on present value. For this suggested escape, besides being entirely conjectural, is instinct with certainty of injustice either to the community or the Railways. The possibility of such injustice admonishes us, as it did in deciding the constitutional questions concerning interstate commerce, that rate regulation is an intensely practical matter. . . .

"*Fifth*. Public officials, investors, and most large businesses are convinced of the practical value of the depreciation charge as a guide to knowledge of the results of operation. Many States require public utilities to make such a charge. But most railroads, some gas and electric companies, and some other concerns deny the propriety of making any annual depreciation charge. They insist that the making of such a charge will serve rather to mislead than to aid in determining the financial result

[203]

of the year's operations. They urge that the current cost of maintaining the plant, whether by repair, renewals, or replacements, should be treated as a part of the maintenance account, at least in systems consisting of large and diversified properties intended for continuous operation and requiring a constant level of efficiency. They insist that, in such systems, retirements, replacements, and renewals attain a uniform rate and tend to be equal each year; that, therefore, no great disproportion in revenues and operating expenses in the various years results if the whole expenditure made for renewals or replacements in any year is treated as an expense of operation of that year and the retirements of property are not otherwise reflected in any specific charge. They admit that it may be desirable to create a special reserve, to enable the company to spread the cost of retiring certain large units of property over a series of years, thus preventing a disproportionate burden upon the operations of a single year. But they say that such a reserve is not properly called a depreciation reserve. Moreover they contend that when a large unit is retired, not because it has been worn out but because some more efficient substitute has been found, the cost of retirement should be spread over the future, so that it may fall upon those who will gain the benefit of the enhanced efficiency. . . . Under the replacement method of accounting advocated by the railroads and others there is no depreciation charge and no depreciation reserve. Operating expenses are charged directly with replacements at their cost. This method does not concern itself with all retirements, but only with retirements which are replaced.

"Despite the seemingly unanswerable logic of a depreciation charge, they oppose its adoption, urging the uncertainties inherent in the predetermination of service life and of salvage value, and the disagreement among experts as to the most equitable plan of distributing the total net plant expense among the several years of service. They point out that each step in the process of fixing a depreciation charge is beset with difficulties, because of the variables which attend every determination involved. The first step is to estimate how long the depreciable plant will remain in service. Engineers calculate with certitude its composite service life by applying weighted averages to the data concerning the several property units. But their exactitude is delusive. Each unit has its individual life dependent upon the effect of physical exhaustion, obsolescence, inadequacy, and public requirement. The physical duration of the life depends largely upon the conditions of the use; and these cannot be foretold. The process of obsolescence is even less predictable. Advances in the arts are constantly being made which would require retirement at some time, even if the unit were endowed with perpetual physical life. But these advances do not proceed at a uniform pace. The normal progress of invention is stimulated or retarded by the ever changing conditions of business. Moreover, it is the practical embodiment of inventions which produces obsolescence; and business conditions determine even more largely the time and the extent to which new inventions are embodied in improved machines. The march toward inadequacy, as distinguished from obsolescence, is likewise erratic.

"The protestants point out that uncertainty is incident also to the second step in the process of fixing the appropriate depreciation charge. A plant unit rarely remains in service until consumed physically. Scrap remains; and this must be accounted for, since it is the net expense of the exhaustion of plant which the depreciation charge is to cover. Such scrap value is often a very large factor in the calculation of plant expense. The probable salvage on the unit when retired at the end of its service life must, therefore, be estimated. But its future value is never knowable.

"And, finally, the protestants show that after the net expense in plant consumption is thus estimated, there remains the task of distributing it equitably over the assumed service life—the allocation of the amount as charges of the several years. There are many recognized methods for calculating these amounts, each method having strenuous advocates; and the amounts thus to be charged, in the aggregate as well as in the successive years, differ widely according to the method adopted. Under the straight line method, the aggregate of the charges of the several years equals the net plant expense for the whole period of service life; and the charge is the same for all the years. Under the sinking fund method, the aggregate of the charges of the several years is less than the net plant expense for the whole period; because the proceeds of each year's charge are deemed to have been continuously invested at compound interest and the balance is assumed to be obtained from interest accumulations. Other methods of distributing the total charge produce still other results in the amount of the charges laid upon the operating expense of the several years of service.

"We have no occasion to decide whether the view taken by the Interstate Commerce Commission in *Telephone and Railroad Depreciation Charges*, 118 I. C. C. 295, or the protest of the railroads, gas, and electric companies should prevail. For in neither event was the Court of Appeals justified in directing an increase in the allowance. The adequacy of a depreciation charge is dependent in large measure upon the practice of the individual concern with respect to its maintenance account. The Commission found that the Railways' property was well maintained and that the allowance of $883,544, together with the usual maintenance charges, would be adequate to keep the property at a constant level of efficiency. It found further, on the basis of the Company's experience, that the charges previously allowed had served 'fairly well' to take care of current depreciation and retirements. The depreciation charge was established by the Railways in 1912 and was fixed by it, of its own motion, at five percent of the gross revenues. The charge at that rate had been continued ever since and had yielded each year an increasing sum. For the gross revenues had grown steadily. In the early years they grew through increase of the number of passengers carried; since 1919, through the repeated increases in the rate of fare. In nearly every year the allowance had exceeded the charges for retirements. After charging retirements, whether placed or not, to the reserve, there remained a credit, on August 31, 1927, of $1,413,793. The allowance of $883,544 is equal to five percent of the estimated gross revenues for 1928. The increase of this allowance for 1928 over that for 1914 was greater proportionately than the increase of the 1928 value of the Railways' property over its 1914 value.

"The estimated charge of $883,544 was thus clearly ample as the year's share of the expense of plant retirement based on cost. But even if the annual depreciation allowance could be made to correspond with the actual consumption of plant, there was nothing in the record to show that the value of the part of plant to be consumed in 1928 would exceed that amount. Nor is there anything in the record or in the findings to show that $883,544, together with the usual maintenance charges and under the improved methods of construction, would be inadequate to provide, at the prices then prevailing, for the replacement required in that year, and also for the year's contribution to a special reserve under the plan advocated by the railroads before the Interstate Commerce Commission. On the contrary, the company's history and the present advances in the street railway industry strongly indicate that, by employing new equipment of lesser value, the Railways could render more efficient service at smaller operating costs. Neither the trial court nor the Court of Appeals made any finding on these matters. The Commission's finding that $883,-544 was an adequate depreciation charge should, therefore, have been accepted by the Court of Appeals, whether the sum allowed be deemed a depreciation charge properly so called, or be treated as the year's contribution to a special reserve to supplement the usual maintenance charges.

"It is clear that the management of the Railways deemed the charge of five percent of gross revenues adequate. On that assumption it paid dividends on the common stock in each year from 1923 through 1927. If the addition to the depreciation charge ordered by the Court of Appeals was proper for the year 1928, it should have also been made in the preceding five years. (The value of the depreciable property in each of the five years preceding 1928 was almost constant and at least equal to that in 1928.) Upon such a recasting of the accounts, no profits were earned after 1924; and there was no surplus fund from which dividends could have been paid legally. If the contention now urged by the Railways is sound, the management misrepresented by its published accounts its financial condition and the results of operation of the several years; and it paid dividends in violation of law."

United Railways & Electric Co. of Baltimore
v. West, et al. Public Service Commission of Maryland
280 U. S. 234, 255

IV. Guaranties of Freedom

Limitations on Free Speech

(Dissenting Opinion, *Schaefer* v. *United States*, 1920)

UNDER THE ESPIONAGE ACT OF 1917 PUBLICATION OF FALSE REPORTS with intent to promote the success of the nation's enemies was punishable by imprisonment. Sentences were imposed on Schaefer (president), Vogel (treasurer), Werner (chief editor), Darkow (managing editor), and Lemke (business manager) of the Philadelphia *Tageblatt* for publishing such reports and conspiring to do so.

While reversing the judgment against Schaefer and Vogel, the Court affirmed it as to the others. The majority opinion of Mr. Justice McKenna referred to Espionage Act decisions where free speech was held to be not an absolute right. Here was "a curious spectacle" of people invoking the protection of the Constitution "to justify the activities of anarchy or of the enemies of the United States," Justice McKenna wrote. The falsifications consisted of changes in accounts clipped from other papers, made to depress patriotic ardor. He upheld the charge given in the trial court that the jurors could rely on their fund of general information in passing on the question of falsity.

To Mr. Justice Clarke, dissenting, this was simply a case of flagrant mistrial. He felt that errors were committed under the strained feeling of war-time and should be corrected at a new and calmer trial. He did not think that peril to the freedom of expression was involved. Mr. Justice Holmes joined in Brandeis' dissent:

WITH the opinion and decision of this Court reversing the judgment against Schaefer and Vogel on the ground that there was no evidence legally connecting them with the publication I concur fully. But I am of opinion that the judgments against

[211]

the other three defendants should also be reversed, because either the demurrers to the several counts should have been sustained or a verdict should have been directed for each defendant on all of the counts.

"The extent to which Congress may, under the Constitution, interfere with free speech, was in *Schenck* v. *United States,* 249 U. S. 47,* declared by a unanimous Court to be this:

> 'The question in every case is whether the words***
> are used in such circumstances and are of such a nature
> as to create a clear and present danger that they will
> bring about the substantive evils that Congress has a
> right to prevent. It is a question of proximity and
> degree.'

"This is a rule of reason. Correctly applied, it will preserve the right of free speech both from suppression by tyrannous, well-meaning majorities, and from abuse by irresponsible, fanatical minorities. Like many other rules for human conduct, it can be applied correctly only by the exercise of good judgment; and to the exercise of good judgment calmness is, in times of deep feeling and on subjects which excite passion, as essential as fearlessness and honesty. The question whether in a particular instance the words spoken or written fall within the permissible curtailment of free speech is, under the rule enunciated by this Court, one of degree; and because it is a question of degree the field in which the jury may exercise its judgment is necessarily a wide one. But its field is not unlimited. The trial provided for is one by judge *and* jury, and the judge may not abdicate his function. If the words were of such a nature and were used under such circumstances that men, judging in calmness, could not reasonably say that they created a clear and present danger that they would bring about the evil which Congress sought and had a right to prevent,

* Included in *The Dissenting Opinions of Mr. Justice Holmes,* p. 231.

then it is the duty of the trial judge to withdraw the case from the consideration of the jury; and, if he fails to do so, it is the duty of the appellate court to correct the error. In my opinion, no jury acting in calmness could reasonably say that any of the publications set forth in the indictment was of such a character or was made under such circumstances as to create a clear and present danger, either that they would obstruct recruiting or that they would promote the success of the enemies of the United States. That they could have interfered with the military or naval forces of the United States or have caused insubordination, disloyalty, mutiny, or refusal of duty in its military or naval services was not even suggested; and there was no evidence of conspiracy, except the cooperation of editors and business manager in issuing the publications complained of.

"The nature and possible effect of a writing cannot be properly determined by culling here and there a sentence and presenting it separated from the context. In making such determination, it should be read as a whole; at least, if it is short like these news items and editorials. Sometimes it is necessary to consider, in connection with it, other evidence which may enlarge or otherwise control its meaning, or which may show that it was circulated under circumstances which gave it a peculiar significance or effect. But no such evidence was introduced by the Government. The writings here in question must speak for themselves. Fifteen publications were set forth in the indictment; and others were introduced in evidence. To reproduce all of them would unduly prolong this opinion. Four are selected which will illustrate the several contentions of the Government. That at least three of these four were deemed by it of special importance is shown by the fact that each of the three was made the subject of a separate count.

"*First.* There were convictions on three counts of willfully obstructing the recruiting and enlistment service. The conviction of the news editor for so obstructing rested wholly upon

[213]

his having inserted the following reprint from a Berlin paper in the *Tageblatt*. [A news item entitled "Yankee Bluff" is quoted.]

"It is not apparent on a reading of this article—which is not unlike many reprints from the press of Germany to which our patriotic societies gave circulation in order to arouse the American fighting spirit—how it could rationally be held to tend even remotely or indirectly to obstruct recruiting. But as this Court has declared and as Professor Chafee has shown in his "Freedom of Speech in War Time," 32 *Harvard Law Review*, 932, 963, the test to be applied—as in the case of criminal attempts and incitement—is not the remote or possible effect. There must be the clear and present danger. Certainly men, judging in calmness and with this test presented to them, could not reasonably have said that this coarse and heavy humor immediately threatened the success of recruiting. . . .

"*Second.* There were convictions on three counts of willfully conveying false reports and statements with intent to promote the success of the enemies of the United States. The *Tageblatt*, like many of the smaller newspapers, was without a foreign or a national news service of any kind, and did not purport to have any. It took such news usually from items appearing in some other paper theretofore published in the German or the English language. It did not in any way indicate the source of its news. The item, if taken from the English press, was of course translated. Sometimes it was copied in full, sometimes in part only, and sometimes it was rewritten, or editorial comment was added. The Government did not attempt to prove that any statement made in any of the news items published in the *Tageblatt* was false in fact. Its evidence, under each count, was limited to showing that the item as published therein varied in some particular from the item as it appeared in the paper from which it had been copied; and no attempt was made to prove the original dispatch to

[214]

the latter paper. The Government contended that solely because of variation from the item copied it was a false report, although the item in the *Tageblatt* did not purport to reproduce an item from another paper, and in no way indicated the source of the news. Each of the three items following illustrates a different method by which the variation was effected:

"1. The publication for which the news editor was convicted on the fifth count by reason of an addition to the item copied. [A reproduction of the item as it was printed in German is given alongside the Government's translation.] The falsification charged is said to consist in having added to the dispatch which was copied from the *Staatszeitung* the words:

'In initiated circles it is said that under no conditions can the new American proposal be accepted, and that the foodstuffs may rot before the ships will be unloaded.'

"But it is obvious, upon comparing the English translation with the German original, that the defendant did no such thing. What occurred was this: The sentence referred to was not made a part of the dispatch in the *Tageblatt*. It followed the dispatch; it was not within the quotation marks, and was separated from it by a dash—a usual method of indicating that what follows is comment or an addition made by the editor. In the English translation, as set forth in the indictment, this sentence, through some inadvertence of the Government's translator or draftsman, was included as part of the dispatch and brought with the quotation therein. Evidently both the jury and the trial judge failed to examine the German original.

"2. One of the publications for which the news editor was convicted on the first count because of an omission from the item copied. [A news item with a St. Petersburg date-line is quoted.] The falsification here is said to consist in the omission from the end of the first paragraph of the following sentence which appeared in the paper from which the item was taken:

'From this it can be concluded that the fall of Riga has united the opposing political factions in Russia.'

"3. The publication for which the news editor was convicted on the sixth count, because of the change of a word in the item copied. [The opinion contains a long dispatch from Washington purporting to quote a speech by Senator LaFollette on increased taxation of war profits.] Falsification is charged solely because the word 'Brot-riots' (translated as 'bread-riots') was used in the eleventh line of the article, instead of the word 'Brodreihen' (translated as 'bread-lines').

"The Act punishes the willful making and conveying of 'false reports and false statements with intent to interfere with the operation or success of the military or naval forces of the United States or to promote the success of its enemies.' Congress sought thereby to protect the American people from being willfully misled to the detriment of their cause by one actuated by the intention to further the cause of the enemy. Willfully untrue statements which might mislead the people as to the financial condition of the Government and thereby embarrass it; as to the inadequacy of the preparations for war or the support of the forces; as to the sufficiency of the food supply; or willfully untrue statements or reports of military operations which might mislead public opinion as to the competency of the army and navy or its leader (see "The Relation Between the Army and the Press in War Time," War College Publication, 1916); or willfully untrue statements or reports which might mislead officials in the execution of the law, or military authorities in the disposition of the forces—such is the kind of false statement, and the only kind, which, under any rational construction, is made criminal by the Act. Could the military and naval forces of the United States conceivably have been interfered with, or the success of the enemy conceivably have been promoted by, any of the three publications set forth above? Surely, neither the addition to the first nor the omission from the second constituted the making of a false statement or report. The mistranslation of 'breadlines' in one passage of the third, if it can be deemed a false report, obviously could not have promoted the success of our enemies. The other publications set out in the indictment were likewise impotent to produce the evil against which the statute aimed.

"Darkow, the news editor, and Werner, the editor, were each sentenced to five years in the penitentiary; Lemke, the business manager, to two years. The jury which found men guilty for publishing news items or editorials like those here in question must have supposed it to be within their province to condemn men, not merely for disloyal acts, but for a disloyal heart; provided only that the disloyal heart was evidenced by some utterance. To prosecute men for such publications reminds of the days when men were hanged for constructive treason. And, indeed, the jury may well have believed from the charge that the Espionage Act had in effect restored the crime of constructive treason. To hold that such harmless additions to or omissions from news items, and such impotent expressions of editorial opinion, as were here shown, can afford the basis even of a prosecution, will doubtless discourage criticism of the policies of the Government. To hold that such publications can be suppressed as false reports, subjects to new perils the constitutional liberty of the press, already seriously curtailed in practice under powers assumed to have been conferred upon the postal authorities. Nor will this grave danger end with the passing of the war. The constitutional right of free speech has been declared to be the same in peace and in war. In peace, too, men may differ widely as to what loyalty to our country demands; and an intolerant majority, swayed by passion or by fear, may be prone in the future, as it has often been in the past, to stamp as disloyal opinions with which it disagrees. Convictions such as these, besides abridging freedom of speech, threaten freedom of thought and of belief."

Schaefer v. United States,
Vogel v. Same, Werner v. Same, Darkow
v. Same, Lemke v. Same
251 U. S. 466, 482

Distributing Leaflets in War Time

(Dissenting Opinion, *Pierce* v. *United States*, 1920)

FOUR MEN WERE ARRESTED IN ALBANY, NEW YORK, FOR MAKING A house-to-house distribution of a leaflet issued by the Chicago head-quarters of the Socialist Party. It was 1917 and the Espionage Act was in force.

The constitutionality of the Act had already been upheld when this case came before the Court. The question here was whether these men could be convicted, under this law, of a conspiracy to cause disloyalty in the military forces of the United States and to disseminate false statements with intent to interfere with the success of those forces. The Court sustained the convictions.

Mr. Justice Pitney held that the "highly colored and sensational document" could be construed fairly "as a protest against the further prosecution of the war by the United States"; it was proper for the jury to determine whether the statements therein had a natural tendency to produce the forbidden consequences. Although the defendants testified that their sole purpose was to gain converts for Socialism "their evidence was far from conclusive and the jury very reasonably might find—as evidently they did—that the protestations of innocence were insincere and that the real purpose of defendants—indeed, the real object of the pamphlet—was to hamper the Government in the prosecution of the war."

Mr. Justice Brandeis delivered the following dissenting opinion (Mr. Justice Holmes concurring):

"WHAT is called 'distributing literature' is a means commonly used by the Socialist Party to increase its membership and otherwise to advance the cause it advocates. To this end the

[219]

national organization with headquarters at Chicago publishes such 'literature' from time to time and sends sample copies to the local organizations. These, when they approve, purchase copies and call upon members to volunteer for service in making the distribution locally. Some time before July 11, 1917, a local of the Socialist Party at Albany, New York, received from the national organization sample copies of a four-page leaflet entitled *The Price We Pay*, written by Irwin St. John Tucker, an Episcopal clergyman and a man of sufficient prominence to have been included in the 1916-1917 edition of *Who's Who in America*. The proposal to distribute this leaflet came up for action at a meeting of the Albany local held on July 11, 1917. A member who was a lawyer called attention to the fact that the question whether it was legal to distribute this leaflet was involved in a case pending in Baltimore in the District Court of the United States; and it was voted 'not to distribute *The Price We Pay* until we know if it is legal.' The case referred to was an indictment under the Selective Draft Act for conspiracy to obstruct recruiting by means of distributing the leaflet. Shortly after the July 11th meeting it became known that District Judge Rose had directed an acquittal in that case; and at the next meeting of the local, held July 25th, it was voted to rescind the motion 'against distributing *The Price We Pay* and call for distributors.' Four members of the local, two of them native Americans, one a naturalized citizen, and the fourth a foreigner who had filed his first naturalization papers, volunteered as distributors. They distributed about 5,000 copies by hand in Albany.

"District Judge Rose in directing an acquittal had said of the leaflet in the Baltimore case:

'I do not think there is anything to go to the jury in this case.

'You may have your own opinions about that circular; I have very strong individual opinions about it, and as to the wisdom and fairness of what is said there; but so far as I can see it is principally a circular intended to induce people to subscribe to Socialist newspapers and to get recruits for the Socialist Party. I do not think that we ought to attempt to prosecute people for that kind of thing. It may be very unwise in its effect, and it may be unpatriotic at that particular time and place, but it would be going very far, indeed, further, I think, than any law that I know of would justify, to hold that there has been made out any case here even tending to show that there was an attempt to persuade men not to obey the law.'

"In New York a different view was taken, and an indictment in six counts was found against the four distributors. Two of the counts were eliminated at the trial. On the other four there were convictions, and on each a sentence of fine and imprisonment. But one of the four counts was abandoned by the Government in this Court. There remain for consideration count 3, which charges a violation of §3 of the Espionage Act, by making false reports and false statements, with the intent 'to interfere with the operation and success of the military and naval forces'; and counts 2 and 6, also involving §3 of the Espionage Act, the one for conspiring, the other for attempting, 'to cause insubordination, disloyalty, and refusal of duty in the military and naval forces.' Demurrers to the several counts and motions that a verdict be directed for the several defendants were overruled.

"In considering the several counts it is important to note that three classes of offenses are included in §3 of the Espionage Act and that the essentials of liability under them differ materially. The first class, under which count 3 is drawn, is the offense of making or conveying false statements or reports with intent to interfere with the operations or success of the military and naval forces. The second, involved in counts 2 and 6, is that of attempting to cause insubordination, disloyalty, mutiny, or refusal of duty. With the third, that of obstructing the recruiting and enlistment service, we have, since the abandonment of the first count, no concern here. Although the uttering or publishing of the words charged be admitted, there necessarily arises in every case—whether the offense charged be of the first class or of the second—the question whether the words were used 'in such circumstances and are of such a nature as to create a clear and present danger that they will bring about the substantive evils that Congress has a right to prevent' (*Schenck* v. *United States*, 249 U. S. 47, 52), and also the question whether the act of uttering or publishing was done willfully, that is, with the intent to produce the result which Congress sought to prevent. But in cases of the first class three additional elements of the crime must be established, namely:

"(1) The statement or report must be of something capable of being proved false in fact. The expression of an opinion, for instance, whether sound or unsound, might conceivably afford a sufficient basis for the charge of attempting to cause insubordination, disloyalty, or refusal of duty, or for the charge of obstructing recruiting; but, because an opinion is not capable of being proved false in fact, a statement of it cannot be made the basis of a prosecution of the first class.

"(2) The statement or report must be proved to be false.

"(3) The statement or report must be known by the defendant to be false when made or conveyed.

"In the case at bar the alleged offense consists wholly in distributing leaflets which had been written and published by others. The fact of distribution is admitted. But every other element of the two classes of crime charged must be established in order to justify conviction. With unimportant exceptions to be discussed later, the only evidence introduced to establish the several elements of both of the crimes charged is the leaflet itself; and the leaflet is unaffected by extraneous evidence which might give to words used therein special meaning or effect. In order to determine whether the leaflet furnishes any evidence to establish any of the above enumerated elements of the offenses charged the whole leaflet must necessarily be read. It is as follows. [The entire document is given, ending with a coupon-request for samples of Socialist Party literature.]

"*First.* From this leaflet, which is divided into six chapters, there are set forth, in count 3, five sentences as constituting the false statements or reports willfully conveyed by defendants with the intent to interfere with the operation and success of the military and naval forces of the United States.

"(*a*) Two sentences are culled from the first chapter. They follow immediately after the words, 'Conscription is upon us; the draft law is a fact'—and a third sentence culled follows a little later. They are:

> 'Into your homes the recruiting officers are coming. They will take your sons of military age and impress them into the army.*** And still the recruiting officers will come; seizing age after age, mounting up to the elder ones and taking the young ones as they grow to soldier size.'

"To prove the alleged falsity of these statements the Government gravely called as a witness a major in the regular army with twenty-eight years' experience, who has been assigned since July 5, 1917, to recruiting work. He testified that 'recruiting' has to do with the volunteer service and has nothing to do with the drafting system and that the word 'impress' has no place in the recruiting service. The subject of his testi-

[223]

mony was a matter, not of fact, but of law, and as a statement of law it was erroneous. That 'recruiting is gaining fresh supplies for the forces, as well by draft as otherwise,' had been assumed by the Circuit Court of Appeals for that circuit in *Masses Publishing Co. v. Patten,* 246 Fed. 24 (decided eleven days before this testimony was given), and was later expressly held by this Court in *Schenck v. United States.* The third of the sentences charged as false was obviously neither a statement nor a report, but a prediction; and it was later verified. [The extension of the draft to persons between the ages of 18 and 45.] That the prediction made in the leaflet was later verified is, of course, immaterial; but the fact shows the danger of extending beyond its appropriate sphere the scope of a charge of falsity.

"(*b*) The fourth sentence set forth in the third count as a false statement was culled from the third chapter of the leaflet and is this:

> 'The Attorney General of the United States is so busy sending to prison men who do not stand up when the Star Spangled Banner is played, that he has not time to protect the food supply from gamblers.'

"To prove the falsity of this statement the Government called the United States attorney for that district, who testified that no Federal law makes it a crime not to stand up when the 'Star Spangled Banner' is played and that he has no knowledge of anyone being prosecuted for failure to do so. The presiding judge supplemented this testimony by a ruling that the Attorney General, like every officer of the Government, is presumed to do his duty, and not to violate his duty, and that this presumption should obtain unless evidence to the contrary was adduced. The Regulations of the Army (No. 378, Edition of 1913, p. 88) provide that if the National Anthem

[224]

is played in any place those present, whether in uniform or in civilian clothes, shall stand until the last note of the anthem. The regulation is expressly limited in its operation to those belonging to the military service, although the practice was commonly observed by civilians throughout the war. There was no Federal law imposing such action upon them. The Attorney General, who does not enforce Army Regulations, was therefore not engaged in sending men to prison for that offense. But, when the passage in question is read in connection with the rest of the chapter, it seems clear that it was intended, not as a statement of fact, but as a criticism of the Department of Justice for devoting its efforts to prosecution for acts or omissions indicating lack of sympathy with the war, rather than to protecting the community from profiteering by prosecuting violators of the Food Control Act. (Act August 10, 1917, c. 53, 40 Stat. 276.) Such criticism of governmental operations, though grossly unfair as an interpretation of facts or even wholly unfounded in fact, are not 'false reports and false statements with intent to interfere with the operation or success of the military or naval forces.'

"(c) The remaining sentence, set forth in count 3 as a false statement, was culled from the sixth chapter of the leaflet and is this:

'Our entry into it was determined by the certainty that if the Allies do not win, J. P. Morgan's loans to the Allies will be repudiated, and those American investors who bit on his promises would be hooked.'

"To prove the falsity of this statement the Government introduced the address made by the President to Congress on April 2, 1917, which preceded the adoption of the Joint Resolution of April 6, 1917, declaring that a state of war exists between the United States and the Imperial German Govern-

[225]

ment. (40 Stat. 1, c. 1.) This so-called statement of fact—which is alleged to be false—is merely a conclusion or a deduction from facts. True it is the kind of conclusion which courts call a conclusion of fact, as distinguished from a conclusion of law, and which is sometimes spoken of as a finding of ultimate fact, as distinguished from an evidentiary fact. But in its essence it is the expression of a judgment—like the statements of many so-called historical facts. To such conclusions and deductions the declaration of this Court in *American School of Magnetic Healing* v. *McAnnulty,* 187 U. S. 94, 104, is applicable. [The passage next quoted refers to opinions on subjects incapable of proof as to their falsity.]

"The cause of a war—as of most human action—is not single. War is ordinarily the result of many cooperating causes, many different conditions, acts, and motives. Historians rarely agree in their judgment as to what was the determining factor in a particular war, even when they write under circumstances where detachment and the availability of evidence from all sources minimize both prejudice and other sources of error; for individuals, and classes of individuals, attach significance to those things which are significant to them. And, as the contributing causes cannot be subjected, like a chemical combination in a test tube, to qualitative and quantitative analysis so as to weigh and value the various elements, the historians differ necessarily in their judgments. One finds the determining cause of war in a great man; another in an idea, a belief, an economic necessity, a trade advantage, a sinister machination, or an accident. It is for this reason largely that men seek to interpret anew in each age, and often with each generation, the important events in the world's history.

"That all who voted for the Joint Resolution of April 6, 1917, did not do so for the reasons assigned by the President in his address to Congress on April 2, is demonstrated by the discussions in the House and in the Senate. That debate discloses also that both in the Senate and in the House the loans to the Allies and the desire to insure their repayment in full were declared to have been instrumental in bringing about in our country the sentiment in favor of the war. However strongly we may believe that these loans were not the slightest makeweight, much less a determining factor, in the country's decision, the fact that some of our representatives in the Senate and the House declared otherwise on one of the most solemn occasions in the history of the Nation should help us to understand that statements like that here charged to be false are in essence matters of opinion and judgment, not matters of fact to be determined by a jury upon or without evidence, and that even the President's address, which set forth high moral grounds justifying our entry into the war, may not be accepted as establishing beyond a reasonable doubt that a statement ascribing a base motive was criminally false. All the alleged false statements were an interpretation and discussion of public facts of public interest. If the proceeding had been for libel, the defense of privilege might have been interposed. . . . There is no reason to believe that Congress, in prohibiting a special class of false statements, intended to interfere with what was obviously comment as distinguished from a statement.

"The presiding judge ruled that expressions of opinion were not punishable as false statements under the Act; but he left it to the jury to determine whether the five sentences in question were statements of facts or expressions of opinion. As this determination was to be made from the reading of the leaflet unaffected by any extrinsic evidence, the question was one for the court. To hold that a jury may make punishable statements of conclusions or of opinion, like those here involved, by declaring them to be statements of facts and to be false would practically deny members of small political parties freedom of criticism and of discussion in times when feelings run high and the questions involved are deemed fundamental. There is nothing in the Act compelling or indeed justifying such a construction of it, and I cannot believe that Congress in passing, and the President in approving it, conceived that such a construction was possible.

"*Second.* But, even if the passages from the leaflet set forth in the third count could be deemed false statements within the meaning of the Act, the convictions thereon were unjustified because evidence was wholly lacking to prove any one of the other essential elements of the crime charged. Thus there was not a particle of evidence that the defendants knew that the statements were false. They were mere distributors of the leaflet. It had been prepared by a man of some prominence. It had been published by the national organization. Not one of the defendants was an officer even of the local organization. One of them, at least, was absent from the meetings at which the proposal to distribute the leaflet was discussed. There is no evidence that the truthfulness of the statements contained in the leaflet had ever been questioned before this indictment was found. The statement mainly relied upon to sustain the conviction—that concerning the effect of our large loans to the Allies—was merely a repetition of what had been declared with great solemnity and earnestness in the Senate and in the House while the Joint Resolution was under discussion. The fact that the President had set forth in his noble address worthy grounds for our entry into the war was not evidence that these defendants knew to be false the charge that base motives had also been operative. The assertion that the great financial interests exercise a potent, subtle, and sinister influence in the important decisions of our Government had often been made by men high in authority. Mr. Wilson, himself a historian, said before he was President and repeated in *The New Freedom* that:

'The masters of the Government of the United States are the combined capitalists and manufacturers of the United States.'

"We may be convinced that the decision to enter the great war was wholly free from such base influences, but we may not, because such is our belief, permit a jury to find, in the absence of evidence, that it was proved beyond a reasonable doubt that these defendants *knew* that a statement in this leaflet to the contrary was false.

"Nor was there a particle of evidence that these statements were made with intent to interfere with the operation or success of the military and naval forces. So far as there is any evidence bearing on the matter of intent, it is directly to the contrary. The fact that the local refused to distribute the pamphlet until Judge Rose had directed a verdict for acquittal in the Baltimore case shows that its members desired to do only that which the law permitted. The tenor of the leaflet itself shows that the intent of the writer and of the publishers was to advance the cause of Socialism, and each defendant testified that this was his only purpose in distributing the pamphlet. Furthermore, the nature of the words used and the circumstances under which they were used showed affirmatively that they did not 'create a clear and present danger', that thereby the operations or success of our military and naval forces would be interfered with.

"The gravamen of the third count is the charge of willfully conveying in time of war false statements with the intent to interfere with the operation and success of our military or naval forces. One who did that would be called a traitor to his country. The defendants, humble members of the Socialist Party, performed as distributors of the leaflet what would ordinarily be deemed merely a menial service. To hold them guilty under the third count is to convict not them alone, but, in effect, their party, or at least its responsible leaders, of treason, as that word is commonly understood. I cannot believe that there is any basis in our law for such a condemnation on this record.

"*Third.* To sustain a conviction on the second or on the sixth count it is necessary to prove that by cooperating to distribute the leaflet the defendants conspired or attempted willfully to 'cause insubordination, disloyalty, mutiny, or refusal of duty in the military or naval forces.' No evidence of intent so to do was introduced unless it be found in the leaflet itself. What has been said in respect to the third count as to the total lack of evidence of evil intent is equally applicable here.

"A verdict should have been directed for the defendants on these counts also because the leaflet was not distributed under such circumstances, nor was it of such a nature, as to create a clear and present danger of causing either insubordination, disloyalty, mutiny, or refusal of duty in the military or naval forces. The leaflet contains lurid and perhaps exaggerated pictures of the horrors of war. Its arguments as to the cause of this war may appear to us shallow and grossly unfair. The remedy proposed may seem to us worse than the evil which, it is argued, will be thereby removed. But the leaflet, far from counseling disobedience to the law, points to the hopelessness of protest, under the existing system, pictures the irresistible power of the military arm of the Government, and indicates that acquiescence is a necessity. Insubordination, disloyalty, mutiny, and refusal of duty in the military or naval forces are very serious crimes. It is not conceivable that any man of ordinary intelligence and normal judgment would be induced by anything in the leaflet to commit them and thereby risk the severe punishment prescribed for such offenses. Certainly there was no clear and present danger that such would be the result. The leaflet was not even distributed among those in the military or the naval service. It was distributed among civilians;

and since the conviction on the first count has been abandoned here by the Government, we have no occasion to consider whether the leaflet might have discouraged voluntary enlistment or obedience to the provisions of the Selective Draft Act.

"The fundamental right of free men to strive for better conditions through new legislation and new institutions will not be preserved, if efforts to secure it by argument to fellow citizens may be construed as criminal incitement to disobey the existing law—merely because the argument presented seems to those exercising the judicial power to be unfair in its portrayal of existing evils, mistaken in its assumptions, unsound in reasoning, or intemperate in language. No objections more serious than these can, in my opinion, reasonably be made to the arguments presented in *The Price We Pay*."

Pierce, et al. v. *United States*
252 U. S. 239, 253

Teaching the Doctrine of Pacifism

(Dissenting Opinion, *Gilbert* v. *State of Minnesota,* 1920)

IN APRIL, 1917, MINNESOTA PASSED A LAW FORBIDDING PUBLIC speeches against enlistment and the teaching of abstinence from war. Its constitutionality was attacked by one who was convicted under it. To the contention that the State had encroached upon subject-matter under the exclusive control of Congress, Mr. Justice McKenna replied that each State has the power of cooperation against the enemies of all; the law was a simple exertion of Minnesota's police power. To the assertion that the State had invaded the right of free discussion of governmental functions, he answered by citing *Schenck* v. *United States* and other cases limiting that right. Here was another "curious spectacle" like the one in *Schaefer* v. *United States,* Justice McKenna said: "The Nation was at war with Germany, armies were recruiting, and the speech was the discouragement of that."

Mr. Justice Holmes, who had written the opinion for the unanimous court in the *Schenck Case,* concurred in the result. Chief Justice White believed that when the Espionage Act was passed Congress occupied the entire field; so he dissented.

This is the dissenting opinion of Mr. Justice Brandeis:

"JOSEPH GILBERT, manager of the organization department of the Nonpartisan League, was sentenced to fine and imprisonment for speaking on August 18, 1917, at a public meeting of the league, words held to be prohibited by chapter 463 of the laws of Minnesota, approved April 20, 1917. Gilbert was a citizen of the United States, and apparently of a State other than Minnesota. He claimed seasonably that the statute violated rights guaranteed to him by the Federal Constitution. This claim has been denied; and, in my opinion, erroneously.

"The Minnesota statute was enacted during the World War; but it is not a war measure. The statute is said to have been enacted by the State under its police power to preserve the peace; but it is in fact an act to prevent teaching that the abolition of war is possible. Unlike the Federal Espionage Act of June 15, 1917, it applies equally whether the United States is at peace or at war. It abridges freedom of speech and of the press, not in a particular emergency, in order to avert a clear and present danger, but under all circumstances. The restriction imposed relates to the teaching of the doctrine of pacifism, and the Legislature in effect proscribes it for all time. The statute does not in terms prohibit the teaching of the doctrine. Its prohibition is more specific and is directed against the teaching of certain applications of it. This specification operates, as will be seen, rather to extend than to limit the scope of the prohibition.

"Sections 1 and 2 prohibit teaching or advocating by printed matter, writing, or word of mouth that men should not enlist in the military or naval forces of the United States. The prohibition is made to apply whatever the motive, the intention, or the purpose of him who teaches. It applies alike to the preacher in the pulpit, the professor at the university, the speaker at a political meeting, the lecturer at a society or club gathering. Whatever the nature of the meeting and whether it be public or private, the prohibition is absolute, if five persons are assembled. The reason given by the speaker for advising against enlistment is immaterial. Young men, considering whether they should enter these services as a means of earning a livelihood or as a career, may not be told that, in the opinion of the speaker, they can serve their country and themselves better by entering the civil service of State or Nation, or by studying for one of the professions, or by engaging in the

[233]

transportation service, or in farming or in business, or by becoming a workman in some productive industry. Although conditions may exist in the army or the navy which are undermining efficiency, which tend to demoralize those who enter the service and would render futile their best efforts, the State forbids citizens of the United States to advocate that men should not enlist unless existing abuses or defects are remedied. The prohibition imposed by the Minnesota statute has no relation to existing needs or desires of the Government. It applies although recruiting is neither in process nor in contemplation. For the statute aims to prevent, not acts, but beliefs. The prohibition imposed by §3 is even more far-reaching than that provided in §§1 and 2. Section 3 makes it punishable to teach in any place a single person that a citizen should not aid in carrying on a war, no matter what the relation of the parties may be. Thus the statute invades the privacy and freedom of the home. Father and mother may not follow the promptings of religious belief, of conscience or of conviction, and teach son or daughter the doctrine of pacifism. If they do, any police officer may summarily arrest them.

"That such a law is inconsistent with the conceptions of liberty hitherto prevailing seems clear. But it is said that the guaranty against abridging freedom of speech contained in the First Amendment of the Federal Constitution applies only to Federal action; that the legislation here complained of is that of a State; that the validity of the statute has been sustained by its highest court as a police measure; that the matter is one of State concern; and that consequently this Court cannot interfere. But the matter is not one merely of State concern. The State law affects directly the functions of the Federal Government. It affects rights, privileges, and immunities of one who is a citizen of the United States; and it deprives him of an important part of his liberty. These are rights which are guaranteed protection by the Federal Constitution; and they are invaded by the statute in question.

"Congress has the exclusive power to legislate concerning the army and navy of the United States, and to determine, among other things, the conditions of enlistment. It has likewise exclusive power to declare war, to determine to what extent citizens shall aid in its prosecution and how effective aid may best be secured. Congress, which has power to raise an army and naval forces by conscription when public safety demands, may, to avert a clear and present danger, prohibit interference by persuasion with the process of either compulsory or voluntary enlistment. As an incident of its power to declare war it may, when the public safety demands, require from every citizen full support, and may, to avert a clear and present danger, prohibit interference by persuasion with the giving of such support. But Congress might conclude that the most effective army and navy would be one composed wholly of men who had enlisted with full appreciation of the limitations and obligations which the service imposes, and in the face of efforts to discourage their doing so. It might conclude that the most effective army would be one composed exclusively of men who are firmly convinced that war is sometimes necessary if honor is to be preserved, and also that the particular war in which they are engaged is a just one. Congress, legislating for a people justly proud of liberties theretofore enjoyed and suspicious or resentful of any interference with them, might conclude that even in times of great danger, the most effective means of securing support from the great body of citizens is to accord to all full freedom to criticize the acts and administration of their country, although such freedom may be used by a few to urge upon their fellow citizens not to aid the Government in carrying on a war, which reason or faith tells them is wrong, and will therefore bring misery upon their country.

"The right to speak freely concerning functions of the Federal Government is a privilege of immunity of every citizen of the United States which, even before the adoption of the Fourteenth Amendment, a State was powerless to curtail. It was held in *Crandall* v. *Nevada*, 6 Wall. 35, that the United States has the power to call to the seat of Government or elsewhere any citizen to aid it in the conduct of public affairs; that every citizen has a correlative right to go there or anywhere in the pursuit of public or private business; and that 'no power can exist in a State to obstruct this right which would not enable it to defeat the purpose for which the Government was established.' The right of a citizen of the United States to take part, for his own or the country's benefit, in the making of Federal laws and in the conduct of the Government, necessarily includes the right to speak or write about them; to endeavor to make his own opinion concerning laws existing or contemplated prevail; and, to this end, to teach the truth as he sees it. Were this not so, 'the right of the people to assemble for the purpose of petitioning Congress for a redress of grievance or for anything else connected with the powers or duties of the national Government' would be a right totally without substance. . . . Full and free exercise of this right by the citizen is ordinarily also his duty; for its exercise is more important to the Nation than it is to himself. Like the course of the heavenly bodies, harmony in national life is a resultant of the struggle between contending forces. In frank expression of conflicting opinion lies the greatest promise of wisdom in governmental action; and in suppression lies ordinarily the greatest peril. There are times when those charged with the responsibility of Government, faced with clear and present danger, may conclude that suppression of divergent opinion is imperative; because the emergency does not permit reliance upon the slower conquest of error by truth. And in such emergencies the power to suppress exists. But the responsibility for the maintenance of the army and navy, for the conduct of war and for the preservation of government, both State and Federal, from 'malice domestic and foreign levy,' rests upon Congress. It is true that the States have the power of self-preservation inherent in any government to suppress insurrection and repel invasion; and to that end they may maintain such a force of militia as Congress may prescribe and arm. . . . But the duty of preserving the State governments falls ultimately upon the Federal Government. . . . And the superior responsibility carries with it the superior right. The States act only under the express direction of Congress. See National Defense Act, June 3, 1916, c. 134, 39 Stat. 166; Selective Service Act, May 18, 1917, c. 15, 40 Stat. 76. The fact that they may stimulate and encourage recruiting, just as they may stimulate and encourage interstate commerce, does not give them the power by police regulations or otherwise to exceed the authority expressly granted to them by the Federal Government. . . . Congress, being charged with responsibility for those functions of government, must determine whether a paramount interest of the Nation demands that free discussion in relation to them should be curtailed. No State may trench upon its province.

"Prior to the passage of the Minnesota statute it had been the established policy of the United States, departed from only once in the life of the Nation, to raise its military and naval forces in times of war as in peace exclusively by voluntary enlistment. Service was deemed a privilege of Americans, not a duty exacted by law. Specific provision had been made to ensure that enlistment should be the result of free, informed, and deliberate choice. The law of the United States left an American as free to advise his fellows not to enter the army or the navy as he was free to recommend their enlistment. The Government had exacted from American citizens no service except the prompt payment of taxes. Although war had been declared, such was still the policy and the law of the United States when Minnesota enacted the statute here in question.

"The Minnesota statute was, when enacted, inconsistent

[237]

with the law of the United States because at that time Congress permitted free discussion of these governmental functions. Later, and before Gilbert spoke the words complained of, the Federal Espionage Law was enacted, but the Minnesota statute was also inconsistent with it. The Federal Act did not prohibit the teaching of any doctrine; it prohibited only certain tangible obstructions to the conduct of the existing war with the German Empire committed with criminal intent. It was so understood and administered by the Department of Justice. Under the Minnesota law, teaching or advice that men should not enlist is made punishable although the jury should find (1) that the teaching or advocacy proved wholly futile and no obstruction resulted; (2) that there was no intent to obstruct; and the court, taking judicial notice of facts, should rule (3) that, when the words were written or spoken, the United States was at peace with all the world. That this conflict was not merely a technical one, but a cause of real embarrassment and danger to the Federal Government, we learn from one of the officials entrusted with the administration of the Espionage Act:

'In the State of Minnesota because of what was claimed to be either inadequate Federal law or inadequate Federal administration, State laws of a sweeping character were passed and enforced with severity. Whether justified or not in adopting this policy of repression, the result of its adoption increased discontent, and the most serious cases of alleged interference with civil liberty were reported to the Federal Government from that State.' (Report of New York Bar Ass'n, vol. 42, p. 296.)

"In *Johnson* v. *Maryland*, 254 U. S. 51, decided November 8, 1920, this Court held that the power of Congress to establish post roads precluded the State from requiring of a Post Office employee using the State highway in the transportation of mail the customary evidence of competency to drive a motor-truck, although the danger to public safety was obvious and it did not appear that the Federal Government had undertaken to deal with the matter by statute or regulation. The prohibition of State action rests, as the Court pointed out there, 'not upon any consideration of degree, but upon the entire absence of power on the part of the States to touch the instrumentalities of the United States.' As exclusive power over enlistments in the army and the navy of the United States and the responsibility for the conduct of war are vested by the Federal Constitution in Congress, legislation by a State on this subject is necessarily void unless authorized by Congress. It is so when Congress makes no regulation, because by omitting to make regulations Congress signifies its intention that, in this respect, the action of the citizens shall be untrammeled. This would be true even if the subject in question were one over which Congress and the States have concurrent power. For where Congress has occupied a field theretofore open also to State legislation, it necessarily excludes all such. . . . Here Congress not only had exclusive power to act on the subject; it had exercised that power directly by the Espionage Law before Gilbert spoke the words for which he was sentenced. The provisions of the Minnesota statute and its title preclude a contention that its purpose was to prevent breaches of the peace. . . . But neither the fact that it was a police regulation (*New York Central Railroad Co.* v. *Winfield,* 244 U. S. 147), nor the fact that it was legislation in aid of congressional action, would, if true, save the statute. For 'when the United States has exercised its exclusive powers*** so far as to take possession of the field, the States no more can supplement its requirements than they can annul them.' . . . The exclusiveness of the power of the Federal Government with

[239]

which the Legislature of Minnesota appears to have put into roots of political sovereignty. The States may not punish treason against the United States, although indirectly acts of treason may affect them vitally. . . . No more may they arrogate to themselves authority to punish the teaching of pacifism that category. Compare *Schaefer* v. *United States* [*supra*].

"As the Minnesota statute is in my opinion invalid because it interferes with Federal functions and with the right of a citizen of the United States to discuss them, I see no occasion to consider whether it violates also the Fourteenth Amendment. But I have difficulty in believing that the liberty guaranteed by the Constitution, which has been held to protect against State denial the right of an employer to discriminate against a workman because he is a member of a trade union (*Coppage* v. *Kansas*, 236 U. S. 1, 35), the right of a business man to conduct a private employment agency (*Adams* v. *Tanner* [See page 3]), or to contract outside the State for insurance of his property (*Allgeyer* v. *Louisiana*, 165 U. S. 578, 589), although the Legislature deems it inimical to the public welfare, does not include liberty to teach, either in the privacy of the home or publicly, the doctrine of pacifism; so long, at least, as Congress has not declared that the public safety demands its suppression. I cannot believe that the liberty guaranteed by the Fourteenth Amendment includes only liberty to acquire and to enjoy property."

Gilbert v. *State of Minnesota*
254 U. S. 325, 334

Postmaster's Power Over Newspapers

(Dissenting Opinion, *Milwaukee Social Dem. Pub. Co.*
v. *Burleson*, 1920)

THE *Milwaukee Leader's* SECOND-CLASS MAIL PRIVILEGE WAS RE-
voked by the Post Office Department in 1917 on the ground that the
paper was "non-mailable" under the Espionage Act. Its publisher sought
a writ to compel Postmaster General Burleson to restore the privilege,
claiming that his order was unconstitutional because issued without a
trial in court and because it resulted in a denial of the right of free
speech and a deprivation of property without due process of law. All
of these contentions were rejected by the Court.

Mr. Justice Clarke, who delivered its opinion, found that the Postmaster General had the power to revoke the second-class mail privilege,
and that the evidence of the paper's opposition to the war justified his
exercise of that power. Articles published in the paper conveyed to its
readers, he said, "false reports and false statements with intent to promote the success of the enemies of the United States" and "constituted
a willful attempt to cause disloyalty and refusal of duty in the military
and naval forces and to obstruct the recruiting and enlistment service."

The Court held that it was impractical to examine each issue of a
newspaper in advance to detect violations; the *Leader* had brought
its troubles on itself; it could use other classes of mail, "mend its ways,"
conform to the law, and apply anew for the second-class rate.

Mr. Justice Holmes, dissenting, regarded the Post Office order
as unjustified by statute,* and he agreed in substance with the view
expressed by Mr. Justice Brandeis, as follows:

"THIS CASE arose during the World War; but it presents no
legal question peculiar to war. It is important, because what

* See page 41, *The Dissenting Opinions of Mr. Justice Holmes.*

[241]

we decide may determine in large measure whether in times of peace our press shall be free.

"The denial to a newspaper of entry as second-class mail, or the revocation of an entry previously made, does not deny to the paper admission to the mail; nor does it deprive the publisher of any mail facility. It merely deprives him of the very low postal rates, called second-class, and compels him to pay postage for the same service at the rate called third-class, which was, until recently, from eight to fifteen times as high as the second-class rate. Such is the nature and the only effect of an order denying or revoking the entry. See Postal Laws and Regulations, §§421, 422, and 423. In this case entry to the second-class mail was revoked because the paper had, in the opinion of the Postmaster General, systematically inserted editorials and news items which he deemed unmailable. The question presented is: Did Congress confer upon the Postmaster General authority to deny second-class postal rates on that ground? The question is one of statutory construction. No such authority is granted in terms in the statutes which declare what matter shall be unmailable. Is there any provision of the postal laws from which the intention of Congress to grant such power may be inferred? The specific reason why the Postmaster General deemed these editorials and news items unmailable was that he considered them violative of Title xii of the Espionage Act. But it is not contended that this specific reason is of legal significance. The scope of the Postmaster General's alleged authority is confessedly the same whether the reason for the non-mailable quality of the matter inserted in a newspaper is that it violates the Espionage Act, or the copyright laws, or that it is part of a scheme to defraud, or concerns lotteries, or is indecent, or is in any other respect matter which Congress has declared shall not be admitted to the mails. The question of the scope of the Postmaster General's power is presented to us on the following record:

"Some years prior to 1917 the *Milwaukee Leader*, a daily newspaper published by the Milwaukee Social Democratic Publishing Company, made application to use the second-class mail, was declared entitled to do so, and thereafter used it continuously. It built up a large circulation, of which about 9,000 copies were distributed daily through the second-class mail. In September, 1917, its publisher was directed to show cause

'why the authorization of admission*** to second-class mail (matter) should not be revoked upon the following ground:
'The publication is not a "newspaper or other periodical publication" within the meaning of the law governing mailable matter of the second class, it being in conflict with the provisions of the law embodied in §481½, Postal Laws and Regulations.'

"That section relates, not specifically to the second-class mail, but to all mail. It recites the provisions of Title xii of the Espionage Act of June 15, 1917, c. 30, 40 Stat. 217, 230, which declares unmailable all letters, pictures, publications and things 'in violation of any of the provisions' of the Act, and prescribes fine and imprisonment as punishment for the use or attempt to use the postal service for the transmission of such unmailable matter. On this notice to show cause the Third Assistant Postmaster General held the customary informal hearing. The publisher of the *Milwaukee Leader* had not been convicted by any court of violating the Espionage Law; and its representative denied that it had ever committed any act in violation of it. But the Third Assistant Postmaster General issued on October 3, 1917, to the postmaster at Milwaukee the instruction that the *Milwaukee Leader*

'is not entitled to transmission in the mail at second-

[243]

class rates of postage because it appears from the evidence in possession of the department that the publication is not a "newspaper or other periodical publication" within the meaning of the law governing mailable matter of the second class, it being in conflict with the provisions of the law embodied in §481½, Postal Laws and Regulations.'

"This determination and action were confirmed by the Postmaster General and the postmaster at Milwaukee thereafter denied to the publication transmission at the rates provided by law for second-class mail. The order did not forbid to the *Milwaukee Leader* all use of the mails, nor did it limit in any way the use of the mail facilities. It merely revoked the so-called second-class mailing permit, and the effect of this was to impose a higher rate of postage on every copy of the newspaper thereafter mailed.

"The return filed herein by the Postmaster General alleges that this order 'involved the exercise of judgment and discretion on his part' and is 'not subject to be reviewed, set aside, or controlled by a court of law'; but he gives this justification for his action:

'By representations and complaints from sundry good and loyal citizens of the United States and from personal reading and consideration of the issues of the said relator's publication, from the date of the declaration of war down to the time of the service of the citation upon it and the hearing granted in pursuance thereof, it seems to this respondent in the exercise of his judgment and discretion and in obedience to the duty on him reposed, as well by the general statutes as by the special provisions of said Espionage Law, that the provisions of the latter Act were systematically and continually violated by the relator's publication.'

[244]

"It thus appears that the Postmaster General, in the exercise of a supposed discretion, refused to carry at second-class mail rates all future issues of the *Milwaukee Leader,* solely because he believed it had systematically violated the Espionage Act in the past. It further appears that this belief rested partly upon the contents of past issues of the paper filed with the return and partly upon 'representations and complaints from sundry good and loyal citizens,' whose statements are not incorporated in this record and which do not appear to have been called to the attention of the publisher of the *Milwaukee Leader* at the hearing or otherwise. It is this general refusal thereafter to accept the paper for transmission at the second-class mail rates which is challenged as being without warrant in law.

"In discussing whether Congress conferred upon the Postmaster General the authority which he undertook to exercise in this case, I shall consider, first, whether he would have had the power to exclude the paper altogether from all future mail service on the ground alleged; and, second, whether he had power to deny the publisher the second-class rate.

"*First.* Power to exclude from the mails has never been conferred in terms upon the Postmaster General. Beginning with the Act of March 3, 1865, c. 89, §16, 13 Stat. 507, relating to obscene matter, and the Act of July 27, 1868, c. 246, §13, 15 Stat. 196, concerning lotteries, Congress has from time to time forbidden the deposit in the mails of certain matter. In each instance, in addition to prescribing fine and imprisonment as a punishment for sending or attempting to send the prohibited matter through the mail, it declared that such matter should not be conveyed in the mail, nor delivered from any post office nor by any letter carrier. By §6 of the Act of June 8, 1872 (Rev. Stats., §396), the Postmaster General was empowered to 'superintend the business of the department, and execute all laws relative to the postal service.' As a matter of administration the Postmaster General, through his subordinates, rejects matter offered for mailing, or removes matter already in the mail, which in his judgment is unmailable. The existence in the Postmaster General of the power to do this cannot be doubted. The only question which can arise is whether in the individual case the power has been illegally exercised. But while he may thus exclude from the mail specific matter which he deems of the kind declared by Congress to be unmailable, he may not, either as a preventive measure or as a punishment, order that in the future mail tendered by a particular person or the future issues of a particular paper shall be refused transmission.

"Until recently, at least, this appears never to have been questioned and the Post Office Department has been authoritatively advised that the power of excluding matter from the mail was limited to such specific matter as upon examination was found to be unmailable and that the Postmaster General could not make an exclusion order operative upon future issues of a newspaper.

"In 1890 Tolstoi's *Kreutzer Sonata* had been excluded from the mails as indecent. Certain newspapers began to publish the book in installments and their position was referred to the Attorney General. He replied:

'***I do not see that it necessarily follows that every installment of the story thus published is obscene, because the story as a whole is declared to be so. It may be, indeed, that one or more chapters of this story are entirely unexceptionable in character. If so, the exclusion, as unmailable, of newspapers containing them might involve serious consequences to yourself.' (19 Op. Atty. Gen. 667, 668.)

"Again, in 1908, President Roosevelt asked the Attorney

General if the law permitted him to deny the mails to an anarchist newspaper published in the Italian language, in which appeared articles advocating the murder of the police force of Paterson and the burning of the city. The Attorney General advised him that such an article constitutes a seditious libel (it has since been made criminal by statute, Act of March 4, 1911, c. 241, §2, 36 Stat. 1339), and that

> 'The Postmaster General [would] be justified in excluding from the mails any issue of a periodical, otherwise entitled to the privilege of second-class mail matter, which shall contain any article constituting a seditious libel and counseling such crimes as murder, arson, riot, and treason.' (26 Op. Atty. Gen. 555.)

"But the Attorney General was careful to point out that the law gave no authority to exclude issues of the paper which should contain no objectionable matter:

> 'It must be premised that the Postmaster General clearly has no power to close the mails to any class of persons, however reprehensible may be their practices or however detestable their reputation; if the question were whether the mails could be closed to all issues of a newspaper, otherwise entitled to admission, by reason of an article of this character in any particular issue, there could be no doubt that the question must be answered in the negative.' (Page 565.)

"If such power were possessed by the Postmaster General, he would, in view of the practical finality of his decisions, become the universal censor of publications. For a denial of the use of the mail would be, for most of them, tantamount to a denial of the right of circulation. Congress has not granted to the Postmaster General power to deny the right of sending matter by mail even to one who has been convicted by a jury and sentenced by a court for unlawful use of the mail and who has been found by the Postmaster General to have been habitually using the mail for frauds or lotteries and is likely to do so in the future. It has, in order to protect the public, directed postmasters to return to the sender mail addressed to the one found by the Postmaster General to be engaged in a scheme to defraud or in a lottery enterprise. But beyond this Congress has never deemed it wise, if, indeed, it has considered it constitutional, to interfere with the civil right of using the mail for lawful purposes.

"The Postmaster General does not claim here the power to issue an order directly denying a newspaper all mail service for the future. Indeed, he asserts that the mail is still open to the *Milwaukee Leader* upon payment of first, third, or fourth-class rates. He contends, however, that in regard to second-class rates special provisions of law apply under which he may deny that particular rate at his discretion. This contention will now be considered.

"*Second.* The second-class mail rate is confined to newspapers and other periodicals, which possess the qualifications and comply with the conditions prescribed by Congress. In the present case the Postmaster General insists that by reason of alleged past violations of Title xii of the Espionage Act, two of the conditions had ceased to be fulfilled. His reasons are these: The Mail Classification Act of March 3, 1879, c. 180, 20 Stat. 359, provides by §14 that a newspaper to be mailable at the second-class rates 'must be regularly issued at stated intervals as frequently as four times a year,' and that it must be 'originated and published for the dissemination of information of a public character.' If any issue of a paper has contained matter violative of the Espionage Act, the paper is no longer 'regularly issued'; and likewise it has ceased to be a paper 'published for the dissemination of information of a public character.' The argument is obviously unsound. The requirement that the newspaper be 'regularly issued' refers, not to the propriety of the reading matter, but to the fact that publication periodically at stated intervals must be intended and that the intention must be carried out. Similarly, the requirement that the paper be 'published for the dissemination of information of a public character' refers not to the reliability of the information or the soundness of the opinions expressed therein, but to the general character of the publication. The Classification Act does not purport to deal with the effect of, or the punishment for, crimes committed through a publication. It simply provides rates and classifies the material which may be sent at the respective rates. The Act says what shall constitute a newspaper. Undoubtedly the Postmaster General has latitude of judgment in deciding whether a publication meets the definition of a newspaper laid down by the law, but the courts have jurisdiction to decide whether the reasons which an administrative officer gives for his actions agree with the requirements of the statute under which he purports to act. . . . The fact that material appearing in a newspaper is unmailable under wholly different provisions of law can have no effect on whether or not the publication is a newspaper. Although it violates the law, it remains a newspaper. If it is a bad newspaper, the Act which makes it illegal, and not the Classification Act, provides the punishment.

"There is also presented, in brief and argument, a much broader claim in support of the action of the Postmaster General. It is insisted that a citizen uses the mail at second-class rates, not as of right, but by virtue of a privilege or permission, the granting of which rests in the discretion of the Postmaster General. Because the payment made for this governmental service is less than it costs, it is assumed that a properly qualified person has not the right to the service so long as it is of-

[249]

fered, and may not complain if it is denied to him. The service is called the second-class privilege. The certificate evidencing such freedom is spoken of as a permit. But, in fact, the right to the lawful postal rates is a right independent of the discretion of the Postmaster General. The right and conditions of its existence are defined and rest wholly upon mandatory legislation of Congress. It is the duty of the Postmaster General to determine whether the conditions prescribed for any rate exist. This determination in the case of the second-class rate may involve more subjects of inquiry, some of them, perhaps, of greater difficulty, than in cases of other rates. But the function of the Postmaster General is the same in all cases. In making the determination he must, like a court or a jury, form a judgment whether certain conditions prescribed by Congress exist, on controverted facts or by applying the law. The function is a strictly judicial one, although exercised in administering an executive office. And it is not a function which either involves or permits the exercise of discretionary power. The so-called permit is mere formal notice of his judgment, but indispensable to the publisher because without it the local postmaster will not transmit the publication at second-class rates. The same sort of permit is necessary for the same bulk service at first, third, or fourth-class rates. There is nothing, in short, about the second-class rate which furnishes the slightest basis in law for differentiating it from the other rates so far as the discretion of the Postmaster General to grant or withhold it is concerned.

"*Third*. Such is the legislation of Congress. It clearly appears that there was no express grant of power to the Postmaster General to deny second-class mail rates to future issues of a newspaper because in his opinion it had systematically violated the Espionage Act in the past, and it seems equally clear that there is no basis for the contention that such power is to be implied. In respect to newspapers mailed by a publisher at second-class rates there is clearly no occasion to imply this drastic power. For a publisher must deposit with the local postmaster, before the first mailing of every issue, a copy of the publication which is now examined for matter subject to a higher rate and in order to determine the portion devoted to advertising. (Act of March 3, 1879, c. 180, §12, 20 Stat. 359.) If there is illegal material in the newspaper, here is ample opportunity to discover it and remove the paper from the mail. Indeed, of the four classes of mail, it is the second alone which affords to the postal officials full opportunity of ascertaining, before deposit in the mail, whether that which it is proposed to transmit is mailable matter. But even if the statutes were less clear in this respect than they seem to me, I should be led to adopt that construction because of the familiar rule that

'where a statute is susceptible of two constructions, by one of which grave and doubtful constitutional questions arise and by the other of which such questions are avoided, our duty is to adopt the latter.' *United States v. Delaware & Hudson Co.*, 213 U. S. 366, 408.

"For adoption of the construction urged by the Postmaster General would raise not only a grave question, but a 'succession of constitutional doubts,' as suggested in *Harriman v. Interstate Commerce Commission*, 211 U. S. 407, 422. It would in practice seriously abridge the freedom of the press. Would it not also violate the First Amendment? It would in practice deprive many publishers of their property without due process of law. Would it not also violate the Fifth Amendment? It would in practice subject publishers to punishment without a hearing by any court. Would it not also violate Article III of the Constitution? It would in practice subject publishers to severe punishment for an infamous crime without trial by jury. Would it not also violate the Sixth Amendment? And the punishment inflicted—denial of a civil right—is certainly unusual.

[251]

Would it not also violate the Eighth Amendment? If the construction urged by the Postmaster General is rejected, these questions need not be answered; but it seems appropriate to indicate why the doubts raised by them are grave.

"(*a*) The power to police the mails is an incident of the postal power. Congress may, of course, exclude from the mails matter which is dangerous or which carries on its face immoral expressions, threats, or libels. It may go further, and through its power of exclusion exercise, within limits, general police power over the material which it carries, even though its regulations are quite unrelated to the business of transporting mails. . . . As stated in *Ex parte Jackson*, 96 U. S. 727, 732:

'The difficulty attending the subject arises, not from the want of power in Congress to prescribe regulations as to what shall constitute mail matter, but from the necessity of enforcing them consistently with rights reserved to the people, of far greater importance than the transportation of the mail.'

"In other words, the postal power, like all its other powers, is subject to the limitations of the Bill of Rights. . . . Congress may not through its postal police power put limitations upon the freedom of the press which, if directly attempted, would be unconstitutional. This Court also stated in *Ex parte Jackson* that

'Liberty of circulating is as essential to that freedom as liberty of publishing; indeed, without the circulation, the publication would be of little value.'

"It is argued that, although a newspaper is barred from the second-class mail, liberty of circulation is not denied, because the first and third-class mail and also other means of

[252]

transportation are left open to a publisher. Constitutional rights should not be frittered away by arguments so technical and unsubstantial. 'The Constitution deals with substance, not shadows. Its inhibition was leveled at the thing, not the name.' (*Cummings* v. *State of Missouri*, 4 Wall. 277, 325.) The Government might, of course, decline altogether to distribute newspapers, or it might decline to carry any at less than the cost of the service, and it would not thereby abridge the freedom of the press, since to all papers other means of transportation would be left open. But to carry newspapers generally at a sixth of the cost of the service, and to deny that service to one paper of the same general character, because to the Postmaster General views therein expressed in the past seem illegal, would prove an effective censorship and abridge seriously freedom of expression.

"How dangerous to liberty of the press would be the holding that the second-class mail service is merely a privilege, which Congress may deny those views it deems to be against public policy, is shown by the following contention made in 1912 by the Solicitor General in the *Lewis Case* [229 U. S. 316]:

'A possible abuse of power is no argument against its existence, but we may as well observe that a denial of the mails to a paper because of its ownership or the views held by its owners may well be illegal as having no relation to the thing carried in the mails *unless the views are expressed in the paper*; but *if such views are expressed in the paper* Congress can doubtless exclude them, just as Congress could now exclude all papers advocating lotteries, prohibition, anarchy, or a protective tariff if a majority of Congress thought such views against public policy.' (Italics in the original.)

[253]

"(*b*) The right which Congress has given to all properly circumstanced persons to distribute newspapers and periodicals through the mails is a substantial right. . . . It is of the same nature as—indeed, it is a part of—the right to carry on business which this Court has been jealous to protect against what it has considered arbitrary deprivations. . . . A law by which certain publishers were unreasonably or arbitrarily denied the low rates would deprive them of liberty or property without due process of law; and it would likewise deny them equal protection of the laws. . . . The Court might hold that a statute which conferred upon the Postmaster General the power to do this, because of supposed past infractions of law, was unreasonable and arbitrary; particularly in respect to second-class mail which affords ample opportunity for preventing the transmission of unmailable matter; and hence obnoxious to the Fifth Amendment.

"The contention that, because the rates are non-compensatory, use of the second-class mail is not a right but a privilege, which may be granted or withheld at the pleasure of Congress, rests upon an entire misconception when applied to individual members of a class. The fact that it is largely gratuitous makes clearer its position as a right; for it is paid for by taxation.

"(*c*) The order revoking the entry of the *Milwaukee Leader* to second-class was clearly a punitive, not a preventive, measure, as all classes of mail except the second were, as the Postmaster General states, left open to it, provided it had sufficient financial resources. Of the three left available, the third class, being for 'miscellaneous printed matter,' was an appropriate one for distributing newspapers and was the cheapest. But the additional cost to the publisher involved in distributing daily 9,000 copies, by the third-class mail would be a very serious one. The actual and intended effect of the order was merely to impose a very heavy fine, possibly $150 a day, for supposed transgression in the past. But the trial and punishment of crimes is a function which the Constitution (Article III, §2, cl. 3) intrusts to the judiciary. I am not aware that any other civil administrative officer has assumed, in any country in which the common law prevails, the power to inflict upon a citizen severe punishment for an infamous crime. Possibly the Court would hold that Congress could not, in view of Article III of the Constitution, confer upon the Postmaster General, as a mere incident in the administration of his Department, authority to issue an order which could operate only as a punishment. . . .

"(*d*) The Sixth Amendment guarantees that, in all criminal prosecutions, the accused shall enjoy the right to a speedy and public trial by an impartial jury of the State and district wherein the crime shall have been committed, and that he shall be confronted with the witnesses against him. It is only in the case of petty offenses that the jury may be dispensed with. . . . What is in effect a very heavy fine has been imposed by the Postmaster General. It has been imposed because he finds that the publisher has committed the crime of violating the Espionage Act. And that finding is based in part upon 'representations and complaints from sundry good and loyal citizens' with whom the publisher was not confronted. It may be that the Court would hold, in view of Article VI in our Bill of Rights, that Congress is without power to confer upon the Postmaster General, or even upon a court, except upon the verdict of a jury and upon confronting the accused with the witnesses against him, authority to inflict indirectly such a substantial punishment as this. . . .

"(*e*) The punishment inflicted is not only unusual in character; it is, so far as known, unprecedented in American legal history. Every fine imposed by a court is definite in amount. Every fine prescribed by Congress is limited in amount. Statutes frequently declare that each day's continuation of an offense shall constitute a new crime. But here a fine imposed for a past

[255]

offense is made to grow indefinitely each day—perhaps throughout the life of the publication. Already, having grown at the rate of say $150 a day, it may aggregate, if the circulation has been maintained, about $180,000 for the three years and four months since the order was entered; and its growth continues. It was assumed in *Waters-Pierce Oil Co.* v. *Texas* (*No.* 1) 212 U. S. 86, 111, that an excessive fine, even if definite, would violate the Eighth Amendment. Possibly the Court, applying the Eighth Amendment, might again, as in *Weems* v. *United States,* 217 U. S. 349, 381, make clear the 'difference between unrestrained power and that which is exercised under the spirit of constitutional limitations formed to establish justice.'

"The suggestion is made that, if a new application for entry to second-class mail had been made, the publishers might have been granted a certificate. It is no bar to proceedings to set aside an illegal sentence that an application to the Executive for clemency might have resulted in a pardon.

"In conclusion I say again—because it cannot be stressed too strongly—that the power here claimed is not a war power. There is no question of its necessity to protect the country from insidious domestic foes. To that end Congress conferred upon the Postmaster General the enormous power contained in the Espionage Act of entirely excluding from the mails any letter, picture, or publication which contained matter violating the broad terms of that Act. But it did not confer—and the Postmaster General concedes that it did not confer—the vague and absolute authority practically to deny circulation to any publication which in his opinion is likely to violate in the future any postal law. The grant of that power is construed into a postal statute passed forty years ago which has never before been suspected of containing such implications. I cannot believe that in establishing postal classifications in 1879 Congress intended to confer upon the Postmaster General authority to issue the order here complained of. If, under the Constitution, administrative officers may, as a mere incident of the peace-time administration of their departments, be vested with the power to issue such orders as this, there is little of substance in our Bill of Rights, and in every extension of governmental functions lurks a new danger to civil liberty."

United States ex rel. Milwaukee Social
Democratic Publishing Co. v. Burleson,
Postmaster General of the United States
255 U. S. 407, 417

Membership in Revolutionary Parties

(Concurring Opinion, *Whitney v. California*, 1927)

FOR HELPING TO ORGANIZE A BRANCH OF THE COMMUNIST LABOR Party at Oakland, Charlotte Anita Whitney was convicted of violating the California Criminal Syndicalism Act of 1919. The Act made it a felony to organize or knowingly become a member of an organization formed to advocate the commission of crime, sabotage, or unlawful acts of force or terrorism as a means of accomplishing industrial or political change. The contention that the Act violated the due process and equal protection clauses of the Fourteenth Amendment was rejected by the Court. Mr. Justice Sanford wrote: "We cannot hold that, as here applied, the Act is an unreasonable or arbitrary exercise of the police power of the State, unwarrantably infringing any right of free speech, assembly or association, or that those persons are protected from punishment by the due process clause who abuse such rights by joining and furthering an organization thus menacing the peace and welfare of the State."

While concurring in the result on the record before the Court, Justice Brandeis took occasion to insist on the extreme constitutional protection owing to freedom of speech and assembly. Mr. Justice Holmes joined in his opinion:

"MISS WHITNEY was convicted of the felony of assisting in organizing, in the year 1919, the Communist Labor Party of California, of being a member of it, and of assembling with it. These acts are held to constitute a crime, because the party was formed to teach criminal syndicalism. The statute which made these acts a crime restricted the right of free speech and

[258]

of assembly theretofore existing. The claim is that the statute, as applied, denied to Miss Whitney the liberty guaranteed by the Fourteenth Amendment.

"The felony which the statute created is a crime very unlike the old felony of conspiracy or the old misdemeanor of unlawful assembly. The mere act of assisting in forming a society for teaching syndicalism, of becoming a member of it, or assembling with others for that purpose is given the dynamic quality of crime. There is guilt although the society may not contemplate immediate promulgation of the doctrine. Thus the accused is to be punished, not for attempt, incitement, or conspiracy, but for a step in preparation, which, if it threatens the public order at all, does so only remotely. The novelty in the prohibition introduced is that the statute aims, not at the practice of criminal syndicalism, nor even directly at the preaching of it, but at association with those who propose to preach it.

"Despite arguments to the contrary which had seemed to me persuasive, it is settled that the due process clause of the Fourteenth Amendment applies to matters of substantive law as well as to matters of procedure. Thus all fundamental rights comprised within the term 'liberty' are protected by the Federal Constitution from invasion by the States. The right of free speech, the right to teach, and the right of assembly are, of course, fundamental rights. . . . These may not be denied or abridged. But, although the rights of free speech and assembly are fundamental, they are not in their nature absolute. Their exercise is subject to restriction, if the particular restriction proposed is required in order to protect the State from destruction or from serious injury, political, economic, or moral. That the necessity which is essential to a valid restriction does not exist unless speech would produce, or is intended to produce, a clear and imminent danger of some substantive evil which the State constitutionally may seek to prevent has been settled. . . .

"It is said to be the function of the Legislature to determine

[259]

whether at a particular time and under particular circumstances the formation of, or assembly with, a society organized to advocate criminal syndicalism constitutes a clear and present danger of substantive evil; and that by enacting the law here in question the Legislature of California determined that question in the affirmative. . . . The Legislature must obviously decide, in the first instance, whether a danger exists which calls for a particular protective measure. But where a statute is valid only in case certain conditions exist, the enactment of the statute cannot alone establish the facts which are essential to its validity. Prohibitory legislation has repeatedly been held invalid, because unnecessary, where the denial of liberty involved was that of engaging in a particular business. The power of the courts to strike down an offending law are no less when the interests involved are not property rights, but the fundamental personal rights of free speech and assembly.

"This Court has not yet fixed the standard by which to determine when a danger shall be deemed clear; how remote the danger may be and yet be deemed present; and what degree of evil shall be deemed sufficiently substantial to justify resort to abridgment of free speech and assembly as the means of protection. To reach sound conclusions on these matters, we must bear in mind why a State is, ordinarily, denied the power to prohibit dissemination of social, economic, and political doctrine which a vast majority of its citizens believes to be false and fraught with evil consequence.

"Those who won our independence believed that the final end of the State was to make men free to develop their faculties, and that in its government the deliberative forces should prevail over the arbitrary. They valued liberty both as an end and as a means. They believed liberty to be the secret of happiness and courage to be the secret of liberty. They believed that freedom to think as you will and to speak as you think are means indispensable to the discovery and spread of political truth; that without free speech and assembly discussion would be futile; that with them, discussion affords ordinarily adequate protection against the dissemination of noxious doctrine; that the greatest menace to freedom is an inert people; that public discussion is a political duty; and that this should be a fundamental principle of the American Government. They recognized the risks to which all human institutions are subject. But they knew that order cannot be secured merely through fear of punishment for its infraction; that it is hazardous to discourage thought, hope, and imagination; that fear breeds repression; that repression breeds hate; that hate menaces stable government; that the path of safety lies in the opportunity to discuss freely supposed grievances and proposed remedies; and that the fitting remedy for evil counsels is good ones. Believing in the power of reason as applied through public discussion, they eschewed silence coerced by law—the argument of force in its worst form. Recognizing the occasional tyrannies of governing majorities, they amended the Constitution so that free speech and assembly should be guaranteed.

"Fear of serious injury cannot alone justify suppression of free speech and assembly. Men feared witches and burnt women. It is the function of speech to free men from the bondage of irrational fears. To justify suppression of free speech there must be reasonable ground to fear that the serious evil will result if free speech is practiced. There must be reasonable ground to believe that the danger apprehended is imminent. There must be reasonable ground to believe that the evil to be prevented is a serious one. Every denunciation of existing law tends in some measure to increase the probability that there will be violation of it. Condonation of a breach enhances the probability. Expressions of approval add to the probability. Propagation of the criminal state of mind by teaching syndicalism increases it. Advocacy of law-breaking heightens it still further. But even advocacy of violation, however reprehensible morally, is not a justification for denying free speech where the advocacy falls short of incitement and there is nothing to indicate that the advocacy would be immediately acted on. The wide difference between advocacy and incitement, between preparation and attempt, between assembling and conspiracy, must be borne in mind. In order to support a finding of clear and present danger it must be shown either that immediate serious violence was to be expected or was advocated, or that the past conduct furnished reason to believe that such advocacy was then contemplated.

"Those who won our independence by revolution were not cowards. They did not fear political change. They did not exalt order at the cost of liberty. To courageous, self-reliant men, with confidence in the power of free and fearless reasoning applied through the processes of popular government, no danger flowing from speech can be deemed clear and present, unless the incidence of the evil apprehended is so imminent that it may befall before there is opportunity for full discussion. If there be time to expose through discussion the falsehood and fallacies, to avert the evil by the processes of education, the remedy to be applied is more speech, not enforced silence. Only an emergency can justify repression. Such must be the rule if authority is to be reconciled with freedom. Such, in my opinion, is the command of the Constitution. It is therefore always open to Americans to challenge a law abridging free speech and assembly by showing that there was no emergency justifying it.

"Moreover, even imminent danger cannot justify resort to prohibition of these functions essential to effective democracy, unless the evil apprehended is relatively serious. Prohibition of free speech and assembly is a measure so stringent that it would be inappropriate as the means for averting a relatively trivial harm to society. A police measure may be unconstitutional merely because the remedy, although effective as means of protection, is unduly harsh or oppressive. Thus, a State might, in the exercise of its police power, make any trespass upon the land of another a crime, regardless of the results or of the intent or purpose of the trespasser. It might, also, punish an attempt, a conspiracy, or an incitement to commit the trespass. But it is hardly conceivable that this Court would hold constitutional a statute which punished as a felony the mere voluntary assembly with a society formed to teach that pedestrians had the moral right to cross uninclosed, unposted, waste lands and to advocate their doing so, even if there was imminent danger that advocacy would lead to a trespass. The fact that speech is likely to result in some violence or in destruction of property is not enough to justify its suppression. There must be the probability of serious injury to the State. Among free men, the deterrents ordinarily to be applied to prevent crime are education and punishment for violations of the law, not abridgment of the rights of free speech and assembly.

"The California Syndicalism Act recites in §4:

'Inasmuch as this act concerns and is necessary to the immediate preservation of the public peace and safety, for the reason that at the present time large numbers of persons are going from place to place in this state advocating, teaching, and practicing criminal syndicalism, this act shall take effect upon approval by the Governor.'

"This legislative declaration satisfies the requirement of the Constitution of the State concerning emergency legislation. . . . But it does not preclude inquiry into the question whether, at the time and under the circumstances, the conditions existed which are essential to validity under the Federal Constitution. As a statute, even if not void on its face, may be challenged because invalid as applied (*Dahnke-Walker Mill-*

[263]

ing Co. v. *Bondurant,* 257 U. S. 282), the result of such an inquiry may depend upon the specific facts of the particular case. Whenever the fundamental rights of free speech and assembly are alleged to have been invaded, it must remain open to a defendant to present the issue whether there actually did exist at the time a clear danger, whether the danger, if any, was imminent, and whether the evil apprehended was one so substantial as to justify the stringent restriction interposed by the Legislature. The legislative declaration, like the fact that the statute was passed and was sustained by the highest court of the State, creates merely a rebuttable presumption that these conditions have been satisfied.

"Whether in 1919, when Miss Whitney did the things complained of, there was in California such clear and present danger of serious evil, might have been made the important issue in the case. She might have required that the issue be determined either by the court or the jury. She claimed below that the statute as applied to her violated the Federal Constitution; but she did not claim that it was void because there was no clear and present danger of serious evil, nor did she request that the existence of these conditions of a valid measure thus restricting the rights of free speech and assembly be passed upon by the court or a jury. On the other hand, there was evidence on which the court or jury might have found that such danger existed. I am unable to assent to the suggestion in the opinion of the Court that assembling with a political party, formed to advocate the desirability of a proletarian revolution by mass action at some date necessarily far in the future, is not a right within the protection of the Fourteenth Amendment. In the present case, however, there was other testimony which tended to establish the existence of a conspiracy, on the part of members of the Industrial Workers of the World, to commit present serious crimes, and likewise to show that such a conspiracy would be furthered by the activity of the society of which Miss Whitney was a member. Under these circumstances the judgment of the State court cannot be disturbed.

"Our power of review in this case is limited not only to the question whether a right guaranteed by the Federal Constitution was denied, but to the particular claims duly made below, and denied. . . . We lack here the power occasionally exercised on review of judgments of lower Federal courts to correct in criminal cases vital errors, although the objection was not taken in the trial court. . . . This is a writ of error to a State court. Because we may not inquire into the errors now alleged, I concur in affirming the judgment of the State court."

Whitney v. *California*
274 U. S. 357, 372

"Capricious Exercise of Power"

(Dissenting Opinion, *Myers* v. *United States*, 1926)

A CONSTITUTIONAL QUESTION OF PRIME IMPORTANCE, UNSETTLED
for 136 years, was presented by a suit to recover salary claimed to be
owed to a postmaster who during the term for which he was appointed,
had been removed from office by the President, without any action by
the Senate. The statute under which he was appointed provided that
postmasters "shall be appointed and may be removed by the President
by and with the advice and consent of the Senate and shall hold their
offices for four years unless sooner removed or suspended according to
law." The only ground on which the Government resisted the suit was
that the power of the President to remove inferior officers was a part
of the executive power granted to him by the Constitution which could
not be taken away nor conditioned by Act of Congress. This contention
was upheld by the Court.

The opinion of Chief Justice Taft for the majority, and those of
Justices McReynolds and Brandeis, who dissented, are lengthy and
fully documented studies of the early debates on the power of the
President and of the long history of Congressional legislation on the
removal of officers. To Justice Holmes, who agreed with the conclusion
of the "exhaustive research" of his brothers McReynolds and Brandeis,
the "arguments drawn from the executive power of the President"
seemed "spiders' webs inadequate to control the dominant facts"—that
the office owes its existence, and the President his power of appointment,
to Congress.*

Here are the concluding paragraphs of Justice Brandeis' opinion:

"THE separation of the powers of government did not make
each branch completely autonomous. It left each in some meas-

* See page 179, *The Dissenting Opinions of Mr. Justice Holmes.*

ure, dependent upon the others, as it left to each power to exercise, in some respects, functions in their nature executive, legislative, and judicial. Obviously the President cannot secure full execution of the laws if Congress denies to him adequate means of doing so. Full execution may be defeated because Congress declines to create offices indispensable for that purpose. Or because Congress, having created the office, declines to make the indispensable appropriation. Or because Congress, having both created the office and made the appropriation, prevents, by restrictions which it imposes, the appointment of officials who in quality and character are indispensable to the efficient execution of the law. If, in any such way, adequate means are denied to the President, the fault will lie with Congress. The President performs his full constitutional duty, if, with the means and instruments provided by Congress and within the limitations prescribed by it, he uses his best endeavors to secure the faithful execution of the laws enacted. . . .

"Checks and balances were established in order that this should be 'a government of laws and not of men.' As White said in the House in 1789, an uncontrollable power of removal in the Chief Executive 'is a doctrine not to be learned in American governments.' Such power had been denied in colonial charters, and even under proprietary grants and royal commissions. It had been denied in the thirteen States before the framing of the Federal Constitution. The doctrine of the separation of powers was adopted by the convention of 1787 not to promote efficiency but to preclude the exercise of arbitrary power. The purpose was not to avoid friction, but, by means of the inevitable friction incident to the distribution of the governmental powers among three departments, to save the people from autocracy. In order to prevent arbitrary executive action, the Constitution provided in terms that presidential appointments be made with the consent of the Senate, unless Congress should otherwise provide; and this clause was construed by Alexander Hamilton in

The Federalist, No. 77, as requiring like consent to removals. Limiting further executive prerogatives customary in monarchies, the Constitution empowered Congress to vest the appointment of inferior officers, 'as we think proper, in the President alone, in the Courts of Law, or in the Heads of Departments.' Nothing in support of the claim of uncontrollable power can be inferred from the silence of the Convention of 1787 on the subject of removal. For the outstanding fact remains that every specific proposal to confer such uncontrollable power upon the Presdent was rejected. In America, as in England, the conviction prevailed then that the people must look to representative assemblies for the protection of their liberties. And protection of the individual, even if he be an official, from the arbitrary or capricious exercise of power was then believed to be an essential of free government."

Myers, Administratrix, v. United States
272 U. S. 52, 240

The Government Instigates Crime

(Dissenting Opinion, *Casey* v. *United States*, 1928)

An attorney in Seattle, suspected of providing prisoners in a jail with narcotics, was trapped by Federal agents and convicted of purchasing morphine in violation of the Harrison Anti-Narcotic Law. That law makes the absence of the required stamps *prima facie* evidence of its violation by the person in possession of the drug.

This provision was held valid by the Court, which sustained the conviction. Mr. Justice Holmes said: "It is consistent with all the Constitutional protections of accused men to throw on them the burden of proving facts peculiarly within their knowledge and hidden from discovery by the Government." The suggestion that the Government induced the crime, he said, was not established by the record. There was evidence to show that the jailers had reason to suspect that the defendant was an habitual offender. "We are not persuaded that the conduct of the officials was different from or worse than ordering a drink of a suspected bootlegger."

Dissenting opinions, differing in part, but all taking the view that the evidence and the presumption did not establish the Government's case, were written by McReynolds, Butler, and Sanford, JJ. Justice Butler concurred in the dissenting opinion of Justice Brandeis:

"The question presented is whether possession within the district of morphine not in the original stamped package is evidence sufficient to sustain the charge that it was illegally purchased therein. I have no occasion to consider that question. For, in my opinion, the prosecution must fail because officers of the Government instigated the commission of the alleged crime.

"These are facts disclosed by the Government's evidence: In the Western District of Washington, Northern Division, prisoners awaiting trial for Federal offenses are commonly detained at King county jail. The prisoners' lawyers frequently come there for consultation with clients. At the request of prisoners, the jailer telephones the lawyers to come for that purpose. A small compartment—called the attorneys' cage—is provided. Prior to the events here in question, the jailer had, upon such request, telephoned Casey, from time to time, to come to see prisoners accused of crimes other than violation of the Narcotic Act. He had doubtless telephoned also, upon request of prisoners who were accused of these crimes, for Casey had acted as attorney in a number of narcotic cases. The jailer observed— or thought he did—that after Casey came some of those visited were under the influence of narcotics. He suspected that Casey had brought them the drug. To entrap him, the following scheme was devised by Patterson and Close, Federal narcotic officers, and carried out with the aid of George Cicero, a convicted felon and drug addict, then in the jail on a charge of forgery, and Mrs. Nelson, the alleged sister-in-law of Roy Nelson, another prisoner and drug addict.

"On December 29th Patterson and Close installed a dictaphone in the attorney's cage, and arranged so that, from an adjacent room, they could both hear conversations in the cage and see occupants. Then they deposited with the superintendent of the jail $20 to Cicero's credit; arranged with him to request the jailer to summon Casey to come to the jail; and also that, when Casey came, Cicero would ask him to procure some morphine and would pay him the $20 for that purpose. The jailer telephoned Casey as requested. Thereafter the Federal agents were in waiting. Casey did not come until about ten o'clock on the morning of the 31st. Cicero talked from the attorney's cage with Casey, and gave him an order for the $20. By arrangement, Casey talked there also with Roy Nelson, who gave him an order on the superintendent for $50. Both orders were immediately cashed. Mrs. Nelson talked with Casey in the corridor.

"The testimony of Patterson, Close, Cicero, and Mrs. Nelson, if believed, is sufficient to prove that Cicero and Roy Nelson asked Casey to procure morphine for them; that he agreed to do so; that the money paid was for that purpose; that it was arranged that the morphine should be smuggled into the jail in laundry; and that Mrs. Nelson arranged with Casey that she would call at his office in the afternoon. She did call, having first gone to the office of the narcotic agents and conferred with them. She testified that she saw at Casey's office a Chinaman or a Japanese; that Casey gave her the package for Roy Nelson; and that she took it immediately to the Federal narcotic office. A Federal narcotic agent who is a chemist testified that upon soaking one of the towels in the package brought to the office by Mrs. Nelson he found that it contained morphine.

"I am aware that courts—mistaking relative social values and forgetting that a desirable end cannot justify foul means—have, in their zeal to punish, sanctioned the use of evidence obtained through criminal violation of property and personal rights or by other practices of detectives even more revolting. But the objection here is of a different nature. It does not rest merely upon the character of the evidence or upon the fact that the evidence was illegally obtained. The obstacle to the prosecution lies in the fact that the alleged crime was instigated by officers of the Government; that the act for which the Government seeks to punish the defendant is the fruit of their criminal conspiracy to induce its commission. The Government may set decoys to entrap criminals. But it may not provoke or create a crime and then punish the criminal, its creature. If Casey is guilty of the crime of purchasing 3.4 grains of morphine on December 31st, as charged, it is because he yielded to the temptation presented by the officers. Their conduct is not a defense to him. For no officer of the Government has power to authorize the violation of an Act of Congress and no conduct of an officer can excuse the violation. But it does not follow that the Court must suffer a detective-made criminal to be punished. To permit that would be tantamount to a ratification by the Government of the officers' unauthorized and unjustifiable conduct. . . .

"This case is unlike those where a defendant confessedly intended to commit a crime and the Government, having knowledge thereof, merely presented the opportunity and set its decoy. So far as appears, the officers had, prior to the events on December 31st, no basis for a belief that Casey was violating the law, except that the jailer harbored a suspicion. Casey took the witness stand and submitted himself to cross-examination. He testified that he had 'never bought, sold, given away, or possessed a single grain of morphine or other opiate,' and that he had 'never procured, or suggested to any one else to procure morphine or narcotics of any kind.' He testified that the payments made on orders from Cicero and Roy Nelson were payments on account of services to be rendered as counsel for the defense in the prosecutions against them then pending. He denied every material fact testified to by witnesses for the prosecution and supported his oath by other evidence. The Government's witnesses admitted that the conversations in the attorneys' cage were carried on in the ordinary tone of voice; that there was no effort to lower the voice or to speak privately or secretly; and that they could have heard all that was said without the use of the dictaphone. They admitted that, when the narcotic agents searched Casey's office under a search warrant on the evening of December 31st, they did not find any narcotics or any trace of them or any other incriminating article; and that when, at about the same time, they arrested Casey, he was taking supper with his wife and daughter at his home seven miles from Seattle. Whether the charge against Casey is true we may not inquire. But if, under such circumstances, the mere suspicion of the jailer could justify entrapment, little would be left of the doctrine.

"The fact that no objection on the ground of entrapment was taken by the defendant either below or in this Court, is without legal significance. This prosecution should be stopped, not because some right of Casey's has been denied, but in order to protect the Government. To protect it from illegal conduct of its officers. To preserve the purity of its courts. In my opinion, the judgment should be vacated with direction to quash the indictment. . . ."

Casey v. United States
276 U. S. 413, 421

Tapping Wires to Obtain Evidence

(Dissenting Opinion, *Olmstead* v. *United States*, 1928)

THE TAPPING OF TELEPHONE WIRES BY FEDERAL AGENTS ENABLED
the Government to obtain evidence which resulted in the defendants'
conviction for conspiring to violate the National Prohibition Act. By a
vote of five to four, the convictions were sustained by the Supreme
Court. The majority, speaking through Chief Justice Taft, decided
that the guaranty of the Fourth Amendment against unreasonable
searches and seizures and that of the Fifth Amendment against self-
incrimination gave no protection to the defendants. There was no
searching and no seizure; the wire tapping was done outside of their
homes and offices; there was no trespass; the men were not compelled
to talk over the telephones. The claim that the evidence should be
rejected because the Federal agents violated a law of the State of
Washington was rejected by applying the common-law rule that the
illegality of the method of obtaining evidence does not affect its
admissibility.

Four Justices dissented: Holmes,* Brandeis, Butler, and Stone.
Brandeis wrote:

"THE defendants were convicted of conspiring to violate
the National Prohibition Act. Before any of the persons now
charged had been arrested or indicted, the telephones by means
of which they habitually communicated with one another and
with others had been tapped by Federal officers. To this end,
a lineman of long experience in wire tapping was employed,
on behalf of the Government and at its expense. He tapped
eight telephones, some in the homes of the persons charged,

* See page 184, *The Dissenting Opinions of Mr. Justice Holmes.*

some in their offices. Acting on behalf of the Government and in their official capacity, at least six other prohibition agents listened over the tapped wires and reported the messages taken. Their operations extended over a period of nearly five months. The typewritten record of the notes of conversations overheard occupies 775 typewritten pages. By objections seasonably made and persistently renewed, the defendants objected to the admission of the evidence obtained by wire tapping, on the ground that the Government's wire tapping constituted an unreasonable search and seizure, in violation of the Fourth Amendment, and that the use as evidence of the conversations overheard compelled the defendants to be witnesses against themselves, in violation of the Fifth Amendment.

"The Government makes no attempt to defend the methods employed by its officers. Indeed, it concedes that, if wire tapping can be deemed a search and a seizure within the Fourth Amendment, such wire tapping as was practiced in the case at bar was an unreasonable search and seizure, and that the evidence thus obtained was inadmissible. But it relies on the language of the Amendment, and it claims that the protection given thereby cannot properly be held to include a telephone conversation.

" 'We must never forget,' said Mr. Chief Justice Marshall in *McCulloch* v. *Maryland*, 4 Wheat. 316, 407, 'that it is a Constitution we are expounding.' Since then this Court has repeatedly sustained the exercise of power by Congress, under various clauses of that instrument, over objects of which the Fathers could not have dreamed. . . . We have likewise held that general limitations on the powers of government, like those embodied in the due process clauses of the Fifth and Fourteenth Amendments, do not forbid the United States or the States from meeting modern conditions by regulations which 'a century ago, or even half a century ago, probably would have been rejected as arbitrary and oppressive.' (*Village of Euclid* v. *Ambler Realty Co.*, 272 U. S. 365, 387.) . . . Clauses guaranteeing to the individual protection against specific abuses of power, must have a similar capacity of adaptation to a changing world. It was with reference to such a clause that this Court said in *Weems* v. *United States*, 217 U. S. 349, 373:

> 'Legislation, both statutory and constitutional, is enacted, it is true, from an experience of evils, but its general language should not, therefore, be necessarily confined to the form that evil had theretofore taken. Time works changes, brings into existence new conditions and purposes. Therefore a principle to be vital must be capable of wider application than the mischief which gave it birth. This is peculiarly true of Constitutions. They are not ephemeral enactments, designed to meet passing occasions.' [The quotation further points out the danger of converting the principles of the Constitution into "impotent and lifeless formulas."]

"When the Fourth and Fifth Amendments were adopted, 'the form that evil had theretofore taken' had been necessarily simple. Force and violence were then the only means known to man by which a government could directly effect self-incrimination. It could compel the individual to testify—a compulsion effected, if need be, by torture. It could secure possession of his papers and other articles incident to his private life—a seizure effected, if need be, by breaking and entry. Protection against such invasion of 'the sanctities of a man's home and the privacies of life' was provided in the Fourth and Fifth Amendments by specific language. . . . But 'time works changes, brings into existence new conditions and purposes.' Subtler and more far-reaching means of invading privacy have become available to the Government. Discovery and invention have made it possible for the Government by means far more

[276]

effective than stretching upon the rack, to obtain disclosure in court of what is whispered in the closet.

"Moreover, 'in the application of a Constitution, our contemplation cannot be only of what has been, but of what may be.' The progress of science in furnishing the Government with means of espionage is not likely to stop with wire tapping. Ways may some day be developed by which the Government, without removing papers from secret drawers, can reproduce them in court, and by which it will be enabled to expose to a jury the most intimate occurrences of the home. Advances in the psychic and related sciences may bring means of exploring unexpressed beliefs, thoughts, and emotions. 'That places the liberty of every man in the hands of every petty officer' was said by James Otis of much lesser intrusions than these. To Lord Camden a far slighter intrusion seemed 'subversive of all the comforts of society.' Can it be that the Constitution affords no protection against such invasions of individual security?

"A sufficient answer is found in *Boyd* v. *United States,* 116 U. S. 616, 627-30, a case that will be remembered as long as civil liberty lives in the United States. This Court there reviewed the history that lay behind the Fourth and Fifth Amendments. We said with reference to Lord Camden's judgment in *Entick* v. *Carrington,* 19 Howell's State Trials, 1030:

'The principles laid down in this opinion affect the very essence of constitutional liberty and security. They reach farther than the concrete form of the case there before the court, with its adventitious circumstances; they apply to all invasions on the part of the Government and its employees of the sanctities of a man's home and the privacies of life. It is not the breaking of his doors, and the rummaging of his drawers, that constitutes the essence of the offense; but it is the invasion of his indefeasible right of personal security, personal liberty and private property, where that right has never been forfeited by his conviction of some public offense—it is the invasion of this sacred right which underlies and constitutes the essence of Lord Camden's judgment. Breaking into a house and opening boxes and drawers are circumstances of aggravation; but any forcible and compulsory extortion of a man's own testimony or of his private papers to be used as evidence of a crime or to forfeit his goods, is within the condemnation of that judgment. In this regard the Fourth and Fifth Amendments run almost into each other.'

"In *Ex parte Jackson*, 96 U. S. 727, it was held that a sealed letter intrusted to the mail is protected by the Amendments. The mail is a public service furnished by the Government. The telephone is a public service furnished by its authority. There is, in essence, no difference between the sealed letter and the private telephone message. As Judge Rudkin said below:

'True, the one is visible, the other invisible; the one is tangible, the other intangible; the one is sealed, the other unsealed; but these are distinctions without a difference.'

"The evil incident to invasion of the privacy of the telephone is far greater than that involved in tampering with the mails. Whenever a telephone line is tapped, the privacy of the persons at both ends of the line is invaded, and all conversations between them upon any subject, and although proper, confidential, and privileged, may be overheard. Moreover, the tapping of one man's telephone line involves the tapping of the telephone of every other person whom he may call, or who may call him. As a means of espionage, writs of assistance

[278]

and general warrants are but puny instruments of tyranny and oppression when compared with wire tapping.

"Time and again this Court, in giving effect to the principle underlying the Fourth Amendment, has refused to place an unduly literal construction upon it. This was notably illustrated in the *Boyd* case itself. Taking language in its ordinary meaning, there is no 'search' or 'seizure' when a defendant is required to procure a document in the orderly process of a court's procedure. 'The right of the people to be secure in their persons, houses, papers, and effects, against unreasonable searches and seizures' would not be violated, under any ordinary construction of language, by compelling obedience to a subpoena. But this Court holds the evidence inadmissible simply because the information leading to the issue of the subpoena has been unlawfully secured. . . . Literally, there is no 'search' or 'seizure' when a friendly visitor abstracts papers from an office; yet we held in *Gouled* v. *United States*, 255 U. S. 298, that evidence so obtained could not be used. No court which looked at the words of the Amendment rather than at its underlying purpose would hold, as this Court did in *Ex parte Jackson* that its protection extended to letters in the mails. The provision against self-incrimination in the Fifth Amendment has been given an equally broad construction. The language is: 'No person*** shall be compelled in any criminal case to be a witness against himself.'

"Yet we have held not only that the protection of the Amendment extends to a witness before a grand jury, although he has not been charged with crime (*Counselman* v. *Hitchcock*, 142 U. S. 547, 562, 586) but that:

'It applies alike to civil and criminal proceedings, wherever the answer might tend to subject to criminal responsibility him who gives it. The privilege protects a mere witness as fully as it does one who is also a party defendant.' *McCarthy* v. *Arndstein*, 266 U. S. 34, 40.

"The narrow language of the Amendment has been consistently construed in the light of its object, 'to insure that a person should not be compelled, when acting as a witness in any investigation, to give testimony which might tend to show that he himself had committed a crime. The privilege is limited to criminal matters, but it is as broad as the mischief against which it seeks to guard.' (*Counselman* v. *Hitchcock*, p. 562.)

"Decisions of this Court applying the principle of the *Boyd Case* have settled these things. Unjustified search and seizure violates the Fourth Amendment, whatever the character of the paper; whether the paper when taken by the Federal officers was in the home, in an office, or elsewhere; whether the taking was effected by force, by fraud, or in the orderly process of a court's procedure. From these decisions, it follows necessarily that the Amendment is violated by the officer's reading the paper without a physical seizure, without his even touching it, and that use, in any criminal proceeding of the contents of the paper so examined—as where they are testified to by a Federal officer who thus saw the document or where, through knowledge so obtained, a copy has been procured elsewhere—any such use constitutes a violation of the Fifth Amendment.

"The protection guaranteed by the Amendments is much broader in scope. The makers of our Constitution undertook to secure conditions favorable to the pursuit of happiness. They recognized the significance of man's spiritual nature, of his feelings, and of his intellect. They knew that only a part of the pain, pleasure, and satisfactions of life are to be found in material things. They sought to protect Americans in their beliefs, their thoughts, their emotions, and their sensations. They conferred, as against the Government, the right to be let

[280]

alone—the most comprehensive of rights and the right most valued by civilized men. To protect that right, every unjustifiable intrusion by the Government upon the privacy of the individual, whatever the means employed, must be deemed a violation of the Fourth Amendment. And the use, as evidence in a criminal proceeding, of facts ascertained by such intrusion must be deemed a violation of the Fifth.

"Applying to the Fourth and Fifth Amendments the established rule of construction, the defendants' objections to the evidence obtained by wire tapping must, in my opinion, be sustained. It is, of course, immaterial where the physical connection with the telephone wires leading into the defendants' premises was made. And it is also immaterial that the intrusion was in aid of law enforcement. Experience should teach us to be most on our guard to protect liberty when the Government's purposes are beneficent. Men born to freedom are naturally alert to repel invasion of their liberty by evil-minded rulers. The greatest dangers to liberty lurk in insidious encroachment by men of zeal, well-meaning but without understanding.

"Independently of the constitutional question, I am of opinion that the judgment should be reversed. By the laws of Washington, wire tapping is a crime. Pierce's Code 1921, §8976 (18). To prove its case, the Government was obliged to lay bare the crimes committed by its officers on its behalf. A Federal court should not permit such a prosecution to continue. . . .

"The situation in the case at bar differs widely from that presented in *Burdeau* v. *McDowell*, 256 U. S. 465. There only a single lot of papers was involved. They had been obtained by a private detective while acting on behalf of a private party, without the knowledge of any Federal official, long before any one had thought of instituting a Federal prosecution. Here the evidence obtained by crime was obtained at the Government's expense, by its officers, while acting on its behalf; the

[281]

officers who committed these crimes are the same officers who were charged with the enforcement of the National Prohibition Act; the crimes of these officers were committed for the purpose of securing evidence with which to obtain an indictment and to secure a conviction. The evidence so obtained constitutes the warp and woof of the Government's case. The aggregate of the Government evidence occupies 306 pages of the printed record. More than 210 of them are filled by recital of the details of the wire tapping and of facts ascertained thereby. There is literally no other evidence of guilt on the part of some of the defendants except that illegally obtained by these officers. As to nearly all the defendants (except those who admitted guilt), the evidence relied upon to secure a conviction consisted mainly of that which these officers had so obtained by violating the State law.

"As Judge Rudkin said below:

'Here we are concerned with neither eavesdroppers nor thieves. Nor are we concerned with the acts of private individuals.*** We are concerned only with the acts of Federal agents, whose powers are limited and controlled by the Constitution of the United States.'

"The Eighteenth Amendment has not in terms empowered Congress to authorize anyone to violate the criminal laws of a State. And Congress has never purported to do so. . . . The terms of appointment of Federal prohibition agents do not purport to confer upon them authority to violate any criminal law. Their superior officer, the Secretary of the Treasury, has not instructed them to commit crime on behalf of the United States. It may be assumed that the Attorney General of the United States did not give any such instruction.

"When these unlawful acts were committed they were crimes only of the officers individually. The Government was

[282]

innocent, in legal contemplation; for no Federal official is authorized to commit a crime on its behalf. When the Government, having full knowledge, sought, through the Department of Justice, to avail itself of the fruits of these acts in order to accomplish its own ends, it assumed moral responsibility for the officers' crimes. . . . Compare *Gambino* v. *United States,* 275 U. S. 310. And if this Court should permit the Government, by means of its officers' crimes, to effect its purpose of punishing the defendants, there would seem to be present all the elements of a ratification. If so, the Government itself would become a lawbreaker.

"Will this Court, by sustaining the judgment below, sanction such conduct on the part of the executive? The governing principle has long been settled. It is that a court will not redress a wrong when he who invokes its aid has unclean hands. The maxim of unclean hands comes from courts of equity. But the principle prevails also in courts of law. Its common application is in civil actions between private parties. Where the Government is the actor, the reasons for applying it are even more persuasive. Where the remedies invoked are those of the criminal law, the reasons are compelling.

"The door of a court is not barred because the plaintiff has committed a crime. The confirmed criminal is as much entitled to redress as his most virtuous fellow citizen; no record of crime, however long, makes one an outlaw. The court's aid is denied only when he who seeks it has violated the law in connection with the very transaction as to which he seeks legal redress. Then aid is denied despite the defendant's wrong. It is denied in order to maintain respect for law; in order to promote confidence in the administration of justice; in order to preserve the judicial process from contamination. The rule is one, not of action, but of inaction. It is sometimes spoken of as a rule of substantive law. But it extends to matters of procedure as well. A defense may be waived. It is waived

[283]

when not pleaded. But the objection that the plaintiff comes with unclean hands will be taken by the court itself. It will be taken despite the wish to the contrary of all the parties to the litigation. The court protects itself.

"Decency, security, and liberty alike demand that Government officials shall be subjected to the same rules of conduct that are commands to the citizen. In a government of law, existence of the government will be imperiled if it fails to observe the law scrupulously. Our Government is the potent, the omnipresent teacher. For good or for ill, it teaches the whole people by its example. Crime is contagious. If the Government becomes a lawbreaker, it breeds contempt for law; it invites every man to become a law unto himself; it invites anarchy. To declare that in the administration of the criminal law the end justifies the means—to declare that the Government may commit crimes in order to secure the conviction of a private criminal—would bring terrible retribution. Against that pernicious doctrine this Court should resolutely set its face."

Olmstead, et al. v. *United States*
277 U. S. 438, 471

V. Prohibition and Taxation

Physicians' Prescriptions

(Opinion of the Court, *Lambert* v. *Yellowley*, 1926)

"THE NATIONAL PROHIBITION ACT, Oct. 28, 1919. c. 85, title II, §7, 41 Stat. 305, 311, provides: 'No one but a physician holding a permit to prescribe liquor shall issue any prescription for liquor.*** Not more than a pint of spirituous liquor to be taken internally shall be prescribed for use by the same person within any period of ten days and no prescription shall be filled more than once.' The supplemental Act of November 23, 1921, c. 134, §2, 42 Stat. 222, has a related but broader restriction to which reference will be made later on. Violation of the provision subjects the offender to fine or imprisonment or both. The limitation as to amount applies only to alcoholic liquor 'fit for use for beverage purposes.' (National Prohibition Act, tit. II, §1.) 'Medicinal preparations manufactured in accordance with formulas prescribed by the United States Pharmacopœia, National Formulary, or the American Institute of Homeopathy that are unfit for use for beverage purposes,' and 'patented, patent, and proprietary medicines that are unfit for use for beverage purposes' are specifically exempted from the operation of the provision. (§4, *b* and *c*.) Moreover, the limitation does not apply to prescriptions for such liquor to be administered in certain hospitals. (§6.)

"In November, 1922, Samuel W. Lambert, of New York City, a distinguished physician, brought in the Federal court for that district this suit to enjoin Edward Yellowley, the acting Federal Prohibition Director, and other officials, 'from inter-

[287]

fering with complainant in his acts as a physician in prescribing vinous or spirituous liquors to his patients for medicinal purposes, upon the ground that the quantities prescribed for the use of any one person in any period of ten days exceed the limits fixed by said Acts, or either of them.' As the basis for this relief the bill set forth Dr. Lambert's qualifications and experience as a physician; his belief that in certain cases, including some subject to his professional advice, the use of spirituous liquor internally as a medicine in an amount exceeding one pint in ten days is necessary for the proper treatment of patients in order to afford relief from human ailments; and that he does not intend to prescribe the use of liquor for beverage purposes. It alleged that to treat the diseases of his patients and to promote their physical well-being, according to the untrammeled exercise of his best skill and scientifically trained judgment, and, to that end, to advise the use of such medicines and medical treatment as in his opinion are best calculated to effect their cure and establish their health, is an essential part of his constitutional rights as a physician.

"In May, 1923, the case was heard upon an application for an interlocutory injunction and a motion to dismiss. The District Court issued the injunction. . . . In December, 1924, the United States Circuit Court of Appeals for the Second Circuit reversed the decree, and directed that the bill be dismissed. . . . In the interval, this Court had decided *Hixon* v. *Oakes*, 265 U. S. 254, and *Everard's Breweries* v. *Day*, 265 U. S. 545. In the latter Dr. Lambert's counsel was permitted to file a brief, and to present an oral argument. The appeal in the case at bar was taken under §§128 and 241 of the Judicial Code and was allowed before the passage of the Act of February 13, 1925, c. 229, 43 Stat. 936. The claim is that the provision assailed is unconstitutional, because it has no real or substantial relation to the appropriate enforcement of the Eighteenth Amendment; that in enacting the provision

Congress exceeded the powers delegated to it by the Amendment; and that thereby complainant's fundamental rights are violated.

"The Eighteenth Amendment, besides prohibiting by §1 the manufacture, sale, and transportation of intoxicating liquors for beverage purposes, confers upon Congress by §2, in terms, the power to enforce the prohibition by appropriate legislation. That the limitation upon the amount of liquor which may be prescribed for medicinal purposes is a provision adapted to promote the purpose of the Amendment is clear. That the provision is not arbitrary appears from the evidence considered by Congress which embodies, among other things, the lessons of half a century of experience in the several States in dealing with the liquor problem. That evidence disclosed that practicing physicians differ about the value of malt, vinous, and spirituous liquors for medicinal purposes, but that the preponderating opinion is against their use for such purposes; and that among those who prescribe them there are some who are disposed to give prescriptions where the real purpose is to divert the liquor to beverage uses. Indeed, the American Medical Association, at its meeting in 1917, had declared that the use of alcoholic liquor as a therapeutic agent was without 'scientific basis' and 'should be discouraged,' and, at its meeting in June, 1921, had adopted a resolution saying 'reproach has been brought upon the medical profession by some of its members, who have misused the law which permits the prescription of alcohol.' With this as the situation to be met, the Judiciary Committee of the House of Representatives reported with favorable recommendation the bill which became the Act of November 23, 1921, whereby the prescription of intoxicating malt liquor for medicinal purposes is entirely prohibited, and the prescription of other intoxicating liquors is subject to the following restrictions. [In essence, the Act limits the liquor indicated in any prescription to 24 percent alcohol content or one-half pint of alcohol and limits the number of prescription blanks for use within ninety days to one hundred, with a provision for emergencies. Justice Brandeis' opinion then quotes the committee's report on the bill; the report referred to the sparing use which physicians had been making of prescription permits and the necessity of curbing abuse on the part of physicians lacking high ethical standards. The quotation ends with: "In view of the fact that most of the States have more stringent provisions than the one contained in §2, this legislation will work no hardship upon the profession."]

"In *Everard's Breweries* v. *Day*, 265 U. S. 545, the validity of the provision prohibiting the prescription of malt liquor was assailed as going beyond the power of Congress and impinging upon the reserved powers of the States, in that it is an interference with the regulation of health and the practice of medicine, both of which are within the domain of State power and outside the legislative power of Congress. The suit was against the Commissioner of Internal Revenue and other Federal officers, and its chief purpose was to enjoin them from enforcing the provision prohibiting the prescription of malt liquor for medicinal purposes. This Court, besides observing that the 'ultimate and controlling question' in the case was whether the provision prohibiting physicians from prescribing intoxicating malt liquors for medicinal purposes is within the power given to Congress by the Eighteenth Amendment, to enforce by 'appropriate legislation' its prohibition of the manufacture, sale, etc., of intoxicating liquor for beverage purposes, proceeded to consider every phase of the question, and in conclusion held that the provision was appropriate legislation for the purpose and within the power of Congress, although affecting subjects which, but for the Amendment, would be entirely within State control. The Court referred to the settled rule that where the means adopted by Congress in exerting an express power are calculated to effect its purpose, it is not admissible for the judiciary to inquire into the degree of their necessity, and then said (p. 560):

> 'We cannot say that prohibiting traffic in intoxicating malt liquors for medicinal purposes has no real or substantial relation to the enforcement of the Eighteenth Amendment, and is not adapted to accomplish that end and make the constitutional prohibition effective. The difficulties always attendant upon the suppression of traffic in intoxicating liquors are notorious. . . . The Federal Government in enforcing prohibition is confronted with difficulties similar to those encountered by the States. (*Ruppert* v. *Caffey*, 251 U. S. 262.) The opportunity to manufacture, sell, and prescribe intoxicating malt liquors for "medicinal purposes" opens many doors to clandestine traffic in them as beverages under the guise of medicines, facilitates many frauds, subterfuges and artifices; aids evasion, and thereby and to that extent hampers and obstructs the enforcement of the Eighteenth Amendment.'

"The Court further held that Congress must be regarded as having concluded—as it well might do in the absence of any consensus of opinion among physicians and in the presence of the absolute prohibition in many of the States—that malt liquor has no substantial medicinal qualities making its prescription necessary, and that this made it impossible to say the provision was an unreasonable and arbitrary exercise of power.

"We have spoken of that case at length because the decision was by a unanimous Court and if adhered to disposes of the present case. If Congress may prohibit the manufacture and sale of intoxicating malt liquor for medicinal purposes by way of enforcing the Eighteenth Amendment, it equally and to the same end may restrict the prescription of other intoxicating liquor for medicinal purposes. In point of power there is no difference; if in point of expediency there is a difference, that is a matter which Congress alone may consider. Experience has shown that the opportunities for doing what the Constitution forbids are present in both instances, and that advantage not infrequently is taken of those opportunities. Congress, in deference to the belief of a fraction of the medical profession that vinous and spirituous liquors have some medicinal value, has said that they may be prescribed in limited quantities according to stated regulations; but it also has said that they shall not be prescribed in larger quantities, nor without conforming to the regulations, because this would be attended with too much risk of the diversion of liquor to beverage uses. Not only so, but the limitation as to quantity must be taken as embodying an implicit congressional finding that such liquors have no such medicinal value as gives rise to a need for larger or more frequent prescriptions. Such a finding, in the presence of the well-known diverging opinions of physicians, cannot be regarded as arbitrary or without a reasonable basis. On the whole, therefore, we think it plain that the restrictions imposed are admissible measures for enforcing the prohibition ordained by the Eighteenth Amendment.

"A later case applying like principles is *Selzman* v. *United States*, 268 U. S. 466. There a section of the National Prohibition Act forbidding the sale of denatured alcohol without a compliance with certain regulations was assailed as beyond the authority of Congress under the Eighteenth Amendment upon the ground that the Amendment relates only to traffic in intoxicating liquor for beverage purposes, and that, as denatured alcohol is not usable as a beverage, authority to prevent or regulate its sale is not given to Congress by the Amendment, but remains exclusively in the States. This Court held the section valid for the following reasons:

'The power of the Federal Government, granted by the Eighteenth Amendment, to enforce the prohibition of the manufacture, sale, and transportation of intoxicating liquor carries with it power to enact any legislative measures reasonably adapted to promote the purpose. The denaturing in order to render the making and sale of industrial alcohol compatible with the enforcement of prohibition of alcohol for beverage purposes is not always effective. The ignorance of some, the craving and the hardihood of others, and the fraud and cupidity of still others, often tend to defeat its object. It helps the main purpose of the Amendment, therefore, to hedge about the making and disposition of the denatured article every reasonable precaution and penalty to prevent the proper industrial use of it from being perverted to drinking it.'

"From the authority of these cases Dr. Lambert seeks to escape by pointing out that he is a physician and believes that the use of spirituous liquor as a medicinal agent is at times both advisable and necessary. He asserts that to control the medical practice in the States is beyond the power of the Federal Government. Of course his belief in the medicinal value of such liquor is not of controlling significance; it merely places him in what was shown to Congress to be the minor fraction of his profession. Besides, there is no right to practice medicine which is not subordinate to the police power of the States . . . and also to the power of Congress to make laws necessary and proper for carrying into execution the Eighteenth Amendment. When the United States exerts any of the powers conferred upon it by the Constitution, no valid objection can be based upon the fact that such exercise may be attended by some or all of the incidents which attend the exercise by a State of its police power. . . . The Eighteenth Amendment confers upon the Federal Government the power to prohibit the sale of intoxicating liquor for beverage purposes. Under it, as under the necessary and proper clause of Article I, §8, of the Constitution, Congress has power to enforce prohibition 'by appropriate legislation.' High medical authority being in conflict as to the medicinal value of spirituous and vinous liquors taken as a beverage, it would, indeed, be strange if Congress lacked the power to determine that the necessities of the liquor problem require a limitation of permissible prescriptions, as by keeping the quantity that may be prescribed within limits which will minimize the temptation to resort to prescriptions as pretexts for obtaining liquor for beverage uses. Compare *Jacobson* v. *Massachusetts*, 197 U. S. 11."

[Mr. Justice Sutherland wrote a dissenting opinion, McReynolds, Butler, and Stone, JJ., concurring.]

Lambert v. *Yellowley, et al.*
272 U. S. 581

Income Tax on Stock Dividends

(Dissenting Opinion, *Eisner* v. *Macomber*, 1920)

UNDER THE REVENUE ACT OF 1916, WHICH CLASSED STOCK DIVIDENDS with income, a tax was imposed on Mrs. Myrtle H. Macomber, who had received fifty percent of the number of shares she held in the Standard Oil Company of California as a dividend. She paid under protest, contending that the new stock was not income within the meaning of the Sixteenth (Income Tax) Amendment and that the Act violated Article I of the Constitution, which requires direct taxes to be apportioned according to population.

The judgment she won in the District Court was affirmed by the Supreme Court. Five Justices were of opinion that stock dividends were not income, on authority of *Towne* v. *Eisner*, 245 U. S. 418, which dealt with a similar tax under the Revenue Act of 1913. Speaking for the Court, Mr. Justice Pitney said that the issue of new stock to stockholders in proportion to their previous holdings was an increase in the value of capital investment; it represented no profit until a money dividend was declared on the stock or until the stock was sold.

Mr. Justice Holmes, who had written the *Towne* v. *Eisner* opinion, pointed out that "the construction of the statute then before the Court might be different from that of the Constitution." He thought that the Amendment justified the tax.* Mr. Justice Day agreed with him.

Mr. Justice Brandeis also dissented (Mr. Justice Clarke concurring):

"FINANCIERS, with the aid of lawyers, devised long ago two different methods by which a corporation can, without increasing its indebtedness, keep for corporate purposes accumulated

* See page 215, *The Dissenting Opinions of Mr. Justice Holmes.*

[295]

profits, and yet, in effect, distribute these profits among its stockholders. One method is a simple one. The capital stock is increased; the new stock is paid up with the accumulated profits; and the new shares of paid-up stock are then distributed among the stockholders *pro rata* as a dividend. If the stockholder prefers ready money to increasing his holding of the stock in the company, he sells the new stock received as a dividend. The other method is slightly more complicated. Arrangements are made for an increase of stock to be offered to stockholders *pro rata* at par, and, at the same time, for the payment of a cash dividend equal to the amount which the stockholder will be required to pay to the company if he avails himself of the right to subscribe for his *pro rata* of the new stock. If the stockholder takes the new stock, as is expected, he may endorse the dividend check received to the corporation and thus pay for the new stock. In order to ensure that all the new stock so offered will be taken, the price at which it is offered is fixed far below what it is believed will be its market value. If the stockholder prefers ready money to an increase of his holdings of stock, he may sell his right to take new stock *pro rata*, which is evidenced by an assignable instrument. In that event the purchaser of the rights repays to the corporation, as the subscription price of the new stock, an amount equal to that which it had paid as a cash dividend to the stockholder.

"Both of these methods of retaining accumulated profits while in effect distributing them as a dividend had been in common use in the United States for many years prior to the adoption of the Sixteenth Amendment. They were recognized equivalents. Whether a particular corporation employed one or the other method was determined sometimes by requirements of the law under which the corporation was organized; sometimes it was determined by preferences of the individual officials of the corporation; and sometimes by stock market conditions. Whichever method was employed the resultant

[296]

distribution of the new stock was commonly referred to as a stock dividend. How these two methods have been employed may be illustrated by the action in this respect (as reported in *Moody's Manual,* 1918 *Industrial,* and the *Commercial and Financial Chronicle*) of some of the Standard Oil companies, since the disintegration pursuant to the decision of this Court in 1911. . . . [Justice Brandeis describes three stock distributions.]

"It thus appears that among financiers and investors the distribution of the stock, by whichever method effected, is called a stock dividend; that the two methods by which accumulated profits are legally retained for corporate purposes and at the same time distributed as dividends are recognized by them to be equivalents; and that the financial results to the corporation and to the stockholders of the two methods are substantially the same—unless a difference results from the application of the Federal income tax law.

[Justice Brandeis then relates that Mrs. Macomber received a dividend "paid by direct issue of the stock to her according to the simple method described above."]

"It is conceded that if the stock dividend paid to Mrs. Macomber had been made by the more complicated method pursued by the Standard Oil Company of Kentucky, that is, issuing rights to take new stock *pro rata* and paying to each stockholder simultaneously a dividend in cash sufficient in amount to enable him to pay for this *pro rata* of new stock to be purchased—the dividend so paid to him would have been taxable as income, whether he retained the cash or whether he returned it to the corporation in payment for his *pro rata* of new stock. But it is contended that, because the simple method was adopted of having the new stock issued direct to the stockholders as paid-up stock, the new stock is not to be deemed income, whether she retained it or converted it into cash by sale. If such a different result can flow merely from the differ-

[297]

ence in the method pursued, it must be because Congress is without power to tax as income of the stockholder either the stock received under the latter method or the proceeds of its sale; for Congress has, by the provisions in the Revenue Act of 1916, expressly declared its purpose to make stock dividends, by whichever method paid, taxable as income.

"The Sixteenth Amendment, proclaimed February 25, 1913, declares:

'The Congress shall have power to lay and collect taxes on incomes, from whatever source derived, without apportionment among the several States, and without regard to any census or enumeration.'

"The Revenue Act of September 8, 1916, c. 463, §2a, 39 Stat. 756, 757, provided:

'That the term "dividends" as used in this title shall be held to mean any distribution made or ordered to be made by a corporation*** out of its earnings or profits accrued since March first, nineteen hundred and thirteen, and payable to its shareholders, whether in cash or in stock of the corporation,*** which stock dividend shall be considered income, to the amount of its cash value.'

"Hitherto powers conferred upon Congress by the Constitution have been liberally construed, and have been held to extend to every means appropriate to attain the end sought. In determining the scope of the power the substance of the transaction, not its form, has been regarded. . . . Is there anything in the phraseology of the Sixteenth Amendment or in the nature of corporate dividends which should lead to a departure from these rules of construction and compel this Court to hold that

Congress is powerless to prevent a result so extraordinary as that here contended for by the stockholder?

"*First.* The term 'income,' when applied to the investment of the stockholder in a corporation, had, before the adoption of the Sixteenth Amendment, been commonly understood to mean the returns from time to time received by the stockholder from gains or earnings of the corporation. A dividend received by a stockholder from a corporation may be either in distribution of capital assets or in distribution of profits. Whether it is the one or the other is in no way affected by the medium in which it is paid, nor by the method or means through which the particular thing distributed as a dividend was procured. If the dividend is declared payable in cash, the money with which to pay it is ordinarily taken from surplus cash in the treasury. But (if there are profits legally available for distribution and the law under which the company was incorporated so permits) the company may raise the money by discounting negotiable paper; or by selling bonds, scrip or stock of another corporation then in the treasury; or by selling its own bonds, scrip or stock then in the treasury; or by selling its own bonds, scrip or stock issued expressly for that purpose. How the money shall be raised is wholly a matter of financial management. The manner in which it is raised in no way affects the question whether the dividend received by the stockholder is income or capital; nor can it conceivably affect the question whether it is taxable as income.

"Likewise whether a dividend declared payable from profits shall be paid in cash or in some other medium is also wholly a matter of financial management. If some other medium is decided upon, it is also wholly a question of financial management whether the distribution shall be, for instance, in bonds, scrip or stock of another corporation or in issues of its own. And if the dividend is paid in its own issues, why should there be a difference in result dependent upon whether the distribution

[299]

was made from such securities then in the treasury or from others to be created and issued by the company expressly for that purpose? So far as the distribution may be made from its own issues of bonds, or preferred stock created expressly for the purpose, it clearly would make no difference in the decision of a question whether the dividend was a distribution of profits, that the securities had to be created expressly for the purpose of distribution. If a dividend paid in securities of that nature represents a distribution of profits Congress may, of course, tax it as income of the stockholder. Is the result different where the security distributed is common stock?

"Suppose that a corporation having power to buy and sell its own stock, purchases, in the interval between its regular dividend dates, with monies derived from current profits, some of its own common stock as a temporary investment, intending at the time of purchase to sell it before the next dividend date and to use the proceeds in paying dividends, but later, deeming it inadvisable either to sell this stock or to raise by borrowing the money necessary to pay the regular dividend in cash, declares a dividend payable in this stock; can any one doubt that in such a case the dividend in common stock would be the income of the stockholder and constitutionally taxable as such? . . . And would it not likewise be income of the stockholder subject to taxation if the purpose of the company in buying the stock so distributed had been from the beginning to take it off the market and distribute it among the stockholders as a dividend, and the company actually did so? And proceeding a short step further: Suppose that a corporation decided to capitalize some of its accumulated profits by creating additional common stock and selling the same to raise the working capital, but after the stock has been issued and certificates therefor are delivered to the bankers for sale, general financial conditions make it undesirable to market the stock and the company concludes that it is wiser to husband, for working capital, the cash which it had intended to use in paying the stockholders a dividend, and, instead, to pay the dividend in the common stock which it had planned to sell; would not the stock so distributed be a distribution of profits—and hence, when received, be income of the stockholder and taxable as such? If this be conceded, why should it not be equally income of the stockholder, and taxable as such, if the common stock created by capitalizing profits had been originally created for the express purpose of being distributed as a dividend to the stockholder who afterwards received it?

"*Second.* It has been said that a dividend payable in bonds or preferred stock created for the purpose of distributing profits may be income and taxable as such, but that the case is different where the distribution is in common stock created for that purpose. Various reasons are assigned for making this distinction. One is that the proportion of the stockholder's ownership to the aggregate number of the shares of the company is not changed by the distribution. But that is equally true where the dividend is paid in its bonds or in its preferred stock. Furthermore, neither maintenance nor change in the proportionate ownership of a stockholder in a corporation has any bearing upon the question here involved. Another reason assigned is that the value of the old stock held is reduced approximately by the value of the new stock received, so that the stockholder after receipt of the stock dividend has no more than he had before it was paid. That is equally true whether the dividend be paid in cash or in other property, for instance, bonds, scrip or preferred stock of the company. The payment from profits of a large cash dividend, and even a small one, customarily lowers the then market value of the stock because the undivided property represented by each share has been correspondingly reduced. The argument which appears to be most strongly urged for the stockholders is, that when a stock dividend is made, no portion of the assets of the company is thereby seg-

[301]

regated for the stockholder. But does the issue of new bonds or of preferred stock created for use as a dividend result in any segregation of assets for the stockholder? In each case he receives a piece of paper which entitles him to certain rights in the undivided property. Clearly segregation of assets in a physical sense is not an essential of income. The year's gains of a partner are taxable as income, although there, likewise, no segregation of his share in the gains from that of his partners is had.

"The objection that there has been no segregation is presented also in another form. It is argued that until there is a segregation, the stockholder cannot know whether he has really received gains; since the gains may be invested in plant or merchandise or other property and perhaps be later lost. But is not this equally true of the share of a partner in the year's profits of the firm or, indeed, of the profits of the individual who is engaged in business alone? And is it not true, also, when dividends are paid in cash? The gains of a business, whether conducted by an individual, by a firm, or by a corporation, are ordinarily reinvested in large part. Many a cash dividend honestly declared as a distribution of profits, proves later to have been paid out of capital, because errors in forecast prevent correct ascertainment of values. Until a business venture has been completely liquidated it can never be determined with certainty whether there have been profits unless the returns have at least exceeded the capital originally invested. Business men, dealing with the problem practically, fix necessary periods and rules for determining whether there have been net profits— that is, income or gains. They protect themselves from being seriously misled by adopting a system of depreciation charges and reserves. Then, they act upon their own determination, whether profits have been made. Congress in legislating has wisely adopted their practices as its own rules of action.

"*Third.* The Government urges that it would have been

within the power of Congress to have taxed as income of the stockholder his *pro rata* share of undistributed profits earned, even if no stock dividend representing it had been paid. Strong reasons may be assigned for such a view. . . . The undivided share of a partner in the year's undistributed profits of his firm is taxable as income of the partner, although the share in the gain is not evidenced by any action taken by the firm. Why may not the stockholder's interest in the gains of the company? The law finds no difficulty in disregarding the corporate fiction whenever that is deemed necessary to attain a just result. . . . The stockholder's interest in the property of the corporation differs, not fundamentally, but in form only, from the interest of a partner in the property of the firm. There is much authority for the proposition that, under our law, a partnership or joint stock company is just as distinct and palpable an entity in the idea of the law, as distinguished from the individuals composing it, as is a corporation. No reason appears why Congress, in legislating under a grant of power so comprehensive as that authorizing the levy of an income tax, should be limited by the particular view of the relation of the stockholder to the corporation and its property which may, in the absence of legislation, have been taken by this Court. But we have no occasion to decide the question whether Congress might have taxed to the stockholder his undivided share of the corporation's earnings. For Congress has in this Act limited the income tax to that share of the stockholder in the earnings which is, in effect, distributed by means of the stock dividend paid. In other words, to render the stockholder taxable there must be both earnings made *and* a dividend paid. Neither earnings without dividend —nor a dividend without earnings—subjects the stockholder to taxation under the Revenue Act of 1916.

"*Fourth.* The equivalency of all dividends representing profits, whether paid in cash or in stock, is so complete that serious question of the taxability of stock dividends would probably never have been made if Congress had undertaken to tax only those dividends which represented profits earned during the year in which the dividend was paid or in the year preceding. But this Court, construing liberally, not only the constitutional grant of power, but also the Revenue Act of 1913, held that Congress might tax, and had taxed, to the stockholder dividends received during the year, although earned by the company long before; and even prior to the adoption of the Sixteenth Amendment. . . . That rule, if indiscriminatingly applied to all stock dividends representing profits earned, might, in view of corporate practice, have worked considerable hardship, and have raised serious questions. Many corporations, without legally capitalizing any part of their profits, had assigned definitely some part or all of the annual balances remaining after paying the usual cash dividends, to the uses to which permanent capital is ordinarily applied. Some of the corporations doing this, transferred such balances on their books to 'surplus' account—distinguishing between such permanent 'surplus' and the 'undivided profits' account. Other corporations, without this formality, had assumed that the annual accumulating balances carried as undistributed profits were to be treated as capital permanently invested in the business. And still others, without definite assumption of any kind, had so used undivided profits for capital purposes. To have made the revenue law apply retroactively so as to reach such accumulated profits, if and whenever it should be deemed desirable to capitalize them legally by the issue of additional stock distributed as a dividend to stockholders, would have worked great injustice. Congress endeavored in the Revenue Act of 1916 to guard against any serious hardship which might otherwise have arisen from making taxable stock dividends representing profits earned within the tax year or in the year preceding; but it did limit the taxability to such dividends representing accumulated profits. It did not limit the taxability to stock dividends representing profits earned since

March 1, 1913. Thereby stockholders were given notice that their share also in undistributed profits accumulating thereafter was at some time to be taxed as income. And Congress sought by §3 to discourage the postponement of distribution for the illegitimate purpose of evading liability to surtaxes.

"*Fifth.* The decision of this Court, that earnings made before the adoption of the Sixteenth Amendment, but paid out in cash dividend after its adoption, were taxable as income of the stockholder, involved a very liberal construction of the Amendment. To hold now that earnings both made and paid out after the adoption of the Sixteenth Amendment cannot be taxed as income of the stockholders if paid in the form of a stock dividend, involves an exceeding narrow construction of it. As said by Mr. Chief Justice Marshall in *Brown* v. *Maryland*, 12 Wheat. 419, 446:

'To construe the power so as to impair its efficacy, would tend to defeat an object, in the attainment of which the American public took, and justly took, the strong interest which arose from a full conviction of its necessity.'

"No decision heretofore rendered by this Court requires us to hold that Congress, in providing for the taxation of stock dividends, exceeded the power conferred upon it by the Sixteenth Amendment. The two cases mainly relied upon to show that this was beyond the power of Congress are *Towne* v. *Eisner*, 245 U. S. 418, which involved a question not of constitutional power but of statutory construction, and *Gibbons* v. *Mahon*, 136 U. S. 549, which involved a question arising between life tenant and remainderman. So far as concerns *Towne* v. *Eisner* we have only to bear in mind what was there said (p. 425): 'But it is not necessarily true that income means the same thing in the Constitution and the [an] Act.' *Gibbons* v.

[305]

Mahon is even less an authority for a narrow construction of the power to tax incomes conferred by the Sixteenth Amendment. In that case the Court was required to determine how, in the administration of an estate in the District of Columbia, a stock dividend, representing profits, received after the decedent's death, should be disposed of as between life tenant and remainderman. The question was in essence: What shall the intention of the testator be presumed to have been? On this question there was great diversity of opinion and practice in the courts of English-speaking countries. Three well-defined rules were then competing for acceptance; two of these involved an arbitrary rule of distribution, the third equitable apportionment. See *Cook on Corporations*, 7th Ed., §§552-558.

"1. The so-called English rule, declared in 1799, by *Brander* v. *Brander*, 4 Ves. Jr. 800, that a dividend representing profits, whether in cash, stock or other property, belongs to the life tenant if it was a regular or ordinary dividend, and belongs to the remainderman if it was an extraordinary dividend.

"2. The so-called Massachusetts rule, declared in 1868 by *Minot* v. *Paine*, 99 Mass. 101, that a dividend representing profits, whether regular, ordinary, or extraordinary, if in cash belongs to the life tenant, and if in stock belongs to the remainderman.

"3. The so-called Pennsylvania rule, declared in 1857 by *Earp's Appeal*, 28 Pa. 368, that where a stock dividend is paid, the court shall inquire into the circumstances under which the fund had been earned and accumulated out of which the dividend, whether a regular, an ordinary, or an extraordinary one, was paid. If it finds that the stock dividend was paid out of profits earned since the decedent's death, the stock dividend belongs to the life tenant; if the court finds that the stock dividend was paid from capital or from profits earned before

[306]

the decedent's death, the stock dividend belongs to the remainderman.

"This Court adopted in *Gibbons* v. *Mahon* as the rule of administration for the District of Columbia, the so-called Massachusetts rule, the opinion being delivered in 1890 by Mr. Justice Gray. Since then the same question has come up for decision in many of the States. The so-called Massachusetts rule, although approved by this Court, has found favor in only a few States. The so-called Pennsylvania rule, on the other hand, has been adopted since by so many of the States (including New York and California) that it has come to be known as the 'American rule.' Whether, in view of these facts and the practical results of the operation of the two rules as shown by the experience of the thirty years which have elapsed since the decision in *Gibbons* v. *Mahon*, it might be desirable for this Court to reconsider the question there decided, as some other courts have done (see 29 *Harvard Law Review* 551), we have no occasion to consider in this case. For, as this Court there pointed out (136 U. S. 560), the question involved was one 'between the owners of successive interests in particular shares,' and not, as in *Bailey* v. *Railroad Co.*, 22 Wall. 604, a question 'between the corporation and the Government, and [which] depended upon the terms of a statute carefully framed to prevent corporations from evading payment of the tax upon their earnings.'

"We have, however, not merely argument; we have examples which should convince us that 'there is no inherent, necessary and immutable reason why stock dividends should always be treated as capital.' (*Tax Commissioner* v. *Putnam*, 227 Mass. 522, 533.) The Supreme Judicial Court of Massachusetts has steadfastly adhered, despite ever-renewed protest, to the rule that every stock dividend is, as between life tenant and remainderman, capital and not income. But in construing the

Massachusetts Income Tax Amendment, which is substantially identical with the Federal Amendment, that court held that the Legislature was thereby empowered to levy an income tax upon stock dividends representing profits. The courts of England have, with some relaxation, adhered to their rule that every extraordinary dividend is, as between life tenant and remainderman, to be deemed capital. But in 1913 the Judicial Committee of the Privy Council held that a stock dividend representing accumulated profits was taxable like an ordinary cash dividend. . . . In dismissing the appeal these words of the Chief Justice of the Supreme Court of Western Australia were quoted, which show that the facts involved were identical with those in the case at bar:

'Had the company distributed the £101,450 among the shareholders and had the shareholders repaid such sums to the company as the price of the 81,160 new shares, the duty on the £101,450 would clearly have been payable. Is not this virtually the effect of what was actually done? I think it is.'

"*Sixth*. If stock dividends representing profits are held exempt from taxation under the Sixteenth Amendment, the owners of the most successful businesses in America, will, as the facts in this case illustrate, be able to escape taxation on a large part of what is actually their income. So far as their profits are represented by stock received as dividends they will pay these taxes not upon their income but only upon the income of their income. That such a result was intended by the people of the United States when adopting the Sixteenth Amendment is inconceivable. Our sole duty is to ascertain their intent as therein expressed. In terse, comprehensive language befitting the Constitution, they empowered Congress 'to lay and collect taxes on incomes from whatever source derived.' They intended to include thereby everything which by reasonable understanding can fairly be regarded as income. That stock dividends representing profits are so regarded, not only by the plain people, but by investors and financiers, and by most of the courts of the country, is shown, beyond peradventure, by their acts and by their utterances. It seems to me clear, therefore, that Congress possesses the power which it exercised to make dividends representing profits, taxable as income, whether the medium in which the dividend is paid be cash or stock, and that it may define, as it has done, what dividends representing profits shall be deemed income. It surely is not clear that the enactment exceeds the power granted by the Sixteenth Amendment. And, as this Court has so often said, the high prerogative of declaring an Act of Congress invalid, should never be exercised except in a clear case.

'It is but a decent respect due to the wisdom, the integrity, and the patriotism of the legislative body, by which any law is passed, to presume in favor of its validity, until its violation of the Constitution is proved beyond all reasonable doubt.' (*Ogden* v. *Saunders*, 12 Wheat. 213, 270.)"

Eisner, as Collector of United States Internal Revenue for the Third District of the State of New York, v. *Macomber*
252 U. S. 189, 220

State Taxation of Corporations

(Dissenting Opinion, *Quaker City Cab Co.* v. *Pennsylvania*, 1928)

TRANSPORTATION COMPANIES, ORGANIZED AS CORPORATIONS, WERE subjected by a Pennsylvania statute passed in 1889 to a tax on their gross receipts derived from passengers and freight transported wholly within the state. A Philadelphia taxicab company appealed to the Supreme Court from a judgment of the State court assessing the tax against it. Because its competitors, who were doing business as individuals and partnerships, were not subject to the tax, the company claimed that it was denied the equal protection of the laws, in violation of the Fourteenth Amendment.

Six members of the Court decided that the statute was unconstitutional. Their spokesman was Mr. Justice Butler. Pointing to the fact that the discrimination between corporations and those conducting the same business under other forms of organization was based solely on the character of the owner, he concluded that the statute "fails to meet the requirement that a classification to be consistent with the equal protection clause must be based on a real and substantial difference having reasonable relation to the subject of the legislation."

Holmes,* Brandeis, and Stone, JJ., wrote dissenting opinions. That of Mr. Justice Brandeis follows:

"IT HAS BEEN the consistent policy of Pennsylvania since 1840 to subject businesses conducted by corporations to heavier taxation than like businesses conducted by individuals. It has likewise been the consistent policy of the State since 1864 to subject some kinds of businesses conducted by corporations to heavier taxation than other businesses conducted by corporations. Pur-

* See page 141, *The Dissenting Opinions of Mr. Justice Holmes.*

suant to this policy, the Legislature of Pennsylvania laid, in 1889, upon public service corporations furnishing transportation for hire, a gross receipts tax of eight mills on each dollar of gross receipts earned wholly within the State. (Act of June 1, 1889, P. L. 1889, pp. 420, 431.) That statute has remained unchanged so far as affects the question here involved. It applies equally to every corporation engaged in the same kind of business, and makes no discrimination between foreign and domestic corporations. But neither this specific tax, nor any equivalent tax, is laid upon individuals or partnerships engaged in the same business. Nor is this tax or an equivalent laid upon corporations which supply certain other public services.

"The Supreme Court of the State has construed this statute as applicable to all taxicab corporations; and has held the Quaker City Cab Company, a foreign corporation doing an intrastate business in Pennsylvania since the year 1917, liable for taxes accrued on that business for the last six months of 1923, which was agreed on as a test period. The Company claims that the statute as construed and applied violates the Federal Constitution. There is no contention that it violates either the commerce clause or the due process clause. The claim is that it denies equal protection of the laws; and the contention is rested specifically upon the ground that the exaction 'is not a tax peculiar to corporations.'

"As the statute applies equally to domestic and to foreign corporations, cases like *Southern Ry. Co.* v. *Greene,* 216 U. S. 400; *Kentucky Finance Corporation* v. *Paramount Auto Exchange,* 262 U. S. 544; *Hanover Fire Insurance Co.* v. *Harding,* 272 U. S. 494; and *Power Manufacturing Co.* v. *Saunders,* 274 U. S. 490, have no application. And no claim is made that the Federal Constitution prevents a State from taxing corporations engaged in one class of business more heavily than those engaged in another. . . . The fundamental question requiring decision is a general one. Does the equality clause prevent a State from imposing a heavier burden of taxation upon corporations engaged exclusively in intrastate commerce, than upon individuals engaged under like circumstances in the same kind of business? The narrower question presented is, whether this heavier burden may be imposed by a form of tax 'not peculiarly applicable to corporations.' That is, by a tax of such a character that it might have been extended to individuals if the Legislature had seen fit to do so.

"The equality clause does not forbid a State to classify for purposes of taxation. Discrimination through classification is said to violate that clause only where it is such as to preclude the assumption that it was made 'in the exercise of legislative judgment and discretion.' . . . In other words, the equality clause requires merely that the classification shall be reasonable. We call that action reasonable which an informed, intelligent, just-minded, civilized man could rationally favor. In passing upon legislation assailed under the equality clause we have declared that the classification must rest upon a difference which is real, as distinguished from one which is seeming, specious, or fanciful, so that all actually situated similarly will be treated alike, that the object of the classification must be the accomplishment of a purpose or the promotion of a policy which is within the permissible functions of the State, and that the difference must bear a relation to the object of the legislation which is substantial, as distinguished from one which is speculative, remote, or negligible. Subject to this limitation of reasonableness, the equality clause has left unimpaired, both in range and in flexibility, the State's power to classify for purposes of taxation. Can it be said that the classification here in question is unreasonable?

"The difference between a business carried on in corporate form and the same business carried on by natural persons is, of course, a real and important one.*** Because of this difference, Congress has repeatedly discriminated against incorporated concerns and in favor of the unincorporated. The Corporation Tax of August 5, 1909, c. 6, §38, 36 Stat. 11, 112, imposed a tax of one percent on the net income of corporations when a corresponding tax was not imposed upon the income of individuals. Since the adoption of the Sixteenth Amendment, the net income of both corporations and individuals has been subjected to taxes of the same nature; but the tax imposed has discriminated heavily against at least many of the businesses which are incorporated.

"The imposition of the heavier tax on corporations by means of an annual tax in the form of a franchise tax declared to be for the privilege of doing business in corporate form is common, and, since *Home Insurance Co.* v. *New York,* 134 U. S. 594, 606, 607, the validity of such a tax has not been questioned. This heavier burden the State may impose by means of an annual franchise tax in addition to the ordinary property and excise taxes imposed upon all persons, natural and artificial. Or it may impose the heavier burden by means of a franchise tax which will be the sole tax upon the corporation; that is, it may make the franchise tax so high as to include both the tax representing the special privilege of doing business in corporate form and the equivalent for taxes borne by natural persons engaged in the same occupation. Few propositions are better settled than the rule that, in determining whether a State tax violates the Federal Constitution, we are to look at the operation or effect of the tax and not at its name or form. . . . Since a State is permitted to impose upon the corporation more than a *pro rata* share of the common burden of taxation, I find nothing in the Federal Constitution which prohibits it from adopting any of the familiar kinds of taxes as the means of the heavier imposition. Surely, there is nothing inherently objectionable in the long-established, commonly used, gross earnings tax, which should prevent its being selected for that purpose.

"Why Pennsylvania should have chosen to impose upon

corporations a heavier tax than upon individuals or partnerships engaged under like circumstances in the same line of business, or why it should have selected this particular form of tax as the means of doing so, we have no occasion to enquire. The State may have done this because, in view of the advantages inherent in corporate organization, the Legislature believed that course necessary in order to insure a just distribution of the burdens of government. In *Flint* v. *Stone-Tracy Co.*, 220 U. S. 107, 162, this Court listed the advantages which justify the imposition of special taxes on corporations: 'The continuity of the business, without interruption by death or dissolution, the transfer of property interests by the disposition of shares of stock, the advantages of business controlled and managed by corporate directors, the general absence of individual liability, these and other things inhere in the advantages of business thus conducted, which do not exist when the same business is conducted by private individuals or partnerships.'

"In Pennsylvania the practice of imposing heavier burdens upon corporations dates from a time when there, as elsewhere in America, the fear of growing corporate power was common. The present heavier imposition may be a survival of an early effort to discourage the resort to that form of organization. The apprehension is now less common. But there are still intelligent, informed, just-minded and civilized persons who believe that the rapidly growing aggregation of capital through corporations constitutes an insidious menace to the liberty of the citizen; that it tends to increase the subjection of labor to capital; that, because of the guidance and control necessarily exercised by great corporations upon those engaged in business, individual initiative is being impaired and creative power will be lessened; that the absorption of capital by corporations, and their perpetual life, may bring evils similar to those which attended mortmain; that the evils incident to the accelerating absorption of business by corporations outweigh the benefits thereby secured; and that the process of absorption should be retarded. The Court may think such views unsound. But obviously the requirement that a classification must be reasonable does not imply that the policy embodied in the classification made by the Legislature of a State shall seem to this Court a wise one. It is sufficient for us that there is nothing in the Federal Constitution which prohibits a State from imposing a heavier tax burden upon corporations organized for the purpose of engaging exclusively in intrastate commerce, and that there is nothing inherently objectionable in the instrument which Pennsylvania selected for imposing the heavier burden—the gross receipts tax.

"For these reasons, I should have no doubt that the statute of Pennsylvania was well within its power, if the question were an open one. But it seems to me that the validity of such legislation has been established by a decision of this Court, rendered after much consideration. The contention here sustained differs in no essential respect from that made and overruled in *Flint v. Stone-Tracy Co.*, 220 U. S. 107, 161. There, as here, the tax was imposed merely because the owner of the business was a corporation, as distinguished from an individual or a partnership. There, as here, the character of the owner was the sole fact on which the distinction was made to depend. There, as here, the discrimination was not based on any other difference in the source of the income or in the character of the property employed. The cases differ in but two respects, neither of them material."

Quaker City Cab Co. v. *Commonwealth of Pennsylvania*
277 U. S. 389, 403

VI. STATE AND NATION

"The Specter of a Lack of Uniformity"

(Dissenting Opinion, *Washington* v. *Dawson*, 1924)

THE STATE OF WASHINGTON SOUGHT TO COMPEL A COMPANY EN-
gaged in the business of stevedoring to contribute to the accident fund
provided for by the State Workmen's Compensation Act. The company's employees worked only on board ships in the navigable waters of
the Puget Sound. The Court held in *Southern Pacific Co.* v. *Jensen*, 244
U. S. 205, and *Knickerbocker Ice Co.* v. *Stewart*, 253 U. S. 149, that
Congress could not make subject to State Compensation Laws maritime
accidents, over which the Constitution gives jurisdiction to the Federal
courts. But Congress made a second attempt to do so, this time excepting
from its act the master and members of the crew.

Both State and Federal Supreme Courts found the earlier decisions
controlling, and rejected the claim of the State. The object of the
constitutional grant of jurisdiction, wrote Mr. Justice McReynolds,
was to relieve maritime commerce from unnecessary burdens by making
it subject to one uniform law. Congress has power to enact a general
compensation law for maritime cases; it may not delegate that power
to the States.

Justice Holmes, who had previously alluded to "the specter of a
lack of uniformity," briefly stated that he was not satisfied with the
reasoning of the cases cited,* but had to "leave it to those who think the
principle right to say how far it extends."

Justice Brandeis dissented:

"A CONCERN, doing a general upholstering business in New
York, directs one of its regular employees, resident there, to
make repairs on a vessel lying alongside a New York dock.

---

* His stand in the *Southern Pacific* and *Knickerbocker Ice* cases is expressed in *The
Dissenting Opinions of Mr. Justice Holmes.*

The ship, then temporarily out of commission, is owned and enrolled in New York, and when used is employed only within the State. While on the vessel engaged in making the repairs, the employee is injured without the fault of any one and is disabled for life. A statute of New York provides that, in such a case, he and his dependents shall receive compensation out of funds which employers are obliged to provide. To such State legislation Congress has, in express terms, given its sanction. Under the rule announced by the Court, the Federal Constitution prohibits recovery. If, perchance, the accident had occurred while the employee so engaged was on the dock, the Constitution would permit recovery. Or, if happily he had been killed and the accident had been due to the employer's negligence, recovery (which is provided for by another State statute) would likewise be permitted under the Constitution, even though the accident had occurred on board the vessel.

"The Constitution contains, of course, no provision which, in terms, deals, in any way, with the subject of workmen's compensation. The prohibition found by the Court rests solely upon a clause in §2 of Article 3: 'The judicial power [of the United States] shall extend*** to all cases of admiralty and maritime jurisdiction'.

"The conclusion that the State law violates the Constitution and that the consent of Congress cannot save it, is reached solely by a process of deduction. The chain of reasoning involved is a long one. The argument is that the grant of judicial power to the United States confers upon Congress, by implication, legislative power over the substantive maritime law; that this legislative power in Congress (while not necessarily exclusive) precludes State legislation which 'works material prejudice to the characteristic features of the general maritime law or interferes with the proper harmony and uniformity of that law in its international or interstate relations' [quoting a case cited by the majority]; that there is a rule of the general maritime law by which an employer is not liable, except in case of negligence, for an occupational injury occurring on board a vessel; that the rule applies whenever the vessel on which the injury occurs is afloat on navigable water, even if the vessel, made fast to a dock, is out of commission; that the rule applies to occupations which, like upholstering, are not in their nature inherently maritime; that the rule governs the relations not only of the ship and its owners to their employees, but also the relations of independent contractors to their employees who customarily work on land; that this rule is a characteristic feature of the general maritime law; that for a State to change the rule, even as applied to independent contractors doing work on craft moored to a dock, temporarily disabled, and normally employed wholly within the State, interferes with the proper harmony and uniformity of the general maritime law in its international and interstate relations; and that hence a statute of a State, which provides that employers within it shall be liable to employees within it for occupational accidents occurring within it, violates the Federal Constitution, notwithstanding the State statute is expressly sanctioned by Congress.

"Such is the chain of reasoning. Every link of the chain is essential to the conclusion stated. If any link fails, the argument falls. Several of the links are, in my opinion, unfounded assumption, which crumbles at the touch of reason. How can a law of New York, making a New York employer liable to a New York employee for every occupational injury occurring within the State, mar the proper harmony and uniformity of the assumed general maritime law in its interstate and international relations, when neither a ship, nor a ship owner, is the employer affected, even though the accident occurs on board a vessel on navigable waters? The relation of the independent contractor to his employee is a matter wholly of State concern. The employer's obligation to pay and the employee's right to receive compensation are not dependent upon any act or omission of the ship or of its owners. To impose upon such employer the obligation to make compensation in case of an occupational injury in no way affects the operation of the ship. Nor can it affect the shipowners in any respect, except as every other tax, direct or indirect, laid by a State or municipality may affect, by increasing the cost of living and of doing business, every one who has occasion to enter it and many who have not. This is true of the application of the Workmen's Compensation Law, whether the service rendered by the independent contractor is in its nature non-maritime, like upholstering, or is inherently maritime, like stevedoring. The requirement by the State is a regulation of the business of upholstering or stevedoring. It is not a regulation of shipping. It in no respect attempts to modify, or deal with, admiralty jurisdiction or procedure, or the substantive maritime law. It is but an exercise of the local police power. To impose upon the independent employer the obligation to provide compensation for accidents occurring on a vessel in port, while the vessel is made fast to the dock, in fact, cannot conceivably interfere with the proper harmony and uniformity of the general maritime law in its international or interstate relations.

"Moreover, it is not a characteristic feature of the general maritime law that the employer, in case of accident, is liable to an employee only for negligence. The characteristic feature is the very contrary. To one of the crew, the vessel and her owners are liable, even in the absence of negligence, maintenance, care, and wages—at least, so long as the voyage is continued. To him, they are liable, also, even in the absence of negligence, for indemnity or damages, if the injury results from unseaworthiness of the ship or from failure to supply and keep in order the proper appliances. The legal rights, in case of accident to persons other than members of the crew, were not determined by the maritime law until recently. The admiralty court, instead of extending to these persons this characteristic feature, borrowed the rule of negligence from the common-law courts, making modifications conformable to its views of justice.

"The mere fact that the accident is an incident of a maritime contract, and the service performed thereunder is inherently maritime, does not preclude the application of the workmen's compensation law. The stevedore can recover under the workmen's compensation law if the injury happens to occur on land, although the contract of the stevedoring concern is confessedly a maritime one, and the stevedore is employed in a maritime service quite as much while he is on the dock as after he crosses the gangplank and enters the ship. Underlying the whole chain of reasoning by which the conclusion is reached that the State and Federal statutes are unconstitutional, will be found the legally indefensible assumption that the liability under the Workmen's Compensation Law is governed by the law of the locality in which the accident happened; that is, by the rule that in tort the test of admiralty jurisdiction is presence on navigable waters. There is no more reason why the mere fact that the injury occurs on navigable waters should make applicable the maritime law to liabilities arising under the Workmen's Compensation Law than that it should make the maritime law applicable, in such cases, to the liability under a general accident insurance policy. Tort is, in fact, not an element in the liability created by the Workmen's Compensation Law. On the contrary, the basis of this legislation is liability without fault. Nor does the Workmen's Compensation Law create a status between employer and employee. It provides an incident to the employment which is often likened to a contractual obligation, even where the Workmen's Compensation Law is not of the class called optional. It will hardly be contended that an act occurring beyond the geographical limits of a State cannot be made the basis for the creation of rights to be enjoyed or enforced within it. Workmen's Compensation Laws which provide for compensation for injuries occurring in States other than that of the residence of the employer and the employee are held constitutional. Why should they not be deemed valid where they provide for accidents occurring within the State, but upon navigable waters?

"A further assumption is that Congress, which has power to make and to unmake the general maritime law, can have no voice in determining which of its provisions require adaptation to peculiar local needs and as to which absolute uniformity is an essential of the proper harmony of international and interstate maritime relations. This assumption has no support in reason; and it is inconsistent (at least in principle) with the powers conferred upon Congress in other connections. The grant 'of the*** judicial power*** to all cases of admiralty and maritime jurisdiction' is surely no broader in terms than the grant of power 'to regulate commerce with foreign nations and among the several States.' Yet as to commerce, Congress may, at least in large measure, determine whether uniformity of regulation is required or diversity is permissible. Likewise, Congress is given exclusive power of legislation over its forts, arsenals, dockyards, and other needful places and buildings. But it may permit the diverse laws of the several States to govern the relations of men within them. Congress has exclusive power to legislate concerning the Army and Navy of the United States, to declare war, to determine to what extent citizens shall aid in its prosecution, and how effective aid can best be secured. But State legislation directly affecting these subjects has been sustained. In respect to bankruptcy, duties, imposts, excises, and naturalization the Constitution prescribes uniformity. Still the provision in the Bankruptcy Law giving effect to the divergent exemption laws of the several States was held valid. Absolute uniformity in things maritime is confessedly not essential to the proper harmony of the maritime law in its interstate and international relations. This is illustrated both by the cases which hold constitutional State regulation of pilotage and liens created by State laws in aid of maritime contracts, and by those which hold that there are broad fields of maritime activity to which admiralty jurisdiction does not extend. A notable instance of the latter is the liability in tort for injuries inflicted by a ship to a dock, or to maritime workers on the dock engaged in the inherently maritime operation of stevedoring.

"The recent legislation of Congress seeks, in a statesmanlike manner, to limit the practical scope and effect of our decisions in *Southern Pacific Co.* v. *Jensen, Knickerbocker Ice Co.* v. *Stewart,* and later cases, by making them hereafter applicable only to the relations of the ship to her master and crew. To hold that Congress can effect this result by sanctioning the application of State Workmen's Compensation Laws to accidents to any other class of employees occurring on the navigable waters of the State would not, in my judgment, require us to overrule any of these cases. It would require merely that we should limit the application of the rule therein announced, and that we should declare our disapproval of certain expressions used in the opinions. Such limitation of principles previously announced, and such express disapproval of *dicta,* are often necessary. It is an unavoidable incident of the search by courts of last resort for the true rule. The process of inclusion and exclusion, so often applied in developing a rule, cannot end with its first enunciation. The rule as announced must be deemed tentative. For the many and varying facts to which it will be applied cannot be foreseen. Modification implies growth. It is the life of the law.

"If the Court is of opinion that this Act of Congress is in necessary conflict with its recent decisions, those cases should be frankly overruled. The reasons for doing so are persuasive. Our experience in attempting to apply the rule, and helpful discussion by friends of the Court, have made it clear that the rule declared is legally unsound; that it disturbs legal principles long established; and that if adhered to, it will make a serious addition to the classes of cases which this Court is required to review. Experience and discussion have also made apparent how unfortunate are the results, economically and socially. It has, in part, frustrated a promising attempt to alleviate some of the misery, and remove some of the injustice, incident to the conduct of industry and commerce. These far-reaching and unfortunate results of the rule declared in *Southern Pacific Co.* v. *Jensen* cannot have been foreseen when the decision was rendered. If adhered to, appropriate legislative provision, urgently needed, cannot be made until another amendment of the Constitution shall have been adopted. For no Federal workmen's compensation law could satisfy the varying and peculiar economic and social needs incident to the diversity of conditions in the several States.

"The doctrine of *stare decisis* should not deter us from overruling that case and those which follow it. The decisions are recent ones. They have not been acquiesced in. They have not created a rule of property around which vested interests have clustered. They affect solely matters of a transitory nature. On the other hand, they affect seriously the lives of men, women, and children, and the general welfare. *Stare decisis* is ordinarily a wise rule of action. But it is not a universal, inexorable command. The instances in which the Court has disregarded its admonition are many. The existing admiralty jurisdiction rests, in large part, upon like action of the Court in *The Genesee Chief*, 12 How. 443, 456. In that case the Court overruled *The Thomas Jefferson*, 10 Wheat. 428, and *The Steamboat Orleans* v. *Phoebus*, 11 Pet. 175; and a doctrine declared by Mr. Justice Story with the concurrence of Chief Justice Marshall, and approved by Chancellor Kent, was abandoned when found to be erroneous, although it had been acted on for twenty-six years."

State of Washington v. *W. C. Dawson & Co.*
264 U. S. 219, 228

The "Delicate Adjustment" of State and Federal Regulation

(Dissenting Opinion, *Di Santo* v. *Pennsylvania,* 1927)

A PENNSYLVANIA STATUTE REQUIRED A LICENSE OF EVERY PERSON OR corporation, other than a railroad or steamship company, engaged within the State in the sale of steamship tickets. Before a license could be granted, the applicant was compelled to furnish proof of good moral character and to put up a bond to protect from fraud those who dealt with him. An annual fee of $50 was charged..

A steamship agent was convicted of selling tickets without a license. He claimed that the statute was in conflict with the clause in the Constitution which gives to Congress the power to regulate interstate and foreign commerce. The Supreme Court, in an opinion delivered by Mr. Justice Butler, upheld his contention. The sale of tickets was said to be so directly related to foreign commerce that the sole power to regulate it was in Congress.

Justices Holmes, Brandeis and Stone dissented, the latter two writing opinions with which both the others agreed. Brandeis wrote:

"THE STATUTE is an exertion of the police power of the State. Its evident purpose is to prevent a particular species of fraud and imposition found to have been practiced in Pennsylvania upon persons of small means, unfamiliar with our language and institutions. Much of the immigration into the United States is effected by arrangements made here for remittance of the means of travel. The individual immigrant is often an advance guard. After gaining a foothold here, he has his wife

[328]

and children, aged parents, brothers, sisters or other relatives follow. To this end he remits steamship tickets or orders for transportation. The purchase of the tickets involves trust in the dealer. This is so not only because of the nature of the transaction, but also because a purchaser when unable to pay the whole price at one time makes successive deposits on account, the ticket or order not being delivered until full payment is made. The facilities for remitting both cash and steamship tickets are commonly furnished by private bankers of the same nationality as the immigrant. It was natural that the supervision of persons engaged in the business of supplying steamship tickets should be committed by the statute to the Commissioner of Banking.

"Although the purchase made is of an ocean steamship ticket, the transaction regulated is wholly intrastate—as much so as if the purchase were of local real estate or of local theatre tickets. There is no purpose on the part of the State to regulate foreign commerce. The statute is not an obstruction to foreign commerce. It does not discriminate against foreign commerce. It places no direct burden upon such commerce. It does not affect the commerce except indirectly. Congress could, of course, deal with the subject, because it is connected with foreign commerce. But it has not done so. Nor has it legislated on any allied subject. Thus, there can be no contention that Congress has occupied the field. And obviously, also, this is not a case in which the silence of Congress can be interpreted as a prohibition of State action—as a declaration that in the sale of ocean steamship tickets fraud may be practiced without let or hindrance. If Pennsylvania must submit to seeing its citizens defrauded, it is not because Congress has so willed, but because the Constitution so commands. I cannot believe that it does.

"Unlike the ordinance considered in *Texas Transport Co. v. New Orleans*, 264 U. S. 150, this statute is not a revenue measure. The license fee is small. The whole of the proceeds is required to defray the expense of supervising the business. Unlike the measure considered in *Real Silk Mills* v. *Portland*, 268 U. S. 325, 336, this statute is not an instrument of discrimination against interstate or foreign commerce. Unlike that considered in *Shafer* v. *Farmers' Grain Co.*, 268 U. S. 189, 199, it does not affect the price of articles moving in interstate commerce. The licensing and supervision of dealers in steamship tickets is in essence an inspection law. . . .

"The fact that the sale of the ticket is made as a part of the transaction in foreign or interstate commerce does not preclude application of State inspection laws, where, as here, Congress has not entered the field, and the State regulation neither obstructs, discriminates against, nor directly burdens the commerce. . . . To require that the dealer in tickets be licensed in order to guard against fraud in the local sale of tickets certainly affects interstate or foreign commerce less directly than to provide a test of the locomotive engineer's skill, *Smith* v. *Alabama*, 124 U. S. 465; or eyesight, *Nashville, Chattanooga, & St. Louis Ry.* v. *Alabama*, 128 U. S. 96; or requiring that passenger cars be heated and guard posts placed on bridges, *N. Y., N. H., & H. R. R. Co.* v. *New York*, 165 U. S. 628; or requiring every railway to cause three of its regular passenger trains to stop each way daily at every village containing over three thousand inhabitants, *Lake Shore & Michigan Southern R. R. Co.* v. *Ohio*, 173 U. S. 285; or to require trains to limit within a city their speed to six miles an hour, *Erb.* v. *Morasch*, 177 U. S. 584; or to establish a standard for the locomotive headlight, *Atlantic Coast Line R. R.* v. *Georgia*, 234 U. S. 280; or to prescribe 'full crews,' *Chicago, Rock Island & Pacific Ry.* v. *Arkansas*, 219 U. S. 453; *St. Louis, Iron Mountain & Southern Ry. Co.* v. *Arkansas*, 240 U. S. 518; or to compel the providing of separate coaches for whites and colored persons, *South Covington, etc., Ry.* v. *Kentucky*, 252

[330]

U. S. 399; or to compel a railroad to eliminate grade crossings, although the expense involved may imperil its solvency, *Erie R. R. Co.* v. *Public Utility Commissioners*, 254 U. S. 394, 409-412—State requirements sustained by this Court. . . .

"It is said that *McCall* v. *California*, 136 U. S. 104, requires that the Pennsylvania statute be held void. McCall was an employee of the railroad, not an independent solicitor or dealer. Di Santo, as the State court found the facts, was not an employee of a steamship company, nor an agent authorized to act for one; and it ruled, as a matter of statutory construction, that, if he had been such, he would not have been required by the statute to be licensed. It found him to be an independent dealer or contractor, 'a free lance,' authorized by the several steamship companies 'to sell tickets or orders entitling the persons therein named to passage upon steamers,' but 'with no obligation to any particular company,' except to remit the net amount payable by him to the company for a ticket or order sold. Moreover, the fee imposed by the San Francisco ordinance was an occupation tax, not an inspection fee. Here the Pennsylvania court found that the statute did not produce any revenue.

"On the facts, the *McCall Case* is distinguishable from that at bar. If, because of its reasoning, it is thought not to be distinguishable, it should be disregarded. The doctrine of *stare decisis* presents no obstacle. Disregard of the *McCall Case* would not involve unsettlement of any constitutional principle or of any rule of law, properly so called. It would involve merely refusal to repeat an error once made in applying a rule of law—an error which has already proved misleading as a precedent. While the question whether a particular statute has the effect of burdening interstate or foreign commerce directly presents always a question of law, the determination upon which the validity or invalidity of the statute depends, is largely

[331]

or wholly one of fact. The rule of law which governs the *McCall Case* and the one at bar is the same. It is that a State may not obstruct, discriminate against or directly burden interstate or foreign commerce. The question at bar is whether as applied to existing facts, this particular statute is a direct burden. The decision as to State regulations of this character, depends often, as was said in *Southern Railway* v. *King*, 217 U. S. 524, 533, 'upon their effect upon interstate commerce.' In that case, the Georgia blow post law was held constitutional, as not being a direct burden. In *Seaboard Air Line Ry.* v. *Blackwell*, 244 U. S. 310, the same statute was held, on other facts, to be void, because shown to be a direct burden. Each case required the decision of the question of law. Each involved merely an appreciation of the facts. Neither involved the declaration of a rule of law.

"It is usually more important that a rule of law be settled than that it be settled right. Even where the error in declaring the rule is a matter of serious concern, it is ordinarily better to seek correction by legislation. Often this is true although the question is a constitutional one. The human experience embodied in the doctrine of *stare decisis* teaches us, also, that often it is better to follow a precedent, although it does not involve the declaration of a rule. This is usually true so far as it concerns a particular statute, whether the error was made in construing it or in passing upon its validity. But the doctrine of *stare decisis* does not command that we err again when we have occasion to pass upon a different statute. In the search for truth through the slow process of inclusion and exclusion, involving trial and error, it behooves us to reject, as guides, the decisions upon such questions which prove to have been mistaken. This course seems to me imperative when, as here, the decision involves the delicate adjustment of conflicting claims of the Federal Government and the State to regulate commerce. The many cases on the commerce clause in which this Court has overruled or explained away its earlier decisions show that the wisdom of this course has been heretofore recognized. In the case at bar, also, the logic of words should yield to the logic of realities."

Di Santo v. *Pennsylvania*
273 U. S. 34, 37

VII. IDEAS EXPRESSED BEFORE 1916

The Oregon Brief

(*Muller* v. *Oregon*, 208 U. S. 412)

WHEN AN OREGON STATUTE, LIMITING THE LENGTH OF THE WORK-
day for women, was assailed in 1907 by a laundry which had violated
the law, Louis D. Brandeis was called in to prepare a brief in behalf of
the State. Up to this time labor laws had been argued in the abstract,
according to principles of property rights, freedom of contract, and
class legislation. Brandeis did an extraordinary thing. He corralled
relevant facts. He amassed what he called "the world's experience" and
offered these data to the Supreme Court of the United States.

Mr. Justice Brewer rendered the decision of the Court upholding
the validity of the statute on February 24, 1908. The Justice made
mention of the able argument of Mr. Brandeis and said, "We take
judicial cognizance of all matters of general knowledge."

The brief, prepared by Josephine Goldmark under the direction of
Mr. Brandeis, is given below. Asterisks indicate the omission of the
quotations from factory reports and other sources, too numerous for
inclusion in this volume. The editor's purpose is not to present the
testimony of experts but rather to acquaint readers with the nature
of this historic document.

"THIS CASE presents the single question whether the Statute
of Oregon, approved February 19, 1903, which provides that
'no female [shall] be employed in any mechanical establishment or factory or laundry' 'more than ten hours during the
day,' is unconstitutional and void as violating the Fourteenth
Amendment of the Federal Constitution.

"The decision in this case will, in effect, determine the constitutionality of nearly all the statutes in force in the United States, limiting the hours of labor of adult women, namely: [Excerpts are given from laws enacted by Massachusetts, Rhode Island, Louisiana, Connecticut, Maine, New Hampshire, Maryland, Virginia, Pennsylvania, New York, Nebraska, Washington, Wisconsin, North Dakota, South Dakota, Oklahoma, New Jersey, Colorado and South Carolina.]

ARGUMENT

"The legal rules applicable to this case are few and are well established, namely—

"*First:* The right to purchase or to sell labor is a part of the 'liberty' protected by the Fourteenth Amendment of the Federal Constitution. (*Lochner* v. *New York*, 198 U. S. 45, 53.)

"*Second:* The right to 'liberty' is, however, subject to such reasonable restraint of action as the State may impose in the exercise of the police power for the protection of health, safety, morals, and the general welfare. (*Lochner* v. *New York*, 198 U. S. 45, 53, 67.)

"*Third:* The mere assertion that a statute restricting 'liberty' relates, though in a remote degree, to the public health, safety, or welfare does not render it valid. The act must have a 'real or substantial relation to the protection of the public health and the public safety.' (*Jacobson* v. *Massachusetts*, 187 U. S. 11, 31.) It must have a 'more direct relation, as a means to an end, and the end itself must be appropriate and legitimate.' (*Lochner* v. *New York*, 198 U. S. 45, 56, 57, 61.)

"*Fourth:* Such a law will not be sustained if the Court can see that it has no real or substantial relation to public health, safety, or welfare, or that it is 'an unreasonable, unnecessary and arbitrary interference with the right of the individual to his personal liberty or to enter into those con-

[338]

tracts in relation to labor which may seem to him appropriate or necessary for the support of himself or his family.'

"But 'If the end which the Legislature seeks to accomplish be one to which its power extends, and if the means employed to that end, although not the wisest or the best, are yet not plainly and palpably unauthorized by law, then the Court cannot interfere. In other words, when the validity of a statute is questioned, the burden of proof, so to speak, is upon those' who assail it. (*Lochner* v. *New York*, 198 U. S. 45-68.)

"*Fifth:* The validity of the Oregon statute must therefore be sustained unless the Court can find that there is no 'fair ground, reasonable in and of itself, to say that there is material danger to the public health (or safety), or to the health (or safety) of the employees (or as to the general welfare), if the hours of labor are not curtailed.' (*Lochner* v. *New York*, 198 U. S. 45, 61.)

"The Oregon statute was obviously enacted for the purpose of protecting the public health, safety and welfare. Indeed, it declares:

'Section 5. Inasmuch as the female employees in the various establishments are not protected from overwork, an emergency is hereby declared to exist, and this act shall be in full force and effect from and after its approval by the Governor.'

"The facts of common knowledge of which the Court may take judicial notice (see *Holden* v. *Hardy*, 169 U. S. 366; *Jacobson* v. *Massachusetts*, 197 U. S. 11; *Lochner* v. *New York*, 198 U. S. 48) establish, we submit, conclusively, that there is reasonable ground for holding that to permit women in Oregon to work in a 'mechanical establishment, or factory, or laundry' more than ten hours in one day is dangerous to the public health, safety, morals, or welfare.

"These facts of common knowledge will be considered under the following heads:

"Part I. Legislation (foreign and American), restricting the hours of labor for women.

"Part II. The world's experience upon which the legislation limiting the hours of labor for women is based.

PART FIRST

I. *The Foreign Legislation*

"The leading countries in Europe in which women are largely employed in factory or similar work have found it necessary to take action for the protection of their health and safety and the public welfare, and have enacted laws limiting the hours of labor for adult women.

"About two generations have elapsed since the enactment of the first law. In no country in which the legal limitation upon the hours of labor of adult women was introduced has the law been repealed. Practically without exception every amendment of the law has been in the line of strengthening the law or further reducing the working time. [Historical surveys of such laws are given for Great Britain, France, Switzerland, Austria, Holland, Italy, and Germany.]

II. *The American Legislation*

"Twenty States of the Union, including nearly all of those in which women are largely employed in factory or similar work, have found it necessary to take action for the protection of their health and safety and the public welfare, and have enacted laws limiting the hours of labor for adult women.

"This legislation has not been the result of sudden impulse or passing humor,—it has followed deliberate consideration, and been adopted in the face of much opposition. More than a generation has elapsed between the earliest and the latest of these acts.

"In no instance has any such law been repealed. Nearly every amendment in any law has been in the line of strengthening the law or further reducing the working time.

"The earliest statute in the United States which undertook to limit the hours of labor for women in mechanical or manufacturing establishments was Wisconsin Statute, 1867, chap. 83, which fixed the hours of labor as eight. The Act, however, provided a penalty only in case of compelling a woman to work longer hours. (See present Wisconsin Law, *supra*.)

"The earliest act which effectively restricted the hours of labor for women was Massachusetts Statute, 1874, chap. 34, which fixed the limit at ten hours. The passage of the Massachusetts Act was preceded by prolonged agitation and repeated official investigations. The first legislative inquiry was made as early as 1865.

"After the Massachusetts Act had been in force six years, an elaborate investigation of its economic effects was undertaken by the Massachusetts Bureau of Labor Statistics, under the supervision of its chief, Mr. Carroll D. Wright. His report, published in 1881 (Twelfth Annual Report of the Massachusetts Bureau of Labor Statistics), to the effect that the reduction of the hours of labor had not resulted in increasing the cost of living or reducing wages, led to the passage, in 1885 and 1887, of the ten-hour law for women in Rhode Island, Maine, New Hampshire, and Connecticut, and largely influenced the legislation in other States. (See present laws, *supra*.)

"In the United States, as in foreign countries, there has been a general movement to strengthen and to extend the operation of these laws. In no State has any such law been held unconstitutional, except in Illinois, where, in *Ritchie* v. *People*, 154 Ill. 98, the Act of June 17, 1893, entitled 'An Act to regulate the manufacture of clothing, wearing apparel, and other articles in this State,' etc., was held unconstitutional. That Act provided (§5) that 'No female shall be employed in any factory or workshop more than eight hours in any one day or forty-eight hours in any one week.'

PART SECOND

I. *The Dangers of Long Hours*

"The dangers of long hours for women arise from their special physical organization taken in connection with the strain incident to factory or similar work.

"Long hours of labor are dangerous for women primarily because of their special physical organization. In structure and function women are differentiated from men. Besides these anatomical and physiological differences, physicians are agreed that women are fundamentally weaker than men in all that makes for endurance; in muscular strength, in nervous energy, in the powers of persistent attention and application. Overwork, therefore, which strains endurance to the utmost, is more disastrous to the health of women than of men, and entails upon them more lasting injury. [The brief quotes from the following sources.]

> *Report of Committee on Shops Early Closing Bill.* British House of Commons, 1895.
> *Report of Committee on Early Closing of Shops Bill.* British House of Lords, 1901.
> *Report of the Maine Bureau of Industrial and Labor Statistics.* 1888.
> *Report of the Massachusetts Bureau of Labor Statistics.* 1875.
> *Report of the Nebraska Bureau of Labor and Industrial Statistics.* 1901-1902.
> *Hygiene of Occupations.* By Dr. Theodore Weyl. Jena, 1894.

Travail de Nuit des Femmes dans l'Industrie. Prof. Etienne Bauer. Jena, 1903.

Man and Woman. Havelock Ellis.

History of Factory Legislation. Hutchins and Harrison, 1903.

Report of the British Chief Inspector of Factories and Workshops, 1903, *on the Thirtieth International Congress of Hygiene and Demography.*

Hygiene of Occupation in Reference Handbook of the Medical Sciences. George M. Price, M.D., Medical Sanitary Inspector, Health Department of the City of New York. Vol. VI.

"Such being their physical endowment, women are affected to a far greater degree than men by the growing strain of modern industry. Machinery is increasingly speeded up, the number of machines tended by individual workers grows larger, processes become more and more complex as more operations are performed simultaneously. All these changes involve correspondingly greater physical strain upon the worker.

* * *

[These asterisks indicate the omission of further references to the sources used, including factory reports, social surveys, and other studies.]

"The fatigue which follows long hours of labor becomes chronic and results in general deterioration of health. Often ignored, since it does not result in immediate disease, this weakness and anaemia undermines the whole system; it destroys the nervous energy most necessary for steady work, and effectually predisposes to other illness. The long hours of standing, which are required in many industries, are universally denounced by physicians as the cause of pelvic disorders.

* * *

"The evil effect of overwork before as well as after marriage upon childbirth is marked and disastrous.

* * *

"Accidents to working women occur most frequently at the close of the day, or after a long period of uninterrupted work. The coincidence of casualties and fatigue due to long hours is thus made manifest.

* * *

"The effect of overwork on morals is closely related to the injury to health. Laxity of moral fibre follows physical debility. When the working day is so long that no time whatever is left for a minimum of leisure or home life, relief from the strain of work is sought in alcoholic stimulants and other excesses.

* * *

"The experience of manufacturing countries has illustrated the evil effect of overwork upon the general welfare. Deterioration of any large proportion of the population inevitably lowers the entire community physically, mentally, and morally. When the health of women has been injured by long hours, not only is the working efficiency of the community impaired, but the deterioration is handed down to succeeding generations. Infant mortality rises, while the children of married working-women, who survive, are injured by inevitable neglect. The overwork of future mothers thus directly attacks the welfare of the nation.

(1) The State's Need of Protecting Women

* * *

II. *Shorter Hours the Only Possible Protection*

[344]

"This needed protection to women can be afforded only through shortening the hours of labor. A decrease of the intensity of exertion is not feasible.

* * *

III. *The General Benefits of Short Hours*

"History, which has illustrated the deterioration due to long hours, bears witness no less clearly to the regeneration due to the shorter working day. To the individual and to society alike, shorter hours have been a benefit wherever introduced. The married and unmarried working woman is enabled to obtain the decencies of life outside of working hours. With the improvement in home life, the tone of the entire community is raised. Wherever sufficient time has elapsed since the establishment of the shorter working day, the succeeding generation has shown extraordinary improvement in physique and morals.

* * *

IV. *Economic Aspects of Short Hours*

"The universal testimony of manufacturing countries tends to prove that the regulation of the working day acts favorably upon output. With long hours, output declines; with short hours, it rises. The heightened efficiency of the workers, due to the shorter day, more than balances any loss of time. Production is not only increased, but improved in quality.

* * *

"Wherever the employment of women has been prohibited for more than ten hours in one day, a more equal distribution of work throughout the year has followed. The supposed need

[345]

of dangerously long and irregular hours in the season-trades is shown to be unnecessary. In place of alternating periods of idleness, employers have found it possible to avoid such irregularities by foresight and management.

* * *

"Experience shows how the demands of customers yield to the requirements of a fixed working day. When customers are obliged to place orders sufficiently in advance to enable them to be filled without necessitating overtime work, compliance with this habit becomes automatic.

* * *

"The regulation of the working day has acted as a stimulus to improvement in the processes of manufacture. Invention of new machinery and perfection of old methods have followed the introduction of shorter hours.

* * *

"The establishment of a legal limit to the hours of woman's labor does not result in contracting the sphere of her work.

* * *

V. *Uniformity of Restriction*

"The arguments in favor of allowing overtime in seasonal trades or in cases of supposed emergency have gradually yielded to the dictates of experience which show that uniformity of restriction is essential to carrying out the purpose of the Act.

* * *

"In order to establish enforceable restrictions upon working hours of women, the law must fix a maximum working day. Without a fixed limit of hours, beyond which employment is prohibited, regulation is practically nullified. Exemptions of special trades from the restriction of hours not only subject the workers in such industries to injurious overwork, but go far to destroy the whole intent of the law.

"The difficulties of inspection become insuperable.

* * *

"To grant exceptions from the restriction of hours to certain industries places a premium upon irregularity and the evasions of law. When restrictions are uniform, the law operates without favor and without injury to individuals. Few employers are able to grant their employees reductions of hours, even if they are convinced of its advantages, when their competitors are under no such obligation. Justice to the employer as to the employee therefore requires that the law set a fixed limit of hours for working women and a fixed limit for all alike.

* * *

VI. *The Reasonableness of the Ten-hour Day*

"Factory inspectors, physicians, and working women are unanimous in advocating the ten-hour day wherever it has not yet been established. Some indeed consider ten hours too long a period of labor; but as opposed to the unregulated or longer day, there is agreement that ten hours is the maximum number of working hours compatible with health and efficiency.

(1) Opinions of Physicians and Officials

* * *

(2) Opinions of Employees

[347]

* * *

(3) Opinions of Employers

* * *

VII. *Laundries*

"The specific prohibition in the Oregon Act of more than ten hours' work in laundries is not an arbitrary discrimination against that trade. Laundries would probably not be included under the general terms of 'manufacturing' or 'mechanical establishments'; and yet the special dangers of long hours in laundries, as the business is now conducted, present strong reasons for providing a legal limitation of the hours of work in that business.

* * *

CONCLUSION

"We submit that in view of the facts above set forth and of legislative action extending over a period of more than sixty years in the leading countries of Europe, and in twenty of our States, it cannot be said that the Legislature of Oregon had no reasonable ground for believing that the public health, safety, or welfare did not require a legal limitation on women's work in manufacturing and mechanical establishments and laundries to ten hours in one day. (See *Holden* v. *Hardy*, 169 U. S. 366, 395, 397.)"

Savings Bank Insurance

On OCTOBER 26, 1905, LOUIS D. BRANDEIS, AS COUNSEL FOR A protective committee formed by policyholders in a life insurance company, delivered an address before the Commercial Club of Boston on the subject, "Life Insurance: The Abuses and the Remedies." While emphasizing the wasteful management and unfair practices of the companies of that day, he called attention to the facility and economy by which savings banks could issue policies. The project originated by Mr. Brandeis was authorized by Massachusetts three years later and has been adopted by a number of banks in that State with a consequent lowering of premiums.

Extracts from the 1905 address* are given below:

"LIFE INSURANCE is but a method of saving. The savings banks manage the funds until such time as they shall be demanded by the depositor—the insurance company ordinarily until the depositor's death. The savings bank pays back to the depositor his deposit with interest, less the necessary expense of management. The insurance company in theory does the same. The difference is merely that the savings bank undertakes to repay to each individual depositor the whole of his deposit with interest, while the insurance company undertakes to pay to those who do not reach the average age more than they have deposited (including interest) and to those who exceed the average age less than they have deposited (including interest).

"How many wage-earners would insure in these companies if they were told that for every dollar they pay, forty cents will go to the stockholders, officers' and agents' salaries, or for

* For complete address, see p. 108, *Business—A Profession*, by Louis D. Brandeis.

[349]

other running expenses? How many wage-earners would assume the burden of premiums if they knew that there is but one chance in twelve that they will carry their policies to maturity?

"How idle is the boast sometimes made by these companies that they have returned to the policyholder the whole of his premium. It is as if the savings banks should boast of returning to the depositor all of his deposit but without any interest. Such practically is what the Equitable, the New York Life, and the Mutual Life do today. The average expense of the three companies, exclusive of taxes and fees, was 4.03 percent of their aggregate assets, while the average of the return of the three companies on investments was 4.2 percent. It means in plain English that the company takes as compensation for the care of the policyholder's money all that that money earns.***

"In order to get rid of the abuses, the measures to be applied must be radical and comprehensive. The changes must be fundamental. [Among those suggested were:] *First*—the recognition of the true nature of the life insurance business; namely, that its sole province is to manage temporarily with absolute safety and at a minimum cost the savings of the people deposited to make appropriate provision in case of death, and that since its province is mainly to aid persons of small means, it should be conducted as a beneficent, not as a money-making, institution.

"*Second*—the issuance of deferred dividend policies should be discontinued. The legitimate business of a life insurance company is to insure the life of the individual and to issue life annuities. It should not be used as an investment company or as a means of gambling on the misfortunes of others. The deferred dividend policy with its semi-tontine provision is open to these objections and to others.***

"If our people cannot secure life insurance at a proper cost and through private agencies which deal fairly with them, or if they cannot procure it through private agencies except at the price of erecting financial monsters which dominate the business world and corrupt our political institutions, they will discard the private agency and resort to State insurance.

"Despite your or my protest, the extension of Government activity into fields now occupied by private business is urged on every side. Of all services which the community requires, there is none in which the State could more easily engage than that of insuring the lives of its citizens. Stripped of the mysteries with which it has been permeated, the business of life insurance is one of extraordinary simplicity. To conduct it successfully requires neither energy nor initiative, and if pursued by the State does not even call for the exercise of any high degree of business judgment. The sole requisites would be honesty, accuracy, and economy.

"The business of life insurance, which the companies now make so incomprehensible to the insured, consists properly only of three elements:

1. The initial medical examination.
2. The calculation of the so-called net premium or insurance and mortality reserve.
3. The investment of funds.

"The first is the province of the physician; the second, a mere matter of arithmetic worked out by the actuary and now actually performed in large part also by our insurance departments as a necessary incident of their supervision; the third, the proper investment of funds, would ordinarily require a high degree of judgment. But if the business were conducted by the State, the proper investment of funds would not, at least in Massachusetts, present any difficulty. The State and municipal loans would take up all insurance reserve. The net indebtedness

[351]

of the Commonwealth on December 31, 1904, was $74,335,-130.12, that of our cities and towns $141,658,601. This aggregate of $215,993,731.12 presents a fund far greater than is required as the legal reserve for all the policies now outstanding in this Commonwealth. The net value of all outstanding legal reserve life insurance in Massachusetts on January 1, 1905, was only $122,727,918. The aggregate premiums paid in Massachusetts during the three years ending January 1, 1905, to the thirty-three old line companies was $79,033,991; but the increase during those years of legal reserve requirement was only $23,122.089. The increase of the net State debt and of the gross municipal debt during those years aggregated $34,798,132.74. If the State had done this life insurance business, the three years' increase of legal reserve would not have sufficed to meet the increased borrowings of the State and the municipalities. In Massachusetts, at least, a safe investment for our insurance funds would thus be assured.

"The net return from such investment of the funds by the State would compare not unfavorably with that now received by the leading insurance companies. It is true that the interest return on Massachusetts State and municipal bonds is less than the present average return of the life insurance companies on investments; but that return in case of State insurance would be net. There would, as to the reserve funds, be no expense of management. Furthermore, the investment return of the insurance companies is being almost steadily reduced, and the insurance reserve on new business is being calculated on the basis of three and one-half or three percent, which is as low as the average return on State and municipal bonds.

"In my opinion, the extension of the functions of the State to life insurance is at the present time highly undesirable. Our Government does not yet grapple successfully with the duties which it has assumed, and should not extend its operations at least until it does. But whatever and however strong our conviction against the extension of governmental functions may be, we shall inevitably be swept farther toward socialism unless we can curb the excesses of our financial magnates. The talk of the agitator alone does not advance socialism a step; but the formation of great trusts—the huge consolidations—the insurance 'racers' with the attendant rapacity or the dishonesty of their potent managers, and their frequent corruption of councils and legislatures is hastening us almost irresistibly into socialistic measures. The great captains of industry and of finance, who profess the greatest horror of the extension of governmental functions, are the chief makers of socialism. Socialistic thinkers smile approvingly at the operations of Morgan, Perkins, and Rockefeller, and of the Hydes, McCalls, and McCurdys. They see approaching the glad day when monopoly shall have brought all industry and finance under a single head, so that with the cutting of a single neck, as Nero vainly wished for his Christian subjects, destruction of the enemy may be accomplished. Our great trust-building, trust-abusing capitalists have in their selfish shortsightedness become the makers of socialism, proclaiming by their acts, like the nobles of France, 'After us, the Deluge.' "

———————

The first of a series of magazine articles Mr. Brandeis wrote on savings bank insurance appeared September 15, 1906, in *Collier's Weekly*. After pointing out the waste in industrial insurance—the high cost of premium collection and the large percentage of lapses—he wrote:

"THE THRIFTY workingman, like people of larger means, should have the opportunity of obtaining life insurance at more nearly its necessary cost.

"The sacrifice incident to the present industrial insurance

[353]

system can be avoided only by providing an institution for insurance which will recognize that its function is not to induce working people to take insurance regardless of whether they really want it or can afford to carry it, but rather to supply insurance upon proper terms to those who do want it and can carry it,—an institution which will recognize that the best method of increasing the demand for life-insurance is not eloquent, persistent persuasion, but, as in the case of other necessaries of life, is to furnish a good article at a low price.

"Massachusetts, in its 189 savings banks, and the other States with savings banks similarly conducted, have institutions which, with a slight enlargement of their powers, can at a minimum of expense fill the great need of life insurance for workingmen.

"The only proper elements of the industrial insurance business not common to the savings bank business are simple, and can be supplied at a minimum of expense in connection with our existing savings banks. They are:

(*a*) Fixing the terms on which insurance shall be given.

(*b*) The initial medical examination.

(*c*) Verifying the proof of death.

"The last involves an inquiry similar in character to that now performed by the clerks of savings banks in the identification of depositors.

"The second is the work of a physician, who is available at no greater expense to the savings bank than to the insurance company.

"The first is the work of an insurance actuary, who would be equally available to the savings bank as he is to insurance companies, if the former undertook the insurance business. And the present cost of actuarial service can be greatly reduced; first, by limiting the forms of insurance to two or three standard forms of simple policies, uniform throughout the State;

and, secondly, by providing for the appointment of a State actuary, who, in connection with the insurance commissioner, shall serve all the savings insurance banks. The work of such an actuary is, indeed, now necessarily performed in large part in each State by the insurance department, as an incident of supervising life insurance companies.

"The savings banks could thus enter upon the insurance business under circumstances singularly conducive to extending to the workingman the blessing of safe life insurance at a low cost, because:

"*First.* The insurance department of savings banks would be managed by experienced trustees and officers who had been trained to recognize that the business of investing the savings of persons of small means is a quasi-public trust which should be conducted as a beneficent and not as a selfish money-making institution.

"*Second.* The insurance department of savings banks would be managed by trustees and officers who in their administration of the savings of persons of small means had already been trained to the practice of the strictest economy.

"*Third.* The insurance business of the savings banks, although kept entirely distinct as a matter of investment and accounting, would be conducted with the same plant and the same officials, without any large increase of clerical force or incidental expense, except such as would be required if the bank's deposits were increased. Until the insurance business attained considerable dimensions, probably the addition of even a single clerk might not be necessary. The business of life insurance could thus be established as an adjunct of a savings bank without incurring that heavy expense which has ordinarily proved such a burden in the establishment of a new insurance company.

"If the individual risks were limited at first to, say, $150 on a single life, the business could be begun safely on a purely mutual basis as soon as a few hundred lives were insured, or earlier if a guaranty fund were provided. As the business increased, the limit of single risks could be correspondingly increased, but should probably not exceed $500.

"*Fourth.* The insurance department of savings banks would open with an extensive and potent good will, and with the most favorable conditions for teaching, at slight expense, the value of life insurance. For instance, in Massachusetts the holders of the 1,829,487 savings accounts, a number equal to three-fifths of the whole population of the State, would at once become potential policyholders; and a small amount of advertising would soon suffice to secure a reasonably large business without solicitors.

"*Fifth.* With an insurance clientele composed largely of thrifty savings bank depositors, house-to-house collection of premiums could be dispensed with. The more economical monthly payments of premiums could also probably be substituted for weekly payments.

"*Sixth.* A small initiation fee could be charged, as in assessment and fraternal associations, to cover necessary initial expenses of medical examination and issue of policy. This would serve both as a deterrent to the insured against allowing policies to lapse and as a protection to persisting policyholders from unjust burdens which the lapse of policies casts upon them.

"*Seventh.* The safety of savings banks would, of course, be in no way imperilled by extending their functions to life insurance. Life insurance rests upon substantial certainty, differing in this respect radically from fire, accident, and other kinds of insurance.***

"The causes of failure in life insurance companies since Elizur Wright established the science have been excessive expense, unsound investment, or rapacious or dishonest management. To the risk of these abuses all financial institutions are necessarily subject, but they are evils from which our savings banks have been remarkably free. This practical freedom of our savings banks from these evils affords a strong reason for utilizing them to supply the kindred service of life insurance.

"The theoretical risk of a mortality loss in a single institution greater than that provided for in the insurance reserve could be absolutely guarded against, however, by providing a general guaranty fund, to which all savings-insurance banks within a State would make small *pro rata* contributions,—a provision similar to that prevailing in other countries, where all banks of issue contribute to a common fund which guarantees all outstanding bank notes.

"*Eighth.* In other respects, also, cooperation between the several savings insurance banks within a State would doubtless, under appropriate legislation, be adopted; for instance, by providing that each institution could act as an agent for the others to receive and forward premium payments.

"*Ninth.* The law authorizing the establishment of an insurance department in connection with savings banks should, obviously, be permissive merely. No savings bank should be required to extend its functions to industrial insurance until a majority of its trustees are convinced of the wisdom of so doing.

"The savings banks are not, however, the only existing class of financial institutions which could be utilized for the purpose of supplying, at a low expense rate, insurance in small amounts under a system requiring frequent premium payments. Cooperative banks, as operated in Massachusetts and in some other States, would, under appropriate legislation, be admirably adapted to supply a part of the required service. The excellent record of these institutions in Massachusetts presents a most encouraging exhibit of the achievements of financial democracy when applied to small units and when operating under a wise system of supervision.***

"If an opportunity for cheaper life insurance is afforded by means of an extension of the functions of our savings banks, the present industrial insurance companies may be permitted to pursue their efforts at inculcating thrift in accordance with the system which seems to them wise, and their claim that the present huge waste is inevitable will be duly tested.

"But if we fail to offer to workingmen some opportunity for cheaper insurance through private or quasi-private institutions, the ever-ready remedy of State insurance is certain to be resorted to soon; and there is no other sphere of business now deemed private upon which the State could so easily and so justifiably enter as that of life insurance.

"However great the waste in present life insurance methods, our workingmen will not be induced to abandon life insurance. To them, as to others, life insurance has become a prime need. It must be continued. It should be encouraged. In spite of the disastrous results of this form of savings investment, the industrial insurance business has assumed enormous proportions. On December 31, 1904, the number of industrial life policies outstanding in the three great companies (Metropolitan, Prudential, and John Hancock) was 14,731,463, as against a total of only about 5,258,255 ordinary life policies outstanding in the ninety legal reserve companies.*** In Massachusetts the predominance of industrial policies is even greater than the average. With a population of 3,000,680 there were outstanding December 31, 1904, 1,080,003 industrial policies; that is, one for every three inhabitants, counting men, women, and children, and of ordinary life policies only 257,792 were outstanding.

"The demand of workingmen for life insurance will continue and will grow; but the yearly tribute of the workingmen to Prudential stockholders of dividends equivalent to 219.78 percent on the capital actually paid into the company, the yearly waste of millions in lapsed policies, in fruitless solicita-tion and in needless collections, will cease. The question is merely whether the remedy shall be applied through properly regulated private institutions or whether the State must itself enter upon the business of life insurance."

———————

In *The Independent* for December 20, 1906, Mr. Brandeis was able to record that a number of public-spirited citizens had organized the Massachusetts Savings-Insurance League for the purpose of securing the passage of a permissive law, and that the plan had been submitted to the Recess Insurance Committee of the State Legislature. He also wrote in part:

"THE supporters of the present system of industrial insurance declare that a reduction of expenses and of lapses is impossible. They insist that the loss to the insured and the heavy burden borne by the persisting policyholders from lapses, as well as from the huge cost of premium collection, must all be patiently borne as being inevitable incidents of the beneficent institution of life insurance, when applied to the workingman. It is obvious that a remedy cannot come from men holding such views—from men who refuse to recognize that the best method of increasing the demand for life insurance is not eloquent persistent persuasion, but to furnish a good article at a low price. A remedy can be provided only by some institution which will proceed upon the principle that its function is to supply insurance upon proper terms to those who want it and can carry it, and not to induce working people to take insurance regardless of their real interests. To attain satisfactory results the change of system must be radical.

"The savings banks established on the plan prevailing in New York and generally throughout the New England States are managed on principles and under conditions upon which alone a satisfactory system of life insurance for workingmen can be established. These savings banks have no stockholders, being operated solely for the benefit of the depositors. They are managed by trustees, usually men of large business experience and high character, who serve without pay, recognizing that the business of collecting and investing the savings of persons of small means is a quasi-public trust, which should be conducted as a beneficent, and not as a money-making institution. The trustees, the officers, and the employees of the savings banks have been trained in the administration of these savings to the practice of the strictest economy."

[The following excerpt is from an article by
Mr. Brandeis published in the *Bankers'*
Magazine, December, 1906.]

"MASSACHUSETTS laid the foundation of the admirable savings bank system of the United States by chartering, in 1816, the Provident Institution for Savings in the town of Boston, and also established for the world the scientific practice of life insurance by the work of its insurance commissioner, Elizur Wright.

"It is now proposed that another great step be taken in the development through thrift of general prosperity by extending the functions of savings banks to life insurance. The call for such action is imperative and urgent; because the present system under which the workingmen obtain life insurance involves an appalling sacrifice of their hard-earned savings. This may be illustrated by the experience of Massachusetts. In the fifteen years ending December 31, 1905, the workingmen of that State paid to the so-called industrial life insurance companies an aggregate of $61,294,887 in premiums, and received back only an aggregate of $21,819,606. The insurance reserve arising from these premiums still held by the insurance companies does not exceed $9,838,000. It thus appears that, in addition to interest on invested funds, about one-half of the amount paid by the workingmen in premiums has been absorbed in the expense of conducting the business and in dividends to the insurance companies' stockholders.

"If this $61,294,887, instead of being paid to the insurance companies, had been paid into the savings banks, and these depositors had withdrawn from the banks an amount equal to the aggregate of $21,819,606, which they received from the insurance companies during the fifteen years, the balance remaining in the savings banks December 31, 1905, with the accumulated interest, would have amounted to $49,-931,548.35, and this, although the savings banks would have been obliged to pay upon these increased deposits in taxes four times the amount which was actually paid by the insurance companies on account of this insurance.

"The least which the workingman pays for this industrial insurance is about double the cost per $100 of insurance charged (by the companies); and for the earlier periods of the industrial policy the cost rises as high as eight times that ordinarily paid for life insurance.

"Of the more than $40,000,000 thus lost to the workingmen of a single State in fifteen years, the amount which has gone into dividends to stockholders of the insurance companies is comparatively small.*** By far the greater part of the loss to the workingman is due to the extraordinarily wasteful system under which the business is conducted. This waste arises mainly from the fact that the premiums are collected weekly at the home of the insured, and that a large part of the policies, which are secured only after persistent and expensive solicitation, lapse shortly after they are written."

[In the *Bankers' Magazine*, August, 1908,
after Massachusetts adopted the law.]

"A RAPID extension of the system throughout the State is probable, for under the law any savings bank may serve its community as well by becoming an agency for another savings insurance and annuity bank as by establishing a department of its own; and a bank acting as agent merely is relieved of the necessity of providing the guaranty funds and of considerable special insurance work required of the principal.

"The law also provides for the appointment of other agencies, for instance, manufacturing, mercantile, or other business concerns, as well as trade and other organizations; so that the people in any part of the State may secure the privileges of the new system without awaiting action by the local savings bank."

[In the Quarterly Publication, American Statistical
Association, March, 1909]

"THE savings bank policies have other advantages besides the lower rate. They are participating policies, while the industrial insurance policies are non-participating. The savings bank policies provide for 'full immediate benefit'—that is, payment of the face of the policy in case the insured died at any time after the date of the policy; while the industrial insurance policies provide for payment of only one-half of the face of the policy in case of death within six months after the date of the policy. Furthermore, the savings bank life insurance policy is non-forfeitable for failure to pay premium after six monthly premiums have been paid, whereas the industrial insurance policies lapse in case of failure to pay premium at any time within the first three years.

"The Massachusetts savings bank insurance system was

first put into operation on June 18, 1908, when the savings bank of Whitman—a prosperous manufacturing town in southeastern Massachusetts—opened the first insurance department established under the statute.***

"The Massachusetts system of savings bank insurance and annuities was made possible by Chapter 561 of the Acts of 1907, which authorized any savings bank to establish under proper safeguards an insurance department for the issue to residents of Massachusetts of legal reserve life insurance limited to $500 and annuities limited to $200 on any one life. The Act, however, permits the same person to take out life insurance and annuities from more than one bank.***

"The Massachusetts insurance and pension system can attain success only through the full appreciation by the employees, the employer, and the community that provision for old age and life insurance is an integral part of the daily cost of living; that no wage is a living wage which does not permit the workingman to set apart each day or week or month the necessary cost of such provision for the future; that no working man can be truly self-supporting or independent who does not make such provision, and that the savings bank will enable him to make the provision at the lowest possible cost.

"To make general the appreciation of these facts involves an extensive, persistent, and long-continued campaign of education. This educational work was commenced in the fall of 1906 by the Massachusetts Savings Insurance League, when the project of savings bank insurance was first submitted to the public. The long, strenuous campaign which preceded the passage of the Act resulted in a wide discussion of the subject in every part of the State. Nearly 300 labor unions joined in the effort to secure the requisite legislation.*** Leading manufacturers, financiers, and social workers then gave the movement their support, and the educational work commenced has been continued ever since and has been much enlarged. In this educational work employers, employees, social workers, and the churches are all taking part, and upon this widespread and concerted effort rests the confidence in the success of the system."

This success, as of 1914, was related in *Business—A Profession*, by Louis D. Brandeis, published by Small, Maynard & Co. in that year. The following summary has been made from a chapter in that book:

"The project of the Massachusetts system was first published in *Collier's Weekly*, September 15, 1906. Its main purpose was to eliminate or to mitigate so far as possible the evils incident to the system of industrial life insurance as then practiced by private companies. The causes of these evils were investigated; and it was proposed to remove them by creating a competitive system upon a new plan.*** The insured suffered mainly from three evils:

(*a*) The high premium.
(*b*) Over-persuasion leading to taking out of insurance which was bound soon to lapse.
(*c*) Illiberal and oppressive provisions in the policies.***

The discussions incident to the Massachusetts savings bank insurance plan, beginning in September, 1906, the enactment of the legislation on June 26, 1907, and the practical introduction of the system in June, 1908, with the actual and potential competition resulting, have wrought important changes in rates, methods, and practices of the industrial companies which have mitigated in large measure the flagrant abuses at which the reform was aimed, namely:

"1. The cost of industrial insurance furnished by the Metropolitan and other private companies (expressed in the

[364]

amount purchased by a given weekly premium) has been repeatedly reduced since September, 1906; so that today it is (on the average) about twenty percent lower than it was then.

"2. The methods pursued by the private companies in soliciting industrial insurance have improved since September, 1906, so that the lapse rate is materially reduced.***

"3. The provisions of the insurance policies issued by the private companies have been made more just and liberal. For instance, on January 1, 1907, the amount payable in case of death was increased from nothing, if occurring during the first three months, and one-fourth, if occurring during the second three months, to one-half the face value if death occurred at any time within the first six months. And the amount payable in case of death during any part of the second six months was increased from one-half to the full face value of the policy. Under the changes made January 1, 1907, the premiums, which previously had been payable throughout life, were made to cease at age seventy-five.

"4. Paid-up insurance is now granted by the private companies after three years, whereas before September, 1906, no paid-up insurance was granted until after the end of five years from the date of policy. It is noteworthy that this change was effected as of January 1, 1907, although Vice-President Haley Fiske had declared before the Armstrong Committee in 1905 that 'Any law requiring the issue of paid-up policies in industrial insurance after three years would be most unjust' to the persisting policyholders.'

"5. Since September, 1906, the private companies have made their policies incontestible one year after date of issue, whereas theretofore the policies had been incontestible only after two years.

"6. Since September, 1906, extended insurance is said to be granted after three years from the date of policy, whereas none had been granted theretofore.

[365]

"The improvements made by the private industrial insurance companies as the result of the Massachusetts plan have, of course, been extended to their entire business throughout the United States. When it is remembered that the aggregate premium income of the industrial policies in the United States is now about $115,000,000 a year, it seems clear that the industrial policyholders throughout the country are today buying their insurance for at least $20,000,000 a year less than they would have had to pay for the same amount of insurance had the rates prevailing prior to September, 1906, remained in force.*** The gross rates on the monthly premium savings bank policies in Massachusetts are on the average about seventeen percent less than the *now* prevailing rates of the private industrial companies.*** The policies issued by the Massachusetts savings banks are far more liberal even than those *now* written by the private industrial companies. The full face of the policy is payable in case of death at any time after the issue of the policy. Cash surrender value, paid-up insurance, and extended insurance are granted at any time after six months from the date of the issue of the policy. The policies have also a loan value after the end of the first year.

"A recent investigation of the business of the banks shows that of the policies issued and having twelve months' experience, 25.5 percent of the number of policies and 26.2 percent of the amount of insurance are cancelled within a year, whereas in the large industrial companies over fifty percent of the policies written are cancelled within the year.

"Furthermore the so-called cancellations of the savings insurance banks include all policies surrendered within twelve months, whether by lapse, by death, or by surrender for cash. On the bank policies surrendered after six months, $20,336.50 was returned to the policyholders, and other bank policyholders also received by way of amounts applied to purchases paid-up insurance $3,924.23. This $24,260.73 would have been entirely lost to the policyholders had they been insured in the industrial companies.***

"On February 28, 1914, the insurance departments of the four savings banks had outstanding 8,413 policies, representing $3,316,005 insurance and $29,482 annuities.*** Fifteen other savings banks and four trust companies have become public agencies for these four banks, and there are also twenty-three other public agencies and about two hundred private agencies. In two banks, the People's Savings Bank of Brockton and the Whitman Savings Bank, the insurance department has been conducted for more than five years. The effect has been to increase markedly the number of depositors.***

"The business of the savings insurance banks has been developed in large measure through the educational work conducted by the Massachusetts Savings Insurance League. This league was organized November 26, 1906, by public-spirited citizens of Massachusetts to promote the enactment of the savings bank insurance law. Its work was educational. It undertook to familiarize the people of Massachusetts with the evils incident to the then existing system of industrial life insurance, and to point out the advantage of the Massachusetts plan of savings bank insurance. After the law was enacted the league exerted itself to secure the establishment of insurance departments by the People's Savings Bank of Brockton, and by the Whitman Savings Bank, and also the establishment of agencies. Since that time it has been engaged in active educational work throughout the Commonwealth. It is largely through the medium of the league that the advantages of the system have been made known to the people.

"The league has been instrumental in interesting the large number of manufacturers and others who have established unpaid agencies through which the insurance is written. Its purpose is to bring to the attention of the wage-earners of Massachusetts the importance of making wise provision for the future out of current earnings, either through life insurance or old-age pensions; to endeavor by way of suggestion to encourage them to habits of thrift and foresight, and to acquaint them with the value of savings bank insurance as a means to this end.

"Officials of the private industrial insurance companies point to the relatively small number of policies issued by the Massachusetts insurance banks as evidence that the system has not succeeded. The contrary is true. The initiation of the competitive system was so effective in reforming the most flagrant of the abuses of the industrial companies, that competition with them is necessarily much more difficult than it would have been had the old conditions persisted. And the benefit of these reforms is now enjoyed by nearly every industrial policyholder in the United States."

Industrial Democracy

(From an address* before the National Congress of Charities and
Correction, Boston, June 8, 1911)

"POLITICALLY, the American workingman is free—so far as
the law can make him so. But is he really free? Can any man
be really free who is constantly in danger of becoming dependent for mere subsistence upon somebody and something else
than his own exertion and conduct? Financial dependence is
consistent with freedom only where claim to support rests upon
right, and not upon favor.

"President Cleveland's epigram that 'it is the duty of the
citizen to support the Government, not of the Government
to support the citizen' is only qualifiedly true. Universal suffrage necessarily imposes upon the State the obligation of fitting
its governors—the voters—for their task; and the freedom of
the individual is as much an essential condition of successful
democracy as his education. If the Government permits conditions to exist which make large classes of citizens financially
dependent, the great evil of dependence should at least be
minimized by the State's assuming, or causing to be assumed
by others, in some form, the burden incident to its own
shortcomings.

"The cost of attaining freedom is usually high; and the
cost of providing for the workingman, as an essential of freedom, a comprehensive and adequate system of insurance will
prove to be no exception to this general rule. But, however

* Page 51, *Business—A Profession.*

[369]

large the cost, it should be fairly faced and courageously met. For the expense of securing indemnity against the financial losses attending accident, sickness, invalidity, premature death, superannuation, and unemployment should be recognized as a part of the daily cost of living, like the more immediate demands for rent, for food, and for clothing. So far as it is a necessary charge, it should be met as a current expense, instead of being allowed to accumulate as a debt with compound interest to plague us hereafter."

Old Age Pensions

(From an article in *The Independent*, July 25, 1912)

"HALF a century ago nearly every American boy could look forward to becoming independent as a farmer or mechanic, in business or in professional life; and nearly every American girl might expect to become the wife of such a man. Today most American boys have reason to believe, that throughout life they will work in some capacity as employees of others, either in private or public business; and a large percentage of the women occupy like positions. This revolutionary change has resulted from the great growth of manufacturing and mining as compared with farming; from the formation of trusts and other large business concerns; from the development of our transportation and other public utility corporations; from the marked increase in governmental functions; and, finally, from the invasion of women into industry.

"As soon as we awakened to the fact that America had become largely a nation of employees, the need of a comprehensive provision for superannuated wage-earners secured attention. Given the status of employee for life, and the need of an old age pension is obvious. The employee needs the pension because he cannot—or at least does not—provide adequately from his wages for the period of superannuation. The employers need a comprehensive pension system because, while the presence of superannuated employees in a business seriously impairs its efficiency, the dictates both of humanity and of policy prevent discharge unless their financial necessities are provided for. The demand for a pension system grows more pressing as businesses grow more stable; for in older businesses there is a consistent tendency to accumulate superannuated employees. The demand becomes particularly acute when businesses grow large as well as old, for then it becomes difficult to provide for the individual needs of the abnormal employee.***

"Economically, the superannuation provision may be considered as a depreciation charge. Every prudent manufacturer makes an annual charge for the depreciation of his machines, recognizing not merely physical depreciation but lessened value through obsolescence. He looks forward to the time when the machine, though still in existence and in perfect repair, will be unprofitable, and hence must be abandoned. This annual charge for depreciation he treats as a necessary expense of the business.***

"Whether in the adjustment of relations between the employer and the employee this current cost of providing old age pensions should be borne wholly by the employer, or wholly by the employee, or jointly by both, is an open question; but European and American experience makes it clear that under our present industrial system some comprehensive financial provision for the superannuated worker is essential to social if not to industrial solvency. To neglect such a requirement is as dangerous as it is for the manufacturer to ignore the depreciation of his machines.

"For the protection of the wage-earner it is obviously

necessary that the right to a pension shall not depend upon his being in the employ of a particular concern. If his right to an annuity is dependent upon his remaining in a particular employ he loses all protection whenever he ceases to be so employed, whether he leaves voluntarily, or is discharged, or in case the concern discontinues business by failure or for other cause.

"Adequate old-age protection, therefore, cannot be secured to the wage-earner through the promise of a pension from a particular concern. He should have old age insurance which will protect the wage-earner in whosesoever employ he may happen to be when he reaches the period of superannuation. For the protection of the wage-earner it is likewise necessary that the pension system should confer an absolute right. No pension system can be satisfactory which makes the granting—or the continuance of a pension after it has been granted—a matter of discretion.***

"In other words, what the employer should seek to accomplish by the pension is merely to protect his business from the incubus of superannuated employees; and this purpose is accomplished as to each employee if he leaves the employ before he becomes superannuated. If the workingman so leaves, he should in some form carry with him the accrued right to a pension—the proportionate value of the time service—which would ripen into a pension if the workingman or his new employer paid the premiums of later years."

The Menace of the Trusts

(From a statement before a Senate Committee hearing on
trust legislation, December 14, 1911)

"To a greater or less extent in small business the owners are beginning to recognize that there is but one principle by which lasting success can be attained, and it is this: Those who do the work shall get in some fair proportion what they produce. The share to which capital as such is entitled is small. All the rest should go to those, high and low, who do the work.

"This is the idea which our New England people are working out in their modest business concerns and they are thus finding a way to perpetuate their business and get out of it not only satisfaction and contentment on the part of the working people but contentment and success for themselves.***

"If we are to work out a satisfactory system of profit sharing as a means of reconciling capital and labor, it can only be done by reducing the return of capital and the purveyors of capital and letting the people who do the work, be they managers, the skilled handicraftmen, or day laborers, take all that is earned above a reasonable return on the capital invested.

"The management of the steel corporation has not only failed to work out a proper solution of this vexed problem, but its conduct has tended in the opposite direction. The wages in the steel industry through this period of the trust, so far as made public, compared unfavorably with the period before 1892. In many respects they are absolutely lower than 1892. In other respects they are relatively lower, if the cost of living be taken into consideration. The increase in wages of the day laborers from 1892 to 1907 amounted to about eighteen percent, but the cost of living increased in that period four or five percent more. The wages of skilled laborers during the same period were reduced from five to forty percent.

"Nor is this all, or to my mind the most important consideration in the trust's treatment of labor, important as it is. The most serious ground for criticizing the Steel Trust is that the hours of labor have been shockingly increased since 1892.***

"You cannot have true American citizenship, you cannot preserve political liberty, you cannot secure American standards of living unless some degree of industrial liberty accompanies it. And the United States Steel Corporation and these other trusts have stabbed industrial liberty in the back. They have crushed it out among large groups of our people so completely that it will require years to restore our industries to a condition of health. This social unrest is what is really the matter with business. Well-founded unrest; reasoned unrest; but the manifestations of which are often unintelligent and sometimes criminal.***

"Until we had these great trusts, or the great corporations which preceded them, workers could secure justice through their unions. Abuses of the trade unions have been innumerable. Individuals of slight education, of slight training, are elevated many times by shallow popularity to positions which can be filled adequately only by men possessing great minds and great characters. No wonder, then, that these leaders made mistakes; make grievous errors. The extraordinary thing is that they have not made more mistakes. It is one of the most promising symptoms in American democracy that with all the difficulties attending such positions the labor leaders on the whole have done so little that is wrong. And you, gentlemen, Members of the Senate and Members of the House who are called upon to consider questions affecting 'big business,' must weigh well these by-products. For by their by-products shall you know the trusts.***

"If you do anything which tends to accelerate this pace toward the conversion of American capital into stock exchange securities, by just so much will you increase the difficulty of solving the problem of the Money Trust, which already baffles the best minds of the country.

"And there are still other baneful by-products of the industrial trusts. Mr. [George W.] Perkins has asserted that these great corporations are not private businesses but public businesses. He has asserted that the numerous stockholders are partners in the enterprise with J. P. Morgan & Co. and others, as if that were 'a consummation devoutly to be wished.'

"To my mind this is a condition to be regretted rather than to be welcomed and presents features of a highly serious character. Such numerous small stockholding creates in the corporation a condition of irresponsible absentee landlordism; that is, the numerous small stockholders in the steel corporation, in the tobacco company, and in the other trusts occupy a position which is dangerous to society. They have a certain degree of wealth without responsibility. Their only desire is dividends. Their demand upon the managers is at most to maintain or increase the dividends. They have no power or responsibility; they have no relations to the employees; they are remote, often thousands of miles from the people who are toiling for them. Thus we have reproduced in industry the precise conditions which brought all the misery upon Ireland and upon other countries where absentee landlordism has prevailed. Large dividends are the bribes which the managers tender the small investor for the power to use other people's money.***

"The trust problem can never be settled right for the American people by looking at it through the spectacles of bonds and stocks. You must study it through the spectacles of people's rights and people's interests; must consider the effect upon the development of the American democracy. When you do that you will realize the perils to our institutions which attend the trusts; you will realize the danger of letting the people learn that our sacred Constitution protects not only vested rights but vested wrongs. The situation is a very serious one; unless wise legislation is enacted we shall have as a result of that social unrest a condition which will be more serious than that produced by the fall of a few points in stock-exchange quotations."

[375]

Creating Derelicts

(From a statement before the House Committee investigating the
United States Steel Corporation, January 29, 1912)

"THE first question in considering the condition of labor is,
and to my mind must be, the hours of labor. No matter what
men are paid, no matter what the ordinary conditions may be
under which they work, the first question must be, How long
did this man work? Because not only does the excess of hours of
labor entail upon the individual very serious consequences in
respect to health and the ability to endure labor in the future,
but the effect upon the community as a whole is of infinite
importance; in the first place, in determining what is the time
that is left to the individual to devote himself to the needs of
his own family, to aid in the education and the bringing up of
his children; and in the second place, what is the time that is
left to the individual to perform those duties which are in-
cumbent upon him as a citizen of a free country.***

"This industry, in making these derelicts, in creating
widely this demoralization which comes from subjecting its
workers to such conditions, proves itself in the strongest way
to be a parasitic industry. It is not merely, as you called attention, Mr. Chairman, by the fact that we are protecting this
corporation by a tariff, by a duty supposed to be in the interests
of American workingmen. We are bearing a part of its burdens
also—the rest of the community, by paying now and paying
hereafter the taxes which go to support those who have been
made paupers thereby.***

"While this corporation is the greatest example of combination, the most conspicuous instance of combination of capital in the world, it has, as an incident of the power which it
acquires through that combination and through its associations

[376]

with railroads and the financial world, undertaken, and undertaken successfully, to deny the right of combination to the workingmen, and these horrible conditions of labor, which are a disgrace to America, considering the wealth which has surrounded and flown out of the industry, are the result of having killed or eliminated from the steel industry unionism. All the power of capital and all the ability and intelligence of the men who wield and who serve the capital have been used to make practically slaves of these operatives, because it does not mean merely in respect to the way in which they have lived, but the very worst part of all this is the repression. It is a condition of repression, of slavery in the real sense of the word, which is alien to American conditions."

Fixing Minimum Wages

(From a statement before the New York State Factory Investigating Commission, January 22, 1915, in behalf of a minimum wage law)

"I AM unable to see that there is any difference in principle between a minimum wage law and a law governing the hours of labor, or a factory safety law or a child labor law or any of the other laws of this character. We set out with the principle, the fundamental policy, not only in the Constitution, but as the fundamental policy of the Anglo-American people, that liberty should not be restricted except in so far as required, for the public welfare, health, safety, morals, and general public conditions.*** The liberty of each individual must be limited in such a way that it leaves to others the possibility of individual liberty; the right to develop must be subject to that limitation which gives everybody else the right to develop; the restriction is merely an adjustment of the relations of one individual to another.

[377]

"Now, I think that the objection of the manufacturers to this situation is very largely due to the fact that they have not thought out this proposition, what law means and what liberty means and the rest of it. There is also a failure on their part to think out what the law of supply and demand means. Of course, there isn't any such thing as a law of supply and demand as an inexorable rule. It is an economic tendency, a highly important one, and one of the most important of the economic forces; but all the time we see that there are conditions under which the law of supply and demand does not work.*** One reason why the trades union had to come into existence was because the law of supply and demand did not work properly between the opposing forces of the powerful employer and the individual worker. I think it would be found, in talking with men, that half truths expressed in such words as 'liberty of contract' and the 'law of supply and demand' which people, the business men, use but have not thought out, are probably the most important sources of their objections.

"I am convinced that a minimum wage instead of adding to the expense of an establishment would, after the initial period of introduction, reduce the actual expenses of the establishment. Anything which is of better quality, which costs a little more, gives a larger percentage of value than the thing that is cheap. It is one of the curses of the poor that they have to buy poor things; and it is precisely the same in regard to human labor and human service as in regard to merchandise.

"This will operate in two ways. Not only is the employee worth more but the employer exerts himself to make the employee more efficient.***

"We do exactly the same even in regard to inanimate things. Profitable land is the land which people take care of, and which they develop. The truth which has been realized by our people, whenever they have thought about it, is one of the real explanations of our success in America in manufacture, and to a very great extent such success as we have had in agriculture is also attributable to it. The fact that wages were high in America is what made us save labor and what made us able to produce as we have. Schoenhof wrote twenty or more years ago on the great advantages of the economy of high wages. He merely expressed what had been the experience of our people. It seems to me that if there was an appreciation on the part of the community of what advantage there really is in handling men, in developing your help, nobody would want to accept anyone who was not worth at least a living wage.***

"It has been clearly demonstrated, I think, by those who have studied the possible efficiencies and economies in labor, that the distinction between skilled and unskilled is wholly unscientific and unphilosophical. There certainly is nothing that could be deemed to be nearer an unskilled occupation than lifting a pig of iron from the yard and putting it into a car; and yet it has been demonstrated by a study of that particular operation that it was possible with the same amount of exertion, or less, to produce four times the former results by knowing how to do it, by selecting the proper man to do it, by teaching him how to do it, and particularly by teaching him how to rest when he was not actually under load. Now, what is true of the loading of pig iron has been shown to be true of other occupations which are constantly called unskilled, such as the mere shovelling of coal or the mere shovelling of dirt. You could pass through the whole realm of human, manual occupation and find that the difference between the man who is skilled and the man who is unskilled is not in the occupation but is in the man and in the training of men. And in the same way the performance will be largely dependent not only upon skill but upon the physical and mental condition of the individual. As Lord Brassey said many years ago, it depended upon what a man ate as to what his efficiency was, and the cost of building a railroad was practically the same the world over whether you paid a few cents or a few dollars a day to your men. You get about what you pay for.***

"The minimum will never become the maximum unless there is uniformity in individual performance, and uniformity of performance is contrary to nature. It comes only artificially, as when a curb is placed upon production, by restricting output. Men differ and women differ in what they can do and what they will do, if left free to act. When you say to an employer he shall not go beyond a certain limit in wage, the employer will insist upon getting his money's worth. You may feel perfectly sure that nobody will be employed who is not worth the minimum. But there remains the same freedom to pay higher for better service that exists where there is no minimum wage law. If you shall fix a maximum wage you would find that no employee was worth more than that wage; for the employee would limit his output accordingly. But the moment you allow freedom to pay a higher wage and freedom to do more efficient work you will find that the minimum wage will differ from the maximum wage just as it does today."

Absolutism in Industry

(From statements before the United States Commission on Industrial Relations, April 16, 1914, and January 23, 1915)

"SOCIETY and labor should demand continuity of employment, and when we once get to a point where workingmen are paid throughout the year, as the officers of a corporation are paid throughout the year, everyone will recognize that a business cannot be run profitably unless you keep it running, be-

[380]

cause if you have to pay, whether your men are working or not, your men will work.

"It seems to me that industry has been allowed to develop chaotically, mainly because we have accepted irregularity of employment as if it was something inevitable. It is no more inevitable than insistence upon payment for a great many of the overhead charges in a business, whether the business is in daily operation or not.***

"It seems to me that the intensive study of businesses and of the elimination of wage in business must result in regularizing business. Every man who has undertaken to study the problem of his business in the most effective way has come to recognize that what we must do is to keep the business running all the time, keep it full. If it is a retail business, he makes it his effort to make other days in the week than Saturday a great day; he tries to take periods of the year when people do not naturally buy and make them buy, in the off seasons, in order to keep his plant going during the period in which ordinarily and in other places of business it loses money. Now, that effort must proceed in every business, to try by means of invention, and invention involving large investment, to make the business run throughout the year; that is, to regularize the work, avoid the congestion of the extra-busy season, and avoid the dearth in what has been a slack season.

"Now, scientific management must develop regularity; therefore, in developing regularity it will tend to eliminate unemployment. Of course, it also will naturally tend to eliminate that other unemployment, which comes from lack of work to do, because if you are right in supposing that there is plenty of consumptive power but not enough ability to buy the things, then we may be able to produce them cheaply enough and people will want them and will take them.***

"Unrest will be to a certain extent mitigated by anything which improves the condition of the workers, and I cannot see any real solution, ultimate solution, or an approximation of a solution of unrest as long as there exists in this country any juxtaposition of political democracy and industrial absolutism. To my mind, before we can really solve the problem of industrial unrest, the worker must have a part in the responsibility and management of the business, and whether we adopt scientific management, or adopt any other form of obtaining compensation or of increasing productivity, unrest will not be removed as long as we have that inconsistency, as I view it.***

"I do not consider that the holding of stock by employees—what is practically almost an insignificant participation, considering their percentage to the whole body of stockholders in large corporations—improves the condition of labor in those corporations. I think its effect is rather the opposite.***

"Unrest, to my mind, never can be removed—and fortunately never can be removed—by mere improvement of the physical and material condition of the workingman. If it were possible we should run great risk of improving their material condition and reducing their manhood. We must bear in mind all the time that however much we may desire material improvement and must desire it for the comfort of the individual, that the United States is a democracy, and that we must have, above all things, men. It is the development of manhood to which any industrial and social system should be directed. We Americans are committed not only to social justice in the sense of avoiding things which bring suffering and harm, like unjust distribution of wealth; but we are committed primarily to democracy. The social justice for which we are striving is an incident of our democracy, not the main end. It is rather the result of democracy—perhaps its finest expression—but it rests upon democracy, which implies the rule by the people. And therefore the end for which we must strive is the attainment of rule by the people, and that involves industrial democracy as well as political democracy. That means that the problem of

[382]

a trade should not longer be the problems of the employer alone. The problems of his business, and it is not the employer's business alone, are the problems of all in it. The union cannot shift upon the employer the responsibility for conditions, nor can the employer insist upon determining, according to his will the conditions which shall exist. The problems which exist are the problems of the trade; they are the problems of employer and employee. Profit sharing, however liberal, cannot meet the situation. That would merely mean dividing the profits of business. Such a division may do harm or it might do good, dependent on how it is applied.

"There must be a division not only of profits, but a division also of responsibilities. The employees must have the opportunity of participating in the decisions as to what shall be their condition and how the business shall be run. They must learn also in sharing that responsibility that they must bear, too, the suffering arising from grave mistakes, just as the employer must. But the right to assist in making the decisions, the right of making their own mistakes, if mistakes there must be, is a privilege which should not be denied to labor. We must insist upon labor sharing the responsibility for the result of the business.

"Now, to a certain extent we are getting it—in smaller businesses. The grave objection to the large business is that, almost inevitably, the form of organization, the absentee stock-holdings, and its remote directorship prevent participation, ordinarily, of the employees in such management. The executive officials become stewards in charge of the details of the operation of the business, they alone coming into direct relation with labor. Thus we lose that necessary cooperation which naturally flows from contact between employers and employees —and which the American aspirations for democracy demand. It is in the resultant absolutism that you will find the fundamental cause of prevailing unrest; no matter what is done with

[383]

the superstructure, no matter how it may be improved in one way or the other, unless we eradicate that fundamental difficulty, unrest will not only continue, but, in my opinion, will grow worse.***

"From the standpoint of the community, the welfare of the community, and the welfare of the workers in the company, what is called a democratization in the ownership through the distribution of stock is positively harmful. Such a wide distribution of the stock dissipates altogether the responsibility of stockholders, particularly of those with five shares, ten shares, fifteen shares, or fifty shares. They must recognize that they have no influence in a corporation of hundreds of millions of dollars capital. Consequently they consider it immaterial whatever they do, or omit to do. The net result is that the men who are in control it is almost impossible to dislodge, unless there be such a scandal in the corporation as to make it clearly necessary for the people on the outside to combine for self-protection. Probably even that necessity would not be sufficient to ensure a new management. That comes rarely, except when those in control withdraw because they have been found guilty of reprehensible practices resulting in financial failure.

"The wide distribution of stock, instead of being a blessing, constitutes, to my mind, one of the gravest dangers to the community. It is absentee landlordism of the worst kind. It is more dangerous, far more dangerous than the absentee landlordism from which Ireland suffered. There, at all events, control was centered in a few individuals. By the distribution of nominal control among ten thousand or a hundred thousand stockholders there is developed a sense of absolute irresponsibility on the part of the person who holds that stock. The few men that are in position continue absolute control without any responsibility except to their stockholders of continuing and possibly increasing the dividends.

"Now, that responsibility, while proper enough in a way, may lead to action directly contrary to the public interest.***

"Industrial democracy will not come by gift. It has got to be won by those who desire it. And if the situation is such that a voluntary organization like a labor union is powerless to bring about the democratization of a business, I think we have in this fact some proof that the employing organization is larger than is consistent with the public interest. I mean by larger, is more powerful, has a financial influence too great to be useful to the State; and the State must in some way come to the aid of the workingmen if democratization is to be secured.***

"Men must have industrial liberty as well as good wages."

The Right to Regular Employment

(From the *Survey Graphic*, April 1, 1929, "as formulated long since by Louis D. Brandeis")

"FOR EVERY employee who is 'steady in his work' there shall be steady work. The right to regularity in employment is co-equal with the right to regularity in the payment of interest on bonds, in the delivery to customers of the high quality of product contracted for. No business is successfully conducted which does not perform fully the obligations incident to each of these rights. Each of these obligations is a fixed charge. No dividend shall be paid unless each of these fixed charges has been met. The reserve to ensure regularity of employment is as imperative as the reserve for depreciation; and it is equally a part of the fixed charges to make the annual contribution to that reserve. No business is socially solvent which cannot do so."

[385]

Scientific Management and Trusts

(From an address* before the New England Dry Goods
Association at Boston, February 11, 1908)

"FOR EVERY business concern there must be a limit of greatest efficiency. What that limit is differs under varying conditions; but it is clear that an organization may be too large for efficiency and economical management, as well as too small. The disadvantages attendant upon size may outweigh the advantages. Man's works have outgrown the capacity of the individual man. No matter what the organization, the capacity of the individual man must determine the success of a particular enterprise, not only financially to the owners, but in service to the community. Organization can do much to make possible larger efficient concerns; but organization can never be a substitute for initiative and for judgment. These must be supplied by chief executive officers, and nature sets a limit to their possible accomplishment. Any transportation system which is called upon not merely to operate, but to develop its facilities, makes heavy demands upon its executive officers for initiative and for the exercise of sound judgment. And New England needs most emphatically development of its transportation facilities. To aid in this development we need more minds, not less.***

"It has been suggested that we accept the proposed monopoly in transportation but provide safeguards.

"This would be like surrendering liberty and substituting despotism with safeguards. There is no way in which to safeguard people from despotism except to prevent despotism.

* Collected in *Business—A Profession*.

[386]

There is no way to safeguard the people from the evils of a private transportation monopoly except to prevent the monopoly. The objections to despotism and to monoply are fundamental in human nature. They rest upon the innate and ineradicable selfishness of man. They rest upon the fact that absolute power inevitably leads to abuse. They rest upon the fact that progress flows only from struggle.

"Furthermore, the most carefully devised safeguards are in many respects futile. The legislation authorizing the Boston and Albany lease was surrounded by all safeguards which an able governor, legislature, and our business organizations could devise. Have these safeguarding provisions reduced or made more tolerable the wretched service which we have received?"

The Profession of Business

(From an address* at Brown University Commencement Day, 1912)

"IN THE FIELD of modern business, so rich in opportunity for the exercise of man's finest and most varied mental faculties and moral qualities, mere money-making cannot be regarded as the legitimate end. Neither can mere growth in bulk or power be admitted as a worthy ambition. Nor can a man nobly mindful of his serious responsibilities to society view business as a game, since with the conduct of business human happiness or misery is inextricably interwoven.

"Real success in business is to be found in achievements comparable rather with those of the artist or the scientist, of the inventor or the statesman. And the joys sought in the profession of business must be like their joys and not the mere vulgar satisfaction which is experienced in the acquisition of

* Collected in *Business—A Profession.*

money, in the exercise of power, or in the frivolous pleasure of mere winning.***

"As the profession of business develops, the great industrial and social problems expressed in the present social unrest will one by one find solution."

Competition in Transportation

(From an article in the *Boston Journal*, December 13, 1912)

"ADVOCATES of monopoly urge that the days of competition are passed; that to insist upon competition is to go backward, not forward; that (at least as to railroads and our public-service corporations) the path of progress lies in regulation.***

"The policy of regulating public-service companies is sound; but it must not be overworked. The scope of any possible effective regulation of an interstate railroad, either by Federal or by State commissions, is limited to a relatively narrow sphere. Regulation may prevent positive abuses, like discriminations, or excessive rates. Regulation may prevent persistent disregard of definite public demands, like that for specific trains or for stops at certain stations. Regulation may compel the correction of definite evils, like the use of unsanitary cars. But regulation cannot make inefficient business efficient. Regulation cannot convert a poorly managed railroad into a well-managed railroad. Regulation cannot supply initiative or energy. Regulation cannot infuse into railroad executives the will to please the people. Regulation cannot overcome the anæmia or wasting-sickness which attends monopoly. Regulation may curb, but it cannot develop the action of railroad officials.

"For no commission, however broad its powers, however

[388]

able, fearless, and diligent its members, can perform the functions of general manager and the board of directors of a railroad system; or supply the incentive and the eagerness to please the public and that development which results from the necessities of competition. It is to the lack of efficiency, to the lack of appreciation of the community's needs, and to the lack of this eagerness to please its customers that our demoralized transportation service is in large measure due.

"For instance, bad freight service has seriously impaired the prosperity of New England. Deliveries of freight have been almost incredibly slow and unreliable. The effect upon the business concerns has been very serious. Success of individual businesses has been imperilled. Prosperity of all New England has been retarded. All this has happened in a period in which the country has been blessed with an able, fearless, and upright Interstate Commerce Commission, possessing broad legal powers. The recent hearings before the Commission have disclosed the evils from which the community suffers. The recent public disclosures will undoubtedly result in correcting some specific evils which have been pointed out; but the Commission cannot by any order make the railroads give the shippers good service. Regulation cannot produce efficient and enlightened railroad operation in the interests of the public; and without that the community cannot get satisfactory service.***

"No one has recognized more fully than the members of the Interstate Commerce Commission the limitation of accomplishment through railroad regulation. No one recognizes better than they the continuing need of competition to secure satisfactory service.***

"The excellent work which the Commission has so far done has been possible only because existing competition between railroads has to a large extent produced development and supply of reasonable facilities, and, in the main, reasonable rates; each railroad acting, to a certain extent, as a check upon the other. Such is the condition in Wisconsin, where the best success in regulation of railroads has been attained. To abandon competition in transportation and rely upon regulation as a safeguard against the evils of monopoly would be like surrendering liberty and regulating despotism."

Conservation for the Public

(From argument at a hearing before a Congressional Committee investigating the Department of the Interior, May 27, 1910)

"Now, to my mind it is only a small part of the meaning of conservation to plan to avoid the present wasteful use of natural resources. In some ways it would be of little importance whether the resources were preserved or not preserved if when they are preserved they are preserved for the special interests, are preserved to make the rich richer, leaving the great mass of the people of the United States dependent upon certain large capitalists, dependent upon the very limited number of the rich. I see little good in conservation if that is to be the result. Conservation, in its very essence, is preserving things public for the people, preserving them so that the people may have them. To accomplish this is the aim of our Republic. It is the aim of our great democracy that men shall, so far as humanly possible, have equal opportunities, and that the differences in opportunities to which men have been subject elsewhere shall not prevail here.

"This is what conservation means, and it is because conservation means this that Gifford Pinchot and James R. Garfield and others said: 'No; do not patent those lands; depart from an early method of dealing with things public by throwing them in the lap of those able, experienced, and resourceful men who will develop them.' We insist upon new methods, because the old method of distribution and developing of the great resources of the country is creating a huge privileged class that is endangering liberty. There cannot be liberty without financial independence, and the greatest danger to the people of the United States today is in becoming, as they are gradually more and more, a class of employees. Shall the question be: 'Who is to be the master?' Resistance to such conditions is, I take it, what underlies this conservation movement. It is that which gives it its significance. And on that issue where does Mr. Ballinger [Secretary of the Interior]—where do his associates—stand?"

The Fruits of Efficiency

(From brief introduced at Interstate Commerce Commission
hearing, January 3, 1911)

"UNDER scientific management the employee is enabled to earn without greater strain upon his vitality from twenty-five to sixty percent and at times even one hundred percent more than under the old system. The larger wages are made possible by larger production; but this gain in production is not attained by 'speeding up.' It comes largely from removing the obstacles to production which annoy and exhaust the workman—obstacles for which he is not, or should not be made, responsible. The management sees to it that his machine is always in perfect order. The management sees to it that he is always supplied with the necessary materials. The management sees to it that the work comes to him at proper times, with proper instructions and in proper condition. The management sees to it that he is shown the best possible way of doing the job; that is, the

[391]

way which takes least time, which takes least effort, and which produces the best result. Relieved of every unnecessary effort, of every unnecessary interruption and annoyance, the worker is enabled without greater strain to furnish more in production. And under the exhilaration of achievement he develops his capacity.***

"The social gains of the workingman from scientific management are greater even than the financial.***

"The employer gains not only reduced labor cost due to greater productivity of the workingman, but also those incidental benefits which flow from improved service, as from greater celerity and greater punctuality in completing the work. The employer gains much from the lessened need of plant and equipment which follows its fuller and uninterrupted use. He saves in interest and in taxes, and in depreciation charges. He saves in reduced stock of materials, raw and in process. He saves in a lessened strain upon his credit.***

"Unionism does not prevent the method of scientific management. It is true that unions, in some trades, have bitterly opposed the introduction of the piece rate or the bonus system *without scientific management,* just as other unions have opposed the day rate system *without scientific management.* And very intelligent labor leaders have from time to time objected —and objected properly—to ruthless methods of 'speeding up'; but, as shown above, 'speeding up' is not scientific management nor, as also shown above, is the piece rate system, with or without a bonus, scientific management.

"It will always require tact and patience to introduce radically new methods, whether the persons to be affected are organized or unorganized workers or are those 'higher up'."

(From foreword to *Primer of Scientific Management*,
by Frank B. Gilbreth, 1912)

"SCIENTIFIC MANAGEMENT undertakes to secure greater production for the same or less effort. It secures to the workingman that development and rise in self-respect, that satisfaction with his work, which in other lines of human activity accompanies achievement.

"Eagerness and interest take the place of indifference, both because the workman is called upon to do the highest work of which he is capable, and also because in doing this better work he secures appropriate and substantial recognition and reward. Under scientific management men are led, not driven. Instead of working unwillingly for their employer, they work in co-operation with the management for themselves and their employer on what is a 'square deal.' If the fruits of scientific management are directed into proper channels, the workingman will get not only a fair share but a very large share of the industrial profits arising from improved industry.

"In order that the workingman may get this large share of the benefits through higher wages, shorter hours, regular employment, and better working conditions, the labor unions must welcome, not oppose, the introduction of scientific management to the end that the workingman through the unions may participate in fixing those wages, hours, and conditions.

"Unless the workingman is so represented, there must be danger that his interests will not be properly cared for; and he cannot be properly represented except through organized labor. The introduction of scientific management therefore offers to organized labor its greatest opportunity."

Railroads

(From brief and argument heard by the Interstate Commerce Commission on a proposed advance in freight rates, January 3 and 11, 1911)

"IT IS undoubtedly true that under the system of management prevailing among railroads, numerous economies are possible upon each railroad which, if introduced, would result in very large savings to that company—savings far greater in amount than the added expense due to the recent increases in the wage scale. If, for instance, each railroad were now to adopt in each department the best methods and practices now prevailing in any other American railroad, it is clear that the operating expenses of each company would be very largely reduced.

"But a far greater measure of economy would result to each company from the introduction of scientific management by which the efficiency of labor, plant and machinery, and materials would be very largely increased. Scientific management increases efficiency, and economy comes as a by-product.

"The science of management is not new. Some of its principles were discovered and applied a quarter of a century ago by Fred W. Taylor in the Midvale Steel Works. Other principles have been discovered and developed by him and by many others since. ***

"Railroad operation presents an especially favorable opportunity for cooperation through the introduction of scientific management.

"The fact that the railroad business is subject in its accounting to the orders of this Commission makes it possible for this Commission to require that each company ascertain and report to it the simple unit costs of each operation in every department of the road. The further fact that the railroad business is largely non-competitive makes it proper to publish these costs, and to give to each railroad the benefit of knowing the lowest elementary unit cost of each operation attained by any railroad, and how it was attained. The ascertainment of the ultimate unit cost is necessary before an instructive basis of comparison can be had. The knowledge that the average annual cost per locomotive of repairs, renewals, and depreciation on one railroad is $3,832.37, and on another is $2,709.27, would be a very unsafe guide for determining the relative economy of operation on the two railroads. The conditions on the two railroads and standards of renewal and depreciation may vary so that the company expending the greatest sum may actually have conducted its locomotive use and repair more economically than the railroad expending less. What is needed as a basis for comparison are the ultimate unit costs; the cost of turning a wheel, the cost of laying a tie or rail under particular conditions, and even that relatively simple operation must be analyzed and separated into its ultimate simple elements.

"The attainment by each railroad for each operation of the lowest cost attained by any railroad for that operation would not, however, satisfy the demands of scientific management. To attain only the best that has been done presents rather the beginning than the end of economies which scientific management contemplates. With the ascertainment of the lowest existing costs the study must be made whether there are still waste time and effort involved in the best existing method of performing that particular operation, and of eliminating such waste when determined. And when that shall have been done there will still remain the wide field of research for a better way of doing the same thing.

"The railroads have combined to maintain rates. There can be no proper objection to their cooperating in reducing costs—cooperating with a view to dividing among themselves the great task set by scientific management; the task of investigating how in each operation in each particular department

[395]

greater efficiency can be attained, and how costs can be reduced, and then imparting to each of the others the results of such investigations.***

"This investigation has developed clearly that the railroads to meet any existing needs should not look without but within. If their net income is insufficient, the proper remedy is not higher rates, resulting in higher costs and lessened business, but scientific management, resulting in lower costs, in higher wages, and increased business. If their credit is impaired, the proper remedy is not to apply the delusive stimulant of higher rates, but to strengthen their organizations by introducing advanced methods and eliminating questionable practices. Thus they will maintain credit by deserving it.***

"I ask the Commission to consider whether there is not a causal connection between the fact of bigness, the fact of this extraordinary gross, and the fact of the reduced net; whether it is not a fact that the Pennsylvania system, the New York Central system, and indeed, to a less extent, the Baltimore & Ohio system have not exceeded what may be called the limit of greatest efficiency. Because, obviously, in all human institutions there must be a limit of greatest efficiency. These railroads are run by men; and, preëminently, they are determined by one or two men. Everybody in his experience knows his own limitations; knows how much less well he can do many things than a few things. There undoubtedly is a limit with a railroad, as in the case of other institutions, where they may be too small; but there is another limit where they may be too large—where the centrifugal force will be greater than the centripetal, and where, by reason of the multiplicity of problems and the distance to the circumference, looseness of administration arises that overcomes any advantage from size, overcomes it so far as to make it relatively a losing proposition.***

"I say, therefore, may not that be one of the causes of the

trouble which some of the railroads believe themselves to be in? And this question, this bigness, or, as I would be inclined to call it, this curse of bigness, has other incidents than the ones I have mentioned. Growth has been ordinarily obtained by absorption of other lines, at a very high price. We know that this is true in many instances. We know that many of these lines that have been taken over have been taken over under circumstances which gave to the security holders a larger return than they had before, as well as a certain return, operating as a fixed charge, that placed upon these lines burdens which did not hitherto exist.

"One instance by no means a solitary instance, or probably not the most flagrant instance of it, has occurred in connection with our own Boston & Albany Railroad, which, it appeared, had cost the New York Central in five years on an average $1,000,000 a year."

———————

(From argument on behalf of Interstate Commerce Commission in the "Five Per Cent Case," June 26, 1914)

"We have heard a great deal about the fear of Government ownership, but I do not know whether it is to be feared or not. But I feel very certain that no step could be taken which would so advance that time when Government ownership comes as to grant this so-called horizontal increase which is asked. I feel that the question we have before us is not so much the future of the railroads, as to whether they, by the granting of this increase, should get relief, but the more important question of whether governmental regulation of railroads is the method which will be pursued long. It is commission government and commission regulation which is really involved in this application. If, in the light of these facts as they have developed here,

[397]

it should appear that there is no way of taking care of this situation except to continue the abuses that exist and to intensify the injustice with respect to particular traffic and to stretch or go beyond the terms of the law and the delegation which Congress has made, then, indeed, there would be a crisis, and a crisis which would be as unfortunate for the railroads as it would be for the rest of the community. ***

"If you gentlemen will look into the facts, instead of at the generalizations and general statements, you will find that there is nothing whatever in this situation which should prevent your doing what is of such importance to the railroad and to the community, and to us all, and that is to remedy the cause of this trouble, to stop the leeches, and to put an end to injustice, discrimination and waste."

Price and Competition

(From a statement before the House Committee on Interstate and Foreign Commerce, January 9, 1915, in behalf of price regulation)

"UNRESTRICTED COMPETITION, with its abuses and excesses, leads to monopoly, because these abuses and excesses prevent competition from functioning properly as a regulator of business. Competition proper is beneficent, because it acts as an incentive to the securing of better quality or lower cost. It operates also as a repressive of greed, keeping within bounds the natural inclination to exact the largest profit obtainable. Unfair and oppressive competition defeats those purposes. It prevents the natural development which should attend rivalry and which gives success to those who contribute most to the community by their development of their own business and the exercise of moderation in the exaction of profits. It substitutes devious and corrupt methods for honest rivalry and seeks to win, not by superior methods, but by force. Its purpose is not to excel, but to destroy. The Clayton Act and the Federal Trade Commission act are designed to aid in preventing monopoly by preventing unfair and destructive competition, and the worst form of illegitimate competition has been found to be price-cutting. All the investigations in Congress and elsewhere have confirmed this conclusion. Monopoly is the natural outcome of cutthroat competition. With the exception of the railroad rebate, cutthroat competition was the most powerful of all weapons which the Standard Oil Co. employed. It was the most powerful of all weapons employed by the Tobacco Trust. The Standard Oil Trust would cut the price in the districts where a competitor established himself, and thus destroy him, meanwhile reimbursing itself for the cut in that region by charging higher prices elsewhere.***

"The denial of the right to establish standard prices results in granting a privilege to the big concerns; a discrimination in favor of the rich and powerful as against the small man; for the concern with large capital, as the powerful trusts, can secure adherence to the standard price while the small manufacturer or producer can not. The small man needs the protection of the law; but the law becomes the instrument by which he is destroyed. The rule laid down by the Supreme Court [in the *Sanatogen Case, Bauer* v. *O'Donnell*, 229 U. S. 1] is inconsistent with the business policy adopted by this country and recently confirmed by the Clayton Act and the Federal trade act—the policy of regulating competition. The decision must be explained by the fact that the Court did not fully understand the practical application of these rules to the trade facts. The public interest clearly demands that price standardization be permitted; and it demands it in the first place in the interest of the small man—the small manufacturer, the small producer, and the small retailer."

Price and Business Incentive

(From a statement before the House Sub-committee of Committee on
Patents in a hearing on the Oldfield revision of
patent statutes, May 15, 1912)

"TAKE, in the first place, the matter of fixed resale prices.
Now, it seems to me at first blush as if the power of the manufacturer, by reason of the incident that he happens to be
manufacturing a product under a patent, to fix the price at
which that article shall be retailed is a right that is not dangerous to the community. It certainly is to that extent an extension
over what we have known at the common law as the power to
restrict the alienation of property. That is true. And we must
therefore approach the situation with a doubt as to whether
that power is beneficial or not. But when we investigate the
facts, the economy, the business facts, I think we must find that
that power has been beneficial in its operation, so far as it is
here involved, except where certain conditions arose, which
conditions would not be affected directly by the legislation proposed—I mean conditions of general monopoly as distinguished
from the monopoly granted under the patent.

"Take this class of articles on which the committee has
already had much testimony, the razor: On the one hand, the
Gillette safety razor, and, as opposed to it, the Gem, the Auto-Strop, or any one of the other numerous razors which have been
put before the community. There is a definite, fixed price at
which the one or the other should be sold. Now, the fixing of
that price has possibly prevented one retail dealer from selling
the article a little lower than the other, but the fixing of that
price has tended not to suppress but to develop competition,
because it has made it possible in the distribution of those goods
to go to an expense and to open up another sphere of mer-

chandising which would have been absolutely impossible without a fixed price. The whole world can be drawn into the field. Every dealer, every small stationer, every small druggist, every small hardware man, can be made a purveyor of that article by comprehensive advertising, and you have stimulated, through the fixed price, the little man as against the department store, and as against the large unit which may otherwise monopolize that trade. And when you have developed the Gillette razor, and as you develop it, you are inciting the invention, and, what is more important than the invention, you are inciting the commercial development of the competing article. Every success like the Gillette success is constantly inciting a large number of other men to go into that business. You are making a market for invention, and you are doing it by means of the reputation of the particular article which cannot be made and cannot be conserved without some limit upon the price at which the article goes to the community.

"Now, where does the danger come? It comes when one of those concerns or some outsiders undertake to monopolize the safety-razor business. Then all of the advantages which have come from that price fixing to the community vanish, and in their place there comes a large number of dangers, and very serious dangers, to the community.

"When you have four or five or six or eight separate razor concerns you have the most complete guaranty against extortionate prices, because the moment one of those concerns fixes a price higher than it ought to be, there is the incitement to the others to push their goods, and in the course of a comparatively short time the community abandons the one, or tends to abandon the one, and to take up the other.***

"Now, we have got to encourage in every way the individual enterprise, and we have to bear in mind that on the one hand while you are encouraging the enterprise and making for the advance of the country and the prosperity of the indi-

[401]

vidual, the inventor, and the business man; on the other hand, the moment you get these large organizations, these large trusts, you are doing exactly the opposite; you are discouraging invention; you are preventing advance; you are putting an actual damper upon advance, and these great businesses, whether they be the General Electric, the Harvester Company, or the Shoe Machinery Company, with their glittering returns to stockholders, are a distinct menace to the industries of the country.***

"The danger comes in creating an organization in itself so large that it has unlimited funds, connected with other organizations, connected with what has been commonly termed the Money Trust, in such a way that you cannot get capital. That is the inherent danger in the trust as a commercial organization —its money traps.***

"As long as you have freedom, freedom of capital and freedom in the lines of business, you are safe; and if you have not freedom you cannot be safe under any circumstances. It is a battle for life to have freedom and that is the only way we can advance. Anything like changing any of these little things is like putting a patch on here and there. It is merely a delusion. We who are lawyers have a special obligation, and that is to make our law efficient. The disgrace that has come to the law, the discredit, the disrespect which has come to the law, is because it is inefficient, and because we make rules and we do not provide any machinery for enforcing them.***

"I am strenuously opposed to the Government fixing any price in any business that is competitive but I do think that a man who has an individual article, whether it be covered by a patent, copyright, trade-mark, or trade name—something which is known as his article—should have the right to have that article distributed under the conditions which he deems best, including a fixed price, provided always that it is a competitive article; that is, that the field of competition is left open. And one of the dozen restrictions which are perfectly safe in a competitive business at once become instruments of oppression when you have a non-competitive business.

"I should advise providing in the law that, for instance, while every restraint of trade is, under the decision in the Standard Oil and Tobacco cases, not illegal but only if it is an unreasonable restraint of trade, I should provide that the doing of any one of those things should be conclusive evidence of unreasonableness and therefore conclusive evidence of illegality, drawing a marked distinction between the competitive and non-competitive businesses. And the reason is perfectly obvious. On the one hand, where you have a patent, the man is giving something to the community for his monopoly; but when you have formed a combination you have taken away from the community the different lines and different avenues of advance which they previously had.***

"It is in the interest of the community that a man in a free business, in a competitive business, shall have the incentive to make just as much money as he can. If he makes too much money—I mean according to these economic doctrines—he is sure to find some fellow coming in and trying to share it with him. If he has nothing more than the advantage of his ability in producing that article, no advantage of position by which he can compel submission to him, so much the better. You ought to make men devise new methods, efficient methods, of producing results."

Preventing Standardized Prices

(From an article in *Harper's Weekly*, November 15, 1913)

"WHEN A COURT decides a case upon grounds of public policy, the judges become in effect legislators. The question involved is no longer one for lawyers only. It seems fitting, therefore, to inquire whether the common trade practice of maintaining the price of trade-marked articles has been justly condemned.***

"The Supreme Court says that a contract by which a producer binds a retailer to maintain the established selling price of his trade-marked product is void because it prevents competition between retailers of the article and restrains trade.*

"Such a contract does, in a way, limit competition, but no man is bound to compete with himself. And when the same trade-marked article is sold in the same market by one dealer at a less price than by another, the producer in effect competes with himself. To avoid such competition, the producer of a trade-marked article often sells it to but a single dealer in a city or town; or he establishes an exclusive sales agency. No one has questioned the legal right of an independent producer to create such exclusive outlets for his product. But if exclusive selling agencies are legal, why should the individual manufacturer of a trade-marked article be prevented from establishing a marketing system, under which his several agencies for distribution will sell at the same price? There is no difference, in substance, between an agent who retails the article and a dealer who retails it.

"For many business concerns the policy of maintaining a standard price for a standard article is simple. The village baker readily maintained the quality and price of his product, by sale and delivery over his own counter. The great Standard Oil monopoly maintains quality and price (when it desires to do so) by selling throughout the world to the retailer or the consumer from its own tank-wagons. But for most producers the jobber and the retailer are the necessary means of distribution—as necessary as the railroad, the express, or the parcel post. The Standard Oil Company can, without entering into

* *Dr. Miles Medical Co.* v. *Park & Sons Co.*, 220 U. S. 373, *Bauer* v. *O'Donnell*, 229 U. S. 1.

contracts with dealers, maintain the price through its dominant power. Shall the law discriminate against the lesser concerns which have not that power, and deny them the legal right to contract with dealers to accomplish a like result? For in order to insure to the small producer the ability to maintain the price of his product, the law must afford him contract protection, when he deals through the middleman.

"But the Supreme Court says that a contract which prevents a dealer of trade-marked articles from cutting the established selling price, restrains trade. In a sense every contract restrains trade; for after one has entered into a contract, he is not as free in trading as he was before he bound himself. But the right to bind one's self is essential to trade development. And it is not every contract in restraint of trade, but only contracts *unreasonably* in restraint of trade, which are invalid. Whether a contract does unreasonably restrain trade is not to be determined by abstract reasoning. Facts only can be safely relied upon to teach us whether a trade practice is consistent with the general welfare. And abundant experience establishes that the one-price system, which marks so important an advance in the ethics of trade, also has greatly increased the efficiency of merchandising, not only for the producer, but for the dealer and the consumer as well.

"If a dealer is selling unknown goods or goods under his own name, he alone should set the price; but when a dealer has to use somebody else's name or brand in order to sell goods, then the owner of that name or brand has an interest which should be respected. The transaction is essentially one between the two principals—the maker and the user. All others are middlemen or agents; for the product is not really sold until it has been bought by the consumer. Why should one middleman have the power to depreciate in the public mind the value of the maker's brand and render it unprofitable not only for the maker but for other middlemen? Why should one middleman be allowed to indulge in a practice of price-cutting, which tends to drive the maker's goods out of the market and in the end interferes with people getting the goods at all?

"When a trade-marked article is advertised to be sold at less than the standard price, it is generally done to attract persons to a particular store by the offer of an obviously extraordinary bargain. It is a bait—called by the dealers a 'leader.' But the cut-price article would more appropriately be termed a 'mis-leader'; because ordinarily the very purpose of the cut-price is to create a false impression.

"The dealer who sells the Dollar Ingersoll watch for sixty-seven cents necessarily loses money in that particular transaction. He has no desire to sell any article on which he must lose money. He advertises the sale partly to attract customers to his store; but mainly to create in the minds of those customers the false impression that other articles in which he deals and which are not of a standard or known value will be sold upon like favorable terms.***

"A single prominent price-cutter can ruin a market for both the producer and the regular retailer. And the loss to the retailer is serious.

"On the other hand, the consumer's gain from price-cutting is only sporadic and temporary. The few who buy a standard article for less than its value do benefit—unless they have, at the same time, been misled into buying some other article at more than its value. But the public generally is the loser; and the losses are often permanent. If the price-cutting is not stayed, and the manufacturer reduces the price to his regular customers in order to enable them to retain their market, he is tempted to deteriorate the article in order to preserve his own profits. If the manufacturer cannot or will not reduce his price to the dealer, the consumer suffers at least the inconvenience of not being able to buy the article.***

"The position of the independent producer who establishes

the price at which his own trade-marked article shall be sold
to the consumer must not be confused with that of a combination or trust which, controlling the market, fixes the price of a
staple article. The independent producer is engaged in a business open to competition. He establishes the price at his peril—
the peril that, if he sets it too high, either the consumer will
not buy, or, if the article is nevertheless popular, the high
profits will invite even more competition. The consumer who
pays the price established by an independent producer in a
competitive line does so voluntarily; he pays the price asked,
because he deems the article worth that price as compared with
the cost of other competing articles. But when a trust fixes,
through its monopoly power, the price of a staple article in
common use, the consumer does not pay the price voluntarily.
He pays under compulsion. There being no competitor he must
pay the price fixed by the trust, or be deprived of the use of
the article.***

"The competition attained by prohibiting the producer of
a trade-marked article from maintaining his established price
offers nothing substantial. Such competition is superficial
merely. It is sporadic, temporary, delusive. It fails to protect the
public where protection is needed. It is powerless to prevent the
trust from fixing extortionate prices for its product. The great
corporation with ample capital, a perfected organization, and a
large volume of business can establish its own agencies or sell
direct to the consumer, and is in no danger of having its business destroyed by price-cutting among retailers. But the prohibition of price-maintenance imposes upon the small and
independent producer a serious handicap. Some avenue of escape must be sought by them; and it may be found in combination. Independent manufacturers without the capital or the
volume of business requisite for engaging alone in the retail
trade will be apt to combine with existing chains of stores, or

to join with other manufacturers similarly situated in establishing new chains of retail stores through which to market their product direct to the consumer. The process of exterminating the small independent retailer already hard pressed by capitalistic combinations—the mail-order houses, existing chains of stores, and the large department stores—would be greatly accelerated by such a movement. Already the displacement of the small independent business man by the huge corporation with its myriad of employees, its absentee ownership, and its financier control presents a grave danger to our democracy. The social loss is great; and there is no economic gain. But the process of capitalizing free Americans is not an inevitable one. It is largely the result of unwise, man-made, privilege-creating law, which has stimulated existing tendencies to inequality instead of discouraging them. Shall we under the guise of protecting competition, further foster monopoly by creating immunity for the price-cutters?

"Americans should be under no illusions as to the value or effect of price-cutting. It has been a most potent weapon of monopoly—a means of killing the small rival to which the great trusts have resorted most frequently. It is so simple, so effective. Far-seeing organized capital secures by this means the cooperation of the short-sighted unorganized consumer to his own undoing. Thoughtless or weak, he yields to the temptation of trifling immediate gain, and, selling his birthright for a mess of pottage, becomes himself an instrument of monopoly."

Sharing Business Knowledge

(From statement before the House Committee on the Interstate Trade
Commission Bill, January 30, 1914)

"IT HAS SEEMED to me that the purpose of all trust legislation should rather be to prevent than to punish; in other words, to create conditions which will render less likely the restraints of all trade and monopolies rather than to merely correct them when they are discovered. The establishment of a trade commission has a purpose far broader than merely aiding the Department of Justice in the pursuit of its work.***

"The inequality between the great corporations, with huge resources, and the small competitors and others is such that equality before the law will no longer be secured merely by supplying adequate machinery for enforcing the law. To prevent oppression and injustice the Government must be prepared to lend its aid.***

"It would be an aid to the corporation and an aid to the Government—an aid to the industry itself, perhaps, more than anything else—to know the facts. That stands at the very basis of efficiency—to know what an operation costs, to know why it costs that amount, and why it does not cost less and why it is not possible for somebody else to do it for less. As business develops men will talk as freely about the details of advance in business efficiency as physicians now talk about their new discoveries in aid of health. The fact that medical knowledge is open to all does not prevent different physicians from advancing in competition with one another—competition in the larger sense. The fact that the law and the decisions of the courts are public and that we lawyers or any one of us have all the opportunity possible of knowing all that has been decided does not prevent an honorable competition among lawyers. All business is tending today more and more to the recognition of the fact that what we want and what every man should know are the facts of business. No one concern can alone find out the facts which should be known. The Government should aid in advancing that knowledge.***

[409]

"This trade information I speak of relates to facts which ought to be the common knowledge of every man in the business. Every manufacturer in business, for instance, who manufactures a given article, ought to have the opportunity of learning the best way of producing his article. Ought he not just as much as the physician should know the latest cure? That would be a highly desirable result that he should know the best way of doing it. To aid in disseminating that knowledge is a proper function of government in a democracy. We instruct the farmer in the best way of doing his work today; why should we not instruct the manufacturer?"

Consulting Labor

(From an article in *Harper's Weekly*, December 11, 1915)

"IN A DEMOCRATIC community men who are to be affected by a proposed change of conditions should be consulted and the innovators must carry the burden of convincing others at each stage of the process of change that what is being done is right. Labor must have throughout an opportunity of testing whether that which is recorded as a truth, is really a truth, and whether it is the whole truth. Labor must not only be convinced of the industrial truths—which scientific management is disclosing—but most be convinced that those truths are consistent with what may be termed human truth. Is the greater productivity attained clearly consistent with the health of the body, the mind, and the soul of the worker? Is it consistent with greater joy in work, and generally in living? These are questions which must be answered in the affirmative, and to the satisfaction, not of a few, merely, but of the majority of those to be affected."

[410]

Disseminating the Facts of Industry

(From statement before Federal Trade Commission,
April 30, 1915, regarding its work)

"THE DIFFICULTY in deciding any question that comes up is really the difficulty in getting at the facts. Most men can decide any problem correctly if all of the facts be properly set before them. The difficulty in this situation of your passing upon this condition [deciding whether proposed actions are within the prohibition of the anti-trust acts] is two-fold. You are to determine in advance, largely as prophets, what is going to happen. Assuming absolutely good faith on the part of the people who come before you, you are to determine whether that which they are planning to do is going to result in an improper restraint of trade. You cannot decide that fact because you do not know what the facts are going to be, nor the conditions to which they are going to apply them, because they do not even know; because they are going to act, and even in good faith, upon the circumstances as they arise from time to time. For you to say in advance, even if you get a full and fair statement from all of these people as to what they were planning to do, is to predict things on a state of facts which you do not know, because they are in the future.

"But the other point is—and that is the point that we lawyers have to deal with more frequently, and which is constantly impressed upon us—no statement of facts, however honest your people may be, can be relied upon until it has been subjected to the careful study and criticism of people who have a different point of view. Now, these people may be perfectly honest in laying this matter before you. They see it from their side. They do not know the whole field. They only see the difficulties which they have got and which they are trying to overcome. They do

[411]

not see the other side—the evils which may attend their doing of this act. If we are going to get anywhere near the truth and justice in this action, you have got to have the other side fully represented, and that never can be done in advance because the people who are going to be affected by this are not available. They may not exist, I mean. They may not be in existence as an industry or as a commercial force. But even if they are, they cannot be summoned here to take action, and you cannot possibly have the knowledge which would make you wise enough to deal with that situation in such a way as to make it safe. Everybody who has undertaken to deal with this in the past ten years has been confronted with that situation—the practical certainty that if any board—if the Attorney General—or if any board of any kind undertook to deal with this situation the community would get tricked, even with the best of intent on the part of the Government agency.***

"There are several ways in which you can be of immense help. You can get at the facts of any trade, and, in the next place, bring up this question which you and I [to the acting chairman, Edward N. Hurley] were discussing yesterday—the question of the actual costs in business, and in each business, and you will eliminate five-sixths of all the cut-throat competition, and, ultimately, the desire for a combination, just as soon as your people educate themselves to find out what a thing costs. There is something—just such methods as Mr. Hurley has discussed with me: of working out proper methods of book-keeping and accounting for each individual line of business. You can do an immense good, as bearing directly and indirectly on this very problem that you are talking about, because you will eliminate the necessity for a large part of it. Then you make those people not only know when they are losing money, but when they are not losing money, and you are teaching them why they are losing money. You will make these men, who have never done any close thinking before, think as to why it

[412]

has cost so much; why this one element in my total expense has been so large. You will be able to point out to them what that element of expense is with other people, without pointing out who they are; and you will be educating men to do business constantly better. That will be one of the greatest constructive services you can perform. It is a thing that is really very much deeper and more far-reaching in its effect than even industrial education, because it is the greatest education; it is making the man understand his own individual power. Now, you are in a position to lay that whole thing before the people, and when you have taught the people how to do their business you have done away with those things that are driving people into improper company.

"Now, there is another thing you can do in the working out of that situation. You can bring out the actual demand and supply, and the capacity of any given line. Men don't know anything about that. In most lines of business they have a mighty small notion. Our lack of organization in business is a lack of knowledge, and of comprehensive knowledge. The trouble with our business is that men have been keeping as secrets things which would be beneficial for the public to know. Now, I believe that the real way to mend this terrible competition which is leading men to want to make these agreements is to play the game with cards right up on the table. A large part of this whole business can be done by letting the people see what the matter is. Our whole tendency has been to lead people to believe that these things ought to be secret. The Steel Trust did a mighty good thing when they gave out their figures, and they might have given them more in detail than they did without hurting them at all, and helping the whole trade, and themselves, too. There is no reason why facts should not be made public, and you are in a position where you can give to the public, through your investigation, the means of attaining this result, because you can gather the facts together and you can present them, and they would really be an aid to business.

"You stand in that extraordinarily helpful position of being, in the first place, sympathetic. In the next place, you are detached. You have not the sympathy of the fellow inside and who sees only the things around him, and his troubles; but you are on the outside, and you can understand businesses and not be interested in them. That is what other men cannot do. You stand outside; you have the means of knowledge and of getting detailed information; and you can, by laying out the situation in any line of business, tell those men what they need and just point out and say to them, 'Here is this, and here is that.'

"Take a situation such as in the case of these coal lines. The attempt of people in this region [indicating] to market their coal over here [indicating], when the people who want to market their coal there are right around the corner [indicating] is a folly. It is a perfect folly to try and sell their coal three hundred or four hundred miles away. There is bound to be a loss to them and to the people and to the railroads who haul their coal. I don't believe in those unbusinesslike ways simply because men do not know the situation, and because they have not things in their proper relation. That is what is making our business failures so numerous, and it is what is causing the sinking of capital and then later a desire to improve things in a way that simply throws the burden on the community. They are merely shifting the losses.

"So, I believe that this Commission could not do anything which, in its real essence, would be more harmful to business and more dangerous to the Commission itself than to exercise this power, if you have it. But I think it is perfectly clear that you have not got it.***

"I feel, too, that in what you are doing in any line of trade —I mean where it comes to anything that you can make public

—you ought to be in close relation to the trade publications, and to encourage a systematic habit of their reporting fully all that you are doing, so that this may be the clearing house; that those journals may become practically your organs for communicating with all the people in that particular line of business."

INDEX